Node.js, MongoDB and Angular Web Development

Second Edition

Node.js, MongoDB and Angular Web Development

Second Edition

Brad Dayley
Brendan Dayley
Caleb Dayley

Addison-Wesley

Node.js, MongoDB and Angular Web Development, Second Edition

ISBN-13: 978-0-13-465553-6

ISBN-10: 0-13-465553-2

Library of Congress Control Number: 2017954802

Printed in the United States of America

1 17

Trademarks

Warning and Disclaimer

Special Sales

For information about buying this title in bulk quantities, or for special sales opportunities (which may include electronic versions; custom cover designs; and content particular to your business, training goals, marketing focus, or branding interests), please contact our corporate sales department at corpsales@pearsoned.com or (800) 382-3419.

For government sales inquiries, please contact governmentsales@pearsoned.com.

For questions about sales outside the U.S., please contact intlcs@pearson.com.

Editor
Mark Taber

Senior Project Editor
Tonya Simpson

Copy Editor
Geneil Breeze

Indexer
Erika Millen

Compositor
codeMantra

Proofreader
Abigail Manheim

Technical Editor
Jesse Smith

Cover Designer
Chuti Prasertsith

Contents at a Glance

Contents

About the Authors

Brad Dayley is a senior software engineer with more than 20 years of experience developing enterprise applications and web interfaces. He has used JavaScript and jQuery for years and is the author of *Learning Angular, jQuery and JavaScript Phrasebook* and *Sams Teach Yourself AngularJS, JavaScript, and jQuery All in One*. He has designed and implemented a wide array of applications and services, from application servers to complex web applications.

Brendan Dayley is a web application developer who loves learning and implementing the latest and greatest technologies. He is the co-author of *Learning Angular* and *Sams Teach Yourself AngularJS, JavaScript, and jQuery All in One*. He has written a number of web applications using JavaScript, TypeScript, and Angular, and he is exploring the capabilities of new web and mobile technologies such as augmented reality and how to use them for innovative solutions.

Caleb Dayley is a university student studying computer science. He tries to learn all that he can and has taught himself much of what he knows about programming. He has taught himself several languages, including JavaScript, C#, and, using the first edition of this book, *NodeJS, MongoDB and Angular*. He is excited for what the future holds, and the opportunities to help design and create the next generation of innovative software that will continue to improve the way we live, work, and play.

Acknowledgments

I'd like to take this page to thank all those who made this title possible. First, I thank my wonderful wife for the inspiration, love, and support she gives me. I'd never make it far without you. I also want to thank my boys for the help they are when I am writing. Thanks to Mark Taber for getting this title rolling in the right direction.

—Brad Dayley

I'd like to thank all those who helped make this book possible for me. First and foremost, my wife, who pushes me to become greater and gives me all her love. Also my father, who mentored me not just in writing and programming but in life. My mother, who has always been there for me when I need her. And finally, Mark Taber, who gave me the chance to be a part of this.

—Caleb Dayley

Accessing the Free Web Edition

Your purchase of this book in any format includes access to the corresponding Web Edition, which provides several special online-only features:

- The complete text of the book
- Updates and corrections as they become available

The Web Edition can be viewed on all types of computers and mobile devices with any modern web browser that supports HTML5.

To get access to the Web Edition of *Node.js, MongoDB and Angular Web Development* all you need to do is register this book:

1. Go to www.informit.com/register.
2. Sign in or create a new account.
3. Enter the ISBN: 9780134655536.
4. Answer the questions as proof of purchase.
5. The Web Edition will appear under the Digital Purchases tab on your Account page. Click the Launch link to access the product.

Introduction

Welcome to *Node.js, MongoDB and Angular Web Development*. This book is designed to catapult you into the world of using JavaScript—from the server and services to the browser client—in your web development projects. The book covers the implementation and integration of Node.js, MongoDB, and Angular—some of the most exciting and innovative technologies emerging in the world of web development.

This introduction covers

- Who should read this book
- Why you should read this book
- What you will be able to achieve using this book
- What Node.js, MongoDB, and Angular are and why they are great technologies
- How this book is organized
- Where to find the code examples

Let's get started.

Who Should Read This Book

This book is aimed at readers who already have an understanding of the basics of HTML and have done some programming in a modern programming language. Having an understanding of JavaScript will make this book easier to digest but is not required because the book does cover the basics of JavaScript.

Why You Should Read This Book

This book will teach you how to create powerful, interactive websites and web applications—from the webserver and services on the server to the browser-based interactive web applications. The technologies covered here are all open source, and you will be able to use JavaScript for both the server-side and browser-side components.

Typical readers of this book want to master Node.js and MongoDB for the purpose of building highly scalable and high-performing websites. Typical readers also want to leverage the MVC/MVVM (Model-View-Controller/Model-View-View-Model) approach of Angular to implement well-designed and structured webpages and web applications. Overall, Node.js, MongoDB, and Angular provide an easy-to-implement, fully integrated web development stack that allows you to implement amazing web applications.

What You Will Learn from This Book

Reading this book will enable you to build real-world, dynamic websites and web applications. Websites no longer consist of simple static content in HTML pages with integrated images and formatted text. Instead, websites have become much more dynamic, with a single page often serving as an entire site or application.

Using Angular technology allows you to build into your webpage logic that can communicate back to the Node.js server and obtain necessary data from the MongoDB database. The combination of Node.js, MongoDB, and Angular allows you to implement interactive, dynamic webpages. The following are just a few of the things that you will learn while reading this book:

- How to implement a highly scalable and dynamic webserver, using Node.js and Express
- How to build server-side web services in JavaScript
- How to implement a MongoDB data store for you web applications
- How to access and interact with MongoDB from Node.js JavaScript code
- How to define static and dynamic web routes and implement server-side scripts to support them
- How to define your own custom Angular components that extend the HTML language
- How to implement client-side services that can interact with the Node.js webserver
- How to build dynamic browser views that provide rich user interaction
- How to add nested components to your webpages
- How to implement Angular routing to manage navigation between client application views

What Is Node.js?

Node.js, sometimes referred to as just Node, is a development framework that is based on Google's V8 JavaScript engine. You write Node.js code in JavaScript, and then V8 compiles it into machine code to be executed. You can write most—or maybe even all—of your server-side code in Node.js, including the webserver and the server-side scripts and any supporting web application functionality. The fact that the webserver and the supporting web application scripts are running together in the same server-side application allows for much tighter integration between the webserver and the scripts.

The following are just a few reasons Node.js is a great framework:

- **JavaScript end-to-end:** One of the biggest advantages of Node.js is that it allows you to write both server- and client-side scripts in JavaScript. There have always been difficulties in deciding whether to put logic in client-side scripts or server-side scripts. With Node.js you can take JavaScript written on the client and easily adapt it for the server, and vice versa. An added plus is that client developers and server developers are speaking the same language.
- **Event-driven scalability:** Node.js applies a unique logic to handling web requests. Rather than having multiple threads waiting to process web requests, with Node.js they are processed on the same thread, using a basic event model. This allows Node.js webservers to scale in ways that traditional webservers can't.
- **Extensibility:** Node.js has a great following and an active development community. People are providing new modules to extend Node.js functionality all the time. Also, it is simple to install and include new modules in Node.js; you can extend a Node.js project to include new functionality in minutes.
- **Fast implementation:** Setting up Node.js and developing in it are super easy. In only a few minutes you can install Node.js and have a working webserver.

What Is MongoDB?

MongoDB is an agile and scalable NoSQL database. The name Mongo comes from the word "hu**mongo**us," emphasizing the scalability and performance MongoDB provides. MongoDB provides great website backend storage for high-traffic websites that need to store data such as user comments, blogs, or other items because it is quickly scalable and easy to implement.

The following are some of the reasons that MongoDB really fits well in the Node.js stack:

- **Document orientation:** Because MongoDB is document-oriented, data is stored in the database in a format that is very close to what you deal with in both server-side and client-side scripts. This eliminates the need to transfer data from rows to objects and back.
- **High performance:** MongoDB is one of the highest-performing databases available. Especially today, with more and more people interacting with websites, it is important to have a backend that can support heavy traffic.
- **High availability:** MongoDB's replication model makes it easy to maintain scalability while keeping high performance.
- **High scalability:** MongoDB's structure makes it easy to scale horizontally by sharing the data across multiple servers.
- **No SQL injection:** MongoDB is not susceptible to SQL injection (that is, putting SQL statements in web forms or other input from the browser and thereby compromising database security). This is the case because objects are stored as objects, not using SQL strings.

What Is Angular?

Angular is a client-side JavaScript framework developed by Google. The theory behind Angular is to provide a framework that makes it easy to implement well-designed and structured webpages and applications, using an MVC/MVVM framework.

Angular provides functionality to handle user input in the browser, manipulate data on the client side, and control how elements are displayed in the browser view. Here are some of the benefits Angular provides:

- **Data binding:** Angular has a clean method for binding data to HTML elements, using its powerful scope mechanism.
- **Extensibility:** The Angular architecture allows you to easily extend almost every aspect of the language to provide your own custom implementations.
- **Clean:** Angular forces you to write clean, logical code.
- **Reusable code:** The combination of extensibility and clean code makes it easy to write reusable code in Angular. In fact, the language often forces you to do so when creating custom services.
- **Support:** Google is investing a lot into this project, which gives it an advantage over similar initiatives that have failed.
- **Compatibility:** Angular is based on JavaScript and has a close relationship with the JavaScript standard. This makes it easier to begin integrating Angular into your environment and reuse pieces of your existing code within the structure of the Angular framework.

How This Book Is Organized

This book is divided into six main parts:

- Part I, "Getting Started," provides an overview of the interaction between Node.js, MongoDB, and Angular and how these three products form a complete web development stack. Chapter 2 is a JavaScript primer that provides the basics of the JavaScript language that you need when implementing Node.js and Angular code.
- Part II, "Learning Node.js," covers the Node.js language platform, from installation to implementation of Node.js modules. This part gives you the basic framework you need to implement your own custom Node.js modules as well as the webserver and server-side scripts.
- Part III, "Learning MongoDB," covers the MongoDB database, from installation to integration with Node.js applications. This part discusses how to plan your data model to fit your application needs and how to access and interact with MongoDB from your Node.js applications.

- Part IV, "Using Express to Make Life Easier," discusses the Express module for Node.js and how to leverage it as the webserver for your application. You learn how to set up dynamic and static routes to data as well as how to implement security, caching, and other webserver basics.
- Part V, "Learning Angular," covers the Angular framework architecture and how to integrate it into your Node.js stack. This part covers creating custom HTML components and client-side services that can be leveraged in the browser.
- Part VI, "Advanced Angular," covers more advanced Angular development, such as building custom directives and custom services. You also learn about using Angular's built-in HTTP and routing services. This section finishes with some additional rich UI examples, such as building drag-and-drop components and implementing animations.

Getting the Code Examples

Throughout this book, you will find code examples in listings. The title for each listing includes a filename for the source code. The source code is available for download at the book's website.

A Final Word

We hope you enjoy learning about Node.js, MongoDB, and Angular as much as we have. They are great, innovative technologies that are fun to use. Soon, you'll be able to join the many other web developers who use the Node.js-to-Angular web stack to build interactive websites and web applications. Enjoy the book!

1

Introducing the Node.js-to-Angular Stack

To get you off on the right foot, this chapter focuses on the fundamental components of the web development framework and then describes the components of the Node.js-to-Angular stack that will be the basis for the rest of the book. The first section discusses various aspects of the general website/web application development framework from users to backend services. The purpose of first covering the web development framework components is to get you in the mindset to more easily understand how the components of the Node.js-to-Angular stack relate to the pieces of the general framework. This should help you better see the benefits of using the Node.js-to-Angular stack components over the more traditional technologies.

Understanding the Basic Web Development Framework

To get you in the right mindset to understand the benefits of utilizing Node.js, MongoDB, and Angular as your web framework, this section provides an overview of the basic components of most websites. If you are familiar with the full web framework, this section will be old hat, but if you understand only the server side or client side of the web framework, this section gives you a more complete picture.

The main components of any given web framework are the user, browser, webserver, and backend services. Although websites vary greatly on appearance and behavior, all have these basic components in one form or another.

This section is not intended to be in-depth, comprehensive, or technically exact, but rather a high level perspective of the parts involved in a functional website. The components are described in a top-down manner from user down to backend services. Then in the next section we discuss the Node.js-to-Angular stack from the bottom up, and you can get a picture of where each piece fits and why. Figure 1.1 provides a basic diagram to make it easier to visualize the components in a website/web application.

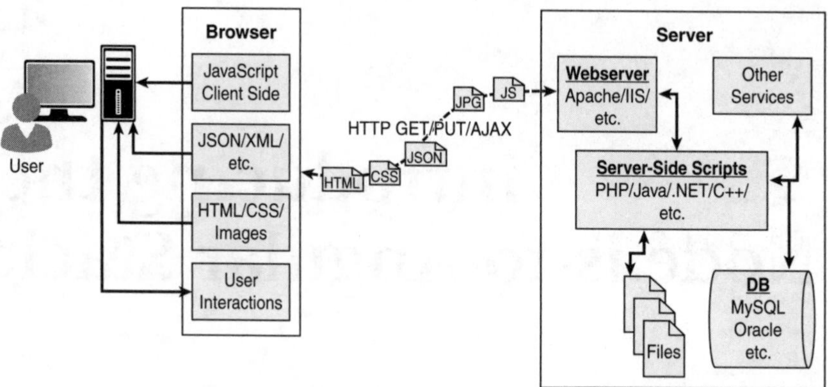

Figure 1.1 Diagram showing the components of a basic website/web application

User

Users are a fundamental part of all websites; they are, after all, the reason websites exist in the first place. User expectations define the requirements for developing a good website, and these expectations have changed a lot over the years. Users used to accept the slow, cumbersome experience of the "world-wide-wait," but no longer. They expect websites to behave closer to applications installed on their computers and mobile devices.

The user role in a web framework is to sit on the visual output and interaction input of webpages. That is, users view the results of the web framework processing and then provide interactions using mouse clicks, keyboard input, and swipes and taps on mobile devices.

Browser

The browser plays three roles in the web framework. First, it provides communication to and from the webserver. Second, it interprets the data from the server and renders it into the view that the user actually sees. Finally, the browser handles user interaction through the keyboard, mouse, touchscreen, or other input device and takes the appropriate action.

Browser to Webserver Communication

Browser-to-webserver communication consists of a series of requests using the HTTP and HTTPS protocols. Hypertext Transfer Protocol (HTTP) defines communication between the browser and the webserver. HTTP defines what types of requests can be made as well as the format of those requests and the HTTP response.

HTTPS adds an additional security layer, SSL/TLS, to ensure secure connections by requiring the webserver to provide a certificate to the browser. The user then can determine whether to accept the certificate before allowing the connection.

The browser makes three main types of requests to the server:

- **GET:** The GET request is typically used to retrieve data from the server, such as .html files, images, or JSON data.
- **POST:** POST requests are used when sending data to the server, such as adding an item to a shopping cart or submitting a web form.
- **AJAX:** Asynchronous JavaScript and XML (AJAX) is actually just a GET or POST request done directly by JavaScript running in the browser. Despite the name, an AJAX request can receive XML, JSON, or raw data in the response.

Rendering the Browser View

The screen that the user actually views and interacts with is often made up of several different pieces of data retrieved from the webserver. The browser reads data from the initial URL and then renders the HTML document to build a Document Object Model (DOM). The DOM is a tree structure object with the HTML document as the root. The structure of the tree basically matches the structure of the HTML document. For example, the `document` will have `html` as a child, and `html` will have `head` and `body` as children, and `body` may have `div`, `p`, or other elements as children, like this:

```
document
  + html
     + head
     + body
       + div
         + p
```

The browser interprets each DOM element and renders it to the user's screen to build the webpage view.

The browser often ends up getting various types of data from multiple webserver requests to build the webpage. The following are the most common types of data the browser uses to render the final user view as well as define the webpage behavior.

- **HTML files:** These provide the fundamental structure of the DOM.
- **CSS files:** These define how each of the elements on the page is to be styled; for example, font, color, borders, and spacing.
- **Client-side scripts:** These are typically JavaScript files. They can provide added functionality to the webpage, manipulate the DOM to change the look of the webpage, and provide any necessary logic required to display the page and provide functionality.
- **Media files:** Image, video, and sound files are rendered as part of the webpage.
- **Data:** Any data, such as XML, JSON, or raw text, can be provided by the webserver as a response to an AJAX request. Rather than sending a request back to the server to rebuild the webpage, new data can be retrieved via AJAX and inserted into the webpage via JavaScript.

- **HTTP headers:** The HTTP protocol defines a set of headers that can be used by the browser and client-side scripts to define the behavior of the webpage. For example, cookies are contained in the HTTP headers. The HTTP headers also define the type of data in the request as well as the type of data expected to be returned back to the browser.

User Interaction

The user interacts with the browser via input devices such as mice, keyboards, and touchscreens. The browser has an elaborate event system that captures these user input events and then takes the appropriate action. Actions vary from displaying a popup menu to loading a new document from the server to executing client-side JavaScript.

Webserver

The webserver's main focus is handling requests from browsers. As described earlier, the browser may request a document, post data, or perform an AJAX request to get a data. The webserver uses the HTTP headers as well as the URL to determine what action to take. This is where things get different depending on the webserver, configuration, and technologies used.

Most out-of-the-box webservers, such as Apache and IIS, are made to serve static files such as .html, .css, and media files. To handle POST requests that modify server data and AJAX requests to interact with backend services, webservers need to be extended with server-side scripts.

A *server-side program* is really anything that can be executed by the webserver to perform the task the browser is requesting. These can be written in PHP, Python, C, C++, C#, Java, ... the list goes on and on. Webservers such as Apache and IIS provide mechanisms to include server-side scripts and then wire them up to specific URL locations requested by the browser.

This is where having a solid webserver framework can make a big difference. It often takes quite a bit of configuration to enable various scripting languages and wire up the server-side scripts so that the webserver can route the appropriate request to the appropriate script.

The server-side scripts either generate the response directly by executing their code or connect with other backend servers such as databases to obtain the necessary information and then use that information to build and send the appropriate response.

Backend Services

Backend services are services that run behind the webserver and provide data used to build responses to the browser. The most common type of backend service is a database that stores information. When a request comes in from the browser that requires information from the database or other backend service, the server-side script connects to the database, retrieves the information, formats it, and then sends it back to the browser. Conversely, when data comes in from a web request that needs to be stored in the database, the server-side script connects to the database and updates the data.

Understanding the Node.js-to-Angular Stack Components

Now that you have the basic structure of the web framework fresh in your mind, it is time to discuss the Node.js-to-Angular stack. The most common—and we believe the best—version of this stack is the Node.js-to-Angular stack comprised of MongoDB, Express, Angular, and Node.js.

In the Node.js-to-Angular stack, Node.js provides the fundamental platform for development. The backend services and server-side scripts are all written in Node.js. MongoDB provides the data store for the website but is accessed via a MongoDB driver Node.js module. The webserver is defined by Express, which is also a Node.js module.

The view in the browser is defined and controlled using the Angular framework. Angular is an MVC framework where the model is made up of JSON or JavaScript objects, the view is HTML/CSS, and the controller is made up of Angular JavaScript.

Figure 1.2 provides a basic diagram of how the Node.js-to-Angular stack fits into the basic website/web application model. The following sections describe each of these technologies and why they were chosen as part of the Node.js-to-Angular stack. Later chapters in the book cover each of the technologies in much more detail.

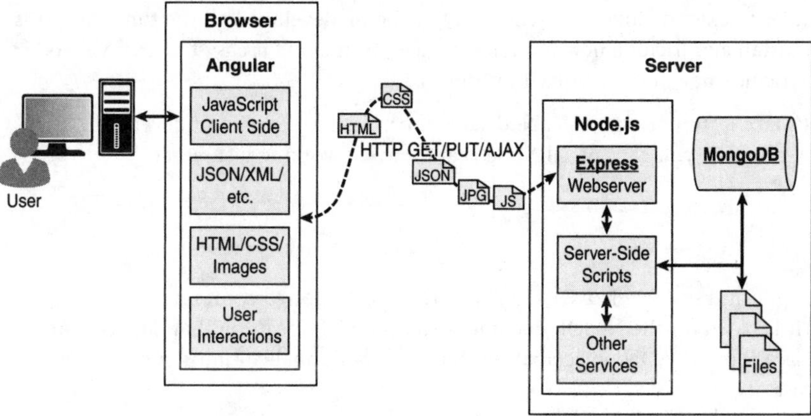

Figure 1.2 Basic diagram showing where Node.js, Express, MongoDB, and Angular fit in the web paradigm

Node.js

Node.js is a development framework based on Google's V8 JavaScript engine. Therefore, Node.js code is written in JavaScript and then compiled into machine code by V8 to be executed.

Many of your backend services can be written in Node.js, as can the server-side scripts and any supporting web application functionality. The nice thing about Node.js is that it is all just

JavaScript, so you can easily take functionality from a client-side script and place it in a server-side script. Also, the webserver can run directly within the Node.js platform as a Node.js module, so it makes it much easier than, say, Apache at wiring up new services or server-side scripts.

The following are just a few reasons why Node.js is a great framework to start from:

- **JavaScript end-to-end:** One of the biggest advantages to Node.js is that it allows you to write both server- and client-side scripts in JavaScript. There have always been difficulties in deciding where to put scripting logic. Too much on the client side makes the client cumbersome and unwieldy, but too much on the server side slows down web applications and puts a heavy burden on the webserver. With Node.js you can take JavaScript written on the client and easily adapt it for the server and vice versa. Also, your client developers and server developers will be speaking the same language.
- **Event-driven scalability:** Node.js applies a different logic to handling web requests. Rather than having multiple threads waiting to process web requests, they are processed on the same thread using a basic event model. This allows Node.js webservers to scale in ways that traditional webservers never can. This is discussed in more detail in later chapters.
- **Extensibility:** Node.js has a great following and an active development community. New modules to extend Node.js functionality are being developed all the time. Also it is simple to install and include new modules in Node.js, making it easy to extend a Node.js project to include new functionality in minutes.
- **Time:** Let's face it, time is valuable. Node.js is super easy to set up and develop in. In only a few minutes, you can install Node.js and have a working webserver.

MongoDB

MongoDB is an agile and scalable NoSQL database. The name Mongo comes from "hu**mongo**us." It is based on the NoSQL document store model, meaning that data is stored in the database as a form of JSON objects rather than the traditional columns and rows of a relational database.

MongoDB provides great website backend storage for high traffic websites that need to store data such as user comments, blogs, or other items because it is fast, scalable, and easy to implement. This book covers using the MongoDB driver library to access MongoDB from Node.js.

Node.js supports a variety of DB access drivers, so the data store could just as easily be MySQL or some other database. However, the following are some of the reasons that MongoDB really fits in the Node.js stack well:

- **Document orientation:** Because MongoDB is document-oriented, the data is stored in the database in a format close to what you will be dealing with in both server-side and client-side scripts. This eliminates the need to transfer data from rows to objects and back.

- **High performance:** MongoDB is one of the highest performing databases available. Especially today when more and more people interact with websites, it is important to have a backend that can support heavy traffic.
- **High availability:** MongoDB's replication model makes it easy to maintain scalability while keeping high performance.
- **High scalability:** MongoDB's structure makes it easy to scale horizontally by sharing the data across multiple servers.
- **No SQL injection:** MongoDB is not susceptible to SQL injection (putting SQL statements in web forms or other input from the browser that compromises the DB security) because objects are stored as objects, not using SQL strings.

Express

The Express module acts as the webserver in the Node.js-to-Angular stack. The fact that it is running in Node.js makes it easy to configure, implement, and control. The Express module extends Node.js to provide several key components for handling web requests. This allows you to implement a running webserver in Node.js with only a few lines of code.

For example, the Express module provides the ability to easily set up destination routes (URLs) for users to connect to. It also provides great functionality on working with the HTTP request and response objects, including things like cookies and HTTP headers.

The following is a partial list of the valuable features of Express:

- **Route management:** Express makes it easy to define routes (URL endpoints) that tie directly to Node.js script functionality on the server.
- **Error handling:** Express provides built-in error handling for documents not found and other errors.
- **Easy integration:** An Express server can easily be implemented behind an existing reverse proxy system such as Nginx or Varnish. This allows it to be easily integrated into your existing secured system.
- **Cookies:** Express provides easy cookie management.
- **Session and cache management:** Express also enables session management and cache management.

Angular

Angular is a client-side framework developed by Google. Angular provides all the functionality needed to handle user input in the browser, manipulate data on the client side, and control how elements are displayed in the browser view. It is written using TypeScript. The entire theory behind Angular is to provide a framework that makes it easy to implement web applications using the MVC framework.

Other JavaScript frameworks could be used with the Node.js platform, such as Backbone, Ember, and Meteor. However, Angular has the best design, feature set, and trajectory at this writing. Here are some of the benefits of Angular:

- **Data binding:** Angular has a clean method to bind data to HTML elements using its powerful scope mechanism.
- **Extensibility:** The Angular architecture allows you to easily extend almost every aspect of the language to provide your own custom implementations.
- **Clean:** Angular forces you to write clean, logical code.
- **Reusable code:** The combination of extensibility and clean code makes it easy to write reusable code in Angular. In fact, the language often forces you to do so when creating custom services.
- **Support:** Google is investing a lot into this project, which gives it an advantage over other similar initiatives.
- **Compatibility:** Angular is based on TypeScript, which makes it easier to begin integrating Angular into your environment and to reuse pieces of your existing code within the structure of the Angular framework.

Summary

This chapter covered the basics of the web development framework. The chapter discussed the interaction between the webserver and the browser as well as the functionality required to make modern websites function.

The chapter also described the Node.js-to-Angular stack, comprising Node.js, MongoDB, Express, and Angular. Node.js provides the platform for the framework, MongoDB provides the backend data store, Express provides the webserver, and Angular provides the client-side framework for modern web applications.

Next

The next chapter provides a primer on the JavaScript language. Since the entire Node.js-to-Angular stack is based on JavaScript, you need to be familiar with the language to follow the examples in the rest of the book.

2

JavaScript Primer

Each component that you will be working with in this book—Node.js, Express, TypeScript, and Angular—is based on the JavaScript language. This makes it easy to implement and reuse code at all levels of your web development stack.

The purpose of this chapter is to familiarize you with some of the language basics of JavaScript, such as variables, functions, and objects. It is not intended as a full language guide, but rather a synopsis of important syntax and idioms. If you are not familiar with JavaScript, this chapter should give you enough information to help you understand the examples throughout the rest of the book. If you already know JavaScript well, you have the option of skipping this chapter or reviewing it as a refresher.

Defining Variables

The first place to begin within JavaScript is defining variables. Variables are a means to name data so that you can use that name to temporarily store and access data from your JavaScript files. Variables can point to simple data types such as numbers or strings, or they can point to more complex data types such as objects.

To define a variable in JavaScript you use the `var` keyword and then give the variable a name, for example:

```
var myData;
```

You can also assign a value to the variable in the same line. For example, the following line of code creates a variable `myString` and assigns it the value of `"Some Text"`:

```
var myString = "Some Text";
```

The following lines work as well:

```
var myString;
myString = "Some Text";
```

Once you have declared the variable, you can use the name to assign the variable a value and access the value of the variable. For example, the following code stores a string into the `myString` variable and then uses it when assigning the value to the `newString` variable:

```
var myString = "Some Text";
var newString = myString + " Some More Text";
```

Your variable names should describe the data stored in them so that it is easy to use them later in your program. The only rules for creating variable names is that they must begin with a letter, `$`, or `_`, and they cannot contain spaces. Also remember that variable names are case sensitive, so using `myString` is different from `MyString`.

Understanding JavaScript Data Types

JavaScript uses data types to determine how to handle data assigned to a variable. The variable type determines what operations you can perform on the variable, such as looping or executing. The following list describes the most common types of variables that you will work with throughout the book:

- **String:** Stores character data as a string. The character data is specified by either single or double quotes. All the data contained in the quotes will be assigned to the string variable. For example:

  ```
  var myString = 'Some Text';
  var anotherString = 'Some More Text';
  ```

- **Number:** Stores the data as a numerical value. Numbers are useful in counting, calculations, and comparisons. Some examples are

  ```
  var myInteger = 1;
  var cost = 1.33;
  ```

- **Boolean:** Stores a single bit that is either true or false. Booleans are often used for flags. For example, you might set a variable to false at the beginning of some code and then check it on completion so see whether the code execution hit a certain spot. The following examples define a `true` and a `false` variable.

  ```
  var yes = true;
  var no = false;
  ```

- **Array:** An indexed array is a series of separate distinct data items all stored under a single variable name. Items in the array can be accessed by their zero-based index using `array[index]`. The following example creates a simple array and then accesses the first element, which is at index `0`.

  ```
  var arr = ["one", "two", "three"]
  var first = arr[0];
  ```

- **Object literal:** JavaScript supports the ability to create and use object literals. When you use an object literal you can access values and functions in the object using the `object.property` syntax. The following example shows how to create and access properties of an object literal:

  ```
  var obj = {"name": "Brendan", "Hobbies":["Video Games", "camping"], "age",
  "Unknown"};
  var name = obj.name;
  ```

- **Null:** At times you do not have a value to store in a variable either because it hasn't been created or you are no longer using it. At this time you can set a variable to `null`. Using `null` is better than assigning the variable a value of `0` or empty string `""` because those may be valid values for the variable. Assigning the variable to `null` allows you to assign no value and check against `null` inside your code.

  ```
  var newVar = null;
  ```

> **Note**
>
> JavaScript is a typeless language. You do not need to specify in the script what data type the variable is as the interpreter automatically figures out the correct data type for the variable. Additionally, you can assign a variable of one type to a value of a different type. For example, the following code defines a string variable and then assigns it to an integer value type:
>
> ```
> var id = "testID";
> id = 1;
> ```

Using Operators

JavaScript operators allow you to alter the value of a variable. You are already familiar with the `=` operator used to assign values to variables. JavaScript provides several different operators that can be grouped into two types: arithmetic and assignment.

Arithmetic Operators

Arithmetic operators are used to perform operations between variables and direct values. Table 2.1 shows a list of the arithmetic operations along with the results that get applied.

Table 2.1 **JavaScript's arithmetic operators, with results based on `y=4` initially**

Operator	Description	Example	Resulting `x`
+	Addition	`x=y+5`	`9`
		`x=y+"5"`	`"45"`
		`x="Four"+y+"4"`	`"Four44"`

Operator	Description	Example	Resulting x
-	Subtraction	x=y-2	2
++	Increment	x=y++	4
		x=++y	5
--	Decrement	x=y--	4
		x=--y	3
*	Multiplication	x=y*4	16
/	Division	x=10/y	2.5
%	Modulus (remainder of Division)	x=y%3	1

Note

The + operator can also be used to add strings or strings and numbers together. This allows you to quickly concatenate strings as well as add numerical data to output strings. Table 2.1 shows that when adding a numerical value and a string value the numerical value is converted to a string and then the two strings are concatenated.

Assignment Operators

Assignment operators are used to assign a value to a variable. In addition to the = operator, several different forms allow you to manipulate the data as you assign the value. Table 2.2 shows a list of the assignment operations along with the results that get applied.

Table 2.2 **JavaScript's assignment operators, with results based on x=10 initially**

Operator	Example	Equivalent Arithmetic Operators	Resulting x
=	x=5	x=5	5
+=	x+=5	x=x+5	15
-=	x-=5	x=x-5	5
*=	x*=5	x=x*5	50
/=	x/=5	x=x/5	2
%=	x%=5	x=x%5	0

Applying Comparison and Conditional Operators

Using conditionals is a way to apply logic to your applications so that certain code will be executed only under the correct conditions. This is done by applying comparison logic to variable values. The following sections describe the comparisons available in JavaScript and how to apply them in conditional statements.

Comparison Operators

A comparison operator evaluates two pieces of data and returns `true` if the evaluation is correct or `false` if the evaluation is not correct. Comparison operators compare the value on the left of the operator against the value on the right.

The simplest way to help you understand JavaScript comparison syntax is to provide a list with some examples. Table 2.3 shows a list of the comparison operators along with some examples.

Table 2.3 **JavaScript's comparison operators, with results based on `x=10` initially**

Operator	Description	Example	Result
`==`	Is equal to (value only)	`x==8`	`false`
		`x==10`	`true`
`===`	Both value and type are equal	`x===10`	`true`
		`x==="10"`	`false`
`!=`	Is not equal	`x!=5`	`true`
`!==`	Both value and type are not equal	`x!=="10"`	`true`
		`x!==10`	`false`
`>`	Is greater than	`x>5`	`true`
`>=`	Is greater than or equal to	`x>=10`	`true`
`<`	Is less than	`x<5`	`false`
`<=`	Is less than or equal to	`x<=10`	`true`

You can chain multiple comparisons together using logical operators and standard parentheses. Table 2.4 shows a list of the logical operators and how to use them to chain comparisons together:

Table 2.4 **JavaScript's comparison operators, with results based on `x=10` and `y=5` initially**

Operator	Description	Example	Result
`&&`	And	`(x==10 && y==5)`	`true`
		`(x==10 && y>x)`	`false`
`||`	Or	`(x>=10 || y>x)`	`true`
		`(x<10 || y>x)`	`false`
`!`	Not	`!(x==y)`	`true`
		`!(x>y)`	`false`

Operator	Description	Example	Result
	Mix	`(x>=10 && y<x || x==y)`	`true`
		`((x<y || x>=10) && y>=5)`	`true`
		`(!(x==y) && y>=10)`	`false`

Using `if` Statements

An `if` statement allows you to separate code execution based on the evaluation of a comparison. In the following lines of code the conditional operators are in `()`, and the code to execute if the conditional evaluates to `true` is in `{}`:

```
if(x==5){
  do_something();
}
```

In addition to only executing code within the `if` statement block, you can specify an `else` block that gets executed only if the condition is `false`. For example:

```
if(x==5){
  do_something();
} else {
  do_something_else();
}
```

You can also chain `if` statements together. To do this add a conditional statement along with an `else` statement, for example:

```
if(x<5){
  do_something();
} else if(x<10) {
  do_something_else();
} else {
  do_nothing();
}
```

Implementing `switch` Statements

Another type of conditional logic is the `switch` statement. The `switch` statement allows you to evaluate an expression once and then, based on the value, execute one of many different sections of code.

The syntax for the `switch` statement is

```
switch(expression){
  case value1:
    <code to execute>
    break
```

```
  case value2:
    <code to execute>
    break;
  default:
    <code to execute if not value1 or value2>
}
```

So here is what is happening. The `switch` statement evaluates the expression entirely and gets a value. The value may be a string, number, Boolean, or even an object. The `switch` expression is then compared to each value specified by the `case` statement. If the value matches, then the code in the `case` statement is executed. If no values match, then the default code is executed.

> **Note**
>
> Typically each `case` statement includes a `break` command at the end to signal a break out of the `switch` statement. If no `break` is found, then code execution continues with the next `case` statement.

Implementing Looping

Looping is a means to execute the same segment of code multiple times. This is useful when you need to perform the same tasks on an array or set of objects.

JavaScript provides functionality to perform `for` and `while` loops. The followings sections describe how to implement loops in your JavaScript.

`while` Loops

The most basic type of looping in JavaScript is the `while` loop. A `while` loop tests an expression and continues to execute the code contained in its {} brackets until the expression evaluates to `false`.

For example, the following `while` loop executes until the value of `i` is equal to `5`:

```
var i = 1;
while (i<5){
  console.log("Iteration " + i + "<br>");
  i++;
}
```

The resulting output to the console is

```
Iteration 1
Iteration 2
Iteration 3
Iteration 4
```

do/while Loops

Another type of while loop is the do/while loop. This is useful if you always want to execute the code in the loop at least once and the expression cannot be tested until the code has executed at least once.

For example, the following do/while loop executes until the value of day is equal to Wednesday:

```
var days = ["Monday", "Tuesday", "Wednesday", "Thursday", "Friday"];
var i=0;
do{
  var day=days[i++];
  console.log("It's " + day + "<br>");
} while (day != "Wednesday");
```

The resulting output to the console is

```
It's Monday
It's Tuesday
It's Wednesday
```

for Loops

The JavaScript for loop allows you to execute code a specific number of times by using a for statement that combines three statements into a single block of execution using the following syntax:

```
for (assignment; condition; update;){
  code to be executed;
}
```

The for statement uses those three statements as follows when executing the loop:

- ***assignment***: Executed before the loop begins and not again. This is used to initialize variables that will be used in the loop as conditionals.
- ***condition***: Expression evaluated before each iteration of the loop. If the expression evaluates to true the loop is executed; otherwise, the for loop execution ends.
- ***update***: Executed each iteration after the code in the loop has executed. This is typically used to increment a counter that is used in statement 2.

The following example illustrates not only a basic for loop but also the ability to nest one loop inside another:

```
for (var x=1; x<=3; x++){
  for (var y=1; y<=3; y++){
    console.log(x + " X " + y + " = " + (x*y) + "<br>");
  }
}
```

The resulting output to the web console is

```
1 X 1 = 1
1 X 2 = 2
1 X 3 = 3
2 X 1 = 2
2 X 2 = 4
2 X 3 = 6
3 X 1 = 3
3 X 2 = 6
3 X 3 = 9
```

`for/in` Loops

Another type of `for` loop is the `for/in` loop. The `for/in` loop executes on any data type that can be iterated on. For the most part, you use the `for/in` loop on arrays and objects. The following example illustrates the syntax and behavior of the `for/in` loop on a simple array:

```
var days = ["Monday", "Tuesday", "Wednesday", "Thursday", "Friday"];
for (var idx in days){
  console.log("It's " + days[idx] + "<br>");
}
```

Notice that the variable `idx` is adjusted each iteration through the loop from the beginning array index to the last. The resulting output is

```
It's Monday
It's Tuesday
It's Wednesday
It's Thursday
It's Friday
```

Interrupting Loops

When working with loops there are times that you need to interrupt the execution of code inside the code itself without waiting for the next iteration. There are two different ways to do this: using the `break` and `continue` keywords.

The `break` keyword stops execution of the `for` or `while` loop completely. The `continue` keyword, on the other hand, stops execution of the code inside the loop and continues on with the next iteration. Consider the following examples:

Using a `break` if the day is Wednesday:

```
var days = ["Monday", "Tuesday", "Wednesday", "Thursday", "Friday"];
for (var idx in days){
  if (days[idx] == "Wednesday")
    break;
  console.log("It's " + days[idx] + "<br>");
}
```

Once the value is Wednesday, loop execution stops completely:

```
It's Monday
It's Tuesday
```

Using a `continue` if the day is Wednesday:

```
var days = ["Monday", "Tuesday", "Wednesday", "Thursday", "Friday"];
for (var idx in days){
  if (days[idx] == "Wednesday")
    continue;
  console.log("It's " + days[idx] + "<br>");
}
```

Notice that the write is not executed for Wednesday because of the `continue` statement; however, the loop execution did complete:

```
It's Monday
It's Tuesday
It's Thursday
It's Friday
```

Creating Functions

One of the most important parts of JavaScript is making code that is reusable by other code. To do this you organize your code into functions that perform specific tasks. A function is a series of code statements combined together in a single block and given a name. The code in the block can then be executed by referencing that name.

Defining Functions

Functions are defined using the `function` keyword followed by a name that describes the use of the function, a list of zero or more arguments in `()`, and a block of one or more code statements in {}. For example, the following is a function definition that writes `"Hello World"` to the console.

```
function myFunction(){
  console.log("Hello World");
}
```

To execute the code in `myFunction()`, all you need to do is add the following line to the main JavaScript or inside another function.

```
myFunction();
```

Passing Variables to Functions

Frequently you need to pass specific values to functions that they will use when executing their code. Values are passed in comma-delimited form to the function. The function definition needs a list of variable names in `()` that match the number being passed in. For example, the following function accepts two arguments, a `name` and `city`, and uses them to build the output string:

```
function greeting(name, city){
  console.log("Hello " + name);
  console.log(". How is the weather in " + city);
}
```

To call the `greeting()` function, you need to pass in a `name` value and a `city` value. The value can be a direct value or a previously defined variable. To illustrate this, the following code executes the `greeting()` function with a `name` variable and a direct string for the `city`:

```
var name = "Brad";
greeting(name, "Florence");
```

Returning Values from Functions

Often, functions need to return a value to the calling code. Adding a `return` keyword followed by a variable or value returns that value from the function. For example, the following code calls a function to format a string, assigns the value returned from the function to a variable, and then writes the value to the console:

```
function formatGreeting(name, city){
  var retStr = "";
  retStr += "Hello <b>" + name +"<b>,<br>);
  retStr += "Welcome to " + city + "!";
 return retStr;
}
var greeting = formatGreeting("Brad", "Rome");
console.log(greeting);
```

You can include more than one `return` statement in the function. When the function encounters a `return` statement, code execution of the function is stopped immediately. If the `return` statement contains a value to return, then that value is returned. The following example shows a function that tests the input and returns immediately if it is zero.

```
function myFunc(value){
  if (value == 0)
    return value;
  <code_to_execute_if_value_nonzero>
  return value;
}
```

Using Anonymous Functions

So far all the examples you have seen are of named functions. JavaScript also provides the ability to create anonymous functions. In a functional language like JavaScript, anonymous functions can be used as parameters to functions, properties of an object, or to return values from a function. These functions have the advantage of being defined directly in the parameter sets when calling other functions. Thus, you do not need a formal definition.

For example, the following code defines a function, `doCalc()`, that accepts three parameters. The first two should be numbers, and the third is a function that will be called and pass the two numbers as arguments:

```
function doCalc(num1, num2, calcFunction){
    return calcFunction(num1, num2);
}
```

You could define a function and then pass the function name without parameters to `doCalc()`, for example:

```
function addFunc(n1, n2){
    return n1 + n2;
}
doCalc(5, 10, addFunc);
```

However, you also have the option to use an anonymous function directly in the call to `doCalc()`, as shown in the following two statements:

```
console.log( doCalc(5, 10, function(n1, n2){ return n1 + n2; }) );
console.log( doCalc(5, 10, function(n1, n2){ return n1 * n2; }) );
```

As you can see, the advantage of using anonymous functions is that you do not need a formal definition because it will not be used anywhere else in your code. This makes JavaScript code more concise and readable.

Understanding Variable Scope

Once you start adding conditions, functions, and loops to your JavaScript applications, you need to understand variable scoping. Variable scope is simply "the value of a specific variable name at the current line of code being executed."

JavaScript allows you to define both a global and a local version of the variable. The global version is defined in the main JavaScript, and local versions are defined inside functions. When you define a local version in a function, a new variable is created in memory. Within that function you reference the local version. Outside that function, you reference the global version.

To understand variable scoping better, consider the following code:

```
var myVar = 1;
function writeIt(){
  var myVar = 2;
  console.log("Variable = " + myVar);
  writeMore();
}
function writeMore(){
  console.log("Variable = " + myVar);
}
writeIt();
```

The global variable `myVar` is defined on line 1; then on line 3 a local version is defined within the `writeIt()` function. Line 4 writes `"Variable = 2"` to the console. Then in line 5, `writeMore()` is called. Since no local version of `myVar` is defined in `writeMore()`, the value of the global `myVar` is written in line 8.

Using JavaScript Objects

JavaScript has several built-in objects such as Number, Array, String, Date, and Math. Each of these built-in objects has member properties and methods. In addition to the JavaScript objects, Node.js, MongoDB, Express, and Angular add their own built-in objects as well.

JavaScript provides a nice object-oriented programming structure for you to create your own custom objects. Using objects rather than just a collection of functions is key to writing clean, efficient, reusable JavaScript code.

Using Object Syntax

To use objects in JavaScript effectively, you need to have an understanding of their structure and syntax. An object is really just a container to group multiple values and, in some instances, functions together. The values of an object are called *properties*, and functions are called *methods*.

To use a JavaScript object, you must first create an instance of the object. Object instances are created using the `new` keyword with the object constructor name. For example, to create a number object, you use the following line of code to create an instance of the built-in `Number` object in JavaScript:

```
var x = new Number ("5");
```

Object syntax is straightforward: You use the object name, followed by a dot, and then the property or method name. For example, the following lines of code get and set the `name` property of an object named `myObj`:

```
var s = myObj.name;
myObj.name = "New Name";
```

You can also get and set object methods of an object in the same manner. For example, the following lines of code call the `getName()` method and then change the method function on an object named `myObj`:

```
var name = myObj.getName();
myObj.getName = function() { return this.name; };
```

You can also create objects and assign variables and functions directly using {} syntax. For example, the following code defines a new object and assigns values and a method function:

```
var obj = {
    name: "My Object",
    value: 7,
    getValue: function() { return this.value; }
};
```

You can also access members of a JavaScript object using the `object[propertyName]` syntax. This is useful when you are using dynamic property names or if the property name must include characters not supported by JavaScript. The following examples access the `"User Name"` and `"Other Name"` properties of an object named `myObj`:

```
var propName = "User Name";
var val1 = myObj[propName];
var val2 = myObj["Other Name"];
```

Creating Custom-Defined Objects

As you have seen so far, using the built-in JavaScript objects has several advantages. As you begin to write code that uses more and more data, you will find yourself wanting to build your own custom objects with specific properties and methods.

JavaScript objects can be defined in a couple different ways. The simplest way is the on-the-fly method: You create a generic object and then add properties to it as needed.

For example, to create a user object and assign a first and last name as well as define a function to return the name, you could use the following code:

```
var user = new Object();
user.first="Brendan";
user.last="Dayley";
user.getName = function() { return this.first + " " + this.last; }
```

You could also accomplish the same thing through direct assignment using the following syntax where the object is enclosed in {} and the properties are defined using `property:value` syntax:

```
var user = {
  first: Brendan,
  last: 'Dayley',
  getName: function() { return this.first + " " + this.last; }};
```

These first two options work well for simple objects that you do not need to reuse later. A better method for reusable objects is to actually enclose the object inside its own function block. This has the advantage of allowing you to keep all the code pertaining to the object local to the object itself. For example:

```
function User(first, last){
  this.first = first;
  this.last = last;
  this.getName = function( ) { return this.first + " " + this.last; }};
var user = new User("Brendan", "Dayley");
```

The end result of these methods is essentially the same: You have an object with properties that that can be referenced using dot syntax as shown here:

```
console.log(user.getName());
```

Using a Prototyping Object Pattern

An even more advanced method of creating objects is using a prototyping pattern. The prototyping pattern is implemented by defining the functions inside the `prototype` attribute of the object instead of the object itself. The advantage of prototyping is that the functions defined in the prototype are created only once when the JavaScript is loaded, instead of each time a new object is created.

The following example shows the code necessary to implement the prototyping pattern. Notice that the object `UserP` is defined and then the `UserP.prototype` is set to include the `getFullName()` function. You can include as many functions in the prototype as you want. Each time a new object is created, those functions will be available.

```
function UserP(first, last){
  this.first = first;
  this.last = last;
}
UserP.prototype = {
  getFullName: function(){
      return this.first + " " + this.last;
    }
};
```

Manipulating Strings

The `String` object is by far the most commonly used object in JavaScript. JavaScript automatically creates a `String` object for you any time you define a variable that has a string data type. For example:

```
var myStr = "Teach Yourself jQuery & JavaScript in 24 Hours";
```

When creating a string, several special characters cannot be directly added to the string. For these characters, JavaScript provides a set of escape codes described in Table 2.5.

Table 2.5 **`String` object escape codes**

Escape	Description	Example	Output String
`\'`	Single quote mark	`"couldn\'t be"`	`couldn't be`
`\"`	Double quote mark	`"I \"think\" I \"am\""`	`I "think" I "am"`
`\\`	Backslash	`"one\\two\\three"`	`one\two\three`
`\n`	New line	`"I am\nI said"`	`I am` `I said`
`\r`	Carriage return	`"to be\ror not"`	`to be` `or not`

Escape	Description	Example	Output String
`\t`	Tab	`"one\ttwo\tthree"`	`one two three`
`\b`	Backspace	`"correctoin\b\b\bion"`	`correction`
`\f`	Form feed	`"Title A\fTitle B"`	`Title A then Title B`

To determine the length of the string, you can use the `length` property of the `String` object, for example:

```
var numOfChars = myStr.length;
```

The `String` object has several functions that allow you to access and manipulate the string in various ways. The methods for string manipulation are described in Table 2.6.

Table 2.6 **Methods to manipulate `String` objects**

Method	Description
`charAt(index)`	Returns the character at the specified index.
`charCodeAt(index)`	Returns the `unicode` value of the character at the specified index.
`concat(str1, str2, ...)`	Joins two or more strings, and returns a copy of the joined strings.
`fromCharCode()`	Converts `unicode` values to actual characters.
`indexOf(subString)`	Returns the position of the first occurrence of a specified `subString` value. Returns `-1` if the substring is not found.
`lastIndexOf(subString)`	Returns the position of the last occurrence of a specified `subString` value. Returns `-1` if the substring is not found.
`match(regex)`	Searches the string and returns all matches to the regular expression.
`replace(subString/regex, replacementString)`	Searches the string for a match of the `subString` or regular expression, and replaces the matched substring with a new substring.
`search(regex)`	Searches the string based on the regular expression and returns the position of the first match.
`slice(start, end)`	Returns a new string that has the portion of the string between the `start` and `end` positions removed.
`split(sep, limit)`	Splits a string into an array of substrings based on a separator character or regular expression. The optional `limit` argument defines the maximum number of splits to make starting from the beginning.

Method	Description
`substr(start,length)`	Extracts the characters from a string, beginning at a specified `start` position, and through the specified `length` of characters.
`substring(from, to)`	Returns a substring of characters between the `from` and `to` index.
`toLowerCase()`	Converts the string to lowercase.
`toUpperCase()`	Converts a string to uppercase.
`valueOf()`	Returns the primitive string value.

To get you started on using the functionality provided in the `String` object, the following sections describe some of the common tasks that can be done using `String` object methods.

Combining Strings

Multiple strings can be combined either by using a + operation or by using the `concat()` function on the first string. For example, in the following code `sentence1` and `sentence2` will be the same:

```
var word1 = "Today ";
var word2 = "is ";
var word3 = "tomorrow\'s";
var word4 = "yesterday.";
var sentence1 = word1 + word2 + word3 + word4;
var sentence2 = word1.concat(word2, word3, word4);
```

Searching a String for a Substring

To tell whether a string is a substring of another, you can use the `indexOf()` method. For example, the following code writes the string to the console only if it contains the word "think":

```
var myStr = "I think, therefore I am.";
if (myStr.indexOf("think") != -1){
  console.log (myStr);
}
```

Replacing a Word in a String

Another common `String` object task is replacing one substring with another. To replace a word or phrase in a string, use `the replace()` method. The following code replaces the text `"<username>"` with the value of the variable `username`:

```
var username = "Brendan";
var output = "<username> please enter your password: ";
output.replace("<username>", username);
```

Splitting a String into an Array

A common task with strings is to split them into arrays using a separator character. For example, the following code splits a time string into an array of its basic parts using the `split()` method on the `":"` separator:

```
var t = "12:10:36";
var tArr = t.split(":");
var hour = t[0];
var minute = t[1];
var second = t[2];
```

Working with Arrays

The `Array` object provides a means of storing and handling a set of other objects. Arrays can store numbers, strings, or other JavaScript objects. There are a few different methods to create JavaScript arrays. For example, the following statements create three identical versions of the same array:

```
var arr = ["one", "two", "three"];
var arr2 = new Array();
arr2[0] = "one";
arr2[1] = "two";
arr2[2] = "three";
var arr3 = new Array();
arr3.push("one");
arr3.push("two");
arr3.push("three");
```

The first method defines `arr` and sets the contents in a single statement using `[]`. The second method creates the `arr2` object and then adds items to it using direct index assignment. The third method creates the `arr3` object and then uses the best option for extending arrays, which is to use the `push()` method to push items onto the array.

To get the number of elements in the array, you can use the `length` property of the `Array` object, for example:

```
var numOfItems = arr.length;
```

Arrays are zero-based indexed, meaning that the first item is at index 0 and so on. For example, in the following code the value of the variable `first` will be `Monday`, and the value of variable `last` will be `Friday`:

```
var week = ["Monday", "Tuesday", "Wednesday", "Thursday", "Friday"];
var first = w [0];
var last = week[week.length-1];
```

The `Array` object has several built-in functions that allow you to access and manipulate the array in various ways. Table 2.7 describes the methods attached to the `Array` object that allows you to manipulate the array contents.

Table 2.7 **Methods to manipulate `Array` objects**

Method	Description
`concat(arr1, arr2, ...)`	Returns a joined copy of the arrays that are passed as arguments.
`indexOf(value)`	Returns the first index of the `value` in the array or `-1` if the item is not found.
`join(separator)`	Joins all elements of an array separated by the separator into a single string. If no separator is specified, then a comma is used.
`lastIndexOf(value)`	Returns the last index of the `value` in the array or `-1` if the value is not found.
`pop()`	Removes the last element from the array and returns that element.
`push(item1, item2, ...)`	Adds one or more new elements to the end of an array and returns the new length.
`reverse()`	Reverses the order of all elements in the array.
`shift()`	Removes the first element of an array and returns that element.
`slice(start, end)`	Returns the elements between the `start` and `end` indexes.
`sort(sortFunction)`	Sorts the elements of the array. The `sortFunction` is optional.
`splice(index, count, item1, item2...)`	At the `index` specified, count number items are removed, and then any optional items passed in as arguments are inserted at `index`.
`toString()`	Returns the string form of the array.
`unshift()`	Adds new elements to the beginning of an array and returns the new length.
`valueOf()`	Returns the primitive value of an array object.

To get you started using the functionality provided in the `Array` object, the following sections describe some of the common tasks that can be done using `Array` object methods.

Combining Arrays

You can combine arrays the same way that you combine `String` objects, using `+` statements or using the `concat()` method. In the following code, `arr3` ends up being the same as `arr4`:

```
var arr1 = [1,2,3];
var arr2 = ["three", "four", "five"]
var arr3 = arr1 + arr2;
var arr4 = arr1.concat(arr2);
```

> **Note**
>
> You can combine an array of numbers and an array of strings. Each item in the array keeps its own object type. However, as you use the items in the array you need to keep track of arrays that have more than one data type so that you do not run into problems.

Iterating Through Arrays

You can iterate through an array using a `for` or a `for/in` loop. The following code illustrates iterating through each item in the array using each method:

```
var week = ["Monday", "Tuesday", "Wednesday", "Thursday", "Friday"];
for (var i=0; i<week.length; i++){
  console.log("<li>" + week[i] + "</li>");
}
for (dayIndex in week){
  console.log("<li>" + week[dayIndex] + "</li>");
}
```

Converting an Array into a String

A useful feature of `Array` objects is the ability to combine the elements of a string together to make a `String` object separated by a specific separator using the `join()` method. For example, the following code results in the time components being joined back together into the format 12:10:36:

```
var timeArr = [12,10,36];
var timeStr = timeArray.join(":");
```

Checking Whether an Array Contains an Item

Often you need to check to see whether an array contains a certain item. This can be done by using the `indexOf()` method. If the item is not found in the list, a `-1` is returned. The following function writes a message to the console if an item is in the `week` array:

```
function message(day){
  var week = ["Monday", "Tuesday", "Wednesday", "Thursday", "Friday"];
  if (week.indexOf(day) == -1){
    console.log("Happy " + day);
  }
}
```

Adding and Removing Items to Arrays

There are several methods to add and remove items from `Array` objects using the various built-in methods. Table 2.8 shows you the various methods used in this book.

Table 2.8 **Array object methods used to add and remove elements from arrays**

Statement	Value of x	Value of arr
`var arr = [1,2,3,4,5];`	undefined	1,2,3,4,5
`var x = 0;`	0	1,2,3,4,5
`x = arr.unshift("zero");`	6 (length)	zero,1,2,3,4,5
`x = arr.push(6,7,8);`	9 (length)	zero,1,2,3,4,5,6,7,8
`x = arr.shift();`	zero	1,2,3,4,5,6,7,8
`x = arr.pop();`	8	1,2,3,4,5,6,7
`x=arr.splice(3,3,"four", "five","six");`	4,5,6	1,2,3,four,five,six,7
`x = arr.splice(3,1);`	four	1,2,3,five,six,7
`x = arr.splice(3);`	five,six,7	1,2,3

Adding Error Handling

An important part of JavaScript coding is adding error handling for instances where there may be problems. By default, if a code exception occurs because of a problem in your JavaScript, the script fails and does not finish loading. This is not usually the desired behavior; in fact, it is often catastrophic. To prevent these types of problems, wrap your code in a `try/catch` block.

`try/catch` Blocks

To prevent your code from totally bombing out, use `try/catch` blocks that can handle problems inside your code. If JavaScript encounters an error when executing code in a `try` block, it jumps down and executes the `catch` portion instead of stopping the entire script. If no error occurs, then all of the `try` block is executed and none of the `catch` block.

For example, the following `try/catch` block tries to assign variable `x` to a value of an undefined variable named `badVarNam`.

```
try{
    var x = badVarName;
} catch (err){
    console.log(err.name + ': "' + err.message +  '" occurred when assigning x.');
}
```

Notice that the `catch` statement accepts an `err` parameter, which is an error object. The error object provides the `message` property that provides a description of the error. The error object also provides a `name` property, which is the name of the error type that was thrown.

The preceding code results in an exception and writes the following message:

```
ReferenceError: "badVarName is not defined occurred when assigning x."
```

Throw Your Own Errors

You can also throw your own errors using a `throw` statement. The following code illustrates how to add `throw` statements to a function to throw an error even if a script error does not occur. The function `sqrRoot()` accepts a single argument `x`. It then tests `x` to verify that it is a `positive` number and returns a string with the square root of `x`. If `x` is not a positive number, then the appropriate error is thrown and the `catch` block returns the error:

```
function sqrRoot(x) {
    try {
        if(x=="")     throw {message:"Can't Square Root Nothing"};
        if(isNaN(x)) throw {message:"Can't Square Root Strings"};
        if(x<0)       throw {message:"Sorry No Imagination"};
        return "sqrt("+x+") = " + Math.sqrt(x);
    } catch(err){
        return err.message;
    }
}
function writeIt(){
    console.log(sqrRoot("four"));
    console.log(sqrRoot(""));
    console.log(sqrRoot("4"));
    console.log(sqrRoot("-4"));
}
writeIt();
```

The following is the console output showing the different errors that are thrown based on input to the `sqrRoot()` function:

```
Can't Square Root Strings
Can't Square Root Nothing
sqrt(4) = 2
Sorry No Imagination
```

Using `finally`

Another valuable tool in exception handling is the `finally` keyword. A `finally` keyword can be added to the end of a `try/catch` block. After the `try/catch` blocks are executed, the `finally` keyword is always executed. It doesn't matter if an error occurs and is caught or if the `try` block is fully executed.

The following is an example of using a `finally` block inside a webpage:

```
function testTryCatch(value){
  try {
    if (value < 0){
      throw "too small";
```

```
    } else if (value > 10){
      throw "too big";
    }
    your_code_here
    catch (err) {
    console.log("The number was " + err.message);
  } finally {
    console.log("This is always written.");
  }
}
```

Summary

Understanding JavaScript is critical to working in the Node.js, MongoDB, Express, and Angular environments. This chapter discussed enough of the basic JavaScript language syntax for you to grasp the concepts in the rest of the book. The chapter discussed creating objects and functions, as well as working with strings and arrays. You also learned how to apply error handling to your scripts, which is critical in the Node.js environment.

Next

In the next chapter, you jump right into the basics of setting up a Node.js project. You also learn a few of the language idioms and a see simple practical example.

3

Getting Started with Node.js

This chapter introduces you to the Node.js environment. Node.js is a website/application framework designed with high scalability in mind. It was designed to take advantage of the existing JavaScript technology in the browser and flow those same concepts all the way down through the webserver into the backend services. Node.js is a great technology that is easy to implement and yet extremely scalable.

Node.js is a modular platform, meaning that much of the functionality is provided by external modules rather than being built in to the platform. The Node.js culture is active in creating and publishing modules for almost every imaginable need. Therefore, much of this chapter focuses on understanding and using the Node.js tools to build, publish, and use your own Node.js modules in applications.

Understanding Node.js

Node.js was developed in 2009 by Ryan Dahl as an answer to the frustration caused by concurrency issues, especially when dealing with web services. Google had just come out with the V8 JavaScript engine for the Chrome web browser, which was highly optimized for web traffic. Dahl created Node.js on top of V8 as a server-side environment that matched the client-side environment in the browser.

The result is an extremely scalable server-side environment that allows developers to more easily bridge the gap between client and server. The fact that Node.js is written in JavaScript allows developers to easily navigate back and forth between client and server code and even reuse code between the two environments.

Node.js has a great ecosystem with new extensions being written all the time. The Node.js environment is clean and easy to install, configure, and deploy. Literally in only an hour or two you can have a Node.js webserver up and running.

Who Uses Node.js?

Node.js quickly gained popularity among a wide variety of companies. These companies use Node.js first and foremost for scalability but also for ease of maintenance and faster development. The following are just a few of the companies using the Node.js technology:

- Yahoo!
- LinkedIn
- eBay
- *New York Times*
- Dow Jones
- Microsoft

What Is Node.js Used For?

Node.js can be used for a wide variety of purposes. Because it is based on V8 and has highly optimized code to handle HTTP traffic, the most common use is as a webserver. However, Node.js can also be used for a variety of other web services such as:

- Web services APIs such as REST
- Real-time multiplayer games
- Backend web services such as cross-domain, server-side requests
- Web-based applications
- Multiclient communication such as IM

What Does Node.js Come With?

Node.js comes with many built-in modules available right out of the box. This book covers many but not all of these modules:

- **Assertion testing:** Allows you to test functionality within your code.
- **Buffer:** Enables interaction with TCP streams and file system operations. (See Chapter 5, "Handling Data I/O in Node.js.")
- **C/C++ add-ons:** Allows for C or C++ code to be used just like any other Node.js module.
- **Child processes:** Allows you to create child processes. (See Chapter 9, "Scaling Applications Using Multiple Processors in Node.js.")
- **Cluster:** Enables the use of multicore systems. (See Chapter 9.)
- **Command line options:** Gives you Node.js commands to use from a terminal.
- **Console:** Gives the user a debugging console.

- **Crypto:** Allows for the creation of custom encryption. (See Chapter 10, "Using Additional Node.js Modules.")
- **Debugger:** Allows debugging of a Node.js file.
- **DNS:** Allows connections to DNS servers. (See Chapter 10.)
- **Errors:** Allows for the handling of errors.
- **Events:** Enables the handling of asynchronous events. (See Chapter 4, "Using Events, Listeners, Timers, and Callbacks in Node.js.")
- **File system:** Allows for file I/O with both synchronous and asynchronous methods. (See Chapter 6, "Accessing the File System from Node.js.")
- **Globals:** Makes frequently used modules available without having to include them first. (See Chapter 10.)
- **HTTP:** Enables support for many HTTP features. (See Chapter 7, "Implementing HTTP Services in Node.js.")
- **HTTPS:** Enables HTTP over the TLS/SSL. (See Chapter 7.)
- **Modules:** Provides the module loading system for Node.js. (See Chapter 3.)
- **Net:** Allows the creation of servers and clients. (See Chapter 8, "Implementing Socket Services in Node.js.")
- **OS:** Allows access to the operating system that Node.js is running on. (See Chapter 10.)
- **Path:** Enables access to file and directory paths. (See Chapter 6.)
- **Process:** Provides information and allows control over the current Node.js process. (See Chapter 9.)
- **Query strings:** Allows for parsing and formatting URL queries. (See Chapter 7.)
- **Readline:** Enables an interface to read from a data stream. (See Chapter 5.)
- **REPL:** Allows developers to create a command shell.
- **Stream:** Provides an API to build objects with the stream interface. (See Chapter 5.)
- **String decoder:** Provides an API to decode buffer objects into strings. (See Chapter 5.)
- **Timers:** Allows for scheduling functions to be called in the future. (See Chapter 4.)
- **TLS/SSL:** Implements TLS and SSL protocols. (See Chapter 8.)
- **URL:** Enables URL resolution and parsing. (See Chapter 7.)
- **Utilities:** Provides support for various apps and modules.
- **V8:** Exposes APIs for the Node.js version of V8. (See Chapter 10.)
- **VM:** Allows for a V8 virtual machine to run and compile code.
- **ZLIB:** Enables compression using Gzip and Deflate/Inflate. (See Chapter 5.)

Installing Node.js

To easily install Node.js, download an installer from the Node.js website at http://nodejs.org. The Node.js installer installs the necessary files on your PC to get Node.js up and running. No additional configuration is necessary to start creating Node.js applications.

Looking at the Node.js Install Location

If you look at the install location, you will see a couple of executable files and a `node_modules` folder. The `node` executable file starts the Node.js JavaScript VM. The following list describes the executables in the Node.js install location that you need to get started:

- **node:** This file starts a Node.js JavaScript VM. If you pass in a JavaScript file location, Node.js executes that script. If no target JavaScript file is specified, then a script prompt is shown that allows you to execute JavaScript code directly from the console.
- **npm:** This command is used to manage the Node.js packages discussed in the next section.
- **node_modules:** This folder contains the installed Node.js packages. These packages act as libraries that extend the capabilities of Node.js.

Verify Node.js Executables

Take a minute and verify that Node.js is installed and working before moving on. To do so, open a console prompt and execute the following command to bring up a Node.js VM:

```
node
```

Next, at the Node.js prompt execute the following to write `"Hello World"` to the screen.

```
>console.log("Hello World");
```

You should see `"Hello World"` output to the console screen. Now exit the console using Ctrl+C in Windows or Cmd+C on a Mac.

Next, verify that the `npm` command is working by executing the following command in the OS console prompt:

```
npm version
```

You should see output similar to the following:

```
{ npm: '3.10.5',
  ares: '1.10.1-DEV',
  http_parser: '2.7.0',
  icu: '57.1',
  modules: '48',
  node: '6.5.0',
  openssl: '1.0.2h',
```

```
uv: '1.9.1',
v8: '5.1.281.81',
zlib: '1.2.8'}
```

Selecting a Node.js IDE

If you are planning on using an Integrated Development Environment (IDE) for your Node.js projects, you should take a minute and configure that now as well. Most developers are particular about the IDE that they like to use, and there will likely be a way to configure at least for JavaScript if not Node.js directly. For example, Eclipse has some great Node.js plugins, and the WebStorm IDE by IntelliJ has some good features for Node.js built in. If you are unsure of where to start, we use Visual Studio Code for the built-in TypeScript functionality required later in this book.

That said, you can use any editor you want to generate your Node.js web applications. In reality, all you need is a decent text editor. Almost all the code you will generate will be .js, .json, .html, and .css. So pick the editor in which you feel the most comfortable writing those types of files.

Working with Node Packages

One of the most powerful features of the Node.js framework is the ability to easily extend it with additional Node Packaged Modules (NPMs) using the Node Package Manager (NPM). That's right, in the Node.js world, NPM stands for two things. This book refers to the Node Packaged Modules as *modules* to make it easier to follow.

What Are Node Packaged Modules?

A Node Packaged Module is a packaged library that can easily be shared, reused, and installed in different projects. Many different modules are available for a variety of purposes. For example, the Mongoose module provides an ODM (Operational Data Model) for MongoDB, Express extends Node's HTTP capabilities, and so on.

Node.js modules are created by various third-party organizations to provide the needed features that Node.js lacks out of the box. This community of contributors is active in adding and updating modules.

Node Packaged Modules include a `package.json` file that defines the packages. The `package.json` file includes informational metadata, such as the name, version author, and contributors, as well as control metadata, such as dependencies and other requirements that the Node Package Manager uses when performing actions such as installation and publishing.

Understanding the Node Package Registry

The Node modules have a managed location called the Node Package Registry where packages are registered. This allows you to publish your own packages in a location where others can use them as well as download packages that others have created.

The Node Package Registry is located at https://npmjs.com. From this location you can view the newest and most popular modules as well as search for specific packages, as shown in Figure 3.1.

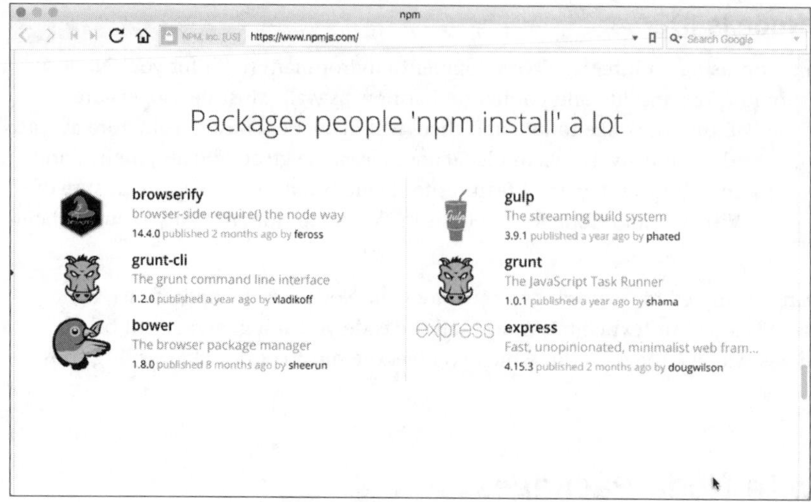

Figure 3.1 The official Node Package Modules website

Using the Node Package Manager

The Node Package Manager you have already seen is a command-line utility. It allows you to find, install, remove, publish, and do everything else related to Node Package Modules. The Node Package Manager provides the link between the Node Package Registry and your development environment.

The simplest way to really explain the Node Package Manager is to list some of the command-line options and what they do. You use many of these options in the rest of this chapter and throughout the book. Table 3.1 lists the Node Package Manager commands.

Table 3.1 **`npm` command-line options (with `express` as the package, where appropriate)**

Option	Description	Example
`search`	Finds module packages in the repository	`npm search express`

`install`	Installs a package either using a `package.json` file, from the repository, or a local location	`npm install`
		`npm install express`
		`npm install express@0.1.1`
		`npm install ../tModule.tgz`

`install -g`	Installs a package globally	`npm install express -g`

Option	Description	Example
`remove`	Removes a module	`npm remove express`
`pack`	Packages the module defined by the `package.json` file into a .tgz file	`npm pack`
`view`	Displays module details	`npm view express`
`publish`	Publishes the module defined by a `package.json` file to the registry	`npm publish`
`unpublish`	Unpublishes a module you have published	`npm unpublish myModule`

`owner`	Allows you to add, remove, and list owners of a package in the repository	`npm add bdayley myModule`
		`npm rm bdayley myModule`
		`npm ls myModule`

Searching for Node Package Modules

You can also search for modules in the Node Package Registry directly from the command prompt using the `npm search` *<search_string>* command. For example, the following command searches for modules related to `openssl` and displays the results as shown in Figure 3.2:

```
npm search openssl
```

```
NAME                DESCRIPTION
bignum              Arbitrary-precision integer arithmetic using OpenSSL

certgen             Certificate generation library that uses the openssl command l
cipherpipe          Thin wrapper around openssl for encryption/decryption
csr                 Read csr file
csr-gen             Generates OpenSSL Certificate Signing Requests
dcrypt              extended openssl bindings
fixedentropy        ```js // V8 supports custom sources of entropy. // by default,

lockbox             Simple, strong encryption.

node-hardcoressl    HardcoreSSL is a package for obtaining low-level asynchronous
nrsa                OpenSSL's RSA encrypt/decrypt routines
openssl             openssl wrapper
openssl-wrapper     OpenSSL wrapper
rsa                 OpenSSL's RSA encrypt/decrypt routines
rsautl              A wrapper for OpenSSL's rsautl
selfsigned          Generate self signed certificates private and public keys
ssh-key-decrypt     Decrypt encrypted ssh private keys

ssl                 Verification of SSL certificates

ssl-keychain        OpenSSL Keychain and Key generation module
ssl-keygen          OpenSSL Key Generation module
ursa                RSA public/private key crypto

x509-keygen         node.js module to generate self-signed certificate via openssl
```

Figure 3.2 Searching for Node.js modules from the command prompt

Installing Node Packaged Modules

To use a Node module in your applications, it must first be installed where Node can find it. To install a Node module, use the `npm install <module_name>` command. This downloads the Node module to your development environment and places it into the `node_modules` folder where the `install` command is run. For example, the following command installs the `express` module:

```
npm install express
```

The output of the `npm install` command displays the dependency hierarchy installed with the module. For example, the following code block shows part of the output from installing the `express` module.

```
C:\express\example
`-- express@4.14.0
  +-- accepts@1.3.3
  | +-- mime-types@2.1.11
  | | `-- mime-db@1.23.0
  | `-- negotiator@0.6.1
  +-- array-flatten@1.1.1
  +-- content-disposition@0.5.1
  +-- content-type@1.0.2
  +-- cookie@0.3.1
  +-- cookie-signature@1.0.6
  +-- debug@2.2.0
  | `-- ms@0.7.1 ...
```

The dependency hierarchy is listed; some of the methods Express requires are `cookie-signature`, `range-parser`, `debug`, `fresh`, `cookie`, and `send` modules. Each of these was downloaded during the install. Notice that the version of each dependency module is listed.

Node.js has to be able to handle dependency conflicts. For example, the `express` module requires `cookie 0.3.1`, but another module may require `cookie 0.3.0`. To handle this situation, a separate copy for the cookie module is placed in each module's folder under another `node_modules` folder.

To illustrate how modules are stored in a hierarchy, consider the following example of how `express` looks on disk. Notice that the `cookie` and `send` modules are located under the `express` module hierarchy, and that since the `send` module requires `mime` it is located under the `send` hierarchy:

```
./
./node_modules
./node_modules/express
./node_modules/express/node_modules/cookie
./node_modules/express/node_modules/send
./node_modules/express/node_modules/send/node_modules/mime
```

Using package.json

All Node modules must include a package.json file in their root directory. The package.json file is a simple JSON text file that defines the module including dependencies. The package.json file can contain a number of different directives to tell the Node Package Manager how to handle the module.

The following is an example of a package.json file with a name, version, description, and dependencies:

```
{
    "name": "my_module",
    "version": "0.1.0",
    "description": "a simple node.js module",
    "dependencies" : {
        "express"   :  "latest"
    }
}
```

The only required directives in the package.json file are name and version. The rest depend on what you want to include. Table 3.2 describes the most common directives:

Table 3.2 **Directives used in the package.json file**

Directive	Description	Example
name	Unique name of package.	"name": "camelot"
preferGlobal	Indicates this module prefers to be installed globally.	"preferGlobal": true
version	Version of the module.	"version": 0.0.1
author	Author of the project.	"author": "arthur@???.com"
description	Textual description of module.	"description": "a silly place"
contributors	Additional contributors to the module.	"contributors": [{ "name": "gwen", "email": "gwen@???.com"}]
bin	Binary to be installed globally with project.	"bin: { "excalibur": "./bin/excalibur"}
scripts	Specifies parameters that execute console apps when launching node.	"scripts" { "start": "node ./bin/excalibur", "test": "echo testing"}
main	Specifies the main entry point for the app. This can be a binary or a .js file.	"main": "./bin/excalibur"

Directive	Description	Example

`repository`	Specifies the repository type and location of the package.	`"repository": {`
		`"type": "git",`
		`"location":`
		`"http://???.com/c.git"}`

`keywords`	Specifies keywords that show up in the `npm` search.	`"keywords": [` `"swallow", "unladen" ]`

`dependencies`	Modules and versions this module depends on. You can use the `*` and `x` wildcards.	`"dependencies": {`
		`"express": "latest",`
		`"connect": "2.x.x,`
		`"cookies": "*" }`

`engines`	Version of `node` this package works with.	`"engines": {` `"node": ">=6.5"}`

A great way to use `package.json` files is to automatically download and install the dependencies for your Node.js app. All you need to do is create a `package.json` file in the root of your project code and add the necessary dependencies to it. For example, the following `package.json` requires the `express` module as a dependency.

```
{
    "name": "my_module",
    "version": "0.1.0",
    "dependencies" : {
        "express"  :  "latest"
    }
}
```

Then you run the following command from root of your package, and the `express` module is automatically installed.

```
npm install
```

Notice that no module is specified in the `npm install`. That is because `npm` looks for a `package.json` file by default. Later, as you need additional modules, all you need to do is add those to the `dependencies` directive and then run `npm install` again.

Creating a Node.js Application

Now you have enough information to jump into a Node.js project and get your feet wet. In this section, you create your own Node Packaged Module and then use that module as a library in a Node.js application.

The code in this exercise is kept to a minimum so that you can see exactly how to create a package, publish it, and then use it again.

Creating a Node.js Packaged Module

To create a Node.js Packaged Module you need to create the functionality in JavaScript, define the package using a `package.json` file, and then either publish it to the registry or package it for local use.

The following steps take you through the process of building a Node.js Packaged Module using an example called `censorify`. The `censorify` module accepts text and then replaces certain words with asterisks:

1. Create a project folder named `.../censorify`. This is the root of the package.
2. Inside that folder, create a file named `censortext.js`.
3. Add the code from Listing 3.1 to `censortext.js`. Most of the code is just basic JavaScript; however, note that lines 18–20 export the functions `censor()`, `addCensoredWord()`, and `getCensoredWords()`. The `exports.censor` is required for Node.js applications using this module to have access to the `censor()` function as well as the other two.

Listing 3.1 `censortext.js`: **Implementing a simple** `censor` **function and exporting it for other modules using the package**

```
01 var censoredWords = ["sad", "bad", "mad"];
02 var customCensoredWords = [];
03 function censor(inStr) {
04   for (idx in censoredWords) {
05     inStr = inStr.replace(censoredWords[idx], "****");
06   }
07   for (idx in customCensoredWords) {
08     inStr = inStr.replace(customCensoredWords[idx], "****");
09   }
10   return inStr;
11 }
12 function addCensoredWord(word){
13   customCensoredWords.push(word);
14 }
15 function getCensoredWords(){
16   return censoredWords.concat(customCensoredWords);
17 }
18 exports.censor = censor;
19 exports.addCensoredWord = addCensoredWord;
20 exports.getCensoredWords = getCensoredWords;
```

4. Once the module code is completed, you need to create a `package.json` file that is used to generate the Node.js Packaged Module. Create a `package.json` file in the

.../censorify folder. Then add contents similar to Listing 3.2. Specifically, you need to add the name, version, and main directives as a minimum. The main directive needs to be the name of the main JavaScript module that will be loaded, in this case censortext. Note that the .js is not required, Node.js automatically searches for the .js extension.

Listing 3.2 package.json: **Defining the Node.js module**

```
{
  "author": "Brendan Dayley",
  "name": "censorify",
  "version": "0.1.1",
  "description": "Censors words out of text",
  "main": "censortext",
  "dependencies": {},
  "engines": {
      "node": "*"
  }
}
```

5. Create a file named README.md in the .../censorify folder. You can put whatever read me instructions you want in this file.
6. Navigate to the .../censorify folder in a console window and run the npm pack command to build a local package module.
7. The npm pack command creates a censorify-0.1.1.tgz file in the .../censorify folder. This is your first Node.js Packaged Module.

Publishing a Node.js Packaged Module to the NPM Registry

In the previous section you created a local Node.js Packaged Module using the npm pack command. You can also publish that same module to the NPM repository at http://npmjs.com/.

When modules are published to the NPM registry, they are accessible to everyone using the NPM manager utility discussed earlier. This allows you to distribute your modules and applications to others more easily.

The following steps describe the process of publishing the module to the NPM registry. These steps assume that you have completed steps 1 through 5 from the previous section:

1. Create a public repository to contain the code for the module. Then push the contents of the .../censorify folder up to that location. The following is an example of a Github repository URL:

   https://github.com/username/projectname/directoryName/ch03/censorify

2. Create an account at https://npmjs.org/signup.
3. Use the npm adduser command from a console prompt to add the user you created to the environment.

4. Type in the username, password, and email that you used to create the account in step 2.
5. Modify the `package.json` file to include the new repository information and any keywords that you want made available in the registry search as shown in lines 7–14 in Listing 3.3.

Listing 3.3 `package.json`: **Defining the Node.js module that includes the repository and keywords information**

```
01 {
02   "author": "Brad Dayley",
03   "name": "censorify",
04   "version": "0.1.1",
05   "description": "Censors words out of text",
06   "main": "censortext",
07   "repository": {
08     "type": "git",
09     //"url": "Enter your github url"
10   },
11   "keywords": [
12     "censor",
13     "words"
14   ],
15   "dependencies": {},
16   "engines": {
17       "node": "*"
18   }
19 }
```

6. Publish the module using the following command from the `.../censor` folder in the console:

   ```
   npm publish
   ```

Once the package has been published you can search for it on the NPM registry and use the `npm install` command to install it into your environment.

To remove a package from the registry make sure that you have added a user with rights to the module to the environment using `npm adduser` and then execute the following command:

```
npm unpublish <project name>
```

For example, the following command unpublishes the `censorify` module:

```
npm unpublish censorify
```

In some instances you cannot unpublish the module without using the `--force` option. This option forces the removal and deletion of the module from the registry. For example:

```
npm unpublish censorify --force
```

Using a Node.js Packaged Module in a Node.js Application

In the previous sections you learned how to create and publish a Node.js module. This section provides an example of actually using a Node.js module inside your Node.js applications. Node.js makes this simple: All you need to do is install the NPM into your application structure and then use the `require()` method to load the module.

The `require()` method accepts either an installed module name or a path to a .js file located on the file system. For example:

```
require("censorify")
require("./lib/utils.js")
```

The .js filename extension is optional. If it is omitted, Node.js searches for it.

The following steps take you through that process so you can see how easy it is:

1. Create a project folder named `.../readwords`.
2. From a console prompt inside the `.../readwords` folder, use the following command to install the `censorify` module from the `censorify-0.1.1.tgz` package you created earlier:

   ```
   npm install .../censorify/censorify-0.1.1.tgz
   ```

3. Or if you have published the `censorify` module, you can use the standard command to download and install it from the NPM registry:

   ```
   npm install censorify
   ```

4. Verify that a folder named `node_modules` is created along with a subfolder named `censorify`.
5. Create a file named `.../readwords/readwords.js`.
6. Add the contents shown in Listing 3.4 to the `readwords.js` file. Notice that a `require()` call loads the `censorify` module and assigns it to the variable `censor`. Then the `censor` variable can be used to invoke the `getCensoredWords()`, `addCensoredWords()`, and `censor()` functions from the `censorify` module.

Listing 3.4 `readwords.js`: **Loading the** `censorify` **module when displaying text**

```
var censor = require("censorify");
console.log(censor.getCensoredWords());
console.log(censor.censor("Some very sad, bad and mad text."));
censor.addCensoredWord("gloomy");
console.log(censor.getCensoredWords());
console.log(censor.censor("A very gloomy day."));
```

7. Run the `readwords.js` application using the `node readwords.js` command and view the output shown in the following code block. Notice that the censored words are

replaced with `****` and that the new censored word `gloomy` is added to the `censorify` module instance `censor`.

```
C:\nodeCode\ch03\readwords>node readwords
[ 'sad', 'bad', 'mad' ]
Some very *****, ***** and ***** text.
[ 'sad', 'bad', 'mad', 'gloomy' ]
A very *** day.
```

Writing Data to the Console

One of the most useful modules in Node.js during the development process is the `console` module. This module provides a lot of functionality when writing debug and information statements to the console. The `console` module allows you to control output to the console, implement time delta output, and write tracebacks and assertions to the console. This section covers using the `console` module because you need to know it for subsequent chapters in the book.

Because the `console` module is so widely used, you do not need to load it into your modules using a `require()` statement. You simply call the console function using `console.<function>(<parameters>)`. Table 3.3 lists the functions available in the `console` module.

Table 3.3 **Member functions of the `console` module**

Function	Description

`log([data],[...])`	Writes data output to the console. The data variable can be a string or an object that can be resolved to a string. Additional parameters can also be sent. For example:
	`console.log("There are %d items", 5);`
	`>>There are 5 items`

`info([data],[...])`	Same as `console.log`.
`error([data],[...])`	Same as `console.log`; however, the output is also sent to `stderr`.
`warn([data],[...])`	Same as `console.error`.

`dir(obj)`	Writes out a string representation of a JavaScript object to the console. For example:
	`console.dir({name:"Brad", role:"Author"});`
	`>> { name: 'Brad', role: 'Author' }`

`time(label)`	Assigns a current timestamp with ms precision to the string `label`.

Function	Description

timeEnd(label)	Creates a delta between the current time and the timestamp assigned to label and outputs the results. For example:
	console.time("FileWrite");
	f.write(data); //takes about 500ms
	console.timeEnd("FileWrite");
	>> FileWrite: 500ms

trace(label)	Writes out a stack trace of the current position in code to stderr. For example:
	module.trace("traceMark");
	>>Trace: traceMark
	  at Object.<anonymous> (C:\test.js:24:9)
	  at Module._compile (module.js:456:26)
	  at Object.Module._ext.js (module.js:474:10)
	  at Module.load (module.js:356:32)
	  at Function.Module._load (module.js:312:12)
	  at Function.Module.runMain(module.js:497:10)
	  at startup (node.js:119:16)
	  at node.js:901:3

assert(expression, [message])	Writes the message and stack trace to the console if expression evaluates to false.

Summary

This chapter focused on getting you up to speed on the Node.js environment. Node.js Packaged Modules provide the functionality that Node.js does not inherently come with. You can download these modules from the NPM registry, or you can even create and publish your own. The package.json file provides the configuration and definition for every Node.js module.

The examples in this chapter covered creating, publishing, and installing your own Node.js Packaged Modules. You learned how to use the NPM to package a local module as well as publish one to the NPM registry. You then learned how to install the Node.js modules and use them in your own Node.js applications.

Next

The next chapter covers the event-driven nature of Node.js. You see how events work in the Node.js environment and learn how to control, manipulate, and use them in your applications.

4

Using Events, Listeners, Timers, and Callbacks in Node.js

Node.js provides scalability and performance through its powerful event-driven model. This chapter focuses on understanding the model and how it differs from traditional threading models used by most webservers. Understanding the event model is critical because it may force you to change the design thinking for your applications. However, the changes will be well worth the improvement in speed that you get using Node.js.

This chapter also covers the different methods you use to add work to the Node.js event queue. You can add work using event listeners or timers, or you can schedule work directly. You also learn how to implement events in your own custom modules and objects.

Understanding the Node.js Event Model

Node.js applications are run in a single-threaded event-driven model. Although Node.js implements a thread pool in the background to do work, the application itself doesn't have any concept of multiple threads. "Wait, what about performance and scale?" you might ask. At first it may seem counterintuitive, but once you understand the logic behind the Node.js event model it all makes perfect sense.

Comparing Event Callbacks and Threaded Models

In the traditional threaded web model, a request comes in to the webserver and is assigned to an available thread. Then the handling of work for that request continues on that thread until the request is complete and a response is sent.

Figure 4.1 illustrates the threaded model processing two requests, `GetFile` and `GetData`. The `GetFile` request first opens the file, reads the contents, and then sends the data back in a response. All this occurs in order on the same thread. The `GetData` request connects to the DB, queries the necessary data, and then sends the data in the response.

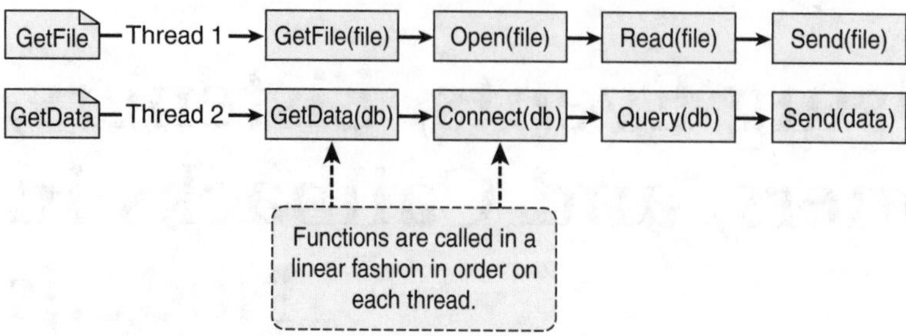

Figure 4.1 Processing two requests on individual threads using the threaded model

The Node.js event model does things differently. Instead of executing all the work for each request on individual threads, work is added to an event queue and then picked up by a single thread running an event loop. The event loop grabs the top item in the event queue, executes it, and then grabs the next item. When executing code that is no longer live or has blocking I/O, instead of calling the function directly, the function is added to the event queue along with a callback that is executed after the function completes. When all events on the Node.js event queue have been executed, the Node application terminates.

Figure 4.2 illustrates the way Node.js handles the `GetFile` and `GetData` requests. The `GetFile` and `GetData` requests are added to the event queue. Node.js first picks up the `GetFile` request, executes it, and then completes by adding the `Open()` callback function to the event queue. Next, it picks up the `GetData` request, executes it, and completes by adding the `Connect()` callback function to the event queue. This continues until there are no callback functions to be executed. Notice in Figure 4.2 that the events for each thread do not necessarily follow a direct interleaved order. For example, the `Connect` request takes longer to complete than the `Read` request, so `Send(file)` is called before `Query(db)`.

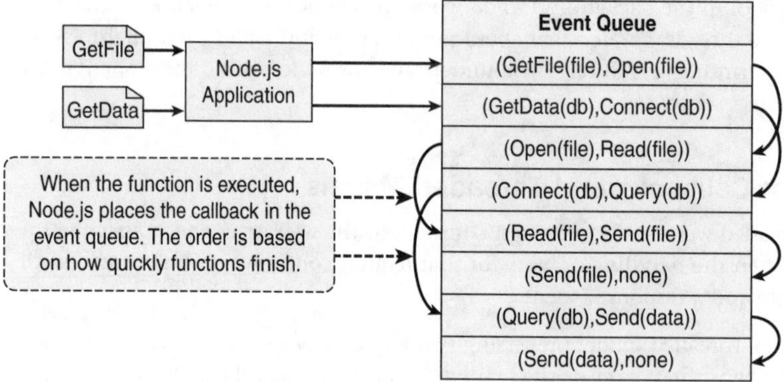

Figure 4.2 Processing two requests on a single event-driven thread using the Node.js event model

Blocking I/O in Node.js

The Node.js event model of using the event callbacks is great until you run into the problem of functions that block waiting for I/O. Blocking I/O stops the execution of the current thread and waits for a response before continuing. Some examples of blocking I/O are

- Reading a file
- Querying a database
- Socket request
- Accessing a remote service

The reason Node.js uses event callbacks is not to have to wait for blocking I/O. Therefore, any requests that perform blocking I/O are performed on a different thread in the background. Node.js implements a thread pool in the background. When an event that requires blocking I/O is retrieved from the event queue, Node.js retrieves a thread from the thread pool and executes the function there instead of on the main event loop thread. This prevents the blocking I/O from holding up the rest of the events in the event queue.

The function executed on the blocking thread can still add events back to the event queue to be processed. For example, a database query call is typically passed a callback function that parses the results and may schedule additional work on the event queue before sending a response.

Figure 4.3 illustrates the full Node.js event model including the event queue, event loop, and the thread pool. Notice that the event loop either executes the function on the event loop thread itself or, for blocking I/O, it executes the function on a separate thread.

The Conversation Example

To help you understand how events work in Node.js versus traditional threaded webservers, consider the example of having different conversations with a large group of people at a party. You are acting the part of the webserver, and the conversations represent the work necessary to process different types of web requests. Your conversations are broken up into several segments with different individuals. You end up talking to one person and then another. Then you go back to the first person and then to a third person, back to the second, and so on.

This example has many similarities to webserver processing. Some conversations end quickly, like a simple request for a piece of data in memory. Others are broken up into several segments as you go back and forth between individuals, similar to a more complex server-side conversation. Still others have long breaks when you are waiting for the other person to respond, similar to blocking I/O requests to the file system, database, or remote service.

Using the traditional webserver threading model in the conversation example sounds great at first because each thread acts like you. The threads/clones can talk back and forth with each person, and it almost seems as though you can have multiple conversations simultaneously. There are two problems with this model.

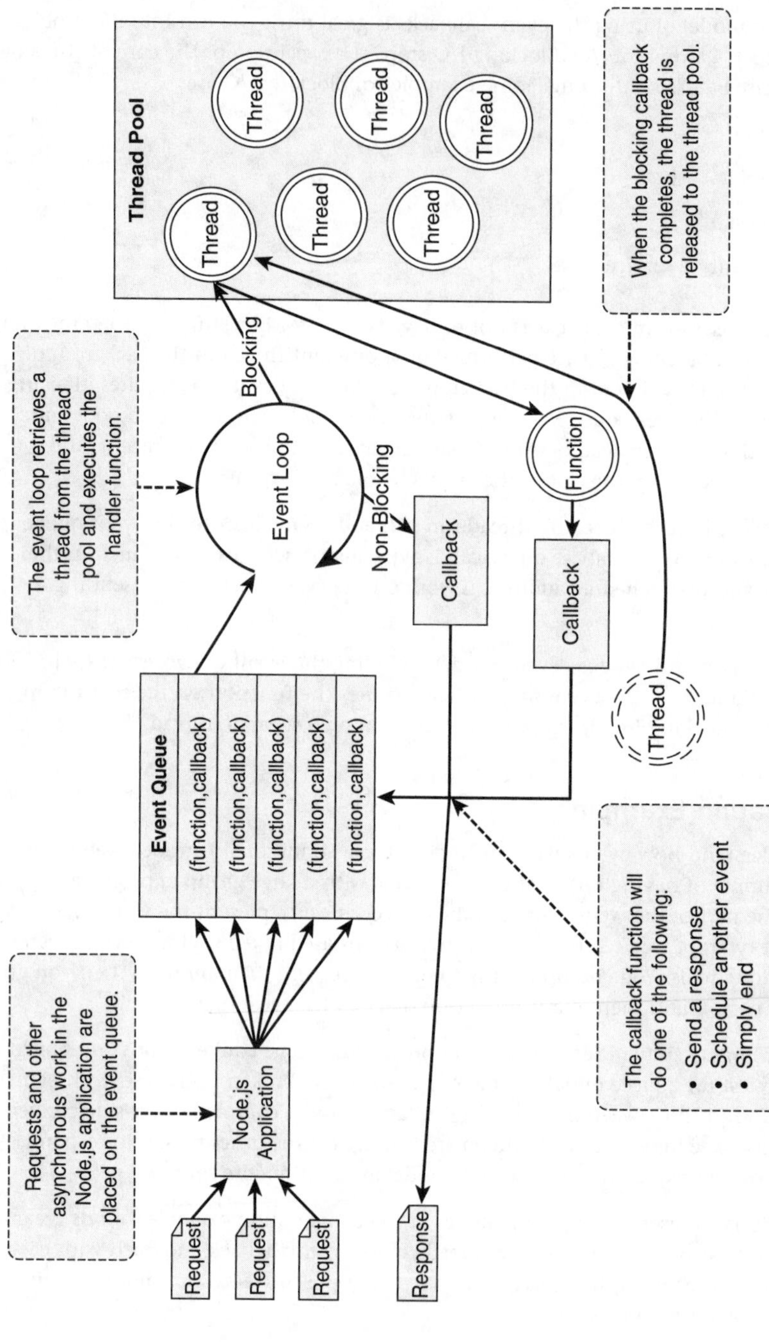

Figure 4.3 In the Node.js event model, work is added as a function with callback to the event queue, and then picked up on the event loop thread. The function is then executed on the event loop thread in the case of non-blocking, or on a separate thread in the case of blocking

First, you are limited by the number of clones. What if you only have five clones? To talk with a sixth person, one clone must completely finish its conversation. The second problem is the limited number of CPUs (or "brains") that the threads ("clones") must share. This means that clones sharing the same brain have to stop talking/listening while other clones are using the brain. You can see that there really isn't a benefit to having clones when they freeze while the other clones are using the brain.

The Node.js event model acts more like real life when compared to the conversation example. First, Node.js applications run on a single thread, which means there is only one of you, no clones. Each time a person asks you a question, you respond as soon as you can. Your interactions are completely event driven, and you move naturally from one person to the next. Therefore, you can have as many conversations going on at the same time as you want by bouncing between individuals. Second, your brain is always focused on the person you are talking to since you aren't sharing it with clones.

So how does Node.js handle blocking I/O requests? That is where the background thread pool comes into play. Node.js hands blocking requests over to a thread in the thread pool so that it has minimal impact on the application processing events. Think about when someone asks you a question that you have to think about. You can still interact with others at the party while trying to process that question in the back of your mind. That processing may impact how fast you interact with others, but you are still able to communicate with several people while processing the longer-lived thought.

Adding Work to the Event Queue

As you create your Node.js applications, keep in mind the event model described in the previous section and apply it to the way you design your code. To leverage the scalability and performance of the event model, make sure that you break work up into chunks that can be performed as a series of callbacks.

Once you have designed your code correctly, you can then use the event model to schedule work on the event queue. In Node.js applications, work is scheduled on the event queue by passing a callback function using one of these methods:

- Make a call to one of the blocking I/O library calls such as writing to a file or connecting to a database.
- Add a built-in event listener to a built-in event such as an `http.request` or `server.connection`.
- Create your own event emitters and add custom listeners to them.
- Use the `process.nextTick` option to schedule work to be picked up on the next cycle of the event loop.
- Use timers to schedule work to be done after a particular amount of time or at periodic intervals.

The following sections discuss implementing timers, `nextTick`, and custom events. They give you an idea of how the event mechanism works. The blocking I/O calls and built-in events are covered in subsequent chapters.

Implementing Timers

A useful feature of Node.js and JavaScript is the ability to delay execution of code for a period of time. This can be useful for cleanup or refresh work that you do not want to always be running. There are three types of timers you can implement in Node.js: timeout, interval, and immediate. The following sections describe each of these timers and how to implement them in your code.

Delaying Work with Timeouts

Timeout timers are used to delay work for a specific amount of time. When that time expires, the callback function is executed and the timer goes away. Use timeouts for work that only needs to be performed once.

Timeout timers are created using the `setTimeout(callback, delayMilliSeconds, [args])` method built into Node.js. When you call `setTimeout()`, the callback function is executed after `delayMilliSeconds` expires. For example, the following executes `myFunc()` after 1 second:

```
setTimeout(myFunc, 1000);
```

The `setTimeout()` function returns a timer object ID. You can pass this ID to `clearTimeout(timeoutId)` at any time before the `delayMilliSeconds` expires to cancel the timeout function. For example:

```
myTimeout =  setTimeout(myFunc, 100000);
…
clearTimeout(myTimeout);
```

Listing 4.1 implements a series of simple timeouts that call the `simpleTimeout()` function, which outputs the number of milliseconds since the timeout was scheduled. Notice that it doesn't matter which order `setTimeout()` is called; the results, shown in Listing 4.1 Output, are in the order that the delay expires.

Listing 4.1 `simple_timer.js`: **Implementing a series of timeouts at various intervals**

```
function simpleTimeout(consoleTimer){
  console.timeEnd(consoleTimer);
}
console.time("twoSecond");
setTimeout(simpleTimeout, 2000, "twoSecond");
console.time("oneSecond");
setTimeout(simpleTimeout, 1000, "oneSecond");
console.time("fiveSecond");
```

```
setTimeout(simpleTimeout, 5000, "fiveSecond");
console.time("50MilliSecond");
setTimeout(simpleTimeout, 50, "50MilliSecond");<Listing First>
```

Listing 4.1 Output `simple_timer.js`: **Timeout functions executed at different delay amounts**

```
C:\books\node\ch04> node simple_timer.js
50MilliSecond: 50.489ms
oneSecond: 1000.688ms
twoSecond: 2000.665ms
fiveSecond: 5000.186ms
```

Performing Periodic Work with Intervals

Interval timers are used to perform work on a regular delayed interval. When the delay time expires, the callback function is executed and is then rescheduled for the delay interval again. Use intervals for work that needs to be performed on a regular basis.

Interval timers are created using the `setInterval(callback, delayMilliSeconds, [args])` method built into Node.js. When you call `setInterval()`, the callback function is executed every interval after `delayMilliSeconds` has expired. For example, the following executes `myFunc()` every second:

```
setInterval(myFunc, 1000);
```

The `setInterval()` function returns a timer object ID. You can pass this ID to `clearInterval(intervalId)` at any time before the `delayMilliSeconds` expires to cancel the timeout function. For example:

```
myInterval = setInterval(myFunc, 100000);
...
clearInterval(myInterval);
```

Listing 4.2 implements a series of simple interval callbacks that update the values of the variables `x`, `y`, and `z` at different intervals. Notice that the values of `x`, `y`, and `z` are changed differently because the interval amounts are different, with `x` incrementing twice as fast as `y`, which increments twice as fast as `z`, as shown in Listing 4.2 Output.

Listing 4.2 `simple_interval.js`: **Implementing a series of update callbacks at various intervals**

```
var x=0, y=0, z=0;
function displayValues(){
  console.log("X=%d; Y=%d; Z=%d", x, y, z);
}
function updateX(){
```

```
  x += 1;
}
function updateY(){
  y += 1;
}
function updateZ(){
  z += 1;
  displayValues();
}
setInterval(updateX, 500);
setInterval(updateY, 1000);
setInterval(updateZ, 2000);
```

Listing 4.2 Output `simple_interval.js`: **Interval functions executed at different delay amounts**

```
C:\books\node\ch04> node simple_interval.js
x=3; y=1; z=1
x=7; y=3; z=2
x=11; y=5; z=3
x=15; y=7; z=4
x=19; y=9; z=5
x=23; y=11; z=6
```

Performing Immediate Work with an Immediate Timer

Immediate timers are used to perform work on a function as soon as the I/O event callbacks are executed, but before any timeout or interval events are executed. This allows you to schedule work to be done after the current events in the event queue are completed. Use immediate timers to yield long-running execution segments to other callbacks to prevent starving the I/O events.

Immediate timers are created using the `setImmediate(callback, [args])` method built into Node.js. When you call `setImmediate()`, the callback function is placed on the event queue and popped off once for each iteration through the event queue loop after I/O events have a chance to be called. For example, the following schedules `myFunc()` to execute on the next cycle through the event queue:

```
setImmediate(myFunc(), 1000);
```

The `setImmediate()` function returns a timer object ID. You can pass this ID to `clearImmediate(immediateId)` at any time before it is picked up off the event queue. For example:

```
myImmediate =  setImmediate(myFunc);
...
clearImmediate(myImmediate);
```

Dereferencing Timers from the Event Loop

Often you do not want timer event callbacks to continue to be scheduled when they are the only events left in the event queue. Node.js provides a useful utility to handle this case. The `unref()` function available in the object returned by `setInterval` and `setTimeout` allows you to notify the event loop to not continue when these are the only events on the queue.

For example, the following dereferences the `myInterval` interval timer:

```
myInterval = setInterval(myFunc);
myInterval.unref();
```

If for some reason you later do not want the program to terminate if the interval function is the only event left on the queue, you can use the `ref()` function to re-reference it:

```
myInterval.ref();
```

> **Warning**
>
> When using `unref()` with `setTimout` timers, a separate timer is used to wake up the event loop. Creating a lot of these can cause an adverse performance impact on your code, so use them sparingly.

Using `nextTick` to Schedule Work

A useful method of scheduling work on the event queue is the `process.nextTick(callback)` function. This function schedules work to be run on the next cycle of the event loop. Unlike the `setImmediate()` method, `nextTick()` executes before the I/O events are fired. This can result in starvation of the I/O events, so Node.js limits the number of `nextTick()` events that can be executed each cycle through the event queue by the value of `process.maxTickDepth`, which defaults to 1000.

Listing 4.3 illustrates the order of events when using a blocking I/O call, timers, and `nextTick()`. Notice that the blocking call `fs.stat()` is executed first, then two `setImmediate()` calls, and then two `nextTick()` calls. Listing 4.3 Output shows that both `nextTick()` calls are executed before any of the others. Then the first `setImmediate()` call is executed followed by the `fs.stat()`, and then on the next iteration through the loop, the second `setImmediate()` call is executed.

Listing 4.3 `nexttick.js`: **Implementing a series of blocking `fs` calls, immediate timers, and `nextTick()` calls to show the order in which they get executed**

```
var fs = require("fs");
fs.stat("nexttick.js", function(){
  console.log("nexttick.js Exists");
});
setImmediate(function(){
  console.log("Immediate Timer 1 Executed");
});
```

```
setImmediate(function(){
  console.log("Immediate Timer 2 Executed");
});
process.nextTick(function(){
  console.log("Next Tick 1 Executed");
});
process.nextTick(function(){
  console.log("Next Tick 2 Executed");
});
```

Listing 4.3 Output `nexttick.js`: **Executing the** `nextTick()` **calls first**

```
c:\books\node\ch04>node nexttick.js
Next Tick 1 Executed
Next Tick 2 Executed
Immediate Timer 1 Executed
Immediate Timer 2 Executed
nexttick.js Exists
```

Implementing Event Emitters and Listeners

In the following chapters you get a chance to implement many of the events built in to the various Node.js modules. This section focuses on creating your own custom events as well as implementing listener callbacks that get implemented when an event is emitted.

Adding Custom Events to Your JavaScript Objects

Events are emitted using an `EventEmitter` object. This object is included in the events module. The `emit(eventName, [args])` function triggers the `eventName` event and includes any arguments provided. The following code snippet shows how to implement a simple event emitter:

```
var events = require('events');
var emitter = new events.EventEmitter();
emitter.emit("simpleEvent");
```

Occasionally you want to add events directly to your JavaScript objects. To do that you need to inherit the `EventEmitter` functionality in your object by calling `events.EventEmitter.call(this)` in your object instantiation as well as adding the `events.EventEmitter.prototype` to your object's prototyping. For example:

```
Function MyObj(){
  Events.EventEmitter.call(this);
}
MyObj.prototype.__proto__ = events.EventEmitter.prototype;
```

You then can emit events directly from instances of your object. For example:

```
var myObj = new MyObj();
myObj.emit("someEvent");
```

Adding Event Listeners to Objects

Once you have an instance of an object that can emit events, you can add listeners for the events that you care about. Listeners are added to an `EventEmitter` object using one of the following functions:

- **`.addListener(eventName, callback)`**: Attaches the `callback` function to the object's listeners. Every time the `eventName` event is triggered, the `callback` function is placed in the event queue to be executed.
- **`.on(eventName, callback)`**: Same as `.addListener()`.
- **`.once(eventName, callback)`**: Only the first time the `eventName` event is triggered, the `callback` function is placed in the event queue to be executed.

For example, to add a listener to an instance of the `MyObject` `EventEmitter` class defined in the previous section you would use the following:

```
function myCallback(){
  …
}
var myObject = new MyObj();
myObject.on("someEvent", myCallback);
```

Removing Listeners from Objects

Listeners are useful and vital parts of Node.js programming. However, they do cause overhead, and you should use them only when necessary. Node.js provides server helper functions on the `EventEmitter` object that allow you to manage the listeners that are included. These include

- **`.listeners(eventName)`**: Returns an array of listener functions attached to the `eventName` event.
- **`.setMaxListeners(n)`**: Triggers a warning if more than `n` listeners are added to an `EventEmitter` object. The default is 10.
- **`.removeListener(eventName, callback)`**: Removes the `callback` function from the `eventName` event of the `EventEmitter` object.

Implementing Event Listeners and Event Emitters

Listing 4.4 demonstrates the process of implementing listeners and custom event emitters in Node.js. The `Account` object is extended to inherit from the `EventEmitter` class and provides two methods to deposit and withdraw that both emit the `balanceChanged` event. Then in lines 15–31, three callback functions are implemented that are attached to the `Account` object instance `balanceChanged` event and display various forms of data.

Notice that the `checkGoal(acc, goal)` callback is implemented a bit differently than the others. This was done to illustrate how to pass variables into an event listener function when the event is triggered. The results of executing the code are shown in Listing 4.4 Output.

Listing 4.4 `emitter_listener.js`: **Creating a custom `EventEmitter` object and implementing three listeners that are triggered when the `balancedChanged` event is triggered**

```
01 var events = require('events');
02 function Account() {
03   this.balance = 0;
04   events.EventEmitter.call(this);
05   this.deposit = function(amount){
06     this.balance += amount;
07     this.emit('balanceChanged');
08   };
09   this.withdraw = function(amount){
10     this.balance -= amount;
11     this.emit('balanceChanged');
12   };
13 }
14 Account.prototype.__proto__ = events.EventEmitter.prototype;
15 function displayBalance(){
16   console.log("Account balance: $%d", this.balance);
17 }
18 function checkOverdraw(){
19   if (this.balance < 0){
20     console.log("Account overdrawn!!!");
21   }
22 }
23 function checkGoal(acc, goal){
24   if (acc.balance > goal){
25     console.log("Goal Achieved!!!");
26   }
27 }
28 var account = new Account();
29 account.on("balanceChanged", displayBalance);
30 account.on("balanceChanged", checkOverdraw);
31 account.on("balanceChanged", function(){
32   checkGoal(this, 1000);
33 });
34 account.deposit(220);
35 account.deposit(320);
36 account.deposit(600);
37 account.withdraw(1200);
```

Listing 4.4 Output `emitter_listener.js`: **The account statements output by the listener callback functions**

```
C:\books\node\ch04>node emmiter_listener.js
Account balance: $220
Account balance: $540
Account balance: $1140
Goal Achieved!!!
Account balance: $-60
Account overdrawn!!!
```

Implementing Callbacks

As you have seen in previous sections, the Node.js event-driven model relies heavily on callback functions. Callback functions can be a bit difficult to understand at first, especially if you want to depart from implementing a basic anonymous function. This section deals with three specific implementations of callbacks: passing parameters to a callback function, handling callback function parameters inside a loop, and nesting callbacks.

Passing Additional Parameters to Callbacks

Most callbacks have automatic parameters passed to them, such as an error or result buffer. A common question when working with callbacks is how to pass additional parameters to them from the calling function. You do this by implementing the parameter in an anonymous function and then call the actual callback with parameters from the anonymous function.

Listing 4.5 illustrates implementing callback parameters. There are two `sawCar` event handlers. Note that the `sawCar` event only emits the `make` parameter. Notice that the `emitter.emit()` function also can accept additional parameters; in this case, `make` is added as shown in line 5. The first event handler on line 16 implements the `logCar(make)` callback handler. To add a color for `logColorCar()`, an anonymous function is used in the event handler defined in lines 17–21. A randomly selected color is passed to the call `logColorCar(make, color)`. You can see the output in Listing 4.5 Output.

Listing 4.5 `callback_parameter.js`: **Creating an anonymous function to add additional parameters not emitted by the event**

```
01 var events = require('events');
02 function CarShow() {
03   events.EventEmitter.call(this);
04   this.seeCar = function(make){
05     this.emit('sawCar', make);
06   };
07 }
08 CarShow.prototype.__proto__ = events.EventEmitter.prototype;
```

```
var show = new CarShow();
function logCar(make){
  console.log("Saw a " + make);
}
function logColorCar(make, color){
  console.log("Saw a %s %s", color, make);
}
show.on("sawCar", logCar);
show.on("sawCar", function(make){
  var colors = ['red', 'blue', 'black'];
  var color = colors[Math.floor(Math.random()*3)];
  logColorCar(make, color);
});
show.seeCar("Ferrari");
show.seeCar("Porsche");
show.seeCar("Bugatti");
show.seeCar("Lamborghini");
show.seeCar("Aston Martin");
```

Listing 4.5 Output `callback_parameter.js`: **The results of adding a** `color` **parameter to the callback**

```
C:\books\node\ch04>node callback_parameter.js
Saw a Ferrari
Saw a blue Ferrari
Saw a Porsche
Saw a black Porsche
Saw a Bugatti
Saw a red Bugatti
Saw a Lamborghini
Saw a black Lamborghini
Saw a Aston Martin
Saw a black Aston Martin
```

Implementing Closure in Callbacks

An interesting problem that asynchronous callbacks have is that of closure. Closure is a JavaScript term that indicates that variables are bound to a function's scope and not the parent function's scope. When you execute an asynchronous callback, the parent function's scope may have changed; for example, when iterating through a list and altering values in each iteration.

If your callback needs access to variables in the parent function's scope, then you need to provide closure so that those values are available when the callback is pulled off the event queue. A basic way of doing that is by encapsulating the asynchronous call inside a function block and passing in the variables that are needed.

Listing 4.6 implements a wrapper function that provides closure to the `logCar()` asynchronous function. Notice that the loop in lines 7–12 implements a basic callback. However, Listing 4.6 Output shows that the car name is always the last item read because the value of `message` changes each time through the loop.

The loop in lines 13–20 implements a wrapper function that is passed `message` as the `msg` parameter and that `msg` value sticks with the callback. Thus the closure shown in Output 4.6 displays the correct message. To make the callback truly asynchronous, the `process.nextTick()` method is used to schedule the callback.

Listing 4.6 `callback_closure.js`: **Creating a wrapper function to provide closure for variables needed in the asynchronous callback**

```
01 function logCar(logMsg, callback){
02   process.nextTick(function() {
03     callback(logMsg);
04   });
05 }
06 var cars = ["Ferrari", "Porsche", "Bugatti"];
07 for (var idx in cars){
08   var message = "Saw a " + cars[idx];
09   logCar(message, function(){
10     console.log("Normal Callback: " + message);
11   });
12 }
13 for (var idx in cars){
14   var message = "Saw a " + cars[idx];
15   (function(msg){
16     logCar(msg, function(){
17       console.log("Closure Callback: " + msg);
18     });
19   })(message);
20 }
```

Listing 4.6 Output `callback_closure.js`: **Adding a closure wrapper function allows the asynchronous callback to access necessary variables**

```
C:\books\node\ch04>node callback_closure.js
Normal Callback: Saw a Bugatti
Normal Callback: Saw a Bugatti
Normal Callback: Saw a Bugatti
Closure Callback: Saw a Ferrari
Closure Callback: Saw a Porsche
Closure Callback: Saw a Bugatti
```

Chaining Callbacks

With asynchronous functions you are not guaranteed the order that they will run if two are placed on the event queue. The best way to resolve that is to implement callback chaining by having the callback from the asynchronous function call the function again until there is no more work to do. That way the asynchronous function is never on the event queue more than once.

Listing 4.7 implements a basic example of callback chaining. A list of items is passed into the function `logCars()`, the asynchronous function `logCar()` is called, and then the `logCars()` function is used as the callback when `logCar()` completes. Thus only one version of `logCar()` is on the event queue at the same time. The output of iterating through the list is shown in Listing 4.7 Output.

Listing 4.7 `callback_chain.js`: **Implementing a callback chain where the callback from an anonymous function calls back into the initial function to iterate through a list**

```
function logCar(car, callback){
  console.log("Saw a %s", car);
  if(cars.length){
    process.nextTick(function(){
      callback();
    });
  }
}
function logCars(cars){
  var car = cars.pop();
  logCar(car, function(){
    logCars(cars);
  });
}
var cars = ["Ferrari", "Porsche", "Bugatti",
            "Lamborghini", "Aston Martin"];
logCars(cars);
```

Listing 4.7 Output `callback_chain.js`: **Using an asynchronous callback chain to iterate through a list**

```
C:\books\node\ch04>node callback_chain.js
Saw a Aston Martin
Saw a Lamborghini
Saw a Bugatti
Saw a Porsche
Saw a Ferrari
```

Summary

The event-driven model that Node.js uses provides scalability and performance. You learned the difference between the event-driven model and the traditional threaded model for webservers. You learned that events can be added to the event queue when blocking I/O is called. And you learned that listeners can be triggered by events or timers or called directly using the `nextTick()` method.

This chapter discussed the three types of timer events: timeout, interval, and immediate. Each of these can be used to delay the execution of work for a period of time. You also saw how to implement your own custom event emitters and add listener functions to them.

Next

In the next chapter you see how to manage data I/O using streams and buffers. You also learn about Node.js functionality that allows you to manipulate JSON, string, and compressed forms of data.

5

Handling Data I/O in Node.js

Most active web applications and services have a lot of data flowing through them. That data comes in the form of text, JSON strings, binary buffers, and data streams. For that reason, Node.js has many mechanisms built in to support handling the data I/O from system to system. It is important to understand the mechanisms that Node.js provides to implement effective and efficient web applications and services.

This chapter focuses on manipulating JSON data, managing binary data buffers, implementing readable and writable streams, and compressing and decompressing data. You learn how to leverage the Node.js functionality to work with different I/O requirements.

Working with JSON

One of the most common data types that you work with when implementing Node.js web applications and services is JSON (JavaScript Object Notation). JSON is a lightweight method to convert JavaScript objects into a string form and then back again. This provides an easy method when you need to serialize data objects when passing them from client to server, process to process, stream to stream, or when storing them in a database.

There are several reasons to use JSON to serialize your JavaScript objects over XML including the following:

- JSON is much more efficient and takes up fewer characters.
- Serializing/deserializing JSON is faster than XML because it's simpler syntax.
- JSON is easier to read from a developer's perspective because it is similar to JavaScript syntax.

The only reasons you might want to use XML over JSON are for complex objects or if you have XML/XSLT transforms already in place.

Converting JSON to JavaScript Objects

A JSON string represents the JavaScript object in string form. The string syntax is similar to code, making it easy to understand. You can use the `JSON.parse(string)` method to convert a string that is properly formatted with JSON into a JavaScript object.

For example, the following code snippet defines `accountStr` as a formatted JSON string and converts it to a JavaScript object using `JSON.parse()`. Then member properties can be accessed via dot notation:

```
var accountStr = '{"name":"Jedi", "members":["Yoda","Obi Wan"], \
                  "number":34512, "location": "A galaxy far, far away"}';
var accountObj = JSON.parse(accountStr);
console.log(accountObj.name);
console.log(accountObj.members);
```

The preceding code outputs the following:

```
Jedi
[ 'Yoda', 'Obi Wan' ]
```

Converting JavaScript Objects to JSON

Node also allows you to convert a JavaScript object into a properly formatted JSON string. Thus the string form can be stored in a file or database, sent across an HTTP connection, or written to a stream/buffer. Use the `JSON.stringify(text)` method to parse JSON text and generate a JavaScript object:

For example, the following code defines a JavaScript object that includes string, numeric, and array properties. Using `JSON.stringify()`, it is all converted to a JSON string:

```
var accountObj = {
  name: "Baggins",
  number: 10645,
  members: ["Frodo, Bilbo"],
  location: "Shire"
};
var accountStr = JSON.stringify(accountObj);
console.log(accountStr);
```

The preceding code outputs the following:

```
{"name":"Baggins","number":10645,"members":["Frodo, Bilbo"],"location":"Shire"}
```

Using the `Buffer` Module to Buffer Data

While JavaScript is Unicode friendly, it is not good at managing binary data. However, binary data is useful when implementing some web applications and services. For example:

- Transferring compressed files

- Generating dynamic images
- Sending serialized binary data

Understanding Buffered Data

Buffered data is made up of a series of octets in big endian or little endian format. That means they take up considerably less space than textual data. Therefore, Node.js provides the `Buffer` module that gives you the functionality to create, read, write, and manipulate binary data in a buffer structure. The `Buffer` module is global, so you do not need to use the `require()` statement to access it.

Buffered data is stored in a structure similar to that of an array but is stored outside the normal V8 heap in raw memory allocations. Therefore a `Buffer` cannot be resized.

When converting buffers to and from strings, you need to specify the explicit encoding method to be used. Table 5.1 lists the various encoding methods supported.

Table 5.1 **Methods of encoding between strings and binary buffers**

Method	Description
`utf8`	Multi-byte encoded Unicode characters used as the standard in most documents and webpages.
`utf16le`	Little endian encoded Unicode characters of 2 or 4 bytes.
`ucs2`	Same as `utf16le`.
`base64`	Base64 string encoding.
`Hex`	Encode each byte as two hexadecimal characters.

Big Endian and Little Endian

Binary data in buffers is stored as a series of octets or a sequence of eight 0s and 1s that can be a hexadecimal value of 0x00 to 0xFF. It can be read as a single byte or as a word containing multiple bytes. Endian defines the ordering of significant bits when defining the word. Big endian stores the least significant word first, and little endian stores the least significant word last. For example, the words `0x0A 0x0B 0x0C 0x0D` would be stored in the buffer as `[0x0A, 0x0B, 0x0C, 0x0D]` in big endian but as `[0x0D, 0x0C, 0x0B, 0x0A]` in little endian.

Creating Buffers

`Buffer` objects are actually raw memory allocations; therefore, their size must be determined when they are created. The three methods for creating `Buffer` objects using the `new` keyword are

```
new Buffer(sizeInBytes)
new Buffer(octetArray)
new Buffer(string, [encoding])
```

For example, the following lines of code define buffers using a byte size, octet buffer, and a UTF8 string:

```
var buf256 = new Buffer(256);
var bufOctets = new Buffer([0x6f, 0x63, 0x74, 0x65, 0x74, 0x73]);
var bufUTF8 = new Buffer("Some UTF8 Text \u00b6 \u30c6 \u20ac", 'utf8');
```

Writing to Buffers

You cannot extend the size of a `Buffer` object after it has been created, but you can write data to any location in the buffer. Table 5.2 describes the three methods you can use when writing to buffers.

Table 5.2 **Methods of writing from `Buffer` objects**

Method	Description
`buffer.write(string, [offset], [length], [encoding])`	Writes `length` number of bytes from the `string` starting at the `offset` index inside the buffer using encoding.
`buffer[offset] = value`	Replaces the data at index `offset` with the value specified.
`buffer.fill(value, [offset], [end])`	Writes the value to every byte in the buffer starting at the `offset` index and ending with the `end` index.

`writeInt8(value, offset, [noAssert])`
`writeInt16LE(value, offset, [noAssert])`
`writeInt16BE(value, offset, [noAssert])`
...
	There is a wide range of methods for `Buffer` objects to write integers, unsigned integers, doubles, and floats of various sizes using little endian or big endian. `value` specifies the value to write, `offset` specifies the index to write to, and `noAssert` specifies whether to skip validation of the `value` and `offset`. `noAssert` should be left at the default `false` unless you are absolutely certain of correctness.

To illustrate writing to buffers better, Listing 5.1 defines a buffer, fills it with zeros, writes some text at the beginning using the `write()` method at line 4, and then adds some additional text using a write that alters part of the existing buffer using `write(string, offset, length)` at line 6. Then in line 8 it adds a `+` to the end by directly setting the value of an index, as shown in Listing 5.1 Output. Notice that the `buf256.write("more text", 9, 9)` statement writes to the middle of the buffer and `buf256[18] = 43` changes a single byte.

Listing 5.1 buffer_write.js: **Various ways to write to a Buffer object**

```
buf256 = new Buffer(256);
buf256.fill(0);
buf256.write("add some text");
console.log(buf256.toString());
buf256.write("more text", 9, 9);
console.log(buf256.toString());
buf256[18] = 43;
console.log(buf256.toString());
```

Listing 5.1 Output buffer_write.js: **Writing data from a Buffer object**

```
C:\books\node\ch05>node buffer_write.js
add some text
add some more text
add some more text+
```

Reading from Buffers

There are several methods for reading from buffers. The simplest is to use the `toString()` method to convert all or part of a buffer to a string. However, you can also access specific indexes in the buffer directly or by using `read()`. Also Node.js provides a `StringDecoder` object that has a `write(buffer)` method that decodes and writes buffered data using the specified encoding. Table 5.3 describes these methods for reading `Buffer` objects.

Table 5.3 **Methods of reading from Buffer objects**

Method	Description
`buffer.toString([encoding], [start], [end])`	Returns a string containing the decoded characters specified by encoding from the `start` index to the `end` index of the buffer. If `start` or `end` is not specified, then `toString()` uses the beginning or end of the buffer.
`stringDecoder.write(buffer)`	Returns a decoded string version of the buffer.
`buffer[offset]`	Returns the octet value in the buffer at the specified `offset`.

`readInt8(offset, [noAssert])`
`readInt16LE(offset, [noAssert])`
`readInt16BE(offset, [noAssert])`
...
	There is a wide range of methods for `Buffer` objects to read integers, unsigned integers, doubles, and floats of various sizes using little endian or big endian. These functions accept the offset to read from an optional `noAssert` Boolean value that specifies whether to skip validation of the offset. `noAssert` should be left at the default `false` unless you are absolutely certain of correctness.

To illustrate reading from buffers, Listing 5.2 defines a buffer with `UTF8` encoded characters, and then uses `toString()` without parameters to read all the buffer, and then with the `encoding`, `start`, and `end` parameters to read part of the buffer. Then in lines 4 and 5 it creates a `StringDecoder` with `UTF8` encoding and uses it to write the contents of the buffer out to the console. Next, a direct access method is used to get the value of the octet at index 18. Listing 5.2 Output shows the output of the code.

Listing 5.2 `buffer_read.js`: **Various ways to read from a `Buffer` object**

```
1 bufUTF8 = new Buffer("Some UTF8 Text \u00b6 \u30c6 \u20ac", 'utf8');
2 console.log(bufUTF8.toString());
3 console.log(bufUTF8.toString('utf8', 5, 9));
4 var StringDecoder = require('string_decoder').StringDecoder;
5 var decoder = new StringDecoder('utf8');
6 console.log(decoder.write(bufUTF8));
```

Listing 5.2 Output `buffer_read.js`: **Reading data from a `Buffer` object**

```
C:\books\node\ch05>node buffer_read.js
Some UTF8 Text ¶ テ €
UTF8
Some UTF8 Text ¶ テ €
e3
e3838620
```

Determining Buffer Length

A common task when dealing with buffers is determining the length, especially when you create a buffer dynamically from a string. The length of a buffer can be determined by calling `.length` on the `Buffer` object. To determine the byte length that a string takes up in a buffer you cannot use the `.length` property. Instead you need to use `Buffer.byteLength(string, [encoding])`. Note that there is a difference between the string length and byte length of a buffer. To illustrate this consider the followings statements:

```
"UTF8 text \u00b6".length;
//evaluates to 11
Buffer.byteLength("UTF8 text \u00b6", 'utf8');
//evaluates to 12
Buffer("UTF8 text \u00b6").length;
//evaluates to 12
```

Notice that the same string evaluates to 11 characters, but because it contains a double-byte character the `byteLength` is 12. Also note that `Buffer("UTF8 text \u00b6").length` evaluates to 12 also. That is because `.length` on a buffer returns the byte length.

Copying Buffers

An important part of working with buffers is the ability to copy data from one buffer into another buffer. Node.js provides the `copy(targetBuffer, [targetStart], [sourceStart], [sourceIndex])` method on `Buffer` objects. The `targetBuffer` parameter is another `Buffer` object, and `targetStart`, `sourceStart`, and `sourceEnd` are indexes inside the source and target buffers.

> **Note**
>
> To copy string data from one buffer to the next, make sure that both buffers use the same encoding or you may get unexpected results when decoding the resulting buffer.

You can also copy data from one buffer to the other by indexing them directly, for example:

```
sourceBuffer[index] = destinationBuffer[index]
```

Listing 5.3 illustrates three examples of copying data from one buffer to another. The first method in lines 4–8 copies the full buffer. The next method in lines 10–14 copies only the middle 5 bytes of a buffer. The third example iterates through the source buffer and only copies every other byte in the buffer. The results are shown in Listing 5.3 Output.

Listing 5.3 `buffer_copy.js`: **Various ways to copy data from one `Buffer` object to another**

```
01 var alphabet = new Buffer('abcdefghijklmnopqrstuvwxyz');
02 console.log(alphabet.toString());
03 // copy full buffer
04 var blank = new Buffer(26);
05 blank.fill();
06 console.log("Blank: " + blank.toString());
07 alphabet.copy(blank);
08 console.log("Blank: " + blank.toString());
09 // copy part of buffer
10 var dashes = new Buffer(26);
11 dashes.fill('-');
12 console.log("Dashes: " + dashes.toString());
13 alphabet.copy(dashes, 10, 10, 15);
14 console.log("Dashes: " + dashes.toString());
15 // copy to and from direct indexes of buffers
16 var dots = new Buffer('--------------------------');
17 dots.fill('.');
18 console.log("dots: " + dots.toString());
19 for (var i=0; i < dots.length; i++){
20   if (i % 2) { dots[i] = alphabet[i]; }
21 }
22 console.log("dots: " + dots.toString());
```

Listing 5.3 Output `buffer_copy.js`: **Copying data from one `Buffer` object to another**

```
C:\books\node\ch05>node buffer_copy.js
abcdefghijklmnopqrstuvwxyz
Blank:
Blank: abcdefghijklmnopqrstuvwxyz
Dashes: --------------------------
Dashes: ----------klmno-----------
dots: .........................
dots: .b.d.f.h.j.l.n.p.r.t.v.x.
```

Slicing Buffers

Another important aspect of working with buffers is the ability to divide them into slices. A *slice* is a section of a buffer between a starting index and an ending index. Slicing a buffer allows you to manipulate a specific chunk.

Slices are created using the `slice([start], [end])` method, which returns a `Buffer` object that points to `start` index of the original buffer and has a length of `end` – `start`. Keep in mind that a slice is different from a copy. If you edit a copy, the original does not change. However, if you edit a slice, the original does change.

Listing 5.4 illustrates using slices. Note that when the slice is altered in lines 5 and 6, it also alters the original buffer, as shown in Listing 5.4 Output.

Listing 5.4 `buffer_slice.js`: **Creating and manipulating slices of a `Buffer` object**

```
1 var numbers = new Buffer("123456789");
2 console.log(numbers.toString());
3 var slice = numbers.slice(3, 6);
4 console.log(slice.toString());
5 slice[0] = '#'.charCodeAt(0);
6 slice[slice.length-1] = '#'.charCodeAt(0);
7 console.log(slice.toString());
8 console.log(numbers.toString());
```

Listing 5.4 Output `buffer_slice.js`: **Slicing and modifying a `Buffer` object**

```
C:\books\node\ch05>node buffer_slice.js
123456789
456
#5#
123#5#789
```

Concatenating Buffers

You can also concatenate two or more `Buffer` objects together to form a new buffer. The `concat(list, [totalLength])` method accepts an array of `Buffer` objects as the first parameter, and `totalLength` defines the maximum bytes in the buffer as an optional second argument. The `Buffer` objects are concatenated in the order they appear in the list, and a new `Buffer` object is returned containing the contents of the original buffers up to `totalLength` bytes.

If you do not provide a `totalLength` parameter, `concat()` figures it out for you. However, it has to iterate through the list, so providing a `totalLength` value is faster.

Listing 5.5 concatenates a base `Buffer` with one buffer and then another, as shown in Listing 5.5 Output.

Listing 5.5 `buffer_concat.js`: **Concatenating `Buffer` objects**

```
var af = new Buffer("African Swallow?");
var eu = new Buffer("European Swallow?");
var question = new Buffer("Air Speed Velocity of an ");
console.log(Buffer.concat([question, af]).toString());
console.log(Buffer.concat([question, eu]).toString());
```

Listing 5.5 Output `buffer_concat.js`: **Concatenating `Buffer` objects**

```
C:\books\node\ch05>node buffer_concat.js
Air Speed Velocity of an African Swallow?
Air Speed Velocity of an European Swallow?
```

Using the Stream Module to Stream Data

An important module in Node.js is the stream module. Data streams are memory structures that are readable, writable, or both. Streams are used all over in Node.js, for example, when accessing files or reading data from HTTP requests and in several other areas. This section covers using the `Stream` module to create streams as well as read and write data from them.

The purpose of streams is to provide a common mechanism to transfer data from one location to another. They also expose events, such as when data is available to be read, when an error occurs, and so on. You can then register listeners to handle the data when it becomes available in a stream or is ready to be written to.

Some common uses for streams are HTTP data and files. You can open a file as a readable stream or access the data from an HTTP request as a readable stream and read bytes out as needed. Additionally, you can create your own custom streams. The following sections describe the process of creating and using readable, writable, duplex, and transform streams.

Readable Streams

Readable streams provide a mechanism to easily read data coming into your application from another source. Some common examples of readable streams are

- HTTP responses on the client
- HTTP requests on the server
- fs read streams
- zlib streams
- crypto streams
- TCP sockets
- Child processes stdout and stderr
- process.stdin

Readable streams provide the read([size]) method to read data where size specifies the number of bytes to read from the stream. read() can return a String, Buffer or null. Readable streams also expose the following events:

- **readable:** Emitted when a chunk of data can be read from the stream.
- **data:** Similar to readable except that when data event handlers are attached, the stream is turned into flowing mode, and the data handler is called continuously until all data has been drained.
- **end:** Emitted by the stream when data will no longer be provided.
- **close:** Emitted when the underlying resource, such as a file, has been closed.
- **error:** Emitted when an error occurs receiving data.

Readable stream objects also provide a number of functions that allow you to read and manipulate them. Table 5.4 lists the methods available on a Readable stream object.

Table 5.4 **Methods available on Readable stream objects**

Method	Description
read([size])	Reads data from the stream. The data can be a String, Buffer, or null, meaning there is no more data left. If a size argument is read, then the data is limited to that number of bytes.
setEncoding(encoding)	Sets the encoding to use when returning String in the read() request.
pause()	This pauses data events from being emitted by the object.
resume()	The resumes data events being emitted by the object.

Method	Description
`pipe(destination, [options])`	This pipes the output of this stream into a `Writable` stream object specified by `destination`. `options` in a JavaScript object. For example, `{end:true}` ends the `Writable` destination when the `Readable` ends.
`unpipe([destination])`	Disconnects this object from the `Writable` destination.

To implement your own custom `Readable` stream object, you need to first inherit the functionality for `Readable` streams. The simplest way to do that is to use the `util` module's `inherits()` method:

```
var util = require('util');
util.inherits(MyReadableStream, stream.Readable);
```

Then you create an instance of the object call:

```
stream.Readable.call(this, opt);
```

You also need to implement a `_read()` method that calls `push()` to output the data from the `Readable` object. The `push()` call should push either a `String`, `Buffer`, or `null`.

Listing 5.6 illustrates the basics of implementing and reading from a `Readable` stream. Notice that the `Answers()` class inherits from `Readable` and then implements the `Answers.prototye._read()` function to handle pushing data out. Also notice that on line 18, a direct `read()` call reads the first item from the stream and then the rest of the items are read by the `data` event handler defined on lines 19–21. Listing 5.6 Output shows the result.

Listing 5.6 `stream_read.js`: Implementing a `Readable` stream object

```
01 var stream = require('stream');
02 var util = require('util');
03 util.inherits(Answers, stream.Readable);
04 function Answers(opt) {
05   stream.Readable.call(this, opt);
06   this.quotes = ["yes", "no", "maybe"];
07   this._index = 0;
08 }
09 Answers.prototype._read = function() {
10   if (this._index > this.quotes.length){
11     this.push(null);
12   } else {
13     this.push(this.quotes[this._index]);
14     this._index += 1;
15   }
16 };
17 var r = new Answers();
18 console.log("Direct read: " + r.read().toString());
19 r.on('data', function(data){
```

```
  console.log("Callback read: " + data.toString());
});
r.on('end', function(data){
  console.log("No more answers.");
});
```

Listing 5.6 Output `stream_read.js`: **Implementing a custom `Readable` object**

```
C:\books\node\ch05>node stream_read.js
Direct read: yes
Callback read: no
Callback read: maybe
No more answers.
```

`Writable` Streams

`Writable` streams are designed to provide a mechanism to write data into a form that can easily be consumed in another area of code. Some common examples of `Writable` streams are

- HTTP requests on the client
- HTTP responses on the server
- `fs` write streams
- `zlib` streams
- `crypto` streams
- TCP sockets
- Child process `stdin`
- `process.stdout`, `process.stderr`

`Writable` streams provide the `write(chunk, [encoding], [callback])` method to write data into the stream, where `chunk` contains the data to write, `encoding` specifies the string encoding if necessary, and `callback` specifies a callback function to execute when the data has been fully flushed. The `write()` function returns `true` if the data was written successfully. `Writable` streams also expose the following events:

- **`drain`:** After a `write()` call returns `false`, the `drain` event is emitted to notify listeners when it is okay to begin writing more data.
- **`finish`:** Emitted when `end()` is called on the `Writable` object; all data is flushed and no more data will be accepted.
- **`pipe`:** Emitted when the `pipe()` method is called on a `Readable` stream to add this `Writable` as a destination.

- **unpipe:** Emitted when the `unpipe()` method is called on a `Readable` stream to remove this `Writable` as a destination.

`Writable` stream objects also provide a number of methods that allow you to write and manipulate them. Table 5.5 lists the methods available on a `Writable` stream object.

Table 5.5 **Methods available on `Writable` stream objects**

Method	Description
`write(chunk, [encoding], [callback])`	Writes the data chunk to the stream object's data location. The data can be a `String` or `Buffer`. If `encoding` is specified, then it is used to encode string data. If `callback` is specified, then it is called after the data has been flushed.
`end([chunk], [encoding], [callback])`	Same as `write()`, except it puts the `Writable` into a state where it no longer accepts data and sends the `finish` event.

To implement your own custom `Writable` stream object, you need to first inherit the functionality for `Writable` streams. The simplest way to do that is to use the `util` module's `inherits()` method:

```
var util = require('util');
util.inherits(MyWritableStream, stream.Writable);
```

Then you create an instance of the object call:

```
stream. Writable.call(this, opt);
```

You also need to implement a `_write(data, encoding, callback)` method that stores the data for the `Writable` object. Listing 5.7 illustrates the basics of implementing and writing to a `Writable` stream. Listing 5.7 Output shows the result.

Listing 5.7 `stream_write.js`: **Implementing a `Writable` stream object**

```
var stream = require('stream');
var util = require('util');
util.inherits(Writer, stream.Writable);
function Writer(opt) {
  stream.Writable.call(this, opt);
  this.data = new Array();
}
Writer.prototype._write = function(data, encoding, callback) {
  this.data.push(data.toString('utf8'));
  console.log("Adding: " + data);
  callback();
};
```

```
var w = new Writer();
for (var i=1; i<=5; i++){
  w.write("Item" + i, 'utf8');
}
w.end("ItemLast");
console.log(w.data);
```

Listing 5.7 Output `stream_ write.js`: **Implementing a custom `Writable` object**

```
C:\books\node\ch05>node stream_write.js
Adding: Item1
Adding: Item2
Adding: Item3
Adding: Item4
Adding: Item5
Adding: ItemLast
[ 'Item1', 'Item2', 'Item3', 'Item4', 'Item5', 'ItemLast' ]
```

`Duplex` Streams

A `Duplex` stream combines `Readable` and `Writable` functionality. A good example of a duplex stream is a TCP socket connection. You can read and write from the socket connection once it has been created.

To implement your own custom `Duplex` stream object, you need to first inherit the functionality for `Duplex` streams. The simplest way to do that is to use the `util` module's `inherits()` method:

```
var util = require('util');
util.inherits(MyDuplexStream, stream.Duplex);
```

Then you create an instance of the object call:

```
stream. Duplex.call(this, opt);
```

The `opt` parameter when creating a `Duplex` stream accepts an object with the property `allowHalfOpen` set to `true` or `false`. If this option is `true`, then the readable side stays open even after the writable side has ended and vice versa. If this option is set to `false`, ending the writable side also ends the readable side and vice versa.

When you implement a `Duplex` stream, you need to implement both a `_read(size)` and a `_write(data, encoding, callback)` method when prototyping your `Duplex` class.

Listing 5.8 illustrates the basics of implementing writing to and reading from a `Duplex` stream. The example is basic but shows the main concepts. The `Duplexer()` class inherits from the `Duplex` stream and implements a rudimentary `_write()` function that stores data in an array in the object. The `_read()` function uses `shift()` to get the first item in the array and then ends by pushing `null` if it is equal to `"stop"`, pushes it if there is a value, or sets a timeout timer to call back to the `_read()` function if there is no value.

In Listing 5.8 Output, notice that the first two writes `"I think, "` and `"therefore"` are read together. This is because both were pushed to the `Readable` before the `data` event was triggered.

Listing 5.8 `stream_duplex.js`: Implementing a `Duplex` stream object

```
var stream = require('stream');
var util = require('util');
util.inherits(Duplexer, stream.Duplex);
function Duplexer(opt) {
  stream.Duplex.call(this, opt);
  this.data = [];
}
Duplexer.prototype._read = function readItem(size) {
  var chunk = this.data.shift();
  if (chunk == "stop"){
    this.push(null);
  } else {
    if(chunk){
      this.push(chunk);
    } else {
      setTimeout(readItem.bind(this), 500, size);
    }
  }
};
Duplexer.prototype._write = function(data, encoding, callback) {
  this.data.push(data);
  callback();
};
var d = new Duplexer();
d.on('data', function(chunk){
  console.log('read: ', chunk.toString());
});
d.on('end', function(){
  console.log('Message Complete');
});
d.write("I think, ");
d.write("therefore ");
d.write("I am.");
d.write("Rene Descartes");
d.write("stop");
```

Listing 5.8 Output `stream_ duplex.js`: **Implementing a custom** `Duplex` **object**

```
C:\books\node\ch05>node stream_duplex.js
read:  I think,
read:  therefore
read:  I am.
read:  Rene Descartes
Message Complete
```

`Transform` Streams

Another type of stream is the `Transform` stream. A `Transform` stream extends the `Duplex` stream but modifies the data between the `Writable` stream and the `Readable` stream. This can be useful when you need to modify data from one system to another. Some examples of `Transform` streams are

- `zlib` streams
- `crypto` streams

A major difference between the `Duplex` and the `Transform` streams is that for `Transforms` you do not need to implement the `_read()` and `_write()` prototype methods. These are provided as pass-through functions. Instead, you implement the `_transform(chunk, encoding, callback)` and `_flush(callback)` methods. The `_transform()` method should accept the data from `write()` requests, modify it, and then `push()` out the modified data.

Listing 5.9 illustrates the basics of implementing a `Transform` stream. The stream accepts JSON strings, converts them to objects, and then emits a custom event named `object` that sends the object to any listeners. The `_transform()` function also modifies the object to include a `handled` property and then sends a string form on. Notice that lines 18–21 implement the `object` event handler function that displays certain attributes. In Listing 5.9 Output, notice that the JSON strings now include the `handled` property.

Listing 5.9 `stream_transform.js`: **Implementing a** `Transform` **stream object**

```
01 var stream = require("stream");
02 var util = require("util");
03 util.inherits(JSONObjectStream, stream.Transform);
04 function JSONObjectStream (opt) {
05   stream.Transform.call(this, opt);
06 };
07 JSONObjectStream.prototype._transform = function (data, encoding, callback) {
08   object = data ? JSON.parse(data.toString()) : "";
09   this.emit("object", object);
10   object.handled = true;
11   this.push(JSON.stringify(object));
12   callback();
```

```
};
JSONObjectStream.prototype._flush = function(cb) {
  cb();
};
var tc = new JSONObjectStream();
tc.on("object", function(object){
  console.log("Name: %s", object.name);
  console.log("Color: %s", object.color);
});
tc.on("data", function(data){
  console.log("Data: %s", data.toString());
});
tc.write('{"name":"Carolinus", "color": "Green"}');
tc.write('{"name":"Solarius", "color": "Blue"}');
tc.write('{"name":"Lo Tae Zhao", "color": "Gold"}');
tc.write('{"name":"Ommadon", "color": "Red"}');
```

Listing 5.9 Output `stream_transform.js`: **Implementing a custom `Transform` object**

```
C:\books\node\ch05>node stream_transform.js
Name: Carolinus
Color: Green
Data: {"name":"Carolinus","color":"Green","handled":true}
Name: Solarius
Color: Blue
Data: {"name":"Solarius","color":"Blue","handled":true}
Name: Lo Tae Zhao
Color: Gold
Data: {"name":"Lo Tae Zhao","color":"Gold","handled":true}
Name: Ommadon
Color: Red
Data: {"name":"Ommadon","color":"Red","handled":true}
```

Piping `Readable` Streams to `Writable` Streams

One of the coolest things you can do with stream objects is to chain `Readable` streams to `Writable` streams using the `pipe(writableStream, [options])` function. This does exactly what the name implies. The output from the `Readable` stream is directly input into the `Writable` stream. The `options` parameter accepts an object with the `end` property set to `true` or `false`. When `end` is `true`, the `Writable` stream ends when the `Readable` stream ends. This is the default behavior. For example:

```
readStream.pipe(writeStream, {end:true});
```

You can also break the pipe programmatically using the `unpipe(destinationStream)` option. Listing 5.10 implements a `Readable` stream and a `Writable` stream and then uses the `pipe()`

function to chain them together. To show you the basic process, the data input from the `_write()` method is output to the console in Listing 5.10 Output.

Listing 5.10 `stream_piped.js`**: Piping a** `Readable` **stream into a** `Writable` **stream**

```
var stream = require('stream');
var util = require('util');
util.inherits(Reader, stream.Readable);
util.inherits(Writer, stream.Writable);
function Reader(opt) {
  stream.Readable.call(this, opt);
  this._index = 1;
}
Reader.prototype._read = function(size) {
  var i = this._index++;
  if (i > 10){
    this.push(null);
  } else {
    this.push("Item " + i.toString());
  }
};
function Writer(opt) {
  stream.Writable.call(this, opt);
  this._index = 1;
}
Writer.prototype._write = function(data, encoding, callback) {
  console.log(data.toString());
  callback();
};
var r = new Reader();
var w = new Writer();
r.pipe(w);
```

Listing 5.10 Output `stream_ piped.js`**: Implementing stream piping**

```
C:\books\node\ch05>node stream_piped.js
Item 1
Item 2
Item 3
Item 4
Item 5
Item 6
Item 7
Item 8
Item 9
Item 10
```

Compressing and Decompressing Data with `Zlib`

When working with large systems or moving large amounts of data around, it is helpful to be able to compress and decompress the data. Node.js provides an excellent library in the `Zlib` module that allows you to easily and efficiently compress and decompress data in buffers.

Keep in mind that compressing data takes CPU cycles. So you should be certain of the benefits of compressing the data before incurring the compression/decompression cost. The compression methods supported by `Zlib` are

- **gzip/gunzip:** Standard gzip compression
- **deflate/inflate:** Standard deflate compression algorithm based on Huffman coding
- **deflateRaw/inflateRaw:** Deflate compression algorithm on a raw buffer

Compressing and Decompressing Buffers

The `Zlib` module provides several helper functions that make it easy to compress and decompress data buffers. These all use the same basic format of *`function(buffer, callback)`*, where *`function`* is the compression/decompression method, *`buffer`* is the buffer to be compressed/decompressed, and *`callback`* is the callback function executed after the compression/decompression occurs.

The simplest way to illustrate buffer compression/decompression is to show you some examples. Listing 5.11 provides several compression/decompression examples, and the size result of each example is shown in Listing 5.11 Output.

Listing 5.11 `zlib_buffers.js`: **Compressing/decompressing buffers using the `Zlib` module**

```
var zlib = require("zlib");
var input = '...............text...............';
zlib.deflate(input, function(err, buffer) {
  if (!err) {
    console.log("deflate (%s): ", buffer.length, buffer.toString('base64'));
    zlib.inflate(buffer, function(err, buffer) {
      if (!err) {
        console.log("inflate (%s): ", buffer.length, buffer.toString());
      }
    });
    zlib.unzip(buffer, function(err, buffer) {
      if (!err) {
        console.log("unzip deflate (%s): ", buffer.length, buffer.toString());
      }
    });
  }
});
```

```

zlib.deflateRaw(input, function(err, buffer) {
  if (!err) {
    console.log("deflateRaw (%s): ", buffer.length, buffer.toString('base64'));
    zlib.inflateRaw(buffer, function(err, buffer) {
      if (!err) {
        console.log("inflateRaw (%s): ", buffer.length, buffer.toString());
      }
    });
  }
});

zlib.gzip(input, function(err, buffer) {
  if (!err) {
    console.log("gzip (%s): ", buffer.length, buffer.toString('base64'));
    zlib.gunzip(buffer, function(err, buffer) {
      if (!err) {
        console.log("gunzip (%s): ", buffer.length, buffer.toString());
      }
    });
    zlib.unzip(buffer, function(err, buffer) {
      if (!err) {
        console.log("unzip gzip (%s): ", buffer.length, buffer.toString());
      }
    });
  }
});
```

Listing 5.11 Output `zilb_ buffers.js`: **Compressing/decompressing buffers**

```
C:\books\node\ch05>node zlib_buffers.js
deflate (18):  eJzT00MBJakVJagiegB9Zgcq
deflateRaw (12):  09NDASWpFSWoInoA
gzip (30):  H4sIAAAAAAAAC9PTQwElqRUlqCJ6AIq+x+AiAAAA
inflate (34):  ...............text...............
unzip deflate (34):  ...............text...............
inflateRaw (34):  ...............text...............
gunzip (34):  ...............text...............
unzip gzip (34):  ...............text...............
```

Compressing/Decompressing Streams

Compressing/decompressing streams using `Zlib` is slightly different from compressing/decompressing buffers. Instead, you use the `pipe()` function to pipe the data from one stream through the compression/decompression object into another stream. This can apply to compressing any `Readable` streams into `Writable` streams.

A good example of doing this is compressing the contents of a file using `fs.ReadStream` and `fs.WriteStream`. Listing 5.12 shows an example of compressing the contents of a file using a `zlib.Gzip()` object and then decompressing back using a `zlib.Gunzip()` object.

Listing 5.12 `zlib_file.js`: **Compressing/decompressing a file stream using the `Zlib` module**

```
var zlib = require("zlib");
var gzip = zlib.createGzip();
var fs = require('fs');
var inFile = fs.createReadStream('zlib_file.js');
var outFile = fs.createWriteStream('zlib_file.gz');
inFile.pipe(gzip).pipe(outFile);
gzip.flush();
outFile.close();
var gunzip = zlib.createGunzip();
var inFile = fs.createReadStream('zlib_file.gz');
var outFile = fs.createWriteStream('zlib_file.unzipped');
inFile.pipe(gunzip).pipe(outFile);
```

Summary

At the heart of most intense web applications and services is a lot of data streaming from one system to another. In this chapter, you learned how to use functionality built into Node.js to work with JSON data, manipulate binary buffer data, and utilize data streams. You also learned about compressing buffered data as well as running data streams through compression/decompression.

Next

In the next chapter, you see how to interact with the file system from Node.js. You get a chance to read/write files, create directories, and read file system information.

6

Accessing the File System from Node.js

Interacting with the file system in Node.js is important especially if you need to manage dynamic files to support a web application or service. Node.js provides a good interface for interacting with the file system in the `fs` module. This module provides the standard file access APIs that are available in most languages to open, read, write, and interact with files.

This chapter provides you with the fundamentals necessary to access the file system from Node.js applications. You should come away with the ability to create, read, and modify files as well as navigate the directory structure. You also learn how to access file and folder information as well as delete, truncate, and rename files and folders.

For all the file system calls discussed in this chapter, you need to have loaded the `fs` module, for example:

```
var fs  = require('fs');
```

Synchronous Versus Asynchronous File System Calls

The `fs` module provided in Node.js makes almost all functionality available in two forms: asynchronous and synchronous. For example, there is the asynchronous form `write()` and the synchronous form `writeSync()`. It is important to understand the difference when you are implementing your code.

Synchronous file system calls block until the call completes and then control is released back to the thread. This has advantages but can also cause severe performance issues in Node.js if synchronous calls block the main event thread or too many of the background thread pool threads. Therefore, synchronous file system calls should be limited in use when possible.

Asynchronous calls are placed on the event queue to be run later. This allows the calls to fit into the Node.js event model; however, this can be tricky when executing your code because the calling thread continues to run before the asynchronous call gets picked up by the event loop.

For the most part, the underlying functionality of both synchronous and asynchronous file system calls is exactly the same. They both accept the same parameters with the exception that all asynchronous calls require an extra parameter at the end, which is a callback function to execute when the file system call completes.

The following list describes the important differences between synchronous and asynchronous file system calls in Node.js:

- Asynchronous calls require a callback function as an extra parameter. The callback function is executed when the file system request completes, and typically contains an error as its first parameter.
- Exceptions are automatically handled by asynchronous calls, and an error object is passed as the first parameter if an exception occurs. Exceptions in synchronous calls must be handled by your own `try/catch` blocks of code.
- Synchronous calls are run immediately, and execution does not return to the current thread until they are complete. Asynchronous calls are placed on the event queue, and execution returns to the running thread code, but the actual call will not execute until picked up by the event loop.

Opening and Closing Files

Node provides synchronous and asynchronous methods for opening files. Once a file is opened, you can read data from it or write data to it depending on the flags used to open the file. To open files in a Node.js app, use one of the following statements for asynchronous or synchronous:

```
fs.open(path, flags, [mode], callback)
fs.openSync(path, flags, [mode])
```

The `path` parameter specifies a standard path string for your file system. The `flags` parameter specifies what mode to open the file in—read, write, append, and so on—as described in Table 6.1. The optional `mode` parameter sets the file access mode and defaults to `0666`, which is readable and writable.

Table 6.1 **Flags that define how files are opened**

Mode	Description
`r`	Open file for reading. An exception occurs if the file does not exist.
`r+`	Open file for reading and writing. An exception occurs if the file does not exist.
`rs`	Open file for reading in synchronous mode. This is not the same as forcing `fs.openSync()`. When used, the OS bypasses the local file system cache. Useful on NFS mounts because it lets you skip the potentially stale local cache. You should only use this flag if necessary because it can have a negative impact on performance.

Mode	Description
rs+	Same as rs except the file is open file for reading and writing.
w	Open file for writing. The file is created if it does not exist or truncated if it does exist.
wx	Same as w but fails if the path exists.
w+	Open file for reading and writing. The file is created if it does not exist or truncated if it exists.
wx+	Same as w+ but fails if path exists.
a	Open file for appending. The file is created if it does not exist.
ax	Same as a but fails if the path exists.
a+	Open file for reading and appending. The file is created if it does not exist.
ax+	Same as a+ but fails if the path exists.

Once a file has been opened, you need to close it to force flushing changes to disk and release the OS lock. Closing a file is done using one of the following methods and passing the file handle to it. In the case of the asynchronous `close()` call, you also need to specify a callback function:

```
fs.close(fd, callback)
fs.closeSync(fd)
```

The following shows an example of opening and closing a file in asynchronous mode. Notice that a `callback` function is specified that receives an `err` and an `fd` parameter. The `fd` parameter is the file descriptor that you can use to read or write to the file:

```
fs.open("myFile", 'w', function(err, fd){
  if (!err){
    fs.close(fd);
  }
});
```

The following shows an example of opening and closing a file in synchronous mode. Notice that a there is no callback function and that the file descriptor used to read and write to the file is returned directly from `fs.openSync()`:

```
var fd = fs.openSync("myFile", 'w');
fs.closeSync(fd);
```

Writing Files

The `fs` module provides four different ways to write data to files. You can write data to a file in a single call, write chunks using synchronous writes, write chunks using asynchronous writes, or stream writes through a `Writable` stream. Each of these methods accepts either a `String` or a `Buffer` object as input. The following sections describe how to use these methods.

Simple File Write

The simplest method for writing data to a file is to use one of the `writeFile()` methods. These methods write the full contents of a `String` or `Buffer` to a file. The following shows the syntax for the `writeFile()` methods:

```
fs.writeFile(path, data, [options], callback)
fs.writeFileSync(path, data, [options])
```

The `path` parameter specifies the path to the file. The `path` can be relative or absolute. The `data` parameter specifies the `String` or `Buffer` object to be written to the file. The optional `options` parameter is an object that can contain `encoding`, `mode`, and `flag` properties that define the string encoding as well as the mode and flags used when opening the file. The asynchronous method also requires a `callback` that is called when the file write has been completed.

Listing 6.1 implements a simple asynchronous `fileWrite()` request to store a JSON string of a `config` object in a file. Listing 6.1 Output shows the output of the code.

Listing 6.1 `file_write.js`: **Writing a JSON string to a file**

```
var fs = require('fs');
var config = {
  maxFiles: 20,
  maxConnections: 15,
  rootPath: "/webroot"
};
var configTxt = JSON.stringify(config);
var options = {encoding:'utf8', flag:'w'};
fs.writeFile('config.txt', configTxt, options, function(err){
  if (err){
    console.log("Config Write Failed.");
  } else {
    console.log("Config Saved.");
  }
});
```

Listing 6.1 Output `file_write.js`: **Writing a configuration file**

```
C:\books\node\ch06\writing>node file_write.js
Config Saved.
```

Synchronous File Writing

The synchronous method of file writing writes the data to the file before returning execution to the running thread. This provides the advantage of allowing you to write multiple times in the same section of code, but this can be a disadvantage if the file writes hold up other threads as discussed earlier.

To write to a file synchronously, first open it using `openSync()` to get a file descriptor and then use `fs.writeSync()` to write data to the file. The following shows the syntax for `fs.writeSync()`:

```
fs.writeSync(fd, data, offset, length, position)
```

The `fd` parameter is the file descriptor returned by `openSync()`. The `data` parameter specifies the `String` or `Buffer` object to be written to the file. The `offset` parameter specifies the index in the input `data` to begin reading from; if you want to begin at the current index in the `String` or `Buffer`, this value should be `null`. The `length` specifies the number of bytes to write; specifying `null` writes until the end of the `data` buffer. The `position` argument specifies the position in the file to begin writing at; specifying `null` for this value uses the current file position.

Listing 6.2 illustrates implementing basic synchronous writing to store a series of string data in a file. Listing 6.2 Output shows the result.

Listing 6.2 `file_write_sync.js`: **Performing synchronous writes to a file**

```
var fs = require('fs');
var veggieTray = ['carrots', 'celery', 'olives'];
fd = fs.openSync('veggie.txt', 'w');
while (veggieTray.length){
  veggie = veggieTray.pop() + " ";
  var bytes = fs.writeSync(fd, veggie, null, null);
  console.log("Wrote %s %dbytes", veggie, bytes);
}
fs.closeSync(fd);
```

Listing 6.2 Output `file_write_sync.js`: **Writing synchronously to a file**

```
C:\books\node\ch06\writing>node file_write_sync.js
Wrote olives  7bytes
Wrote celery  7bytes
Wrote carrots  8bytes
```

Asynchronous File Writing

The asynchronous method of file writing puts the write request on the event queue and then returns control back to the calling code. The actual write does not take place until the event loop picks up the write request and executes it. You need to be careful when performing multiple asynchronous write requests on the same file, since you cannot guarantee what order they will be executed unless you wait for the first write callback before executing the next. Typically the simplest way to do this is to nest writes inside the callback from the previous write. Listing 6.3 illustrates that process.

To write to a file asynchronously, first open it using `open()` and then after the callback from the open request has executed, use `fs.write()` to write data to the file. The following shows the syntax for `fs.write()`:

```
fs.writeSync(fd, data, offset, length, position, callback)
```

The `fd` parameter is the file descriptor returned by `openSync()`. The `data` parameter specifies the `String` or `Buffer` object to be written to the file. The `offset` parameter specifies the index in the input data to begin reading data; if you want to begin at the current index in the `String` or `Buffer`, this value should be `null`. The `length` specifies the number of bytes to write; specifying `null` writes until the end of the buffer. The `position` argument specifies the position in the file to begin writing at; specifying `null` for this value uses the current file position.

The `callback` argument must be a function that can accept two parameters, `error` and `bytes`, where `error` is an error that occurred during the write and `bytes` specifies the number of bytes written.

Listing 6.3 illustrates implementing basic asynchronous writing to store a series of string data in a file. Notice that the callback specified in lines 18–20 in the `open()` callback calls the `writeFruit()` function and passes the file descriptor. Also notice that the `write()` callback specified in lines 6–13 also calls `writeFruit()` and passes the file descriptor. This ensures that the asynchronous write completes before executing another. Listing 6.3 Output shows the output of the code.

Listing 6.3 `file_write_async.js`: **Performing asynchronous writes to a file**

```
01 var fs = require('fs');
02 var fruitBowl = ['apple', 'orange', 'banana', 'grapes'];
03 function writeFruit(fd){
04   if (fruitBowl.length){
05     var fruit = fruitBowl.pop() + " ";
06     fs.write(fd, fruit, null, null, function(err, bytes){
07       if (err){
08         console.log("File Write Failed.");
09       } else {
10         console.log("Wrote: %s %dbytes", fruit, bytes);
11         writeFruit(fd);
12       }
13     });
14   } else {
15     fs.close(fd);
16   }
17 }
18 fs.open('fruit.txt', 'w', function(err, fd){
19   writeFruit(fd);
20 });
```

Listing 6.3 Output `file_write_async.js`: **Writing asynchronously to a file**

```
C:\books\node\ch06\writing>node file_write_async.js
Wrote: grapes  7bytes
Wrote: banana  7bytes
Wrote: orange  7bytes
Wrote: apple  6bytes
```

Streaming File Writing

One of the best methods to use when writing large amounts of data to a file is the streaming method. This method opens the file as a `Writable` stream. As discussed in Chapter 5, "Handling Data I/O in Node.js," `Writable` streams can easily be implemented and linked to `Readable` streams using the `pipe()` method, which makes it easy to write data from a `Readable` stream source such as an HTTP request.

To stream data to a file asynchronously, you first need to create a `Writable` stream object using the following syntax:

```
fs.createWriteStream(path, [options])
```

The `path` parameter specifies the path to the file and can be relative or absolute. The optional `options` parameter is an object that can contain `encoding`, `mode`, and `flag` properties that define the string encoding as well as the mode and flags used when opening the file.

Once you have opened the `Writable` file stream, you can write to it using the standard stream `write(buffer)` methods. When you are finished writing, call the `end()` method to close the stream.

Listing 6.4 illustrates implementing a basic `Writable` file stream. Notice that when the code is finished writing, the `end()` method is executed on line 13, which triggers the `close` event. Listing 6.4 Output shows the output of the code.

Listing 6.4 `file_write_stream.js`: **Implementing a `Writable` stream to allow streaming writes to a file**

```
01 var fs = require('fs');
02 var grains = ['wheat', 'rice', 'oats'];
03 var options = { encoding: 'utf8', flag: 'w' };
04 var fileWriteStream = fs.createWriteStream("grains.txt",  options);
05 fileWriteStream.on("close", function(){
06   console.log("File Closed.");
07 });
08 while (grains.length){
09   var data = grains.pop() + " ";
10   fileWriteStream.write(data);
11   console.log("Wrote: %s", data);
12 }
13 fileWriteStream.end();
```

Listing 6.4 Output `file_write_stream.js`: **Implementing streaming writes to a file**

```
C:\books\node\ch06\writing>node file_write_stream.js
Wrote: oats
Wrote: rice
Wrote: wheat
File Closed.
```

Reading Files

The `fs` module also provides four different ways to read data from files. You can read data in one large chunk, read chunks of data using synchronous writes, read chunks of data using asynchronous writes, or stream reads through a `Readable` stream. Each of these methods is effective. Which one you should use depends on the particular needs of your application. The following sections describe how to use and implement these methods.

Simple File Read

The simplest method for reading data to a file is to use one of the `readFile()` methods. These methods read the full contents of a file into a data buffer. The following shows the syntax for the `readFile()` methods:

```
fs.readFile(path, [options], callback)
fs.readFileSync(path, [options])
```

The `path` parameter specifies the path to the file and can be relative or absolute. The optional `options` parameter is an object that can contain `encoding`, `mode`, and `flag` properties that define the string encoding as well as the mode and flags used when opening the file. The asynchronous method also requires a `callback` that is called when the file read has been completed.

Listing 6.5 illustrates implementing a simple asynchronous `readFile()` request to read a JSON string from a configuration file and then use it to create a `config` object. Listing 6.5 Output shows the output of the code.

Listing 6.5 `file_read.js`: **Reading a JSON string file to an object**

```
var fs = require('fs');
var options = {encoding:'utf8', flag:'r'};
fs.readFile('config.txt', options, function(err, data){
  if (err){
    console.log("Failed to open Config File.");
  } else {
    console.log("Config Loaded.");
    var config = JSON.parse(data);
    console.log("Max Files: " + config.maxFiles);
```

```
    console.log("Max Connections: " + config.maxConnections);
    console.log("Root Path: " + config.rootPath);
  }
});
```

Listing 6.5 Output `file_read.js`: **Reading a configuration file to an object**

```
C:\books\node\ch06\reading>node file_read.js
Config Loaded.
Max Files: 20
Max Connections: 15
Root Path: /webroot
```

Synchronous File Reading

The synchronous method of file reading reads the data from the file before returning execution to the running thread. This provides the advantage of allowing you to read multiple times in the same section of code, but this can be a disadvantage if the file reads hold up other threads as discussed earlier.

To read to a file synchronously, first open it using `openSync()` to get a file descriptor and then use `readSync()` to read data from the file. The following shows the syntax for `readSync()`:

```
fs.readSync(fd, buffer, offset, length, position)
```

The `fd` parameter is the file descriptor returned by `openSync()`. The `buffer` parameter specifies the `Buffer` object that data will be read into from the file. The `offset` parameter specifies the index in the `buffer` to begin writing data; if you want to begin at the current index in the `Buffer` this value should be `null`. The `length` specifies the number of bytes to read; specifying `null` writes until the end of the buffer. The `position` argument specifies the position in the file to begin reading from; specifying `null` for this value uses the current file position.

Listing 6.6 illustrates implementing basic synchronous reading to read a chunk of string data from a file. Listing 6.6 Output shows the output of the code.

Listing 6.6 `file_read_sync.js`: **Performing synchronous reads from a file**

```
var fs = require('fs');
fd = fs.openSync('veggie.txt', 'r');
var veggies = "";
do {
  var buf = new Buffer(5);
  buf.fill();
  var bytes = fs.readSync(fd, buf, null, 5);
  console.log("read %dbytes", bytes);
  veggies += buf.toString();
```

```
} while (bytes > 0);
fs.closeSync(fd);
console.log("Veg g (to get output shown) ies: " + veggies);
```

Listing 6.6 Output `file_read_sync.js`: **Reading synchronously from a file**

```
C:\books\node\ch06\reading>node file_read_sync.js
read 5bytes
read 5bytes
read 5bytes
read 5bytes
read 2bytes
read 0bytes
Veggies: olives celery carrots
```

Asynchronous File Reading

The asynchronous method of file reading puts the read request on the event queue and then returns control back to the calling code. The actual read does not take place until the event loop picks up the read request and executes it. You need to be careful when performing multiple asynchronous read requests on the same file, since you cannot guarantee what order they will be executed unless you wait for the first read callback to execute before executing the next read. Typically the simplest way to do this is to nest reads inside the callback from the previous read. Listing 6.7 illustrates that process.

To read from a file asynchronously, first open it using `open()` and then after the callback from the open request has executed, use `read()` to read data from the file. The following shows the syntax for `read()`:

```
fs.read(fd, buffer, offset, length, position, callback)
```

The `fd` parameter is the file descriptor returned by `openSync()`. The buffer parameter specifies the `Buffer` object that data will be read into from the file. The `offset` parameter specifies the index in the buffer to begin reading data; if you want to begin at the current index in the `Buffer`, this value should be `null`. The `length` specifies the number of bytes to read; specifying `null` reads until the end of the buffer. The `position` argument specifies the position in the file to begin reading from; specifying `null` for this value uses the current file position.

The `callback` argument must be a function that can accept three parameters: `error`, `bytes`, and `buffer`. The `error` parameter is an error that occurred during the read, `bytes` specifies the number of bytes read, and `buffer` is the buffer with data populated from the read request.

Listing 6.7 illustrates implementing basic asynchronous reading to read chunks of data from a file. Notice that the callback specified in lines 16–18 in the `open()` callback calls the `readFruit()` function and passes the file descriptor. Also notice that the `read()` callback specified in lines 5–13 also calls `readFruit()` and passes the file descriptor. This ensures that the asynchronous read completes before executing another. Listing 6.7 Output shows the output of the code.

Listing 6.7 `file_read_async.js`: **Performing asynchronous reads from a file**

```
var fs = require('fs');
function readFruit(fd, fruits){
  var buf = new Buffer(5);
  buf.fill();
  fs.read(fd, buf, 0, 5, null, function(err, bytes, data){
      if ( bytes > 0) {
        console.log("read %dbytes", bytes);
        fruits += data;
        readFruit(fd, fruits);
      } else {
        fs.close(fd);
        console.log ("Fruits: %s", fruits);
      }
  });
}
fs.open('fruit.txt', 'r', function(err, fd){
  readFruit(fd, "");
});
```

Listing 6.7 Output `file_read_async.js`: **Reading asynchronously from a file**

```
C:\books\node\ch06\reading>node file_read_async.js
read 5bytes
read 5bytes
read 5bytes
read 5bytes
read 5bytes
read 2bytes
Fruits: grapes banana orange apple
```

Streaming File Reading

One of the best methods to use when reading large amounts of data from a file is the streaming method. This method opens the file as a `Readable` stream. As discussed in Chapter 5, `Readable` streams can easily be implemented and linked to `Writable` streams using the `pipe()` method. This makes it easy to read data from a file and inject it into a `Writable` stream source such as an HTTP response.

To stream data from a file asynchronously, you first need to create a `Readable` stream object using the following syntax:

```
fs.createReadStream(path, [options])
```

The `path` parameter specifies the path to the file. The `path` can be relative or absolute. The optional `options` parameter is an object that can contain `encoding`, `mode`, and `flag` properties that define the string encoding as well as the mode and flags used when opening the file.

Once you have opened the `Readable` file stream, you can easily read from it using the `readable` event with `read()` requests or by implementing a `data` event handler as shown in Listing 6.8.

Listing 6.8 illustrates implementing a basic `Readable` file stream. Notice that lines 4–7 implement a `data` event handler that continuously reads data from the stream. Listing 6.8 Output shows the output of the code.

Listing 6.8 `file_read_stream.js`: **Implementing a `Readable` stream to allow streaming reads from a file**

```
01 var fs = require('fs');
02 var options = { encoding: 'utf8', flag: 'r' };
03 var fileReadStream = fs.createReadStream("grains.txt",  options);
04 fileReadStream.on('data', function(chunk) {
05   console.log('Grains: %s', chunk);
06   console.log('Read %d bytes of data.', chunk.length);
07 });
08 fileReadStream.on("close", function(){
09   console.log("File Closed.");
10 });
```

Listing 6.8 Output `file_read_stream.js`: **Implementing streaming reads from a file**

```
C:\books\node\ch06\reading>node file_read_stream.js
Grains: oats rice wheat
Read 16 bytes of data.
File Closed.
```

Other File System Tasks

In addition to reading and writing files, the `fs` module also provides functionality for interacting with the file system—for example, listing files in a directory, looking at file information, and much more. The following sections cover the most common file system tasks that you may need to implement when creating Node.js applications.

Verifying Path Existence

Before doing any kind of read/write operation on a file or directory, you might want to verify whether the path exists. This can easily be done using one of the following methods:

```
fs.exists(path, callback)
fs.existsSync(path)
```

The `fs.existsSync(path)` returns `true` or `false` based on the `path` existence. Just as with any other asynchronous file system call, if you use `fs.exists()`, you need to implement a callback that is executed when the call completes. The `callback` is passed a Boolean value of `true` or `false` depending on whether the `path` exists. For example, the following code verifies the existence of a file named `filesystem.js` in the current path and displays the results:

```
fs.exists('filesystem.js', function (exists) {
  console.log(exists ? "Path Exists" : "Path Does Not Exist");
});
```

Getting File Info

Another common task is to get basic information about file system objects such as file size, the mode, modify time, whether the entry is a file or folder, and so on. This information can be obtained using one of the following calls:

```
fs.stats(path, callback)
fs.statsSync(path)
```

The `fs.statsSync()` method returns a `Stats` object, whereas the `fs.stats()` method is executed and the `Stats` object is passed to the callback function as the second parameter. The first parameter is `error` if an error occurs.

Table 6.2 lists some of the most commonly used attributes and methods attached to the `Stats` object.

Table 6.2 **Attributes and methods of `Stats` objects for file system entries**

Attribute/Method	Description
`isFile()`	Returns `true` if the entry is a file
`isDirectory()`	Returns `true` if the entry is a directory
`isSocket()`	Returns `true` if the entry is a socket
`dev`	Specifies the device ID on which the file is located
`mode`	Specifies the access mode of the file
`size`	Specifies the number of bytes in the file
`blksize`	Specifies the block size used to store the file in bytes
`blocks`	Specifies the number of blocks the file is taking on disk
`atime`	Specifies the time the file was last accessed
`mtime`	Specifies the time the file was last modified
`ctime`	Specifies the time the file was created

Listing 6.9 illustrates the use of the `fs.stats()` call by making the call and then outputting the results of the object as a JSON string as well as using the `isFile()`, `isDirector()`, and `isSocket()` calls, as shown in Listing 6.9 Output.

Listing 6.9 `file_stats.js`: **Implementing an `fs.stats()` call to retrieve information about a file**

```
var fs = require('fs');
fs.stat('file_stats.js', function (err, stats) {
  if (!err){
    console.log('stats: ' + JSON.stringify(stats, null, '  '));
    console.log(stats.isFile() ? "Is a File" : "Is not a File");
    console.log(stats.isDirectory() ? "Is a Folder" : "Is not a Folder");
    console.log(stats.isSocket() ? "Is a Socket" : "Is not a Socket");
    stats.isDirectory();
    stats.isBlockDevice();
    stats.isCharacterDevice();
    //stats.isSymbolicLink(); //only lstat
    stats.isFIFO();
    stats.isSocket();
  }
});
```

Listing 6.9 Output `file_stats.js`: **Displaying information about a file**

```
C:\books\node\ch06>node file_stats.js
stats: {
  "dev": 818973644,
  "mode": 33206,
  "nlink": 1,
  "uid": 0,
  "gid": 0,
  "rdev": 0,
  "ino": 1970324837052284,
  "size": 535,
  "atime": "2016-09-14T18:03:26.572Z",
  "mtime": "2013-11-26T21:51:51.148Z",
  "ctime": "2014-12-18T17:30:43.340Z",
  "birthtime": "2016-09-14T18:03:26.572Z"
}
Is a File
Is not a Folder
Is not a Socket
```

Listing Files

Another common task when working with the file system is listing files and folders in a directory. For example, you might want to determine whether the files and folders need to be cleaned up, you might need to dynamically operate on the directory structure, and so on.

To access the files in the file system, use one of the following commands to read a list of entries:

```
fs.readdir(path, callback)
fs.readdirSync(path)
```

If `readdirSync()` is called, an array of strings representing the entry names in the specified `path` is returned. In the case of `readdir()`, the list is passed as the second parameter to the `callback` function and an error, if there is one, is passed as the first.

To illustrate the use of `readdir()`, Listing 6.10 implements a nested callback chain to walk the directory structure and output the entries. Notice that the callback function implements a wrapper to provide closure for the `fullPath` variable, and that the `WalkDirs()` function loops by being called by the asynchronous callback function, as shown in Listing 6.10 Output.

Listing 6.10 `file_readdir.js`: **Implementing a callback chain to walk down and output the contents of a directory structure**

```
var fs = require('fs');
var Path = require('path');
function WalkDirs(dirPath){
  console.log(dirPath);
  fs.readdir(dirPath, function(err, entries){
    for (var idx in entries){
      var fullPath = Path.join(dirPath, entries[idx]);
      (function(fullPath){
        fs.stat(fullPath, function (err, stats){
          if (stats.isFile()){
            console.log(fullPath);
          } else if (stats.isDirectory()){
            WalkDirs(fullPath);
          }
        });
      })(fullPath);
    }
  });
}
WalkDirs("../ch06");
```

Listing 6.10 Output `file_readdir.js`: **Iteratively walking the directory structure using chained asynchronous callbacks**

```
C:\books\node\ch06>node file_readdir.js
../ch06
..\ch06\file_readdir.js
..\ch06\filesystem.js
..\ch06\data
..\ch06\file_stats.js
..\ch06\file_folders.js
..\ch06\renamed
```

```
..\ch06\reading
..\ch06\writing
..\ch06\data\config.txt
..\ch06\data\folderA
..\ch06\data\grains.txt
..\ch06\data\fruit.txt
..\ch06\reading\file_read.js
..\ch06\data\veggie.txt
..\ch06\data\log.txt
..\ch06\data\output.txt
..\ch06\writing\file_write.js
..\ch06\reading\file_read_async.js
..\ch06\reading\file_read_sync.js
..\ch06\reading\file_read_stream.js
..\ch06\writing\file_write_async.js
..\ch06\writing\file_write_stream.js
..\ch06\writing\file_write_sync.js
..\ch06\data\folderA\folderC
..\ch06\data\folderA\folderB
..\ch06\data\folderA\folderB\folderD
..\ch06\data\folderA\folderC\folderE
```

Deleting Files

Another common task when working with files is deleting them to clean up data or make more room on the file system. To delete a file from Node.js, use one of the following commands:

```
fs.unlink(path, callback)
fs.unlinkSync(path)
```

The `unlinkSync(path)` returns `true` or `false` based on whether the delete is successful. The asynchronous `unlink()` call passes back an error value to the callback function if an error is encountered when deleting the file.

The following code snippet illustrates the process of deleting a file named `new.txt` using the `unlink()` asynchronous `fs` call:

```
fs.unlink("new.txt", function(err){
  console.log(err ? "File Delete Failed" :  "File Deleted");
});
```

Truncating Files

Truncating a file means reducing the size of the file by setting the end to a smaller value than the current size. You might want to truncate a file that grows continuously but does not contain critical data, such as a temporary log. To truncate a file, use one the following `fs` calls and pass in the number of bytes you want the file to contain when the truncation completes:

```
fs.truncate(path, len, callback)
fs.truncateSync(path, len)
```

The truncateSync(path) returns true or false based on whether the file is successfully truncated. The asynchronous truncate() call passes an error value to the callback function if an error is encountered when truncating the file.

The following code snippet illustrates the process of truncating a file named log.txt to zero bytes.

```
fs.truncate("new.txt", function(err){
  console.log(err ? "File Truncate Failed" :  "File Truncated");
});
```

Making and Removing Directories

At times you may need to implement a directory structure for files being stored by your Node.js application. The fs module provides the functionality to add and remove directories as necessary.

To add a directory from Node.js, use one of the following fs calls. The path can be absolute or relative. The optional mode parameter allows you to specify the access mode for the new directory.

```
fs.mkdir(path, [mode], callback)
fs.mkdirSync(path, [mode])
```

The mkdirSync(path) returns true or false based on whether the directory is successfully created. The asynchronous mkdir() call passes an error value to the callback function if an error is encountered when creating the directory.

Keep in mind that when using the asynchronous method, you need to wait for the callback for the creation of the directory before creating a subdirectory. The following code snippet shows how to chain the creation of a subdirectory structure together:

```
fs.mkdir("./data/folderA", function(err){
  fs.mkdir("./data/folderA/folderB", function(err){
    fs.mkdir("./data/folderA/folderB/folderD", function(err){
    });
  });
  fs.mkdir("./data/folderA/folderC", function(err){
    fs.mkdir("./data/folderA/folderC/folderE", function(err){
    });
  });
});
```

To delete a directory from Node.js, use one of the following fs calls. The path can be absolute or relative.

```
fs.rmdir(path, callback)
fs.rmdirSync(path)
```

The rmdirSync(path) returns true or false based on whether the directory is successfully deleted. The asynchronous rmdir() call passes an error value to the callback function if an error is encountered when deleting the directory.

Just as with the `mkdir()` calls, keep in mind that when using the asynchronous method, you need to wait for the callback of the deletion of the directory before deleting the parent directory. The following code snippet shows how to chain the deletion of a subdirectory structure together:

```
fs.rmdir("./data/folderA/folderB/folderC", function(err){
  fs.rmdir("./data/folderA/folderB", function(err){
    fs.rmdir("./data/folderD", function(err){
    });
  });
  fs.rmdir("./data/folderA/folderC", function(err){
    fs.rmdir("./data/folderE", function(err){
    });
  });
});
```

Renaming Files and Directories

You might also need to rename files and folders in your Node.js application to make room for new data, archive old data, or apply changes made by a user. Renaming files and folders uses the `fs` calls shown here:

```
fs.rename(oldPath, newPath, callback)
fs.renameSync(oldPath, newPath)
```

The `oldPath` specifies the existing file or directory path, and the `newPath` specifies the new name. The `renameSync(path)` returns `true` or `false` based on whether the file or directory is successfully renamed. The asynchronous `rename()` call passes an error value to the callback function if an error is encountered when renaming the file or directory.

The following code snippet illustrates implementing `fs` calls to rename a file named `old.txt` to `new.txt` and a directory named `testDir` to `renamedDir`:

```
fs.rename("old.txt", "new.txt", function(err){
  console.log(err ? "Rename Failed" :  "File Renamed");
});
fs.rename("testDir", "renamedDir", function(err){
  console.log(err ? "Rename Failed" :  "Folder Renamed");
});
```

Watching for File Changes

Although not entirely stable, the `fs` module provides a useful tool to watch a file and execute a callback function when the file changes. This can be useful if you want to trigger events to occur when a file is modified, but do not want to continually poll from your application directly. This does incur some overhead in the underlying OS, so you should use watches sparingly.

To implement a watch on a file, use the following command passing the `path` to the file you want to watch. You can also pass in `options`, which is an object that contains `persistent` and `interval` properties. The `persistent` property is `true` if you want the process to continue to run as long as files are being watched. The `interval` property specifies the time in milliseconds that you want the file to be polled for changes:

```
fs.watchFile(path, [options], callback)
```

When a file change occurs, the `callback` function is executed and passes a current and previous `Stats` object.

The following code example monitors a file named `log.txt` at an interval of every 5 seconds and uses the `Stats` object to output the current and previous times the file was modified:

```
fs.watchFile("log.txt", {persistent:true, interval:5000}, function (curr, prev) {
  console.log("log.txt modified at: " + curr.mtime);
  console.log("Previous modification was: " + prev.mtime);
});
```

Summary

Node.js provides the `fs` module that allows you to interact with the file system. The `fs` module allows you to create, read, and modify files. You can also use the `fs` module to navigate the directory structure, look at information about files and folders, and change the directory structure by deleting and renaming files and folders.

Next

The next chapter focuses on using the `http` module to implement basic webservers. You see how to parse query strings and also how to implement a basic webserver in Node.js.

7

Implementing HTTP Services in Node.js

One of the most important aspects of Node.js is the ability to quickly implement HTTP and HTTPS servers and services. Node.js provides the `http` and `https` modules out of the box, and they provide the basic framework to do most everything you need from an HTTP and HTTPS standpoint. In fact, it is not difficult to implement a full webserver using just the `http` module.

That said, you will likely use a different module, such as `express`, to implement a full-on webserver. This is because the `http` module is pretty low level. It doesn't provide calls to handle routing, cookies, caching, and so on. When you get to the Express chapters later in this book, you will see the advantages it provides.

What you will more likely be using the `http` module for is implementing backend web services for your applications to use. That is where the `http` module becomes an invaluable tool in your arsenal. You can create basic HTTP servers that provide an interface for communications behind your firewall and then basic HTTP clients that interact with those services.

Therefore, this chapter focuses on understanding the objects that come into play when implementing clients and servers using the `http` module. The examples in this chapter are basic so that they are easy to consume and expand on.

Processing URLs

The Uniform Resource Locator (URL) acts as an address label for the HTTP server to handle requests from the client. It provides all the information needed to get the request to the correct server on a specific port and access the proper data.

The URL can be broken down into several different components, each providing a basic piece of information for the webserver on how to route and handle the HTTP request from the client. Figure 7.1 illustrates the basic structure of a URL and the components that may be included. Not all these components are included in every HTTP request. For example, most requests do not include the `auth` component, and many do not include a `query` string or `hash` location.

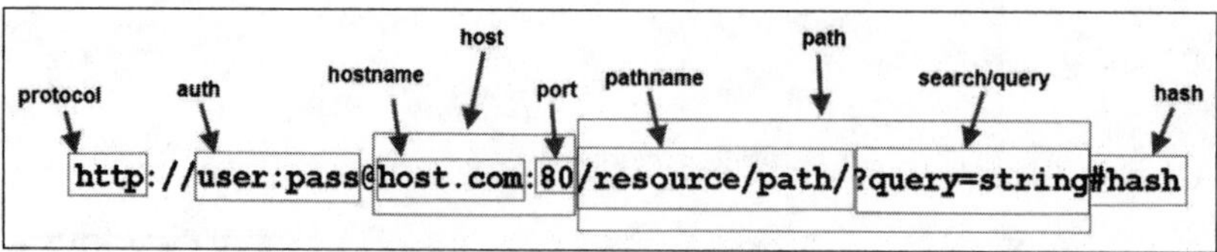

Figure 7.1 Basic components that can be included in a URL

Understanding the `URL` Object

HTTP requests from the client include the URL string with the information shown in Figure 7.1. To use the URL information more effectively, Node.js provides the `url` module that provides functionality to convert the URL string into a `URL` object.

To create a `URL` object from the URL string, pass the URL string as the first parameter to the following method:

```
url.parse(urlStr, [parseQueryString], [slashesDenoteHost])
```

The `url.parse()` method takes the URL string as the first parameter. The `parseQueryString` parameter is a Boolean that when `true` also parses the query string portion of the URL into an object literal. The default is `false`. The `slashesDenoteHost` is also a Boolean that when `true` parses a URL with the format of `//host/path to {host: 'host', pathname: '/path'}` instead of `{pathname: '//host/path'}`. The default is `false`.

You can also convert a `URL` object into a string form using the following `url.parse()` method. Table 7.1 lists the attributes of the `URL` objects created by `url.parse()`:

```
url.format(urlObj)
```

The following shows an example of parsing a URL string into an object and then converting it back into a string:

```
var url = require('url');
var urlStr = 'http://user:pass@host.com:80/resource/path?query=string#hash';
var urlObj = url.parse(urlStr, true, false);
urlString = url.format(urlObj);
```

Table 7.1 **Properties of the `URL` object**

Property	Description
`href`	This is the full URL string that was originally parsed.
`protocol`	The `request` protocol lowercased.
`host`	The full `host` portion of the URL including `port` information lowercased.
`auth`	The `authentication` information portion of a URL.
`hostname`	The `hostname` portion of the host lowercased.
`port`	The `port` number portion of the host.

Property	Description
pathname	The path portion of the URL including the initial slash if present.
search	The query string portion of the URL including the leading question mark.
path	The full path including the pathname and search.
query	This is either the parameter portion of the query string or a parsed object containing the query string parameters and values if the parseQueryString is set to true.
hash	The hash portion of the URL including the pound sign (#).

Resolving the URL Components

Another useful feature of the url module is the ability to resolve URL components in the same manner as a browser would. This allows you to manipulate the URL strings on the server side to make adjustments in the URL. For example, you might want to change the URL location before processing the request because a resource has moved or changed parameters.

To resolve a URL to a new location use the following syntax:

```
url.resolve(from, to)
```

The from parameter specifies the original base URL string. The to parameter specifies the new location where you want the URL to resolve. The following code illustrates an example of resolving a URL to a new location.

```
var url = require('url');
var originalUrl = 'http://user:pass@host.com:80/resource/path?query=string#hash';
var newResource = '/another/path?querynew';
console.log(url.resolve(originalUrl, newResource));
```

The output of the previous code snippet is shown below. Notice that only the resource path and beyond are altered in the resolved URL location:

```
http://user:pass@host.com:80/another/path?querynew
```

Processing Query Strings and Form Parameters

HTTP requests often include query strings in the URL or parameter data in the body for form submissions. The query string can be obtained from the URL object defined in the previous section. The parameter data sent by a form request can be read out of the body of the client request, as described later in this chapter.

The query string and form parameters are just basic key-value pairs. To actually consume these values in your Node.js webserver you need to convert the string into a JavaScript object using the parse() method from the querystring module:

```
querystring.parse(str, [sep], [eq], [options])
```

The `str` parameter is the query or parameter string. The `sep` parameter allows you to specify the separator character used. The default separator character is `&`. The `eq` parameter allows you to specify the assignment character to use when parsing. The default is `=`. The `options` parameter is an object with the property `maxKeys` that allows you to limit the number of keys the resulting object can contain. The default is 1000. If you specify 0, there is no limit.

The following shows an example of using `parse()` to parse a query string:

```
var qstring = require('querystring');
var params = qstring.parse("name=Brad&color=red&color=blue");
The params object created would be:
{name: 'Brad', color: ['red', 'blue']}
```

You can also go back the other direction and convert an object to a query string using the `stringify()` function shown here:

```
querystring.stringify(obj, [sep], [eq])
```

Understanding Request, Response, and Server Objects

To use the `http` module in Node.js applications, you first need to understand the request and response objects. They provide the information and much of the functionality that comes into and out of the HTTP clients and servers. Once you see the makeup of these objects—including properties, events, and methods they provide—it will be simple to implement your own HTTP servers and clients.

The following sections cover the purpose and behavior of the `ClientRequest`, `ServerResponse`, `IncomingMessage`, and `Server` objects. The most important events, properties, and methods that each provides also are covered.

The `http.ClientRequest` Object

The `ClientRequest` object is created internally when you call `http.request()` when building the HTTP client. This object represents the request while it is in progress to the server. You use the `ClientRequest` object to initiate, monitor, and handle the response from the server.

The `ClientRequest` implements a `Writable` stream, so it provides all the functionality of a `Writable` stream object. For example, you can use the `write()` method to write to it as well as pipe a `Readable` stream into it.

To implement a `ClientRequest` object, you use a call to `http.request()` using the following syntax:

```
http.request(options, callback)
```

The `options` parameter is an object whose properties define how to open and send the client HTTP request to the server. Table 7.2 lists the properties that you can specify. The `callback` parameter is a callback function that is called after the request is sent to the server and handles the response back from the server. The only parameter to the callback is an `IncomingMessage` object that will be the response from the server.

The following code shows the basics of implementing the `ClientRequest` object:

```
var http = require('http');
var options = {
  hostname: 'www.myserver.com',
  path: '/',
  port: '8080',
  method: 'POST'
};
var req = http.request(options, function(response){
  var str = ''
  response.on('data', function (chunk) {
    str += chunk;
  });
  response.on('end', function () {
    console.log(str);
  });
});
req.end();
```

Table 7.2 **Options that can be specified when creating a `ClientRequest`**

Property	Description
`host`	The domain name or IP address of the server to issue the request to. Defaults to `localhost`.
`hostname`	Same as `host` but preferred over host to support `url.parse()`.
`port`	Port of remote server. Defaults to 80.
`localAddress`	Local interface to bind for network connections.
`socketPath`	Unix Domain Socket (use one of `host:port` or `socketPath`).
`method`	A string specifying the HTTP request method. For example, `GET`, `POST`, `CONNECT`, `OPTIONS`, etc. Defaults to `GET`.
`path`	A string specifying the requested resource path. Defaults to `/`. This should also include the query string if any. For example: `/book.html?chapter=12`
`headers`	An object containing request headers. For example: `{ 'content-length': '750', 'content-type': 'text/plain' }`
`auth`	Basic authentication in the form of `user:password` used to compute an `Authorization` header.
`agent`	Defines the `Agent` behavior. When an `Agent` is used, request defaults to `Connection:keep-alive`. Possible values are: `undefined` (default): Uses global `Agent`. `Agent` object: Uses specific `Agent` object. `false`: Disables `Agent` behavior.

The `ClientRequest` object provides several events that enable you to handle the various states the request may experience. For example, you can add a listener that is called when the `response` event is triggered by the server's response. Table 7.3 lists the events available on `ClientResponse` objects.

Table 7.3 **Events available on `ClientRequest` objects**

Property	Description
`response`	Emitted when a response to this request is received from the server. The callback handler receives back an `IncomingMessage` object as the only parameter.
`socket`	Emitted after a socket is assigned to this request.
`connect`	Emitted every time a server responds to a request that was initiated with a `CONNECT` method. If this event is not handled by the client, then the connection will be closed.
`upgrade`	Emitted when the server responds to a request that includes an Update request in the headers.
`continue`	Emitted when the server sends a `100 Continue HTTP` response instructing the client to send the request body.

In addition to events, the `ClientRequest` object also provides several methods that can be used to write data to the request, abort the request, or end the request. Table 7.4 lists the methods available on the `ClientRequest` object.

Table 7.4 **Methods available on `ClientRequest` objects**

Method	Description
`write(chunk, [encoding])`	Writes a chunk, `Buffer` or `String` object, of body data into the request. This allows you to stream data into the `Writable` stream of the `ClientRequest` object. If you stream the body data, you should include the `{'Transfer-Encoding', 'chunked'}` header option when you create the request. The encoding parameter defaults to `utf8`.
`end([data], [encoding])`	Writes the optional data out to the request body and then flushes the `Writable` stream and terminates the request.
`abort()`	Aborts the current request.
`setTimeout(timeout, [callback])`	Sets the socket timeout for the request.

Method	Description
`setNoDelay ([noDelay])`	Disables the Nagle algorithm, which buffers data before sending it. The `noDelay` argument is a Boolean that is `true` for immediate writes and `false` for buffered writes.
`setSocketKeepAlive ([enable], [initialDelay])`	Enables and disables the `keep-alive` functionality on the client request. The `enable` parameter defaults to `false`, which is disabled. The `initialDelay` parameter specifies the delay between the last data packet and the first `keep-alive` request.

The `http.ServerResponse` Object

The `ServerResponse` object is created by the HTTP server internally when a `request` event is received. It is passed to the `request` event handler as the second argument. You use the `ServerRequest` object to formulate and send a response to the client.

The `ServerResponse` implements a `Writable` stream, so it provides all the functionality of a `Writable` stream object. For example, you can use the `write()` method to write to it as well as pipe a `Readable` stream into it to write data back to the client.

When handling the client request, you use the properties, events, and methods of the `ServerResponse` object to build and send headers, write data, and send the response. Table 7.5 lists the event and properties available on the `ServerResponse` object. Table 7.6 lists the methods available on the `ServerResponse` object.

Table 7.5 **Events available on `ServerResponse` objects**

Property	Description
`close`	Emitted when the connection to the client is closed prior to sending the `response.end()` to finish and flush the response.
`headersSent`	A Boolean that is `true` if headers have been sent; otherwise, `false`. This is read only.
`sendDate`	A Boolean that, when set to `true`, the `Date` header is automatically generated and sent as part of the response.
`statusCode`	Allows you to specify the response status code without having to explicitly write the headers. For example: `response.statusCode = 500;`

Table 7.6 **Methods available on `ServerResponse` objects**

Method	Description
`writeContinue()`	Sends an `HTTP/1.1 100 Continue` message to the client requesting that the body data be sent.

`writeHead(statusCode, [reasonPhrase], [headers])`	Writes a response header to the request. The `statusCode` parameter is the three-digit HTTP response status code, for example, `200`, `401`, `500`. The optional `reasonPhrase` is a string denoting the reason for the `statusCode`. The `headers` are the response headers object, for example:
	`response.writeHead(200, 'Success', {`
	`  'Content-Length': body.length,`
	`  'Content-Type': 'text/plain' });`

`setTimeout(msecs, callback)`	Sets the socket timeout for the client connection in milliseconds along with a `callback` function to be executed if the timeout occurs.
`setHeader(name, value)`	Sets the value of a specific header where `name` is the HTTP header name and `value` is the header value.
`getHeader(name)`	Gets the value of an HTTP header that has been set in the response.
`removeHeader(name)`	Removes an HTTP header that has been set in the response.
`write(chunk, [encoding])`	Writes a `chunk`, `Buffer` or `String` object, of data out to the response `Writable` stream. This only writes data to the body portion of the response. The default encoding is `utf8`. This returns `true` if the data is written successfully or `false` if the data is written to user memory. If it returns `false`, then a `drain` event is emitted by the `Writable` stream when the buffer is free again.
`addTrailers(headers)`	Adds HTTP trailing headers to the end of the response.
`end([data], [encoding])`	Writes the optional data out to the response body and then flushes the `Writable` stream and finalizes the response.

The `http.IncomingMessage` Object

The `IncomingMessage` object is created either by the HTTP server or the HTTP client. On the server side, the client request is represented by an `IncomingMessage` object, and on the client side the server response is represented by an `IncomingMessage` object. The `IncomingMessage` object can be used for both because the functionality is basically the same.

The `IncomingMessage` implements a `Readable` stream, allowing you to read the client request or server response as a streaming source. This means that the `readable` and `data` events can be listened to and used to read data from the stream.

In addition to the functionality provided by the `Readable` class, the `IncomingMessage` object also provides the properties, events, and methods listed in Table 7.7. These allow you to access information from the client request or server response.

Table 7.7 **Events, properties, and methods available on `IncomingMessage` objects**

Method/Event/Property	Description
`close`	Emitted when the underlying socket is closed.
`httpVersion`	Specifies the version of HTTP used to build the client request/ response.
`headers`	This is an object containing the headers sent with the request/ response.
`trailers`	This is an object containing any trailer headers sent with the request/response.
`method`	Specifies the method for the request/response. For example: `GET`, `POST`, `CONNECT`.
`url`	The URL string sent to the server. This is the string that can be passed to `url.parse()`. This attribute is only valid in the HTTP server handling the client request.
`statusCode`	Specifies the three-digit status code from the server. This attribute is only valid on the HTTP client when handling a server response.
`socket`	This is a handle to the `net.Socket` object used to communicate with the client/server.
`setTimeout(msecs, callback)`	Sets the socket timeout for the connection in milliseconds along with a `callback` function to be executed if the timeout occurs.

The `http.Server` Object

The Node.js HTTP `Server` object provides the fundamental framework to implement HTTP servers. It provides an underlying socket that listens on a port and handles receiving requests and then sends responses out to client connections. While the server is listening, the Node.js application will not end.

The `Server` object implements `EventEmitter` and emits the events listed in Table 7.8. As you implement an HTTP server, you need to handle at least some or all of these events. For example, at a minimum you need an event handler to handle the `request` event that is triggered when a client request is received.

Table 7.8 **Events that can be triggered by `Server` objects**

Event	Description
`request`	Triggered each time the server receives a client request. The callback should accept two parameters. The first is an `IncomingMessage` object representing the client request, and the second is a `ServerResponse` object you use to formulate and send the response. For example: `function callback (request, response){}`
`connection`	Triggered when a new TCP stream is established. The callback receives the socket as the only parameter. For example: `function callback (socket){}`
`close`	Triggered when the server is closed. The callback receives no parameters.
`checkContinue`	Triggered when a request that includes the `Expect: 100-continue` header is received. There is a default event handler that responds with an `HTTP/1.1 100 Continue` even if you do not handle this event. For example: `function callback (request, response){}`
`connect`	Emitted when an HTTP `CONNECT` request is received. The callback receives the request, socket, and head, which is a Buffer containing the first packet of the tunneling stream. For example: `function callback (request, socket, head){}`
`upgrade`	Emitted when the client requests an HTTP upgrade. If this event is not handled clients sending an upgrade request will have their connections closed. The callback receives the request, socket, and head, which is a `Buffer` containing the first packet of the tunneling stream. For example: `function callback (request, socket, head){}`
`clientError`	Emitted when the client connection socket emits an error. The callback receives an error as the first parameter and the socket as the second. For example: `function callback (error, socket){}`

To start the HTTP server, you need to first create a `Server` object using the `createServer()` method shown below. This method returns the `Server` object. The optional `requestListener` parameter is a callback that is executed when the request event is triggered. The callback should accept two parameters. The first is an `IncomingMessage` object representing the client request, and the second is a `ServerResponse` object you use to formulate and send the response:

```
http.createServer([requestListener])
```

Once you have created the `Server` object, you can begin listening on it by calling the `listen()` method on the `Server` object:

```
listen(port, [hostname], [backlog], [callback])
```

The first method `listen(port, [hostname], [backlog], [callback])` is the one that you will most likely use. The following list describes each of the parameters:

- **port:** Specifies the port to listen on.
- **hostname:** Specifies when the hostname will accept connections, and if omitted, the server will accept connections directed to any IPv4 address (INADDR_ANY).
- **backlog:** Specifies the maximum number of pending connections that are allowed to be queued. This defaults to 511.
- **callback:** Specifies the callback handler to execute once the server has begun listening on the specified port.

The following code shows an example of starting an HTTP server and listening on port `8080`. Notice the request callback handler:

```
var http = require('http');
http.createServer(function (req, res) {
  <<handle the request and response here>>
}).listen(8080);
```

Two other methods can be used to listen for connections through the file system. The first accepts a `path` to a file to listen on, and the second accepts an already open file descriptor `handle`:

```
listen(path, [callback])
listen(handle, [callback])
```

To stop the HTTP server from listening once it has started, use the following `close()` method:

```
close([callback]).
```

Implementing HTTP Clients and Servers in Node.js

Now that you understand the `ClientRequest`, `ServerResponse`, and `IncomingMessage` objects, you are ready to implement some Node.js HTTP clients and servers. This section guides you through the process of implementing basic HTTP clients and servers in Node.js. To do this, a client and server are implemented in each section to show you how the two interact.

The examples in the following sections are basic to make it easy for you to grasp the concepts of starting the client/server and then handling the different requests and responses. There is no error handling, protection against attacks, or much of the other functionality built in. However, the examples provide a good variety of the basic flow and structure required to handle general HTTP requests using the `http` module.

Serving Static Files

The most basic type of HTTP server is one that serves static files. To serve static files from Node.js, you need to first start the HTTP server and listen on a port. Then in the request handler, you open the file locally using the `fs` module and write the file contents to the response.

Listing 7.1 shows the basic implementation of a static file server. Notice that line 5 creates the server using `createServer()` and also defines the request event handler shown in lines 6–15. Also notice that the server is listening on port `8080` by calling `listen()` on the `Server` object.

Inside the request event handler on line 6, the `url.parse()` method is used to parse the `url` so that we can use the `pathname` attribute when specifying the path for the file in line 7. The static file is opened and read using `fs.readFile()`, and in the `readFile()` callback the contents of the file are written to the response object using `res.end(data)` on line 14.

Listing 7.1 `http_server_static.js`: **Implementing a basic static file webserver**

```
01 var fs = require('fs');
02 var http = require('http');
03 var url = require('url');
04 var ROOT_DIR = "html/";
05 http.createServer(function (req, res) {
06   var urlObj = url.parse(req.url, true, false);
07   fs.readFile(ROOT_DIR + urlObj.pathname, function (err,data) {
08     if (err) {
09       res.writeHead(404);
10       res.end(JSON.stringify(err));
11       return;
12     }
13     res.writeHead(200);
14     res.end(data);
15   });
16 }).listen(8080);
```

Listing 7.2 shows a basic implementation of an HTTP client that sends a get request to the server to retrieve the file contents. Notice that the options for the request are set in lines 2–6, and then the client request is initiated in lines 16–18 passing the options.

When the request completes, the callback function uses the `on('data')` handler to read the contents of the response from the server and then the `on('end')` handler to log the file contents to a file. Figure 7.2 and Listing 7.2 Output show the output of the HTTP client as well as accessing the static file from a web browser.

Listing 7.2 `http_client_static.js`: **Basic web client retrieving static files**

```
01 var http = require('http');
02 var options = {
03     hostname: 'localhost',
04     port: '8080',
05     path: '/hello.html'
06   };
07 function handleResponse(response) {
08   var serverData = '';
09   response.on('data', function (chunk) {
```

```
    serverData += chunk;
  });
  response.on('end', function () {
    console.log(serverData);
  });
}
http.request(options, function(response){
  handleResponse(response);
}).end();
```

Listing 7.2 Output **Implementing a basic static file webserver**

```
C:\books\node\ch07>node http_server_static.js
<html>
  <head>
    <title>Static Example</title>
  </head>
  <body>
    <h1>Hello from a Static File</h1>
  </body>
</html>
```

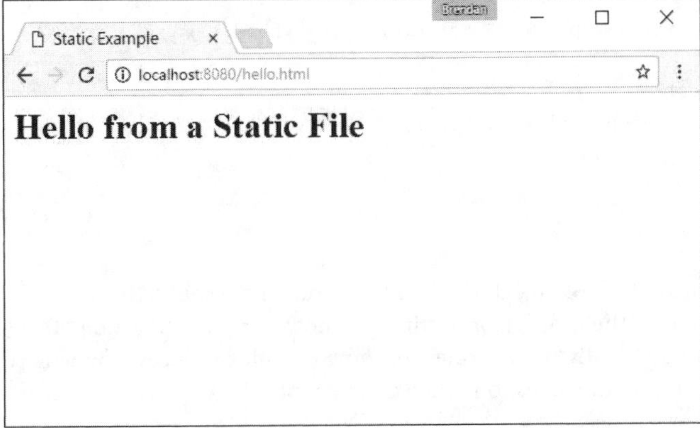

Figure 7.2 Implementing a basic static file web server

Implementing Dynamic GET Servers

More often than not you will use Node.js webservers to serve dynamic content rather than static content. This content may be dynamic HTML files or snippets, JSON data, or a number of other data types. To serve a GET request dynamically, you need to implement code in the request handler that dynamically populates the data you want to send back to the client, writes it out to the response, and then calls end() to finalize the response and flush the Writable stream.

Listing 7.3 shows the basic implementation of a dynamic web service. In this case, the web service simply responds with a dynamically generated HTTP file. The example is designed to show the process of sending the headers, building the response, and then sending the data in a series of `write()` requests.

Notice that line 6 creates the server using `createServer()`, and line 15 begins listening on port `8080` using `listen()`. Inside the request event handler defined in lines 7–15, the `Content-Type` header is set and then the headers are sent with a response code of `200`. In reality you would have already done a lot of processing to prepare the data. But in this case, the data is just the `messages` array defined in lines 2–5.

Notice that in lines 11–13 the loop iterates through the messages and calls `write()` each time to stream the response to the client. Then in line 14 the response is completed by calling `end()`.

Listing 7.3 `http_server_get.js`: **Implementing a basic `GET` webserver**

```
01 var http = require('http');
02 var messages = [
03   'Hello World',
04   'From a basic Node.js server',
05   'Take Luck'];
06 http.createServer(function (req, res) {
07   res.setHeader("Content-Type", "text/html");
08   res.writeHead(200);
09   res.write('<html><head><title>Simple HTTP Server</title></head>');
10   res.write('<body>');
11   for (var idx in  messages){
12     res.write('\n<h1>' + messages[idx] + '</h1>');
13   }
14   res.end('\n</body></html>');
15 }).listen(8080);
```

Listing 7.4 shows a basic implementation of an HTTP client that reads the response from the server in Listing 7.3. This is similar to the example in Listing 7.2; however, note that no path was specified since the service doesn't really require one. For more complex services, you would implement query strings or complex path routes to handle a variety of calls.

Note that on line 11 the `statusCode` from the response is logged to the console. Also on line12 the `headers` from the response are also logged. Then on line 13 the full response from the server is logged. Figure 7.3 and Listing 7.4 Output show the output of the HTTP client as well as accessing the dynamic get server from a web browser.

Listing 7.4 `http_client_get.js`: **Basic web client that makes a `GET` request to the server in Listing 7.3**

```
01 var options = {
02     hostname: 'localhost',
03     port: '8080',
```

```
  };
function handleResponse(response) {
  var serverData = '';
  response.on('data', function (chunk) {
    serverData += chunk;
  });
  response.on('end', function() {
    console.log("Response Status:", response.statusCode);
    console.log("Response Headers:", response.headers);
    console.log(serverData);
  });
}
http.request(options, function(response){
  handleResponse(response);
}).end
```

Listing 7.4 Output **Implementing a basic HTTP GET service**

```
C:\books\node\ch07>node http_server_get.js
Response Status: 200
Response Headers: { 'content-type': 'text/html',
  date: 'Mon, 26 Sep 2016 17:10:33 GMT',
  connection: 'close',
  'transfer-encoding': 'chunked' }
<html><head><title>Simple HTTP Server</title></head><body>
<h1>Hello World</h1>
<h1>From a basic Node.js server</h1>
<h1>Take Luck</h1>
</body></html>
```

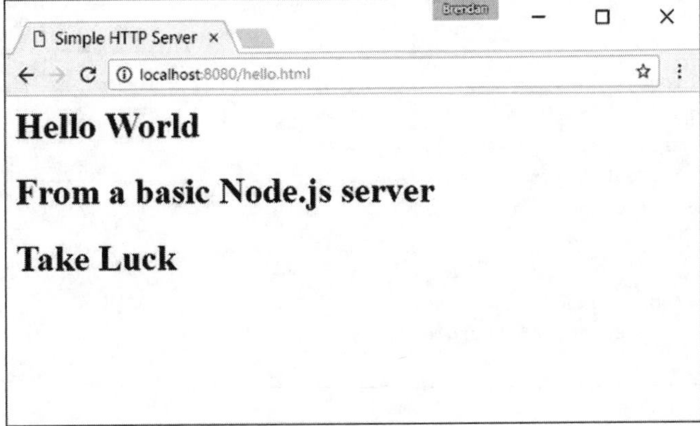

Figure 7.3 Output of a basic HTTP GET server

Implementing POST Servers

Implementing a POST service is similar to implementing a GET server. In fact, you may end up implementing them together in the same code for the sake of convenience. POST services are handy if you need to send data to the server to be updated, as for form submissions. To serve a POST request, you need to implement code in the request handler that reads the contents of the post body out and processes it.

Once you have processed the data, you dynamically populate the data you want to send back to the client, write it out to the response, and then call end() to finalize the response and flush the Writable stream. Just as with a dynamic GET server, the output of a POST request may be a webpage, HTTP snippet, JSON data, or some other data.

Listing 7.5 shows the basic implementation of a dynamic web service handling POST requests. In this case, the web service accepts a JSON string from the client representing an object that has name and occupation properties. The code in lines 4–6 read the data from the request stream, and then in the event handler in lines 7–14, the data is converted to an object and used to build a new object with message and question properties. Then in line 14 the new object is stringified and sent back to the client in the end() call.

Listing 7.5 http_server_post.js: **Implementing a basic HTTP server that handles HTTP POST requests**

```
01 var http = require('http');
02 var options = {
03   host: '127.0.0.1',
04   path: '/',
05   port: '8080',
06   method: 'POST'
07 };
08 function readJSONResponse(response) {
09   var responseData = '';
10   response.on('data', function (chunk) {
11     responseData += chunk;
12   });
13   response.on('end', function () {
14     var dataObj = JSON.parse(responseData);
15     console.log("Raw Response: " +responseData);
16     console.log("Message: " + dataObj.message);
17     console.log("Question: " + dataObj.question);
18   });
19 }
20 var req = http.request(options, readJSONResponse);
21 req.write('{"name":"Bilbo", "occupation":"Burgler"}');
22 req.end();
```

Listing 7.6 shows a basic implementation of an HTTP client that sends JSON data to the server as part of a `POST` request. The request is started in line 20. Then in line 21 a JSON string is written to the request stream, and line 22 finishes the request with `end()`.

Once the server sends the response back, the `on('data')` handler in lines 10–12 reads the JSON response. Then the `on('end')` handler in lines 13–18 parses the response into a JSON object and outputs the raw response, message, and question. Output 7.6 shows the output of the HTTP `POST` client.

Listing 7.6 `http_client_post.js`: **Basic HTTP client that sends JSON data to the server using `POST` and handles the JSON response**

```
01 var http = require('http');
02 var options = {
03   host: '127.0.0.1',
04   path: '/',
05   port: '8080',
06   method: 'POST'
07 };
08 function readJSONResponse (response) {
09   var responseData = '';
10   response.on('data', function (chunk) {
11     responseData += chunk;
12   });
13   response.on('end', function () {
14     var dataObj = JSON.parse(responseData);
15     console.log("Raw Response: " +responseData);
16     console.log("Message: " + dataObj.message);
17     console.log("Question: " + dataObj.question);
18   });
19 }
20 var req = http.request(options, readJSONResponse);
21 req.write('{"name":"Bilbo", "occupation":"Burgler"}');
22 req.end();
```

Listing 7.6 Output **Implementing an HTTP `POST` server serving JSON data**

```
C:\books\node\ch07>node http_server_post.js
Raw Response: {"message":"Hello Bilbo","question":"Are you a good Burgler?"}
Message: Hello Bilbo
Question: Are you a good Burgler?
```

Interacting with External Sources

A common use of the HTTP services in Node.js is to access external systems to get data to fulfill client requests. A variety of external systems provide data that can be used in various ways. In this example, the code connects to the openweathermap.org API to retrieve weather information about a city. To keep the example simple, the output from openweathermap.org is pushed to the browser in a raw format. In reality, you would likely massage the pieces of data needed into your own pages, widgets, or data responses.

Listing 7.7 shows the implementation of the web service that accepts both `GET` and `POST` requests. For the `GET` request, a simple webpage with a form is returned that allows the user to post a city name. Then in the `POST` request the city name is accessed, and the Node.js web client starts up and connects remotely to openweathermap.org to retrieve weather information for that city. Then that info is returned to the server along with the original web form.

The big difference between this example and the previous examples is that the webserver also implements a local web client to connect to the external service and get data used to formulate the response. The webserver is implemented in lines 35–49. Notice that if the method is `POST`, we read the form data from the request stream and use `querystring.parse()` to get the city name and call into the `getWeather()` function.

The `getWeather()` function in lines 27–33 implements the client request to openweathermap.org. Then the `parseWeather()` request handler in lines 17–25 reads the response from openweathermap.org and passes that data to the `sendResponse()` function defined in lines 4–16 that formulates the response and sends it back to the client. Figure 7.4 shows the implementation of the external service in a web browser.

> **Note**
>
> You must go to http://openweathermap.org/ to create an account and get an API key to use the following application.

Listing 7.7 `http_server_external`: **Implementing an HTTP web service that connects remotely to an external source for weather data**

```
01 var http = require('http');
02 var url = require('url');
03 var qstring = require('querystring');
04 var APIKEY = ""//place your own api key within the quotes;
05 function sendResponse(weatherData, res){
06   var page = '<html><head><title>External Example</title></head>' +
07     '<body>' +
08     '<form method="post">' +
09     'City: <input name="city"><br>' +
```

```
    '<input type="submit" value="Get Weather">' +
    '</form>';
  if(weatherData){
    page += '<h1>Weather Info</h1><p>' + weatherData +'</p>';
  }
  page += '</body></html>';
  res.end(page);
}
function parseWeather(weatherResponse, res) {
  var weatherData = '';
  weatherResponse.on('data', function (chunk) {
    weatherData += chunk;
  });
  weatherResponse.on('end', function () {
    sendResponse(weatherData, res);
  });
}
function getWeather(city, res){
  city = city.replace(' ', '-');
  console.log(city);
  var options = {
    host: 'api.openweathermap.org',
    path: '/data/2.5/weather?q=' + city + '&APPID=' + APIKEY
  };
  http.request(options, function(weatherResponse){
    parseWeather(weatherResponse, res);
  }).end();
}
http.createServer(function (req, res) {
  console.log(req.method);
  if (req.method == "POST"){
    var reqData = '';
    req.on('data', function (chunk) {
      reqData += chunk;
    });
    req.on('end', function() {
      var postParams = qstring.parse(reqData);
      getWeather(postParams.city, res);
    });
  } else {
    sendResponse(null, res);
  }
}).listen(8080);
```

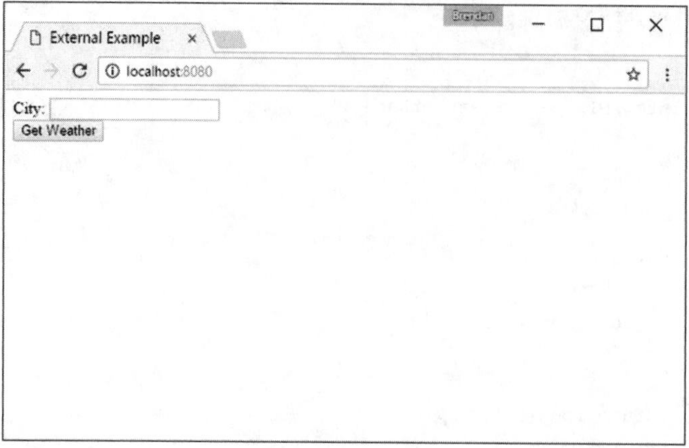

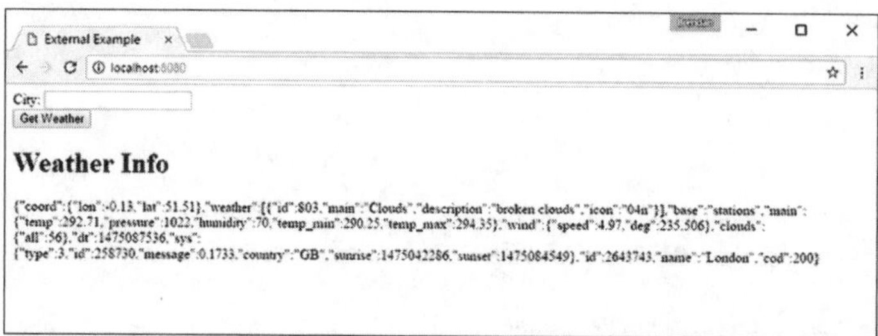

Figure 7.4 Implementing an external web service that connects to a remote source for weather data

Implementing HTTPS Servers and Clients

Hypertext Transfer Protocol Secure (HTTPS) is a communications protocol that provides secure communication between HTTP clients and servers. HTTPS is really just HTTP running on top of the SSL/TLS protocol, which is where it gets its security capabilities. HTTP provides security in two main ways. First, it uses long-term public and secret keys to exchange a short-term session key so that data can be encrypted between client and server. Second, it provides authentication so that you can ensure that the webserver you are connecting to is the one you actually think it is, thus preventing man-in-the-middle attacks where requests are rerouted through a third party.

The following sections discuss implementing HTTP servers and clients in your Node.js environment using the `https` module. Before getting started using HTTPS, you need to generate a private key and a public certificate. There are several ways to do this, depending on your platform. One of the simplest methods is to use the OpenSSL library for your platform.

To generate the private key, first execute the following OpenSSL command:

```
openssl genrsa -out server.pem 2048
```

Next, use the following command to create a certificate signing request file:

```
openssl req -new -key server.pem -out server.csr
```

> **Note**
>
> When creating the certificate signing request file, you will be asked several questions. When prompted for the Common Name, you should put in the domain name of the server you want to connect to. Otherwise, the certificate will not work. Also you can put in additional domain names and IP addresses in the Subject Alternative Names field.

Then to create a self-signed certificate that you can use for your own purpose or for testing, use the following command:

```
openssl x509 -req -days 365 -in server.csr -signkey server.pem -out server.crt
```

> **Note**
>
> The self-signed certificate is fine for testing purposes or internal use. However, if you are implementing an external web service that needs to be protected on the Internet, you may want to get a certificate signed by a certificate authority. If you want to create a certificate that is signed by a third-party certificate authority, you need to take additional steps.

Creating an HTTPS Client

Creating an HTTPS client is almost exactly like the process of creating an HTTP client discussed earlier in this chapter. The only difference is that there are additional options, shown in Table 7.9, that allow you to specify the security options for the client. The most important options you really need to worry about are `key`, `cert`, and `agent`.

The `key` option specifies the private key used for SSL. The `cert` value specifies the x509 public key to use. The global agent does not support options needed by HTTPS, so you need to disable the agent by setting the agent to `null`, as shown here:

```
var options = {
  key: fs.readFileSync('test/keys/client.pem'),
  cert: fs.readFileSync('test/keys/client.crt),
  agent: false
};
```

You can also create your own custom `Agent` object that specifies the agent options used for the request:

```
options.agent = new https.Agent (options);
```

Once you have defined the options with the `cert`, `key`, and `agent` settings, you can call the `https.request(options, [responseCallback])`, and it will work exactly the same as the `http.request()` call. The only difference is that the data between the client and server is encrypted.

```
var options = {
  hostname: 'encrypted.mysite.com',
  port: 443,
  path: '/',
  method: 'GET',
  key: fs.readFileSync('test/keys/client.pem'),
  cert: fs.readFileSync('test/keys/client.crt),
  agent: false
};
var req = https.request(options, function(res)) {
  <handle the response the same as an http.request>
}
```

Table 7.9 **Additional options for `https.request()` and `https.createServer()`**

Event	Description
`pfx`	A string or `Buffer` object containing the private key, certificate, and CA certs of the server in PFX or PKCS12 format.
`key`	A string or `Buffer` object containing the private key to use for SSL.
`passphrase`	A string containing the passphrase for the private key or pfx.
`cert`	A string or `Buffer` object containing the public x509 certificate to use.
`ca`	An `Array` of strings or `Buffers` of trusted certificates in PEM format to check the remote host against.
`ciphers`	A string describing the ciphers to use or exclude.
`rejectUnauthorized`	A Boolean that, when `true`, the server certificate is verified against the list of supplied CAs. An error event is emitted if verification fails. Verification happens at the connection level, before the HTTP request is sent. Defaults to `true`. Only for `https.request()` options.
`crl`	Either a string or list of strings of PEM encoded CRLs (Certificate Revocation List) only for `https.createServer()`.
`secureProtocol`	The SSL method to use. For example, `SSLv3_method` to force SSL version 3.

Creating an HTTPS Server

Creating an HTTPS server is almost exactly like the process of creating an HTTP server discussed earlier in this chapter. The only difference is that there are additional `options` parameters that you must pass into `https.createServer()`. The options, listed previously in Table 7.9, allow you to specify the security options for the server. The most important options you really need to worry about are `key` and `cert`.

The `key` option specifies the private key used for SSL. The `cert` value specifies the x509 public key to use. The following shows an example of creating an HTTPS server in Node.js:

```
var options = {
  key: fs.readFileSync('test/keys/server.pem'),
  cert: fs.readFileSync('test/keys/server.crt')
};
https.createServer(options, function (req, res) {
  res.writeHead(200);
  res.end("Hello Secure World\n");
}).listen(8080);
```

Once the HTTPS server has been created, the request/response handling works the same way as for the HTTP servers described earlier in this chapter.

Summary

An important aspect of Node.js is the ability to quickly implement HTTP and HTTPS servers and services. The `http` and `https` modules provide everything you need to implement webserver basics. For your full webserver, you should use a more extended library, such as Express. However, the `http` and `https` modules work well for some basic web services and are simple to implement.

The examples in this chapter covered the HTTP basics to give you a good start on implementing your own services. You also saw how the `url` and `querystring` modules are used to parse URLs and query strings into objects and back.

Next

In the next chapter, you go a little deeper as the `net` module is discussed. You learn how to implement your own socket services using TCP clients and servers.

8 Implementing Socket Services in Node.js

An important part of backend services is the ability to communicate with each other over sockets. Sockets allow one process to communicate with another process through an IP address and port. This can be useful when implementing interprocess communication (IPC) for two different processes running on the same server or accessing a service running on a completely different server. Node.js provides the `net` module that allows you to create both socket servers and clients that can connect to socket servers. For secure connections, Node.js provides the `tls` module that allows you to implement secure TLS socket servers and clients.

Understanding Network Sockets

Network sockets are endpoints of communication that flow across a computer network. Sockets live below the HTTP layer and provide the actual point-to-point communication between servers. Virtually all Internet communication is based on Internet sockets that flow data between two points on the Internet.

A socket works using a socket address, which is a combination of an IP address and port. There are two types of points in a socket connection: a server that listens for connections and a client that opens a connection to the server. Both the server and the client require a unique IP address and port combination.

The Node.js `net` module sockets communicate by sending raw data using the Transmission Control Protocol (TCP). This protocol is responsible for packaging the data and guaranteeing that it is sent from point to point successfully. Node.js sockets implement the `Duplex` stream, which allows you to read and write streamed data between the server and client.

Sockets are the underlying structure for the `http` module. If you do not need the functionality for handling web requests like `GET` and `POST` and you just need to stream data from point to point, then using sockets gives you a lighter weight solution and a bit more control.

Sockets are also handy when communicating with other processes running on the same computer. Processes cannot share memory directly, so if you want to access the data in one process from another process, you can open up the same socket in each process and read and write data between the two processes.

Understanding TPC Server and `Socket` Objects

To use the `net` module in Node.js applications, you first need to understand the TCP `Server` and `Socket` objects. These objects provide all the framework for starting a TCP server to handle requests and implementing TCP socket clients to make requests to the socket servers. Once you understand the events, properties, methods, and behavior of these objects, it will be simple to implement your own TCP socket servers and clients.

The following sections cover the purpose and behavior of the `net.Socket` and `net.Server` objects. The most important events, properties, and methods that each provides are also covered.

The `net.Socket` Object

`Socket` objects are created on both the socket server and the socket client and allow data to be written and read back and forth between them. The `Socket` object implements a `Duplex` stream, so it provides all the functionality that `Writable` and `Readable` streams provide. For example, you can use the `write()` method to stream writes of data to the server or client and a `data` event handler to stream data from the server or client.

On the socket client, the `Socket` object is created internally when you call `net.connect()` or `net.createConnection()`. This object is intended to represent the socket connection to the server. You use the `Socket` object to monitor the connection, send data to the server, and handle the response back from the server. There is no explicit client object in the Node.js `net` module because the `Socket` object acts as the full client allowing you to send/receive data and terminate the connection.

On the socket server, the `Socket` object is created when a client connects to the server and is passed to the connection event handler. This object is intended to represent the socket connection to the client. On the server, you use the `Socket` object to monitor the client connection as well as send and receive data to and from the client.

To create a `Socket` object, you use one of the following methods. All the calls return a `Socket` object. The only difference is the first parameters that they accept. The final parameter for all of them is a callback function that is executed when a connection is opened to the server. Notice that for each method there is a `net.connect()` and a `net.createConnection()` form. These work exactly the same way:

```
net.connect(options, [connectionListener])
net.createConnection(options, [connectionListener])
net.connect(port, [host], [connectListener])
net.createConnection(port, [host], [connectListener])
net.connect(path, [connectListener])
net.createConnection(path, [connectListener])
```

The first method to create a Socket object is to pass an options parameter, which is an object that contains properties that define the socket connection. Table 8.1 lists the properties that can be specified when creating the Socket object. The second method accepts port and host values, described in Table 8.1, as direct parameters. The third option accepts a path parameter that specifies a file system location that is a Unix socket to use when creating the Socket object.

Table 8.1 **Options that can be specified when creating a Socket**

Property	Description
port	Port number the client should connect to. This option is required.
host	Domain name or IP address of the server that the client should connect to. Defaults to localhost.
localAddress	Local IP address the client should bind to for network connections.
localPort	The local port that it binds to for network connections.
family	Version of IP stack. (default: 4)
lookup	Custom lookup. (default: dns.lookup)

Once the Socket object is created, it provides several events that are emitted during the life cycle of the connection to the server. For example, the connect event is triggered when the socket connects, the data event is emitted when there is data in the Readable stream ready to be read, and the close event is emitted when connection to the server is closed. As you implement your socket server, you can register callbacks to be executed when these events are emitted to handle opening and closing the socket, reading and writing data, and so on. Table 8.2 lists the events that can be triggered on the Socket object.

Table 8.2 **Events that can be triggered on Socket objects**

Event	Description
connect	Emitted when a connection is successfully established with the server. The callback function does not accept any parameters.
data	Emitted when data is received on the socket. If no data event handler is attached, then data can be lost. The callback function must accept a parameter, which is a Buffer object containing the chunk of data that was read from the socket. For example: `function(chunk){}`
end	Emitted when the server terminates the connection by sending a FIN. The callback function does not accept any parameters.
timeout	Emitted when the connection to the server times out due to inactivity.

Event	Description
`drain`	Emitted when the write buffer becomes empty. You can use this event to throttle back the data stream being written to the socket. The callback function does not accept any parameters.
`error`	Emitted when an error occurs on the socket connection. The callback function should accept the error as the only argument. For example: `function(error){}`
`close`	Emitted when the socket has fully closed, either because it was closed by an `end()` or because an error occurred. The callback function does not accept any parameters.

The `Socket` object also includes several methods that allow you to do things like read from and write to the socket as well as pause or end data flow. Many of these are inherited from the `Duplex` stream objects and should be familiar to you. Table 8.3 lists the methods available on the `Socket` object.

Table 8.3 **Methods that can be called on `Socket` Objects**

Method	Description
`setEncoding([encoding])`	When this function is called, data returned from the socket's streams is an encoded `String` instead of a `Buffer` object. Sets the default `encoding` that should be used when writing data to and reading data from the streams. Using this option handles multi-byte characters that might otherwise be mangled when converting the `Buffer` to a string using `buf.toString(encoding)`. If you want to read the data as strings, always use this method.
`write(data, [encoding], [callback])`	Writes a data `Buffer` or `String` to the `Writable` stream of the socket using the encoding if specified. The callback function is executed as soon as the data is written.
`end([data], [encoding])`	Writes a data `Buffer` or `String` to the `Writable` stream of the socket and then flushes the stream and closes the connection.
`destroy()`	This forces the socket connection to shut down. You should only need to use this in the case of failures.
`pause()`	Pauses a `Readable` stream of the socket from emitting `data` events. This allows you to throttle back the upload of data to the stream.
`resume()`	Resumes `data` event emitting on the `Readable` stream of the socket.

Method	Description
`setTimeout(timeout, [callback])`	Specifies a `timeout` in milliseconds that the server will wait before emitting a `timeout` event when the socket is inactive. The `callback` function will be triggered as a `once` event listener. If you want the connection to be terminated on timeout, you should do it manually in the `callback` function.
`setNoDelay([noDelay])`	Disables/enables the Nagle algorithm that buffers data before sending it. Setting this to `false` disables data buffering.
`setKeepAlive([enable], [initialDelay])`	Enables/disables the keep-alive functionality on the connection. The optional `initialDelay` parameter specifies the amount in milliseconds that the socket is idle before sending the first keep-alive packet.
`address()`	Returns the bound address, the address family name, and the port of the socket as reported by the operating system. The return value is an object that contains the port, family, and address properties. For example: `{ port: 8107, family: 'IPv4', address: '127.0.0.1' }`
`unref()`	Calling this method allows the Node.js application to terminate if this socket is the only event on the event queue.
`ref()`	References this socket so that if this socket is the only thing on the event queue, the Node.js application will not terminate.

The `Socket` object also provides several properties that you can access to get information about the object. For example, the address and port the socket is communicating on, the amount of data being written, and the buffer size. Table 8.4 lists the properties available on the `Socket` object.

Table 8.4 **Properties that can be accessed on `Socket` Objects**

Method	Description
`bufferSize`	Returns the number of bytes currently buffered waiting to be written to the socket's stream
`remoteAddress`	IP address of the remote server that the socket is connected to
`remotePort`	Port of the remote server that the socket is connected to
`remoteFamily`	IP of the remote family the socket is connected to
`localAddress`	Local IP address the remote client is using for the socket connection

Method	Description
`localPort`	Local port the remote client is using for the socket connection
`bytesRead`	Number of bytes read by the socket
`bytesWritten`	Number of bytes written by the socket

To illustrate flowing data across a `Socket` object, the following code shows the basics of implementing the `Socket` object on a client. Notice that the `net.connect()` method is called using an `options` object containing a `port` and a `host` attribute. The `connect` callback function logs a message and then writes some data out to the server. To handle data coming back from the server, the `on.data()` event handler is implemented. To handle the closure of the socket, the `on('end')` event handler is implemented:

```
var net = require('net');
var client = net.connect({port: 8107, host:'localhost'}, function() {
  console.log('Client connected');
  client.write('Some Data\r\n');
});
client.on('data', function(data) {
  console.log(data.toString());
  client.end();
});
client.on('end', function() {
  console.log('Client disconnected');
});
```

The `net.Server` Object

The `net.Server` object is used to create a TCP socket server and begin listening for connections to which you will be able to read and write data. The `Server` object is created internally when you call `net.createServer()`. This object represents the socket server and handles listening for connections and then sending and receiving data on those connections to the server.

When the server receives a connection, the `Server` creates a `Socket` object and passes it to any connection event handlers that are listening. Because the `Socket` object implements a `Duplex` stream, you can use the `write()` method to stream writes of data back to the client and a `data` event handler to stream data from the client.

To create a `Server` object, you use the `net.createServer()` method shown here:

```
net.createServer([options], [connectionListener])
```

The options parameter is an object that specifies options to use when creating the socket Server object. Table 8.5 lists the properties of the options object. The second parameter is the connection event callback function, which is executed when a connection is received. This connectionListener callback function is passed to the Socket object for the connecting client.

Table 8.5 **Options that can be specified when creating a net.Server**

Property	Description
allowHalfOpen	A Boolean; when true, the socket won't automatically send a FIN packet when the other end of the socket sends a FIN packet, thus allowing half of the Duplex stream to remain open. Defaults to false.
pauseOnConnect	A Boolean; when true, each socket for each connection is paused, and no data will be read from its handle. This allows processes to pass connections between them without reading any data. Defaults to false.

Once the Server object is created, it provides several events that are triggered during the life cycle of the server. For example, the connection event is triggered when a socket client connects, and the close event is triggered when the server shuts down. As you implement your socket server, you can register callbacks to be executed when these events are triggered to handle connections, errors, and shutdown. Table 8.6 lists the events that can be triggered on the Socket object.

Table 8.6 **Events that can be triggered on Socket objects**

Event	Description
listening	Emitted when the server begins listening on a port by calling the listen() method. The callback function does not accept any parameters.
connection	Emitted when a connection is received from a socket client. The callback function must accept a parameter that is a Socket object representing the connection to the connecting client. For example: function(client){}
close	Emitted when the server closes either normally or on error. This event is emitted until all client connections have ended.
error	Emitted when an error occurs. The close event also is triggered on errors.

The Server object also includes several methods that allow you to do things like read from and write to the socket as well as pause or end data flow. Many of these are inherited from the Duplex stream objects and should be familiar to you. Table 8.7 lists the methods available on the Socket object.

Table 8.7 **Methods that can be called on `Socket` objects**

Method	Description
`listen(port, [host], [backlog], [callback])`	Opens up a port on the server and begins listening for connections. `port` specifies the listening port. If you specify 0 for the port, a random port number is selected. `host` is the IP address to listen on. If it is omitted, the server accepts connections directed to any IPv4 address. `backlog` specifies the maximum number of pending connections the server will allow. The default is 511. The callback function is called when the server has opened the port and begins listening.
`listen(path, [callback])`	Same as the preceding method except that a Unix socket server is started to listen for connections on the file system `path` specified.
`listen(handle, [callback])`	Same as the preceding method except that a handle to a `Server` or `Socket` object has an underlying `_handle` member that points to a file descriptor handle on the server. It assumes that the file descriptor points to a socket file that has been bound to a port already.
`getConnections(callback)`	Returns the number of connections currently connected to the server. The `callback` is executed when the number of connections is calculated and accepts an `error` parameter and a `count` parameter. For example: `function(error, count)`
`close([callback])`	Stops the server from accepting new connections. Current connections are allowed to remain until they complete. The server does not truly stop until all current connections have been closed.
`address()`	Returns the bound address, the address family name, and the port of the socket as reported by the operating system. The return value is an object that contains the port, family, and address properties. For example: `{ port: 8107, family: 'IPv4', address: '127.0.0.1' }`
`unref()`	Calling this method allows the Node.js application to terminate if this server is the only event on the event queue.
`ref()`	References this socket so that if this server is the only thing on the event queue the Node.js application will not terminate.

The `Server` object also provides the `maxConnections` attribute, which allows you to set the maximum number of connections that the server will accept before rejecting them. If a process has been forked to a child for processing using `child_process.fork()`, you should not use this option.

The following code shows the basics of implementing the `Server` object. Notice that the `net.createServer()` method is called and implements a callback that accepts the client `Socket` object. To handle data coming back from the client, the `on.data()` event handler is implemented. To handle the closure of the socket, the `on('end')` event handler is implemented. To begin listening for connections, the `listen()` method is called on port `8107`:

```
var net = require('net');
var server = net.createServer(function(client) {
  console.log(Client connected');
  client.on('data', function(data) {
    console.log('Client sent ' + data.toString());
  });
  client.on('end', function() {
    console.log('Client disconnected');
  });
  client.write('Hello');
});
server.listen(8107, function() {
  console.log('Server listening for connections');
});
```

Implementing TCP Socket Servers and Clients

Now that you understand the `net.Server` and `net.Socket` objects, you are ready to implement some Node.js TCP clients and servers. This section guides you through the process of implementing basic TCP clients and servers in Node.js.

The examples in the following sections are basic to make it easy for you to grasp the concepts of starting the TCP server listening on a port, and then implementing clients that can connect. The examples are designed to help you see the interactions and event handling that need to be implemented.

Implementing a TCP Socket Client

At the most basic level, implementing a TCP socket client involves the process of creating a `Socket` object that connects to the server, writing data to the server, and then handling the data that comes back. Additionally, you should build the socket so that it can also handle errors, the buffer being full, and timeouts. This section discusses each of the steps to implement a socket client using the `Socket` object. Listing 8.1 presents the full code for the following discussion.

The first step is to create the socket client by calling `net.connect()` as shown below. Pass in the `port` and `host` that you want to connect to as well and implement a `callback` function to handle the `connect` event:

```
net.connect({port: 8107, host:'localhost'}, function() {
  //handle connection
});
```

Then inside the callback you should set up the connection behavior. For example, you may want to add a timeout or set the encoding as shown here:

```
this.setTimeout(500);
this.setEncoding('utf8');
```

You also need to add handlers for the `data`, `end`, `error`, `timeout`, and `close` events that you want to handle. For example, to handle the `data` event so that you can read data coming back from the server, you might add the following handler once the connection has been established:

```
this.on('data', function(data) {
  console.log("Read from server: " + data.toString());
  //process the data
  this.end();
});
```

To write data to the server, you implement a `write()` command. If you are writing a lot of data to the server and the write fails, then you may also want to implement a `drain` event handler that begins writing again when the buffer is empty. The following shows an example of implementing a drain handler because of a write failure. Notice that a closure is used to preserve the values of the `socket` and `data` variables once the function has ended.

```
function writeData(socket, data){
  var success = !socket.write(data);
  if (!success){
    (function(socket, data){
      socket.once('drain', function(){
        writeData(socket, data);
      });
    })(socket, data);
  }
}
```

Listing 8.1 shows the full implementation of a basic TCP socket client. All the client does is send a bit of data to the server and receive a bit of data back; however, the example could easily be expanded to support more complex data handling across the socket. Notice that three separate sockets are opened to the server and are communicating at the same time. Notice that each client created gets a different random port number, as shown in Listing 8.1 Output.

Listing 8.1 `socket_client.js`: **Implementing basic TCP socket clients**

```
var net = require('net');
function getConnection(connName){
  var client = net.connect({port: 8107, host:'localhost'}, function() {
    console.log(connName + ' Connected: ');
    console.log('   local = %s:%s', this.localAddress, this.localPort);
    console.log('   remote = %s:%s', this.remoteAddress, this.remotePort);
    this.setTimeout(500);
```

```
    this.setEncoding('utf8');
    this.on('data', function(data) {
      console.log(connName + " From Server: " + data.toString());
      this.end();
    });
    this.on('end', function() {
      console.log(connName + ' Client disconnected');
    });
    this.on('error', function(err) {
      console.log('Socket Error: ', JSON.stringify(err));
    });
    this.on('timeout', function() {
      console.log('Socket Timed Out');
    });
    this.on('close', function() {
      console.log('Socket Closed');
    });
  });
  return client;
}
function writeData(socket, data){
  var success = !socket.write(data);
  if (!success){
    (function(socket, data){
      socket.once('drain', function(){
        writeData(socket, data);
      });
    })(socket, data);
  }
}
var Dwarves = getConnection("Dwarves");
var Elves = getConnection("Elves");
var Hobbits = getConnection("Hobbits");
writeData(Dwarves, "More Axes");
writeData(Elves, "More Arrows");
writeData(Hobbits, "More Pipe Weed");<Listing First>
```

Listing 8.1 Output `socket_client.js`: **Implementing basic TCP socket clients**

```
Elves Connected:
   local = 127.0.0.1:62616
   remote = 127.0.0.1:8107
Dwarves Connected:
   local = 127.0.0.1:62617
   remote = 127.0.0.1:8107
```

```
Hobbits Connected:
   local = 127.0.0.1:62618
   remote = 127.0.0.1:8107
Elves From Server: Sending: More Arrows
Dwarves From Server: Sending: More Axes
Hobbits From Server: Sending: More Pipe Weed
Dwarves Client disconnected
Socket Closed
Elves Client disconnected
Socket Closed
Hobbits Client disconnected
Socket Closed
```

Implementing a TCP Socket Server

At the most basic level, implementing a TCP server client involves the process of creating a `Server` object, listening on a port, and then handling incoming connections, including reading and writing data to and from the connections. Additionally, the socket server should handle the `close` and `error` events on the `Server` object as well as the events that occur in the incoming client connection `Socket` object. This section discusses each of the steps to implement a socket server using the `Server` object. Listing 8.2 presents the full code for the following discussion.

The first step is to create the socket server by calling `net.createServer()` as shown below. You also need to provide a connection callback handler and then call `listen()` to begin listening on the port:

```
var server = net.createServer(function(client) {
  //implement the connection callback handler code here.
});
server.listen(8107, function() {
 //implement the listen callback handler here.
});
```

Inside the `listen` callback handler, you should also add handlers to support the `close` and `error` events on the `Server` object. These may just be log statements, or you may also want to add additional code that is executed when these events occur. The follow shows the basic examples:

```
server.on('close', function(){
  console.log('Server Terminated');
});
server.on('error', function(err){
});
```

Inside the `connection` event callback, you need to set up the connection behavior. For example, you might want to add a timeout or set the encoding as shown here:

```
this.setTimeout(500);
this.setEncoding('utf8');
```

You also need to add handlers for the `data`, `end`, `error`, `timeout`, and `close` events that you want to handle on the client connection. For example, to handle the `data` event so that you can read data coming from the client, you might add the following handler once the connection is established:

```
this.on('data', function(data) {
  console.log("Received from client: " + data.toString());
  //process the data
});
```

To write data to the server, you implement a `write()` command somewhere in your code. If you are writing a lot of data to the client, then you may also want to implement a `drain` event handler that begins writing again when the buffer is empty. This can help if the `write()` returns a failure because the buffer is full, or if you want to throttle back writing to the socket. The following shows an example of implementing a drain handler because of a write failure. Notice that a closure is used to preserve the values of the socket and data variables once the function has ended:

```
function writeData(socket, data){
  var success = !socket.write(data);
  if (!success){
    (function(socket, data){
      socket.once('drain', function(){
        writeData(socket, data);
      });
    })(socket, data);
  }
}
```

The code in Listing 8.2 shows the full implementation of a basic TCP socket server. The socket server accepts connections on port `8107`, reads the data in, and then writes a string back to the client. Although the implementation is basic, it illustrates handling the events as well as reading and writing data in the client connection.

Listing 8.2 `socket_server.js`: **Implementing a basic TCP socket server**

```
var net = require('net');
var server = net.createServer(function(client) {
  console.log('Client connection: ');
  console.log('   local = %s:%s', client.localAddress, client.localPort);
  console.log('   remote = %s:%s', client.remoteAddress, client.remotePort);
  client.setTimeout(500);
  client.setEncoding('utf8');
  client.on('data', function(data) {
    console.log('Received data from client on port %d: %s',
                client.remotePort, data.toString());
    console.log('  Bytes received: ' + client.bytesRead);
```

```
    writeData(client, 'Sending: ' + data.toString());
    console.log('  Bytes sent: ' + client.bytesWritten);
  });
  client.on('end', function() {
    console.log('Client disconnected');
    server.getConnections(function(err, count){
      console.log('Remaining Connections: ' + count);
    });
  });
  client.on('error', function(err) {
    console.log('Socket Error: ', JSON.stringify(err));
  });
  client.on('timeout', function() {
    console.log('Socket Timed Out');
  });
});
server.listen(8107, function() {
  console.log('Server listening: ' + JSON.stringify(server.address()));
  server.on('close', function(){
    console.log('Server Terminated');
  });
  server.on('error', function(err){
    console.log('Server Error: ', JSON.stringify(err));
  });
});
function writeData(socket, data){
  var success = !socket.write(data);
  if (!success){
    (function(socket, data){
      socket.once('drain', function(){
        writeData(socket, data);
      });
    })(socket, data);
  }
}
```

Implementing TLS Servers and Clients

Transport Layer Security/Secure Socket Layer (TLS/SSL) is a cryptographic protocol designed to provide secure communications on the Internet. They use X.509 certificates along with session keys to verify whether the socket server you are communicating with is the one that you want to communicate with. TLS provides security in two main ways. First, it uses long-term public and secret keys to exchange a short-term session key so that data can be encrypted between client and server. Second, it provides authentication so that you can ensure that the webserver you are connecting to is the one you actually think it is, thus preventing man-in-the-middle attacks where requests are rerouted through a third party.

The following sections discuss implementing TLS socket servers and clients in your Node.js environment using the `tls` module. Before getting started using TLS, you need to generate a private key and public certificate for both your clients and your server. There are several ways to do this depending on your platform. One of the simplest methods is to use the OpenSSL library for your platform.

To generate the private key, first execute the following OpenSSL command:

```
openssl genrsa -out server.pem 2048
```

Next, use the following command to create a certificate signing request file:

```
openssl req -new -key server.pem -out server.csr
```

> **Note**
>
> When creating the certificate signing request file, you are asked several questions. When prompted for the Common Name, you should put in the domain name of the server you want to connect to. Otherwise, the certificate will not work. Also you can put in additional domain names and IP addresses in the Subject Alternative Names field.

Then to create a self-signed certificate that you can use for your own purpose or testing, use the following command:

```
openssl x509 -req -days 365 -in server.csr -signkey server.pem -out server.crt
```

> **Note**
>
> The self-signed certificate is fine for testing purposes or internal use. However, if you are implementing an external web service that needs to be protected on the Internet, you may want to get a certificate signed by a certificate authority. If you want to create a certificate that is signed by a third-party certificate authority, you need to take additional steps.

Creating a TLS Socket Client

Creating a TLS client is almost exactly like the process of creating a socket client discussed earlier in this chapter. The only difference is that there are additional options, shown in Table 8.8, that allow you to specify the security options for the client. The most important options you need to worry about are `key`, `cert`, and `ca`.

The `key` option specifies the private key used for SSL. The `cert` value specifies the x509 public key to use. If you are using a self-signed certificate, you need to point the `ca` property at the certificate for the server:

```
var options = {
  key: fs.readFileSync('test/keys/client.pem'),
  cert: fs.readFileSync('test/keys/client.crt'),
  ca: fs.readFileSync('test/keys/server.crt')
};
```

Once you have defined the options with the cert, key, and ca settings, then you can call the tls.connect(options, [responseCallback]), and it will work exactly the same as the net.connect() call. The only difference is that the data between the client and server is encrypted.

```
var options = {
  hostname: 'encrypted.mysite.com',
  port: 8108,
  path: '/',
  method: 'GET',
  key: fs.readFileSync('test/keys/client.pem'),
  cert: fs.readFileSync('test/keys/client.crt'),
  ca: fs.readFileSync('test/keys/server.crt')
};
var req = tls.connect(options, function(res) {
  <handle the connection the same as an net.connect>
})
```

Table 8.8 **Additional options for `tls.connect()`**

Event	Description
pfx	A string or Buffer object containing the private key, certificate, and CA certs of the server in PFX or PKCS12 format.
key	A string or Buffer object containing the private key to use for SSL.
passphrase	A string containing the passphrase for the private key or pfx.
cert	A string or Buffer object containing the public x509 certificate to use.
ca	An array of strings or buffers of trusted certificates in PEM format to check the remote host against.
rejectUnauthorized	A Boolean; when true, the server certificate is verified against the list of supplied CAs. An error event is emitted if verification fails. Verification happens at the connection level, before the HTTP request is sent. Defaults to true.
servername	Specifies the server name for the Server Name Indication SNI TLS extension.
secureProtocol	Specifies the SSL method to use. For example, SSLv3_method will force SSL version 3.

Creating a TLS Socket Server

Creating a TLS socket server is almost exactly like the process of creating a socket server discussed earlier in this chapter. The only differences are that there are additional options parameters that you must pass into https.createServer(), and there are some additional events that can be triggered on the tls.Server object. The options, listed in Table 8.9, allow you to specify the security options for the server. Table 8.10 lists the additional events for the TLS socket server. The most important options you need to worry about are `key`, `cert`, and `ca`.

The `key` option specifies the private key used for SSL. The `cert` value specifies the x509 public key to use. If you are using a self-signed certificate, you need to point the `ca` property at the certificate for the client.

Table 8.9 **Additional options for `tls.createServer()`**

Event	Description
`pfx`	A string or `Buffer` object containing the private key, certificate, and CA certs of the server in PFX or PKCS12 format.
`key`	A string or `Buffer` object containing the private key to use for SSL.
`passphrase`	A string containing the passphrase for the private key or `pfx`.
`cert`	A string or `Buffer` object containing the public x509 certificate to use.
`ca`	An array of strings or buffers of trusted certificates in PEM format to check the remote host against.
`crl`	Either a string or list of strings of PEM encoded CRLs (Certificate Revocation Lists).
`ciphers`	A string describing the ciphers to use or exclude. Using this in conjunction with the `honorCipherOrder` is a good way to prevent BEAST attacks.
`handshakeTimeout`	Specifies the number of milliseconds to wait before aborting the connection if the SSL/TLS handshake does not finish. If the timeout is hit, a `clientError` is emitted on the `tls.Server`.
`honorCipherOrder`	A Boolean; when `true`, the server honors the server's preferences over the client's when choosing a cipher.
`requestCert`	When `true`, the server requests a certificate from clients that connect and attempt to verify that certificate. Default is `false`.
`rejectUnauthorized`	When `true`, the server rejects any connection that is not authorized by the list of supplied CAs. This option only has an effect if `requestCert` is `true`. Default is `false`.
`NPNProtocols`	An `Array` or `Buffer` of possible NPN protocols. Protocols should be ordered by their priority.
`SNICallback`	A function that is called if the client supports the SNI TLS extension. The server name is the only argument passed to the callback.
`sessionIdContext`	A string containing an opaque identifier for session resumption. If `requestCert` is `true`, the default is an MD5 hash value generated from the command line. Otherwise, the default is not provided.
`secureProtocol`	Specifies the SSL method to use. For example, `SSLv3_method` will force SSL version 3.

The following shows an example of creating a TLS socket server in Node.js:

```
var options = {
  key: fs.readFileSync('test/keys/server.pem'),
  cert: fs.readFileSync('test/keys/server.crt'),
  ca: fs.readFileSync('test/keys/client.crt')
};
tls.createServer(options, function (client) {
  client.write("Hello Secure World\r\n");
  client.end();
}).listen(8108);
```

Once the TLS socket server has been created, the request/response handling works basically the same way that the TCP socket servers described earlier in this chapter work. The server can accept connections and read and write data back to the client.

Table 8.10 **Additional events on TLS `Server` objects**

Event	Description
`secureConnection`	Emitted when a new secure connection has been successfully established. The callback accepts a single instance of a `tls.CleartextStream` streaming object that can be written to and read from. For example: `function (clearStream)`
`clientError`	Emitted when a client connection emits an error. The parameters to the callback are the error and a `tls.SecurePair` object. For example: `function (error, securePair)`
`newSession`	Emitted when a new TLS session is created. The callback is passed the `sessionId` and `sessionData` parameters containing the session information. For example: `function (sessionId, sessionData)`
`resumeSession`	Emitted when the client tries to resume a previous TLS session. You can store the session in an external storage so that you can look it up when receiving this event. The callback handler receives two parameters. The first is a `sessionId`, and the second is a `callback` to be executed if the session cannot be established. For example: `function (sessionId, callback)`

Summary

Sockets are useful when implementing backend services in a Node.js application. They allow a service on one system to communicate with a service on another system through an IP address and port. They also provide the ability to implement an IPC between two different processes running on the same server. The `net` module allows you to create `Server` objects that act as socket servers and `Socket` objects that act as socket clients. Since the `Socket` object extends `Duplex` streams, you can read and write data from both the server and the client. For secure connections, Node.js provides the `tls` module that allows you to implement secure TLS socket servers and clients.

Next

In the next chapter, you learn how to implement multiprocessing in a Node.js environment. This allows you to farm work out to other processes on the system to take advantage of multiprocessor servers.

9

Scaling Applications Using Multiple Processors in Node.js

In Chapter 4, "Using Events, Listeners, Timers, and Callbacks in Node.js," you learned that Node.js applications run on a single thread rather than multiple threads. Using the single thread for application processing makes Node.js processes more efficient and faster. But most servers have multiple processors, and you can scale your Node.js applications by taking advantage of them. Node.js allows you to fork work from the main application to separate processes that can then be processed in parallel with each other and the main application.

To facilitate using multiple processes Node.js provides three specific modules. The `process` module provides access to the running processes. The `child_process` module provides the ability to create child processes and communicate with them. The `cluster` module implements clustered servers that share the same port, thus allowing multiple requests to be handled simultaneously.

Understanding the Process Module

The `process` module is a global object that can be accessed from your Node.js applications without the need to use a `require()`. This object gives you access to the running processes as well as information about the underlying hardware architecture.

Understanding Process I/O Pipes

The `process` module provides access to the standard I/O pipes for the process `stdin`, `stdout`, and `stderr`. `stdin` is the standard input pipe for the process, which is typically the console. You can read input from the console using the following code:

```
process.stdin.on('data', function(data){
  console.log("Console Input: " + data);
});
```

When you type in data to the console and press Enter, the data is written back out. For example:

```
some data
Console Input: some data
```

The `stdout` and `stderr` attributes of the `process` module are `Writable` streams that can be treated accordingly.

Understanding Process Signals

A great feature of the `process` module is that it allows you to register listeners to handle signals sent to the process from the OS. This is helpful when you need to perform certain actions, such as clean up before a process is stopped or terminated. Table 9.1 lists the process events that you can add listeners for.

To register for a process signal, simply use the `on(event, callback)` method. For example, to register an event handler for the `SIGBREAK` event, you would use the following code:

```
process.on('SIGBREAK', function(){
  console.log("Got a SIGBREAK");
});
```

Table 9.1 **Events that can be sent to Node.js processes**

Event	Description
`SIGUSR1`	Emitted when the Node.js debugger is started. You can add a listener; however, you cannot stop the debugger from starting.
`SIGPIPE`	Emitted when the process tries to write to a pipe without a process connected on the other end.
`SIGHUP`	Emitted on Windows when the console window is closed, and on other platforms under various similar conditions. Note: Windows terminates Node.js about 10 seconds after sending this event.
`SIGTERM`	Emitted when a request is made to terminate the process. This is not supported on Windows.
`SIGINT`	Emitted when a Break is sent to the process. For example, when Ctrl+C is pressed.
`SIGBREAK`	Emitted on Windows when Ctrl+Break is pressed.
`SIGWINCH`	Emitted when the console has been resized. On Windows, this is emitted only when you write to the console, when the cursor is being moved, or when a readable TTY is used in raw mode.
`SIGKILL`	Emitted on a process kill. Cannot have a listener installed.
`SIGSTOP`	Emitted on a process stop. Cannot have a listener installed.

Controlling Process Execution with the `process` Module

The `process` module also gives you some control over the execution of processes, specifically, the ability to stop the current process, kill another process, or schedule work to run on the event queue. These methods are attached directly to the `process` module. For example, to exit the current Node.js process, you would use:

```
process.exit(0)
```

Table 9.2 lists the available process control methods on the `process` module.

Table 9.2 **Methods that can be called on the `process` module to affect process execution**

Method	Description
`abort()`	Causes the current Node.js application to emit an `abort` event, exit, and generate a memory core.
`exit([code])`	Causes the current Node.js application to exit and return the specified `code`.
`kill(pid, [signal])`	Causes the OS to send a kill signal to the process with the specified `pid`. The default `signal` is SIGTERM, but you can specify another.
`nextTick(callback)`	Schedules the `callback` function on the Node.js application's queue.

Getting Information from the `process` Module

The `process` module provides a wealth of information about the running process and the system architecture. This information can be useful when implementing your applications. For example, the `process.pid` property gives you the process ID that can then be used by your application.

Table 9.3 lists the properties and methods that you can access from the `process` module and describes what they return.

Table 9.3 **Methods that can be called on the `process` module to gather information**

Method	Description
`version`	Specifies the version of Node.js.
`versions`	Provides an object containing the required modules and version for this Node.js application.
`config`	Contains the configuration options used to compile the current node executable.

Method	Description
`argv`	Contains the command arguments used to start the Node.js application. The first element is the node, and the second element is the path to the main JavaScript file.
`execPath`	Specifies the absolute path where Node.js was started from.
`execArgv`	Specifies the node-specific command-line options used to start the application.
`chdir(directory)`	Changes the current working `directory` for the application. This can be useful if you provide a configuration file that is loaded after the application has started.
`cwd()`	Returns the current working directory for the process.
`env`	Contains the key/value pairs specified in the environment for the process.
`pid`	Specifies the current process's ID.
`title`	Specifies the title of the currently running process.
`arch`	Specifies the processor architecture the process is running on (for example, `x64`, `ia32`, or `arm`).
`platform`	Specifies the OS platform (for example, `linux`, `win32`, or `freebsd`).

`memoryUsage()`	Describes the current memory usage of the Node.js process. You need to use the `util.inspect()` method to read in the object. For example:
	`console.log(util.inspect(process.memoryUsage()));`
	`{ rss: 13946880, heapTotal: 4083456, heapUsed: 2190800 }`

`maxTickDepth`	Specifies the maximum number of events schedule by `nextTick()` that will be run before allowing blocking I/O events from being processed. You should adjust this value as necessary to keep your I/O processes from being starved.
`uptime()`	Contains the number of seconds the Node.js processor has been running.
`hrtime()`	Returns a high-resolution time in a tuple `array [seconds, nanoseconds]`. This can be used if you need to implement a granular timing mechanism.
`getgid()`	On POSIX platforms, returns the numerical group ID for this process.
`setgid(id)`	On POSIX platforms, sets the numerical group ID for this process.
`getuid()`	On POSIX platforms, returns the numerical or string user ID for this process.
`setuid(id)`	On POSIX platforms, sets the numerical or string user ID for this process.

Method	Description
`getgroups()`	On POSIX platforms, returns an array of group IDs.
`setgroups(groups)`	On POSIX platforms, sets the supplementary group IDs. Your Node.js application needs root privileges to call this method.
`initgroups(user, extra_group)`	On POSIX platforms, initializes the group access list with the information from `/etc/group`. Your Node.js application needs root privileges to call this method.

To help you understand accessing information using the `process` module, Listing 9.1 makes a series of calls and outputs the results to the console, as shown in Listing 9.1 Output.

Listing 9.1 `process_info.js`: **Accessing information about the process and system using the `process` module**

```
var util = require('util');
console.log('Current directory: ' + process.cwd());
console.log('Environment Settings: ' + JSON.stringify(process.env));
console.log('Node Args: ' + process.argv);
console.log('Execution Path: ' + process.execPath);
console.log('Execution Args: ' + JSON.stringify(process.execArgv));
console.log('Node Version: ' + process.version);
console.log('Module Versions: ' +  JSON.stringify(process.versions));
//console.log(process.config);
console.log('Process ID: ' + process.pid);
console.log('Process Title: ' + process.title);
console.log('Process Platform: ' + process.platform);
console.log('Process Architecture: ' + process.arch);
console.log('Memory Usage: ' + util.inspect(process.memoryUsage()));
var start = process.hrtime();
setTimeout(function() {
  var delta = process.hrtime(start);
  console.log('High-Res timer took %d seconds and %d nanoseconds', delta[0], + delta[1]);
  console.log('Node has been running %d seconds', process.uptime());
}, 1000);
```

Listing 9.1 Output **Accessing information about the process and system using the `process` module**

```
Current directory: C:\Users\CalebTZD\workspace\node\code\ch09
Environment Settings:
Node Args: C:\Program Files\nodejs\node.exe,C:\Users\CalebTZD\workspace\node\code\
ch09\process_info.js
```

```
Execution Path: C:\Program Files\nodejs\node.exe
Execution Args: []
Node Version: v7.8.0
Module Versions: Node Config:
Process ID: 12896
Process Title: C:\Program Files\nodejs\node.exe
Process Platform: win32
Process Architecture: x64
Memory Usage: { rss: 20054016,
  heapTotal: 5685248,
  heapUsed: 3571496,
  external: 8772 }
High-Res timer took 1 seconds and 913430 nanoseconds
Node has been running 1.123 seconds
```

Implementing Child Processes

To take advantage of multiple processors in a server with your Node.js applications, you need to farm work off to child processes. Node.js provides the `child_process` module that allows you to spawn, fork, and execute work on other processes. The following sections discuss the process of executing tasks on other processes.

Keep in mind that child processes do not have direct access to the global memory in each other or the parent process. Therefore, you need to design your applications to run in parallel.

Understanding the `ChildProcess` Object

The `child_process` module provides a new class called `ChildProcess` that acts as a representation of the child processes that can be accessed from the parent. This allows you to control, end, and send messages to the child processes from the parent process that started them.

The `process` module is a `ChildProcess` object as well. This means that when you access `process` from the parent module, it is the parent `ChildProcess` object, but when you access `process` from the child process, it is the `ChildProcess` object.

The purpose of this section is to familiarize you with the `ChildProcess` object so that in subsequent sections you can actually implement multiprocess Node.js applications. The best way to do that is to learn about the events, attributes, and methods of the `ChildProcess` object.

Table 9.4 lists the events that can be emitted on the `ChildProcess` object. You implement handlers for the events to handle when the child process terminates or sends messages back to the parent.

Table 9.4 **Events that can be emitted on `ChildProcess` objects**

Event	Description
`message`	Emitted when a `ChildProcess` object calls the `send()` method to send data. Listeners on this event implement a `callback` that can then read the data sent. For example: `child.on('send': function(message){console.log(message});`
`error`	Emitted when an error occurs in the worker. The handler receives an error object as the only parameter.
`exit`	Emitted when a worker process ends. The handler receives two arguments, `code` and `signal`, that specify the exit code and the signal passed to kill the process if it was killed by the parent.
`close`	Emitted when all the `stdio` streams of a worker process have terminated. Different from exit because multiple processes might share the same stdio streams.
`disconnect`	Emitted when `disconnect()` is called on a worker.

Table 9.5 lists the methods that can be called on the child process. These methods allow you to terminate, disconnect, or send messages to the child process. For example, the following code can be called from the parent process to send an object to the child process:

```
child.send({cmd: 'command data'});
```

Table 9.5 **Methods that can be called on `ChildProcess` objects**

Method	Description
`kill([signal])`	Causes the OS to send a kill signal to the child process. The default signal is `SIGTERM`, but you can specify another. See Table 9.1 for a list of signal strings.
`send(message, [sendHandle])`	Sends a message to the handle. The message can be a string or an object. The optional `sendHandle` parameter allows you to send a TCP `Server` or `Socket` object to the client. This allows the client process to share the same port and address.
`disconnect()`	Closes the IPC channel between the parent and child and sets the connected flag to `false` in both the parent and child processes.

Table 9.6 lists the properties that you can access on a `ChildProcess` object.

Table 9.6 **Properties that can be accessed on `ChildProcess` objects**

Property	Description
`stdin`	An input `Writable` stream.
`stdout`	A standard output `Readable` stream.
`stderr`	A standard output `Readable` stream for errors.
`pid`	An ID of the process.
`connected`	A Boolean that is set to `false` after `disconnect()` is called. When this is `false`, you can no longer `send()` messages to the child.

Executing a System Command on Another Process Using `exec()`

The simplest method of adding work to another process from a Node.js process is to execute a system command in a subshell using the `exec()` function. The `exec()` function can execute just about anything that can be executed from a console prompt; for example, a binary executable, shell script, Python script, or batch file.

When executed, the `exec()` function creates a system subshell and then executes a command string in that shell just as if you had executed it from a console prompt. This has the advantage of being able to leverage the capabilities of a console shell, such as accessing environment variables on the command line.

The syntax for the `exec()` function call is shown below. The `execFile()` function call returns a `ChildProcess` object:

```
child_process.exec(command, [options], callback)
```

The `command` parameter is a string that specifies the command to execute in the subshell. The `options` parameter is an object that specifies settings to use when executing the command, such as the current working directory. Table 9.7 lists the options that can be specified by the `exec()` command.

The `callback` parameter is a function that accepts three parameters: `error`, `stdout`, and `stderr`. The `error` parameter is passed an error object if an error is encountered when executing the command. `stdout` and `stderr` are `Buffer` objects that contain the output from executing the command.

Table 9.7 **Options that can be set when using the `exec()` and `execFile()` Functions**

Property	Description
`cwd`	Specifies the current working directory for the child process to execute within.
`env`	Object whose `property:value` pairs are used as environment key/value pairs.

Property	Description
`encoding`	Specifies the encoding to use for the output buffers when storing output from the command.
`maxBuffer`	Specifies the size of the output buffers for `stdout` and `stderr`. The default value is `200*1024`.
`timeout`	Specifies the number of milliseconds for the parent process to wait before killing the child process if it has not completed. The default is `0`, which means there is no timeout.
`killSignal`	Specifies the kill signal to use when terminating the child process. The default is `SIGTERM`.

The code in Listing 9.2 illustrates an example of executing a system command using the `exec()` function. Listing 9.2 Output shows the result.

Listing 9.2 `child_exec.js`: **Executing a system command in another process**

```
var childProcess = require('child_process');
var options = {maxBuffer:100*1024, encoding:'utf8', timeout:5000};
var child = childProcess.exec('dir /B', options,
                              function (error, stdout, stderr) {
  if (error) {
    console.log(error.stack);
    console.log('Error Code: '+error.code);
    console.log('Error Signal: '+error.signal);
  }
  console.log('Results: \n' + stdout);
  if (stderr.length){
    console.log('Errors: ' + stderr);
  }
});
child.on('exit', function (code) {
  console.log('Completed with code: '+code);
});
```

Listing 9.2 Output `child_exec.js`: **Executing a system command in another process**

```
Completed with code: 0
Results:
chef.js
child_fork.js
child_process_exec.js
child_process_exec_file.js
child_process_spawn.js
```

```
cluster_client.js
cluster_server.js
cluster_worker.js
file.txt
process_info.js
```

Executing an Executable File on Another Process Using `execFile()`

Another simple method of adding work to another process from a Node.js process is to execute an executable file on another process using the `execFile()` function. This is similar to using `exec()` except that no subshell is used. This makes `execFile()` lighter weight, but it also means that the command to execute must be a binary executable. Shell scripts on Linux and batch files on Windows do not work with the `execFile()` function.

The syntax for the `execFile()` function call is shown below. The `execFile()` function returns a `ChildProcess` object:

```
child_process.execFile(file, args, options, callback)
```

The `file` parameter is a string that specifies the path to the executable file that will be executed. The `args` parameter is an array that specifies command-line arguments to be passed to the executable. The `options` parameter is an object that specifies settings to use when executing the command, such as the current working directory. Table 9.7 lists the options that can be specified by the `execFile()` command.

The `callback` parameter is a function that accepts three parameters: `error`, `stdout`, and `stderr`. The `error` parameter is passed an error object if an error is encountered when executing the command. `stdout` and `stderr` are `Buffer` objects that contain the output from executing the command.

Listing 9.3 illustrates executing a system command using the `execFile()` function. Listing 9.3 Output shows the output.

Listing 9.3 `child_process_exec_file.js`: Executing an executable file in another process

```
var childProcess = require('child_process');
var options = {maxBuffer:100*1024, encoding:'utf8', timeout:5000};
var child = childProcess.execFile('ping.exe', ['-n', '1', 'google.com'],
                               options, function (error, stdout, stderr) {
  if (error) {
    console.log(error.stack);
    console.log('Error Code: '+error.code);
    console.log('Error Signal: '+error.signal);
  }
  console.log('Results: \n' + stdout);
  if (stderr.length){
    console.log('Errors: ' + stderr);
```

```
  }
});
child.on('exit', function (code) {
  console.log('Child completed with code: '+code);
});
```

Listing 9.3 Output `child_process_exec_file.js`: **Executing an executable file in another process**

```
Child completed with code: 0
Results:
Pinging google.com [216.58.195.78] with 32 bytes of data:
Reply from 216.58.195.78: bytes=32 time=47ms TTL=55

Ping statistics for 216.58.195.78:
    Packets: Sent = 1, Received = 1, Lost = 0 (0% loss),
Approximate round trip times in milli-seconds:
    Minimum = 47ms, Maximum = 47ms, Average = 47ms
```

Spawning a Process in Another Node.js Instance Using `spawn()`

A more complex method of adding work to another process from a Node.js process is to spawn another process; link the `stdio`, `stdout`, and `stderr` pipes between them; and then execute a file on the new process using the `spawn()` function. That makes spawning a bit heavier than `exec()` but provides some great benefits.

The major differences between `spawn()` and `exec()`/`execFile()` are that the `stdin` for the spawned process can be configured and the `stdout` and `stderr` are `Readable` streams in the parent process. This means that `exec()` and `execFile()` must complete before reading the buffer outputs. However, you can read output data from a `spawn()` process as soon as it is written.

The syntax for the `spawn()` function call is shown below. The `spawn()` function returns a `ChildProcess` object:

```
child_process.spawn(command, [args], [options])
```

The `command` parameter is a string that specifies the command to be executed. The `args` parameter is an array that specifies command-line arguments to be passed to the executable command. The `options` parameter is an object that specifies settings to use when executing the command, such as the current working directory. Table 9.8 lists the options that can be specified by the `spawn()` command.

The `callback` parameter is a function that accepts three parameters: `error`, `stdout`, and `stderr`. The `error` parameter is passed an error object if an error is encountered when executing the command. The `stdout` and `stderr` are defined by the `stdio` option settings; by default they are `Readable` stream objects.

Table 9.8 **Properties of the `options` parameter that can be set when using the `spawn()` function**

Property	Description
`cwd`	A string representing the current working directory of the child process.
`env`	An object whose `property:value` pairs are used as environment key/value pairs.
`detached`	A Boolean; when `true`, this child process is made the leader of a new process group enabling the process to continue even when the parent exits. You should also use `child.unref()` so that the parent process does not wait for the child process before exiting.
`uid`	Specifies the user identity of the process for POSIX processes.
`gid`	Specifies the group identity of the process for POSIX processes.
`stdio`	An array that defines the child process `stdio` configuration (`[stdin, stdout, stderr]`). By default, Node.js opens file descriptors `[0, 1, 2]` for `[stdin, stdout, stderr]`. The strings define the configuration of each input and output stream. For example: `['ipc', 'ipc', 'ipc']` The following list describes each of the options that can be used: **`'pipe'`:** Creates a pipe between the child and parent process. The parent can access the pipe using `ChildProcess.stdio[fd]` where `fd` is the file descriptors `[0, 1, 2]` for `[stdin, stdout, stderr]`. **`'ipc'`:** Creates an IPC channel for passing messages/file descriptors between the parent and child using the `send()` method described earlier. **`'ignore'`:** Does not set up a file descriptor in the child. **`Stream` object:** Specifies a `Readable` or `Writeable` stream object defined in the parent to use. The `Stream` object's underlying file descriptor is duplicated in the child and thus data can be streamed from child to parent and vice versa. **File Descriptor Integer:** Specifies the integer value of a file descriptor to use. **`null`, `undefined`:** Uses the defaults of `[0, 1, 2]` for the `[stdin, stdout, stderr]` values.

Listing 9.4 illustrates executing a system command using the `spawn()` function. Listing 9.4 Output shows the output.

Listing 9.4 `child_process_spawn_file.js`: **Spawning a command in another process**

```
var spawn = require('child_process').spawn;
var options = {
    env: {user:'brad'},
    detached:false,
    stdio: ['pipe','pipe','pipe']
```

```
};
var child = spawn('netstat', ['-e']);
child.stdout.on('data', function(data) {
  console.log(data.toString());
});
child.stderr.on('data', function(data) {
  console.log(data.toString());
});
child.on('exit', function(code) {
  console.log('Child exited with code', code);
});
```

Listing 9.4 Output `child_process_spawn_file.js`: **Spawning a command in another process**

```
Interface Statistics
                             Received            Sent
Bytes                       893521612       951835252
Unicast packets                780762         5253654
Non-unicast packets             94176           31358

Child exited with code 0
Discards                            0               0
Errors                              0               0
Unknown protocols                   0
```

Implementing Child Forks

Node.js also provides a specialized form of process spawning called a *fork*, which is designed to execute Node.js module code inside another V8 instance running on a separate processor. This has the advantage of allowing you to run multiple services in parallel. However, it also takes time to spin up a new instance of V8, and each instance takes about 10MB of memory. Therefore, you should design your forked processes to be longer lived, and not require many of them. Remember that you don't get a performance benefit for creating more processes than you have CPUs in the system.

Unlike `spawn`, you cannot configure the `stdio` for the child process; instead it is expected that you use the `send()` mechanism in the `ChildProcess` object to communicate between the parent and child processes.

The syntax for the `fork()` function call is shown below. The `fork()` function returns a `ChildProcess` object:

```
child_process.fork(modulePath, [args], [options])
```

The `modulePath` parameter is a string that specifies the path to the JavaScript file that is launched by the new Node.js instance. The `args` parameter is an array that specifies command-line arguments to be passed to the `node` command. The `options` parameter is an object that specifies settings to use when executing the command, such as the current working directory. Table 9.9 lists the options that can be specified by the `fork()` command.

The `callback` parameter is a function that accepts three parameters: `error`, `stdout`, and `stderr`. The `error` parameter is passed an error object if an error is encountered when executing the command. The `stdout` and `stderr` are `Readable` stream objects.

Table 9.9 **Properties of the `options` parameter that can be set when using the `fork()` function**

Property	Description
`cwd`	A string representing the current working directory of the child process.
`env`	An object whose `property:value` pairs are used as environment key/value pairs.
`encoding`	Specifies the encoding to use when writing data to the output streams and across the `send()` IPC mechanism.
`execPath`	Specifies the executable to use to create the spawned Node.js process. This allows you to use different versions of Node.js for different processes, although that is not recommended in case the process functionality is different.
`silent`	A Boolean; when `true`, the `stdout` and `stderror` in the forked process are not associated with the parent process. The default is `false`.

Listing 9.5 and Listing 9.6 illustrate examples of forking work off to another Node.js instance running in a separate process. Listing 9.5 uses `fork()` to create three child processes running the code from Listing 9.6. The parent process then uses the `ChildProcess` objects to send commands to the child processes. Listing 9.6 implements the `process.on('message')` callback to receive messages from the parent, and the `process.send()` method to send the response back to the parent process, thus implementing the IPC mechanism between the two.

The output is shown in Listing 9.6 Output.

Listing 9.5 `child_fork.js`**: A parent process creating three child processes and sending commands to each, executing in parallel**

```
var child_process = require('child_process');
var options = {
    env:{user:'Brad'},
    encoding:'utf8'
};
function makeChild(){
  var child = child_process.fork('chef.js', [], options);
  child.on('message', function(message) {
```

```
    console.log('Served: ' + message);
  });
  return child;
}
function sendCommand(child, command){
  console.log("Requesting: " + command);
  child.send({cmd:command});
}
var child1 = makeChild();
var child2 = makeChild();
var child3 = makeChild();
sendCommand(child1, "makeBreakfast");
sendCommand(child2, "makeLunch");
sendCommand(child3, "makeDinner");
```

Listing 9.6 `chef.js`: **A child process handling `message` events and sending data back to the parent process**

```
process.on('message', function(message, parent) {
  var meal = {};
  switch (message.cmd){
    case 'makeBreakfast':
    meal = ["ham", "eggs", "toast"];
    break;
    case 'makeLunch':
    meal = ["burger", "fries", "shake"];
    break;
    case 'makeDinner':
    meal = ["soup", "salad", "steak"];
    break;
  }
  process.send(meal);
});
```

Listing 9.5 Output `chef.js`: **A child process handling `message` events and sending data back to the parent process**

```
Requesting: makeBreakfast
Requesting: makeLunch
Requesting: makeDinner
Served: soup,salad,steak
Served: ham,eggs,toast
Served: burger,fries,shake
```

Implementing Process Clusters

One of the coolest things you can do with Node.js is create a cluster of Node.js instances running in parallel in separate processes on the same machine. You can do that using the techniques you learned about the in the previous section by forking processes and then using the `send(message, serverHandle)` IPC mechanism to communicate `send` messages and pass the underlying TCP server handles between them. However, because that is such a common task, Node.js has provided the `cluster` module that does all that for you automatically.

Using the Cluster Module

The `cluster` module provides the functionality necessary to easily implement a cluster of TCP or HTTP servers running in different processes on the same machine but still using the same underlying socket, thus handling requests on the same IP address and port combination. The `cluster` module is simple to implement and provides several events, methods, and properties that can be used to initiate and monitor a cluster of Node.js servers.

Table 9.10 lists the events that can be emitted in a cluster application.

Table 9.10 **Events that can be emitted by the `cluster` module**

Event	Description
`fork`	Emitted when a new worker has been forked. The `callback` function receives a `Worker` object as the only argument. For example: `function (worker)`
`online`	Emitted when the new worker sends back a message indicating that it has started. The `callback` function receives a `Worker` object as the only argument. For example: `function (worker)`
`listening`	Emitted when the worker calls `listen()` to begin listening on the shared port. The `callback` handler receives the `worker` object as well as an `address` object indicating the port the worker is listening on. For example: `function (worker, address)`
`disconnect`	Emitted after the IPC channel has been disconnected, such as the server calling `worker.disconnect()`. The `callback` function receives a `Worker` object as the only argument. For example: `function (worker)`
`exit`	Emitted when the `Worker` object has disconnected. The `callback` handler receives the `worker`, exit `code`, and `signal` used. For example: `function (worker, code, signal)`
`setup`	Emitted the first time the `setupMaster()` is called.

Table 9.11 lists the methods and properties available in the `cluster` module, allowing you to get information such as whether this node is a worker or the master as well as configuring and implementing the forked processes.

Table 9.11 **Methods and properties of the `cluster` module**

Property	Description
`settings`	Contains the `exec`, `args`, and `silent` property values used to set up the cluster.
`isMaster`	Is `true` if the current process is the cluster master; otherwise, it is `false`.
`isWorker`	Is `true` if the current process is a worker; otherwise, it is `false`.
`setupMaster([settings])`	Accepts an optional settings object that contains `exec`, `args`, and `silent` properties. The `exec` property points to the worker JavaScript file. The `args` property is an array of parameters to pass, and `silent` disconnects the IPC mechanism from the worker thread.
`disconnect([callback])`	Disconnects the IPC mechanism from the workers and closes the handles. The `callback` function is executed when the disconnect finishes.
`worker`	References the current `Worker` object in worker processes. This is not defined in the master process.
`workers`	Contains the `Worker` object, which you can reference by ID from the master process. For example: `cluster.workers[workerId]`

Understanding the `Worker` Object

When a worker process is forked, a new `Worker` object is created in both the master and worker processes. In the worker process, the object is used to represent the current worker and interact with cluster events that are occurring. In the master process, the `Worker` object is used to represent child worker processes so that your master application can send messages to them, receive events on their state changes, and even kill them.

Table 9.12 lists the events that `Worker` objects can emit.

Table 9.12 **Events that can be emitted by `Worker` objects**

Event	Description
`message`	Emitted when the worker receives a new message. The `callback` function is passed the `message` as the only parameter.
`disconnect`	Emitted after the IPC channel has been disconnected on this worker.
`exit`	Emitted when this `Worker` object has disconnected.
`error`	Emitted when an error has occurred on this worker.

Table 9.13 lists the methods and properties available in the `Worker` object, allowing you to get information such as whether this node is a worker or the master as well as configuring and implementing the forked processes.

Table 9.13 **Methods and properties of the `Worker` module**

Property	Description
`id`	Represents the unique ID of this worker.
`process`	Specifies the `ChildProcess` object this worker is running on.
`suicide`	Is set to `true` when `kill()` or `disconnect()` is called on this worker. You can use this flag to determine whether you should break out of loops to try and go down gracefully.
`send(message, [sendHandle])`	Sends a message to the master process.
`kill([signal])`	Kills the current worker process by disconnecting the IPC channel and then exiting. Sets the `suicide` flag to `true`.
`disconnect()`	When called in the worker, closes all servers, waits for the `close` event, and then disconnects the IPC channel. When called from the master, sends an internal message to the worker causing it to disconnect itself. Sets the `suicide` flag.

Implementing an HTTP Cluster

The best way to illustrate the value of the `cluster` module is to show a basic implementation of Node.js HTTP servers. Listing 9.7 implements a basic cluster of HTTP servers. Lines 4–13 register listeners for the `fork`, `listening`, and `exit` events on cluster workers. Then in line 14 `setupMaster()` is called and the worker executable `cluster_worker.js` is specified. Next, lines 15–19 create the workers by calling `cluster.fork()`. Finally, in lines 20–24 the code iterates through the workers and registers an `on('message')` event handler for each one.

Listing 9.8 implements the worker HTTP servers. Notice that the `http` server sends back a response to the client and then also sends a message to the cluster master on line 7.

Listing 9.9 implements a simple HTTP client that sends a series of requests to test the servers created in Listing 9.8. The output of the servers is shown in Listing 9.7 and 9.8 Output, and the output of the clients is shown in Listing 9.9 Output. Notice that Listing 9.9 Output shows that the requests are being handled by different processes on the server.

Listing 9.7 `cluster_server.js`: **A master process creating up to four worker processes**

```
var cluster = require('cluster');
var http = require('http');
if (cluster.isMaster) {
  cluster.on('fork', function(worker) {
    console.log("Worker " + worker.id + " created");
  });
  cluster.on('listening', function(worker, address) {
    console.log("Worker " + worker.id +" is listening on " +
                address.address + ":" + address.port);
  });
  cluster.on('exit', function(worker, code, signal) {
    console.log("Worker " + worker.id + " Exited");
  });
  cluster.setupMaster({exec:'cluster_worker.js'});
  var numCPUs = require('os').cpus().length;
  for (var i = 0; i < numCPUs; i++) {
    if (i>=4) break;
    cluster.fork();
  }
  Object.keys(cluster.workers).forEach(function(id) {
    cluster.workers[id].on('message', function(message){
      console.log(message);
    });
  });
}
```

Listing 9.8 `cluster_worker.js`: **A worker process implementing an HTTP server**

```
var cluster = require('cluster');
var http = require('http');
if (cluster.isWorker) {
  http.Server(function(req, res) {
    res.writeHead(200);
    res.end("Process " + process.pid + " says hello");
    process.send("Process " + process.pid + " handled request");
  }).listen(8080, function(){
    console.log("Child Server Running on Process: " + process.pid);
  });
};
```

Listing 9.9 `cluster_client.js`: **An HTTP client sending a series of requests to test the server**

```
var http = require('http');
var options = { port: '8080' };
function sendRequest(){
  http.request(options, function(response){
    var serverData = '';
    response.on('data', function (chunk) {
      serverData += chunk;
    });
    response.on('end', function () {
      console.log(serverData);
    });
  }).end();
}
for (var i=0; i<5; i++){
  console.log("Sending Request");
  sendRequest();
}
```

Listing 9.7 and 9.8 Output `cluster_server.js`: **A master process creating up to four worker processes**

```
Worker 1 created
Worker 2 created
Worker 3 created
Worker 4 created
Child Server Running on Process: 9012
Worker 1 is listening on null:8080
Child Server Running on Process: 1264
Worker 2 is listening on null:8080
Child Server Running on Process: 5488
Worker 4 is listening on null:8080
Child Server Running on Process: 7384
Worker 3 is listening on null:8080
Process 1264 handled request
Process 7384 handled request
Process 5488 handled request
Process 7384 handled request
Process 5488 handled request
```

Listing 9.9 Output `cluster_client.js`: **An HTTP client sending a series of requests to test the server**

```
Sending Request
Sending Request
Sending Request
Sending Request
Sending Request
Process 10108 says hello
Process 12584 says hello
Process 13180 says hello
Process 10108 says hello
Process 12584 says hello
```

Summary

To make the most out of Node.js performance on servers with multiple processors, you need to be able to farm work off to the other processes. The `process` module allows you to interact with the system process, the `child_process` module allows you to actually execute code on a separate process, and the `cluster` module allows you to create a cluster of HTTP or TCP servers.

The `child_process` module provides the `exec()`, `execFile()`, `spawn()`, and `fork()` functions, which are used to start work on separate processes. The `ChildProcess` and `Worker` objects provide a mechanism to communicate between the parent and child processes.

Next

In the next chapter, you are introduced to some other modules that Node.js provides for convenience. For example, the `os` module provides tools to interact with the OS, and the `util` module provides useful functionality.

10

Using Additional Node.js Modules

This chapter exposes you to some additional built-in capabilities of Node.js. The `os` module provides operating system functionality that can be useful when implementing your applications. The `util` module provides various functionality, such as string formatting. The `dns` module provides the ability to perform DNS lookups and reverse lookups from a Node.js application.

The following sections describe these modules and how to use them in your Node.js applications. Some of the methods will already be familiar to you because you have seen them in previous chapters.

Using the `os` Module

The `os` module provides a useful set of functions that allow you to get information from the operating system (OS). For example, when accessing data from a stream that comes from the OS, you can use the `os.endianness()` function to determine whether the OS is big endian or little endian so that you can use the correct read and write methods.

Table 10.1 lists the methods provided by the `os` module and describes how they are used.

Table 10.1 **Methods that can be called on the `os` module**

Event	Description
`tmpdir()`	Returns a string path to the default temp directory for the OS. Useful if you need to store files temporarily and then remove them later.
`endianness()`	Returns `BE` or `LE` for big endian or little endian, depending on the architecture of the machine.
`hostname()`	Returns the hostname defined for the machine. This is useful when implementing network services that require a hostname.
`type()`	Returns the OS type as a string.

Event	Description
`platform()`	Returns the platform as a string; for example, `win32`, `linux`, or `freeBSD`.
`arch()`	Returns the platform architecture; for example, `x86` or `x64`.
`release()`	Returns the OS version release.
`uptime()`	Returns a timestamp in seconds of how long the OS has been running.
`loadavg()`	On UNIX-based systems, returns an array of values containing the system load value for `[1, 5, 15]` minutes.
`totalmem()`	Returns an integer specifying the system memory in bytes.
`freemem()`	Returns an integer specifying the free system memory in bytes.
`cpus()`	Returns an array of objects that describes the `model`, `speed`, and `times`. This array contains the amount of time the CPU has spent in `user`, `nice`, `sys`, `idle`, and `irq`.
`networkInterfaces()`	Returns an array of objects describing the `address` and `family` of addresses bound on each network interface in your system.
`EOL`	Contains the appropriate End Of Line characters for the operating system; for example, `\n` or `\r\n`. This can be useful to make your application cross-platform compatible when processing string data.

To help you visualize using the `os` module, Listing 10.1 calls each of the `os` module calls, and the output is shown in Listing 10.1 Output.

Listing 10.1 `os_info.js`: **Calling methods on the `os` module**

```
var os = require('os');
console.log("tmpdir :\t" + os.tmpdir());
console.log("endianness :\t" + os.endianness());
console.log("hostname :\t" + os.hostname());
console.log("type :\t\t" + os.type());
console.log("platform :\t" + os.platform());
console.log("arch :\t\t" + os.arch());
console.log("release :\t" + os.release());
console.log("uptime :\t" + os.uptime());
console.log("loadavg :\t" + os.loadavg());
console.log("totalmem :\t" + os.totalmem());
console.log("freemem :\t" + os.freemem());
console.log("EOL :\t" + os.EOL);
console.log("cpus :\t\t" + JSON.stringify(os.cpus()));
console.log("networkInterfaces : " +
            JSON.stringify(os.networkInterfaces()));
```

Listing 10.1 Output **Calling methods on the os module**

```
tmpdir :      C:\Users\CalebTZD\AppData\Local\Temp
endianness :  LE
hostname :    DESKTOP-3I5OR8I
type :        Windows_NT
platform :    win32
arch :        x64
release :     10.0.14393
uptime :      1473719.6450068
loadavg :     0,0,0
totalmem :    12768796672
freemem :     8033443840
EOL :

cpus :
```

Using the `util` Module

The `util` module is a catch-all module that provides functions for formatting strings, converting objects to strings, checking object types, performing synchronous writes to output streams, and some object inheritance enhancements.

The following sections cover most of the functionality in the `util` module. They also explain ways to use the `util` module in your Node.js applications.

Formatting Strings

When handling string data, it is important to be able to format the strings quickly. Node.js provides a rudimentary string formatting method in the `util` module that handles many string formatting needs. The `util.format()` function accepts a formatter string as the first argument and returns a formatted string. The following shows the syntax for the `format()` method, where `format` is the formatter string and then `[...]` represents the following arguments:

```
util.format(format[...args])
```

The `format` argument is a string that can contain zero or more placeholders. Each placeholder begins with a `%` character and is replaced with the converted string value from its corresponding argument. The first formatter placeholder represents the second argument and so on. The following is a list of supported placeholders:

- **`%s`**: Specifies a string
- **`%d`**: Specifies a number (can be integer or float)
- **`%i`**: Specifies an integer
- **`%f`**: Specifies a floating point value
- **`%j`**: Specifies a JSON stringifyable object
- **`%`**: If left empty afterward, does not act as a placeholder

The following is a list of things to keep in mind when using `format()`:

- When there are not as many arguments as placeholders, the placeholder is not replaced. For example:

  ```
  util.format('%s = %s', 'Item1'); // 'Item1:%s'
  ```

- When there are more arguments than placeholders, the extra arguments are converted to strings and concatenated with a space delimiter.

  ```
  util.format('%s = %s', 'Item1', 'Item2', 'Item3'); // 'Item1 = Item2 Item3'
  ```

- If the first argument is not a format string, then `util.format()` converts each argument to a string, concatenates them together using a space delimiter, and then returns the concatenated string. For example:

  ```
  util.format(1, 2, 3); // '1 2 3'
  ```

Checking Object Types

It is often useful to determine whether an object you have received back from a command is of a certain type. To do this, you can use the `isinstanceof` operator, which compares the object types and returns `true` or `false`. For example:

```
([1,2,3] isinstanceof Array) //true
```

Converting JavaScript Objects to Strings

Often, especially when debugging, you need to convert a JavaScript object to a string representation. The `util.inspect()` method allows you to inspect an object and then return a string representation of the object.

The following shows the syntax for the `inspect()` method:

```
util.inspect(object, [options])
```

The `object` parameter is the JavaScript object you want to convert to a string. The `options` method allows you to control certain aspects of the formatting process. `options` can contain the following properties:

- **`showHidden`:** When set to `true`, the non-enumerable properties of the object are also converted to the string. Defaults to `false`.
- **`depth`:** Limits the number of levels deep the inspect process traverses while formatting properties that are also objects. This can prevent infinite loops and also prevent instances where complex objects cost a lot of CPU cycles. Defaults to `2`; if it is `null`, it can recurse forever.
- **`colors`:** When set to `true`, the output is styled with ANSI color codes. Defaults to `false`.
- **`customInspect`:** When set to `false`, any custom `inspect()` functions defined on the objects being inspected are not called. Defaults to `true`.

You can attach your own inspect() function to the object, thus controlling the output. The following code creates an object with first and last properties, but inspect outputs only a name property:

```
var obj = { first:'Caleb', last:'Dayley' };
obj.inspect = function(depth) {
  return '{ name: "' + this.first + " " + this.last + '" }';
};
console.log(util.inspect(obj));
//Outputs: { name: "Caleb Dayley" }
```

Inheriting Functionality from Other Objects

The util module provides the util.inherits() method to allow you to create objects that inherit the prototype methods from another. When you create the new object, the prototype methods are automatically used. You have already seen this in a few examples in the book; for example, when implementing your own custom Readable and Writable streams.

The following shows the format of the util.inherits() method:

```
util.inherits(constructor, superConstructor)
```

The prototype of constructor is set to the prototype of superConstructor and executed when a new object is created. You can access the superConstructor from your custom object constructor using the constructor.super_ property.

Listing 10.2 illustrates using inherits() to inherit the events.EventEmitter object constructor to create a Writable stream. Notice on line 11 the object is an instance of events.EventEmitter. Also notice on line 12 the Writer.super_ value is eventsEmitter. The results are shown in Listing 10.2 Output.

Listing 10.2 util_inherit.js: Using inherits() to inherit the prototypes from events.EventEmitter

```
01 var util = require("util");
02 var events = require("events");
03 function Writer() {
04   events.EventEmitter.call(this);
05 }
06 util.inherits(Writer, events.EventEmitter);
07 Writer.prototype.write = function(data) {
08   this.emit("data", data);
09 };
10 var w = new Writer();
11 console.log(w instanceof events.EventEmitter);
12 console.log(Writer.super_ === events.EventEmitter);
13 w.on("data", function(data) {
14     console.log('Received data: "' + data + '"');
15 });
16 w.write("Some Data!");
```

Listing 10.2 Output `util_inherit.js`: **Using `inherits()` to inherit the prototypes from `events.EventEmitter`**

```
true
true
Received data: "Some Data!"
```

Using the dns Module

If your Node.js application needs to resolve DNS domain names, look up domains, or do reverse lookups, then the dns module is helpful. A DNS lookup contacts the domain name server and requests records about a specific domain name. A reverse lookup contacts the domain name server and requests the DNS name associated with an IP address. The dns module provides functionality for most of the lookups that you may need to perform. Table 10.2 lists the lookup calls and their syntax, and describes how they are used.

Table 10.2 **Methods that can be called on the dns Module**

Event	Description
`lookup(domain, [family], callback)`	Resolves the `domain`. The `family` attribute can be `4`, `6`, or `null`, where `4` resolves into the first found `A` (IPv4) record, 6 resolves into the first round `AAAA` (IPv6) record, and `null` resolves both. The default is `null`. The `callback` function receives an `error` as the first argument and an array of IP `addresses` as the second. For example: `function (error, addresses)`
`resolve(domain, [rrtype], callback)`	Resolves the `domain` into an array of record types specified by `rrtype`. `rrtype` can be ▪ **A:** IPV4 addresses, the default ▪ **AAAA:** IPV6 addresses ▪ **MX:** Mail eXchange records ▪ **TXT:** Text records ▪ **SRV:** SRV records ▪ **PTR:** Reverse IP lookups ▪ **NS:** Name Server records ▪ **CNAME:** Canonical Name records The `callback` function receives an `error` as the first argument and an array of IP `addresses` as the second. For example: `function (error, addresses)`

Event	Description
`resolve4(domain, callback)`	Same as `dns.resolve()` except only for `A` records.
`resolve6(domain, callback)`	Same as `dns.resolve()` except only for `AAAA` records.
`resolveMx(domain, callback)`	Same as `dns.resolve()` except only for `MX` records.
`resolveTxt(domain, callback)`	Same as `dns.resolve()` except only for `TXT` records.
`resolveSrv(domain, callback)`	Same as `dns.resolve()` except only for `SRV` records.
`resolveNs(domain, callback)`	Same as `dns.resolve()` except only for `NS` records.
`resolveCname(domain, callback)`	Same as `dns.resolve()` except only for `CNAME` records.
`reverse(ip, callback)`	Does a reverse lookup on the `ip` address. The `callback` function receives an `error` object if one occurs and an array of `domains` if the lookup is successful. For example: `function (error, domains)`

Listing 10.3 illustrates performing lookups and reverse lookups. In line 3, `resolve4()` is used to look up the IPv4 addresses, and then in lines 5–8, `reverse()` is called on those same addresses and the reverse lookup performed. Listing 10.3 Output shows the result.

Listing 10.3 `dns_lookup.js`: **Performing lookups and then reverse lookups on domains and IP addresses**

```
01 var dns = require('dns');
02 console.log("Resolving www.google.com . . .");
03 dns.resolve4('www.google.com', function (err, addresses) {
04   console.log('IPv4 addresses: ' + JSON.stringify(addresses, false, ' '));
05   addresses.forEach(function (addr) {
06     dns.reverse(addr, function (err, domains) {
07       console.log('Reverse for ' + addr + ': ' + JSON.stringify(domains));
08     });
09   });
10 });
```

Listing 10.3 Output `dns_lookup.js`: **Performing lookups and then reverse lookups on domains and IP addresses**

```
Resolving www.google.com . . .
IPv4 addresses: [
 "172.217.6.68"
]
Reverse for 172.217.6.68: ["sfo07s17-in-f4.1e100.net","sfo07s17-in-f68.1e100.net"]
```

Using the `crypto` Module

The `crypto` module is interesting and fun to play around with. As the name suggests, it creates cryptographic information, or in other words, creates secure communication using secret code. To use `crypto`, you must make sure that it is loaded into your Node project. Although cool, this module isn't necessary, and a Node application can be built without including support for `crypto`. The easiest way to do ensure `crypto` is loaded is to use a simple `try catch (err);` for example:

```
let crypto;
try {
  crypto = require('crypto');
} catch (err) {
  console.log('crypto support is disabled!');
}
```

The `crypto` module includes several classes that provide functionality to encrypt and decrypt data and streams. Table 10.3 lists all the different classes that the `crypto` module provides.

Table 10.3 **Classes that can be used in the `crypto` module**

Class	Description
`certificate`	Used for working with SPKAC (a certificate signing request mechanism) and primarily used to handle output of HTML5.
`cipher`	Used to encrypt data in either a stream that is both readable and writable, or using the `cipher.update` and `cipher.final` methods.
`decipher`	The opposite of `cipher`. Used to decrypt data using either a readable and writable stream or the `decipher.update` and `deciper.final` methods.
`diffieHellman`	Used to create key exchanges for Diffie-Hellman (a specific method for exchanging cryptographic keys).
`eCDH (Elliptical Curve Diffie-Hellman)`	Used to create key exchanges for ECDH (same as Diffie-Hellman, but the two parties use an elliptical curve public-private key pair).

Class	Description
hash	Used to create hash digests of data using a readable and writable stream or hash.update and hash.digest.
hmac	Used to create Hmac digests of data using a readable and writable stream or Hmac.update and Hmac.digest.
sign	Used to generate signatures.
verify	Used in tandem with sign to verify the signatures.

The most common use for the crypto module is to use the Cipher and Decipher classes to create encrypted data that can be stored and decrypted later; for example, passwords. Initially, passwords are entered as text, but it would be foolish to actually store them as text. Instead, passwords are encrypted using an encryption algorithm such as the ('aes192') method. This allows you to store data encrypted so if it is accessed without decrypting, your password is protected from prying minds. Listing 10.4 shows an example of encrypting and decrypting a password string. The output follows in Listing 10.4 Output.

Listing 10.4 encrypt_password.js: **Using** cipher **and** decipher **to encrypt and then decrypt data**

```
var crypto = require('crypto');
var crypMethod = 'aes192';
var secret = 'MySecret';
function encryptPassword(pwd){
  var cipher = crypto.createCipher(crypMethod, secret);
  var cryptedPwd = cipher.update(pwd,'utf8','hex');
  cryptedPwd += cipher.final('hex');
  return cryptedPwd;
}
function decryptPassword(pwd){
  var decipher = crypto.createDecipher(crypMethod, secret);
  var decryptedPwd = decipher.update(pwd,'hex','utf8');
  decryptedPwd += decipher.final('utf8');
  return decryptedPwd;
}
var encryptedPwd = encryptPassword("BadWolf");
console.log("Encrypted Password");
console.log(encryptedPwd);
console.log("\nDecrypted Password");
console.log(decryptPassword(encryptedPwd));
```

Listing 10.4 Output **Using `cipher` and `decipher` to encrypt and then decrypt data**

```
Encrypted Password
0ebc7d846519b955332681c75c834d50

Decrypted Password
BadWolf
```

Other Node Modules and Objects

This section lists some other Node modules and objects that would be beneficial for you to know about:

- **Global:** Object available throughout all the modules. Globals range anywhere from `_dirname`, which gives you the name of the directory, to the `Process` object.
- **V8:** Module used to expose APIs, specifically for the version of V8 that is built in to the Node binary.
- **Debugger:** Module used to debug your Node application. To use, simply start Node with the `debug` argument, like so: `$ node debug myscript.js`.
- **Assertion testing:** Module that provides a basic set of assertion tests used to test invariants.
- **C/C++ add-ons:** Objects that allow you to dynamically link shared objects written in C or C++. They provide an interface that both JavaScript in Node and C/C++ libraries can use, allowing them to work as a regular Node.js applications.
- **REPL (Read Event Print Loop):** Accepts individual lines of input, evaluates them using a user-defined function, and then outputs the results.

Summary

The `os` module allows you to get information about the system, including the operating system type and version, the platform architecture, and programming helps, such as the amount of free memory, temp folder location, and EOL characters. The `util` module is the catch-all library for Node that has methods for synchronous output, string formatting, and type checking. The `dns` module performs DNS lookups and reverse lookups from a Node.js application. The `crypto` module encrypts and decrypts data to secure private data.

Next

In the next chapter, you jump into the world of MongoDB. You learn the MongoDB basics and how to implement it in the Node.js world.

11

Understanding NoSQL and MongoDB

At the core of most large-scale web applications and services is a high-performance data storage solution. The backend data store is responsible for storing everything from user account information to shopping cart items to blog and comment data. Good web applications must store and retrieve data with accuracy, speed, and reliability. Therefore, the data storage mechanism you choose must perform at a level that satisfies user demand.

Several different data storage solutions are available to store and retrieve data needed by your web applications. The three most common are direct file system storage in files, relational databases, and NoSQL databases. The data store chosen for this book is MongoDB, which is a NoSQL database.

The following sections describe MongoDB and discuss the design considerations you need to review before deciding how to implement the structure of data and configuration of the database. The sections cover the questions to ask yourself, and then cover the mechanisms built into MongoDB to satisfy the demands of the answers to those questions.

Why NoSQL?

The concept of NoSQL (Not Only SQL) consists of technologies that provide storage and retrieval without the tightly constrained models of traditional SQL relational databases. The motivation behind NoSQL is mainly simplified designs, horizontal scaling, and finer control of the availability of data.

NoSQL breaks away from the traditional structure of relational databases and allows developers to implement models in ways that more closely fit the data flow needs of their systems. This allows NoSQL databases to be implemented in ways that traditional relational databases could never be structured.

There are several different NoSQL technologies, such as HBase's column structure, Redis's key/value structure, and Neo4j's graph structure. However, in this book MongoDB and the document model were chosen because of great flexibility and scalability when it comes to implementing backend storage for web applications and services. Also MongoDB is one of the most popular and well supported NoSQL databases currently available.

Understanding MongoDB

MongoDB is a NoSQL database based on a document model where data objects are stored as separate documents inside a collection. The motivation of the MongoDB language is to implement a data store that provides high performance, high availability, and automatic scaling. MongoDB is simple to install and implement, as you see in the upcoming chapters.

Understanding Collections

MongoDB groups data together through collections. A *collection* is simply a grouping of documents that have the same or a similar purpose. A collection acts similarly to a table in a traditional SQL database, with one major difference. In MongoDB, a collection is not enforced by a strict schema; instead, documents in a collection can have a slightly different structure from one another as needed. This reduces the need to break items in a document into several different tables, which is often done in SQL implementations.

Understanding Documents

A *document* is a representation of a single entity of data in the MongoDB database. A collection is made up of one or more related objects. A major difference between MongoDB and SQL is that documents are different from rows. Row data is flat, meaning there is one column for each value in the row. However, in MongoDB, documents can contain embedded subdocuments, thus providing a much closer inherent data model to your applications.

In fact, the records in MongoDB that represent documents are stored as BSON, which is a lightweight binary form of JSON, with `field:value` pairs corresponding to JavaScript `property:value` pairs. These `field:value` pairs define the values stored in the document. That means little translation is necessary to convert MongoDB records back into the JavaScript object that you use in your Node.js applications.

For example, a document in MongoDB may be structured similarly to the following with `name`, `version`, `languages`, `admin`, and `paths` fields:

```
{
  name: "New Project",
  version: 1,
  languages: ["JavaScript", "HTML", "CSS"],
  admin: {name: "Brad", password: "****"},
  paths: {temp: "/tmp", project: "/opt/project", html: "/opt/project/html"}
}
```

Notice that the document structure contains fields/properties that are strings, integers, arrays, and objects, just like a JavaScript object. Table 11.1 lists the different data types that field values can be set to in the BSON document.

The field names cannot contain `null` characters, `.` (dots), or `$` (dollar signs). Also, the `_id` field name is reserved for the Object ID. The `_id` field is a unique ID for the system that is made up of the following parts:

- A 4-byte value representing the seconds since the last epoch
- A 3-byte machine identifier
- A 2-byte process ID
- A 3-byte counter, starting with a random value

The maximum size of a document in MongoDB is 16MB, which prevents queries that result in an excessive amount of RAM being used or intensive hits to the file system. Although you may never come close, you still need to keep the maximum document size in mind when designing some complex data types that contain file data.

MongoDB Data Types

The BSON data format provides several different types that are used when storing the JavaScript objects to binary form. These types match the JavaScript type as closely as possible. It is important to understand these types because you can actually query MongoDB to find objects that have a specific property that has a value of a certain type. For example, you can look for documents in a database whose timestamp value is a `String` object or query for ones whose timestamp is a `Date` object.

MongoDB assigns each of the data types an integer ID number from 1 to 255 that is used when querying by type. Table 11.1 shows a list of the data types that MongoDB supports along with the number MongoDB uses to identify them.

Table 11.1 **MongoDB data types and corresponding ID number**

Type	Number
Double	1
String	2
Object	3
Array	4
Binary data	5
Object id	7
Boolean	8
Date	9
Null	10
Regular Expression	11
JavaScript	13

Type	Number
`JavaScript (with scope)`	`15`
`32-bit integer`	`16`
`Timestamp`	`17`
`64-bit integer`	`18`
`Decimal126`	`19`
`Min key`	`-1`
`Max key`	`127`

Another thing to be aware of when working with different data types in MongoDB is the order in which they are compared. When comparing values of different BSON types, MongoDB uses the following comparison order from lowest to highest:

1. `Min Key` (internal type)
2. `Null`
3. `Numbers` (`32-bit integer, 64-bit integer, Double`)
4. `String`
5. `Object`
6. `Array`
7. `Binary Data`
8. `Object ID`
9. `Boolean`
10. `Date`, `Timestamp`
11. `Regular Expression`
12. `Max Key` (internal type)

Planning Your Data Model

Before you begin implementing a MongoDB database, you need to understand the nature of the data being stored, how that data is going to get stored, and how it is going to be accessed. Understanding these concepts allows you to make determinations ahead of time and to structure the data and your application for optimal performance.

Specifically, you should ask yourself the following questions:

- What are the basic objects that my application will be using?
- What is the relationship between the different object types: one-to-one, one-to-many, or many-to-many?

- How often will new objects be added to the database?
- How often will objects be deleted from the database?
- How often will objects be changed?
- How often will objects be accessed?
- How will objects be accessed: by ID, property values, comparisons, and so on?
- How will groups of object types be accessed: by common ID, common property value, and so on?

Once you have the answers to these questions, you are ready to consider the structure of collections and documents inside the MongoDB. The following sections discuss different methods of document, collection, and database modeling you can use in MongoDB to optimize data storage and access.

Normalizing Data with Document References

Data normalization is the process of organizing documents and collections to minimize redundancy and dependency. This is done by identifying object properties that are subobjects and should be stored as a separate document in another collection from the object's document. Typically, this is used for objects that have a one-to-many or many-to-many relationship with subobjects.

The advantage of normalizing data is that the database size will be smaller because only a single copy of an object will exist in its own collection instead of being duplicated on multiple objects in a single collection. Also, if you modify the information in the subobject frequently, you only need to modify a single instance rather than every record in the object's collection that has that subobject.

A major disadvantage of normalizing data is that when looking up user objects that require the normalized subobject, a separate lookup must occur to link the subobject. This can result in a significant performance hit if you are accessing the user data frequently.

An example of when it makes sense to normalize data is a system that contains users that have a favorite store. Each `User` is an object with `name`, `phone`, and `favoriteStore` properties. The `favoriteStore` property is also a subobject that contains `name`, `street`, `city`, and `zip` properties.

However, thousands of users may have the same favorite store, so there is a high one-to-many relationship. Therefore, it doesn't make sense to store the `FavoriteStore` object data in each `User` object because it would result in thousands of duplications. Instead, the `FavoriteStore` object should include an `_id` object property that can be referenced from documents in the user's `FavoriteStore`. The application can then use the reference ID `favoriteStore` to link data from the `Users` collection to `FavoriteStore` documents in the `FavoriteStores` collection.

Figure 11.1 illustrates the structure of the `Users` and `FavoriteStores` collections just described.

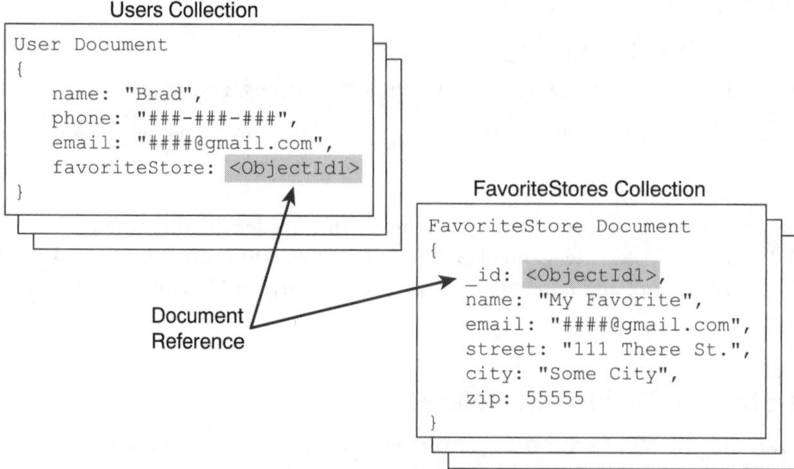

Figure 11.1 Defining normalized MongoDB documents by adding a reference to documents in another collection

Denormalizing Data with Embedded Documents

Denormalizing data is the process of identifying subobjects of a main object that should be embedded directly into the document of the main object. Typically this is done on objects that have a mostly one-to-one relationship or are relatively small and do not get updated frequently.

The major advantage of denormalized documents is that you can get the full object back in a single lookup without the need to do additional lookups to combine subobjects from other collections. This is a major performance enhancement. The downside is that for subobjects with a one-to-many relationship you store a separate copy in each document, which slows down insertion and also takes up additional disk space.

An example of when it makes sense to normalize data is a system that contains users with home and work contact information. The user is an object represented by a `User` document with `name`, `home`, and `work` properties. The `home` and `work` properties are subobjects that contain `phone`, `street`, `city`, and `zip` properties.

The `home` and `work` properties do not change often on the user. You may have multiple users from the same home; however, there likely will not be many of them, and the actual values inside the subobjects are not that big and will not change often. Therefore, it makes sense to store the `home` contact information directly in the `User` object.

The `work` property takes a bit more thinking. How many people are going to have the same work contact information? If the answer is not many, then the `work` object should be embedded with the `User` object. How often are you querying the `User` and need the `work` contact information? If the answer is rarely, then you may want to normalize `work` into its own collection. However, if the answer is frequently or always, then you will likely want to embed `work` with the `User` object.

Figure 11.2 illustrates the structure of the `Users` with `Home` and `work` contact information embedded as just described.

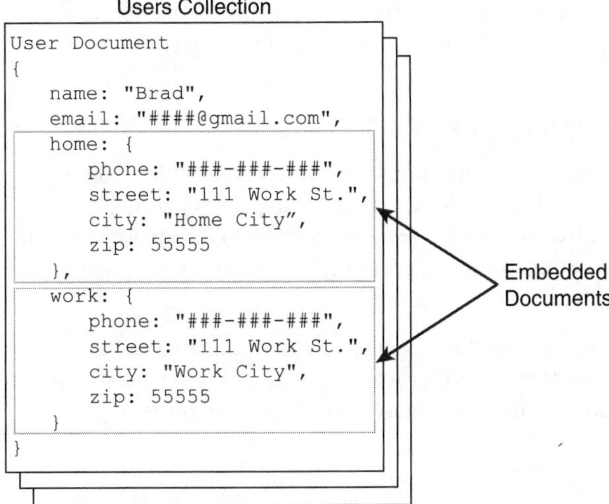

Figure 11.2 Defining denormalized MongoDB documents by implementing embedded objects inside a document

Using Capped Collections

A great feature of MongoDB is the ability to create a *capped collection*, which is a collection that has a fixed size. When a new document that exceeds the size of the collection needs to be written to a collection, the oldest document in the collection is deleted and the new document is inserted. Capped collections work great for objects that have a high rate of insertion, retrieval, and deletion.

The following list contains the benefits of using capped collections:

- Capped collections guarantee that the insertion order is preserved. Queries do not need to use an index to return documents in the order they were stored, thus eliminating indexing overhead.
- Capped collections also guarantee that the insertion order is identical to the order on disk by prohibiting updates that increase the document size. This eliminates the overhead of relocating and managing the new location of documents.
- Capped collections automatically remove the oldest documents in the collection. Therefore, you do not need to implement deletion in your application code.

Be careful using capped collections, though, as they have the following restrictions:

- Documents cannot be updated to a larger size once they have been inserted into the capped collection. You update them, but the data must be the same size or smaller.
- Documents cannot be deleted from a capped collection. That means that the data takes up space on disk even if it is not being used. You can explicitly drop the capped collection to effectively delete all entries, but you need to re-create it to use it again.

A great use of capped collections is as a rolling log of transactions in your system. You can always access the last *X* number of log entries without needing to explicitly clean up the oldest.

Understanding Atomic Write Operations

Write operations are atomic at the document level in MongoDB, which means that only one process can update a single document or a single collection at the same time. This means that writing to documents that are denormalized is atomic. However, writing to documents that are normalized requires separate write operations to subobjects in other collections, and therefore the writes of the normalized object may not be atomic as a whole.

Keep atomic writes in mind when designing your documents and collections to ensure that the design fits the needs of the application. In other words, if you absolutely must write all parts of an object as a whole in an atomic manner, then you need to design the object in a denormalized fashion.

Considering Document Growth

When you update a document, consider what effect the new data will have on document growth. MongoDB provides some padding in documents to allow for typical growth during an update operation. However, if the update causes the document to grow to an amount that exceeds the allocated space on disk, MongoDB has to relocate that document to a new location on the disk, incurring a performance hit on the system. Also, frequent document relocation can lead to disk fragmentation issues—for example, if a document contains an array and you add enough elements to the array.

One way to mitigate document growth is to use normalized objects for the properties that may grow frequently. For example, instead of using an array to store items in a `Cart` object, you could create a collection for `CartItems` and store new items that get placed in the cart as new documents in the `CartItems` collection and then reference the user's `Cart` items within them.

Identifying Indexing, Sharding, and Replication Opportunities

MongoDB provides several mechanisms to optimize performance, scaling, and reliability. As you contemplate your database design, consider each of the following options:

- **Indexing:** Indexes improve performance for frequent queries by building a lookup index that can be easily sorted. The `_id` property of a collection is automatically indexed on since it is a common practice to look items up by ID. However, you also need to consider what other ways users access data and implement indexes that will enhance those lookup methods.

- **Sharding:** Sharding is the process of slicing up large collections of data that can be split between multiple MongoDB servers in a cluster. Each MongoDB server is considered a shard. This provides the benefit of using multiple servers to support a high number of requests to a large system, thus providing horizontal scaling to your database. Look at the size of your data and the amount of requests that will be accessing it to determine whether and how much to shard your collections.
- **Replications:** Replication is the process of duplicating data on multiple MongoDB instances in a cluster. When considering the reliability aspect of your database, you should implement replication to ensure that a backup copy of critical data is always readily available.

Large Collections Versus Large Numbers of Collections

Another important thing to consider when designing your MongoDB documents and collections is the number of collections that the design will result in. There isn't a significant performance hit for having a large number of collections; however, there is a performance hit for having large numbers of items in the same collection. Consider ways to break up your larger collections into more consumable chunks.

For example, say that you store a history of user transactions in the database for past purchases. You recognize that for these completed purchases, you will never need to look them up together for multiple users. You only need them available for the user to look at his or her own history. If you have thousands of users who have a lot of transactions, then it makes sense to store those histories in a separate collection for each user.

Deciding on Data Life Cycles

One of the most commonly overlooked aspects of database design is that of the data life cycle. Specifically, how long should documents exist in a specific collection? Some collections have documents that should be indefinite, for example, active user accounts. However, keep in mind that each document in the system incurs a performance hit when querying a collection. You should define a TTL or time-to-live value for documents in each of your collections.

There are several ways to implement a time-to-live mechanism in MongoDB. One way is to implement code in your application to monitor and clean up old data. Another way is to use the MongoDB TTL setting on a collection, which allows you to define a profile where documents are automatically deleted after a certain number of seconds or at a specific clock time. For collections where you only need the most recent documents, you can implement a capped collection that automatically keeps the size of the collection small.

Considering Data Usability and Performance

Two more important things to consider when designing a MongoDB database are data use and how it will affect performance. The previous sections described different methods for solving some complexities of data size and optimization. The final things you should consider and even reconsider are data usability and performance. Ultimately, these are the two most important aspects of any web solution and, consequently, the storage behind it.

Data usability describes the ability for the database to satisfy the functionality of the website. First, you must make sure that the data can be accessed so that the website functions correctly. Users will not tolerate a website that simply does not do what they want it to. This also includes the accuracy of the data.

Then you can consider performance. Your database must be able to deliver the data at a reasonable rate. You can consult the previous sections when evaluating and designing the performance factors for your database.

In some more complex circumstances, you may find it necessary to evaluate data usability and then performance and then go back and evaluate usability again for a few cycles until you get the balance correct. Also, keep in mind that in today's world, usability requirements can change at any time. Remembering that can influence how you design your documents and collections so that they can become more scalable in the future if necessary.

Summary

In this chapter you learned about MongoDB and design considerations for the structure of data and configuration of a database. You learned about collections, documents, and the types of data that can be stored in them. You also learned how to plan your data model, what questions you need to answer, and the mechanisms built in to MongoDB to satisfy the demands your database needs.

Next

In the next chapter, you install MongoDB. You also learn how to use the MongoDB shell to set up user accounts and access collections and documents.

12

Getting Started with MongoDB

This chapter gets you up to speed with MongoDB. Whereas Chapter 11, "Understanding NoSQL and MongoDB," focused more on the theory side of MongoDB, this chapter is all about practical application. You learn what it takes to install MongoDB, start and stop the engine, and access the MongoDB shell. The MongoDB shell allows you to administer the MongoDB server as well as perform every necessary function on the databases. Using the MongoDB shell is a vital aspect of the development process as well as database administration.

This chapter covers installing MongoDB and accessing the shell. The chapter focuses on some basic administrative tasks such as setting up user accounts and authentication. The chapter then wraps up by describing how to administer databases, collections, and documents.

Building the MongoDB Environment

To get started with MongoDB, the first task is to install it on your development system. Once installed on your development system, you can play around with the functionality, learn the MongoDB shell, and prepare for Chapter 13, "Getting Started with MongoDB and Node.js," in which you begin integrating MongoDB into your Node.js applications.

The following sections cover installation, starting and stopping the database engine, and accessing the shell client. Once you can do those things you are ready to begin using MongoDB in your environment.

Installing MongoDB

The first step in getting MongoDB implemented into your Node.js environment is installing the MongoDB server. There is a version of MongoDB for each of the major platforms, including Linux, Windows, Solaris, and OS X. There is also an enterprise version available for the Red Hat, SuSE, Ubuntu, and Amazon Linux distributions. The enterprise version of MongoDB is subscription-based and provides enhanced security, management, and integration support.

For the purposes of this book and learning MongoDB, the standard edition of MongoDB is perfect. Before continuing, go to the MongoDB website at http://docs.mongodb.org/manual/installation/. Follow the links and instructions to download and install MongoDB in your environment:

As part of the installation and setup process, perform the following steps:

1. Download and extract the MongoDB files.
2. Add the `<mongo_install_location>/bin` to your system path.
3. Create a data files directory: `<mongo_data_location>/data/db`.
4. Start MongoDB using the following command from the console prompt:

```
mongod -dbpath <mongo_data_location>/data/db
```

Starting MongoDB

Once you have installed MongoDB, you need to be able to start and stop the database engine. The database engine starts by executing the `mongod` (`mongod.exe` on Windows) executable in the `<mongo_install_location>/bin` location. This executable starts MongoDB and begins listening for database requests on the configured port.

The `mongod` executable accepts several different parameters that provide methods of controlling its behavior. For example, you can configure the IP `address` and `port` MongoDB listens on as well as logging and authentication. Table 12.1 provides a list of some of the most commonly used parameters.

Here is an example of starting MongoDB with a `port` and `dbpath` parameters:

```
mongod -port 28008 -dbpath <mongo_data_location>/data/db
```

Table 12.1 **mongod command-line parameters**

Parameter	Description
`--help, -h`	Returns basic help and usage text.
`--version`	Returns the version of MongoDB.
`--config <filename>,` `-f <filename>`	Specifies a configuration file that contains runtime-configurations.
`--verbose, -v`	Increases the amount of internal reporting sent to the console and written to the log file specified by `--logpath`.
`--quiet`	Reduces the amount of reporting sent to the console and log file.
`--port <port>`	Specifies a TCP port for `mongod` to listen for client connections. Default: `27017`.

Parameter	Description
`--bind_ip <ip address>`	Specifies the IP address on which mongod will bind to and listen for connections. Default: `All Interfaces`
`--maxConns <number>`	Specifies the maximum number of simultaneous connections that mongod will accept. Max: `20000`
`--logpath <path>`	Specifies a path for the log file. On restart, the log file is overwritten unless you also specify `--logappend`.
`--auth`	Enables database authentication for users connecting from remote hosts.
`--dbpath <path>`	Specifies a directory for the mongod instance to store its data.
`--nohttpinterface`	Disables the HTTP interface.
`--nojournal`	Disables the durability journaling.
`--noprealloc`	Disables the preallocation of data files, which shortens the startup time but can cause significant performance penalties during normal operations.
`--repair`	Runs a repair routine on all databases.

Stopping MongoDB

Each platform has different methods of stopping the mongod executable once it has started. However, one of the best methods is to stop it from the shell client because that cleanly shuts down the current operations and forces the mongod to exit.

To stop the MongoDB database from the shell client, use the following commands to switch to the admin database and then shut down the database engine:

```
use admin
db.shutdownServer()
```

Accessing MongoDB from the Shell Client

Once you have installed, configured, and started MongoDB, you can access it through the MongoDB shell. The MongoDB shell is an interactive shell provided with MongoDB that allows you to access, configure, and administer MongoDB databases, users, and much more. You use the shell for everything from setting up user accounts to creating databases to querying the contents of the database.

The following sections take you through some of the most common administration tasks that you perform in the MongoDB shell. Specifically, you need to be able to create user accounts, databases, and collections to follow the examples in the rest of the book. Also you should be able to perform at least rudimentary queries on documents to help you troubleshoot any problems with accessing data.

To start the MongoDB shell, first make sure that `mongod` is running, and then run the `mongod` command, then execute the `mongo` command from the console prompt. The shell should start up as shown in Figure 12.1.

```
MongoDB shell version: 2.4.8
connecting to: test
Welcome to the MongoDB shell.
For interactive help, type "help".
For more comprehensive documentation, see
        http://docs.mongodb.org/
Questions? Try the support group
        http://groups.google.com/group/mongodb-user
> _
```

Figure 12.1 Starting the MongoDB console shell

Once you have accessed the MongoDB shell, you can administer all aspects of MongoDB. There are a couple of things to keep in mind when using MongoDB. First is that it is based on JavaScript and most of its syntax is available. Second, the shell provides direct access to the database and collections on the server so changes you make directly impact the data on the server.

Understanding MongoDB Shell commands

The MongoDB shell provides several commands that can be executed from the shell prompt. You need to be familiar with these commands as you will use them a lot. The following list describes each command and its purpose:

- **`help <option>`**: Displays syntax help for MongoDB shell commands. The `option` argument allows you to specify an area where you want help.
- **`use <database>`**: Changes the current `database` handle. Database operations are processed on the current database handle.
- **`db.help`**: Displays help options for the database methods.
- **`show <option>`**: Shows a list based on the `option` argument. The value of `option` can be:
  - **`dbs`**: Displays a list of databases.
  - **`collections`**: Displays a list of collections for the current database.
  - **`profile`**: Displays the five most recent `system.profile` entries taking more than 1 millisecond.
  - **`databases`**: Displays a list of all available databases.
  - **`roles`**: Displays a list of all roles for the current database, both built-in and user-defined.
  - **`users`**: Displays a list of all users for that database.
- **`exit`**: Exits the database.

Understanding MongoDB Shell Methods

The MongoDB shell also provides a number of methods to perform administrative functions. These methods can be called directly from the MongoDB shell or from a script executed in the MongoDB shell.

There are many methods that you can use to perform various administrative functions. Some of these are covered in later sections and chapters in this book. For now, you need to be aware of the types of shell methods and how to access them. The following list provides a few examples of shell methods:

- **load(script)**: Loads and runs a JavaScript file inside the shell. This is a great way to script operations for the database.
- **UUID(string)**: Converts a 32-byte hex string into a BSON UUID.
- **db.auth(username, password)**: Authenticates you to the current database.

There are a lot of different shell methods. Many of them are covered in subsequent sections. For a full list of the native methods, check out http://docs.mongodb.org/manual/reference/method/#native.

Understanding Command Parameters and Results

The MongoDB shell is an interactive JavaScript shell that is tightly coupled with the MongoDB data structure. That means that much of the data interaction—from parameters passed to methods to data being returned from methods—is standard MongoDB documents, which are in most respects JavaScript objects. For example, when creating a user you pass in a document similar to the following to define the user:

```
db.createUser( { user: "testUser",
               roles: [ "read" ],
               otherDBRoles: { testDB2: [ "readWrite" ] } } )
```

And when listing the users for a database to the shell, the users are shown as a list of documents similar to this:

```
> use admin
switched to db admin
> db.system.users.find()
{ "_id" : ObjectId("529e71927c798d1dd56a63d9"), "user" : "dbadmin", "pwd" :
"78384f4d73368bd2d3a3e1da926dd269", "roles"
: [  "readWriteAnyDatabase",  "dbAdminAnyDatabase",  "clusterAdmin" ] }
{ "_id" : ObjectId("52a098861db41f82f6e3d489"), "user" : "useradmin", "pwd" :
"0b4568ab22a52a6b494fd54e64fcee9f", "roles
" : [  "userAdminAnyDatabase" ] }
```

Scripting the MongoDB Shell

As you have seen, the commands, methods, and data structure of the MongoDB shell are based on interactive JavaScript. A great method of administering MongoDB is creating scripts that can be run multiple times, or be ready to run at specific times; for example, as for an upgrade.

The script file can contain any number of MongoDB commands using JavaScript syntax such as conditional statements and loops. There are two methods to run a MongoDB shell script. The first is from the console command line using `--eval`. The `--eval` parameter accepts a JavaScript string or a JavaScript file, launches the MongoDB shell, and immediately executes the JavaScript.

For example, the following command starts the MongoDB shell, executes `db.getCollections()` on the test database, and outputs the JSON string results as shown in Figure 12.2:

```
mongo test --eval "printjson(db.getCollectionNames())"
```

> **Note**
>
> If you are using authentication, and you should, the script might need to authenticate to perform the commands.

```
C:\Users\Brad>mongo test --eval "printjson(db.getCollectionNames())"
MongoDB shell version: 2.4.8
connecting to: test
[ "system.indexes", "system.users" ]
```

Figure 12.2 Executing a JavaScript file from the MongoDB console shell command line

The second method is to execute a JavaScript from the MongoDB shell prompt using the `load(script_path)` method. This method loads a JavaScript file and immediately executes it. For example, the following shell command loads and executes the `db_update.js` script file:

```
load("/tmp/db_update.js")
```

Administering User Accounts

Once you have MongoDB up and running, one of the first things you want to do is add users to be able to access the database. MongoDB provides the ability to add, remove, and configure users from the MongoDB shell. The following sections discuss using the MongoDB shell to administer user accounts.

Listing Users

User accounts are stored in the db.system.users collection of each database. The `User` object contains `_id`, `user`, `pwd`, `roles`, and sometimes `otherDBRoles` fields. There are a couple of ways to get a list of user objects. The first is to change to the database you want to list users on and then execute the `show users` command. The following commands show changing to the admin database and listing users, as shown in Figure 12.3:

```
use admin
show users
```

```
>
> use admin
switched to db admin
> show users
{
        "_id" : ObjectId("529e71927c798d1dd56a63d9"),
        "user" : "dbadmin",
        "pwd" : "78384f4d73368bd2d3a3e1da926dd269",
        "roles" : [
                "readWriteAnyDatabase",
                "dbAdminAnyDatabase",
                "clusterAdmin"
        ]
}
{
        "_id" : ObjectId("52a098861db41f82f6e3d489"),
        "user" : "useradmin",
        "pwd" : "0b4568ab22a52a6b494fd54e64fcee9f",
        "roles" : [
                "userAdminAnyDatabase"
        ]
}
> _
```

Figure 12.3 Listing users on the admin database

You can also use a query such as `find` on the `db.system.users` collection. The difference is that `db.system.users.find()` returns a cursor object that you can use to access the `User` documents. For example, the following code gets a cursor for users in the admin database and returns the count of users:

```
use admin
cur = db.system.users.find()
cur.count()
```

Creating User Accounts

You can use the MongoDB shell to create user accounts that can administer, read, and write to the databases. User accounts are added using the `createUser()` method inside the MongoDB shell. The `createUser()` method accepts a `document` object that allows you to specify the username, roles, and password that apply to that user. Table 12.2 lists the fields that can be specified in the document object.

Table 12.2 **Fields used when creating users with the `db.createUser()` method**

Field	Format	Description
`user`	`string`	Specifies a unique username.
`roles`	`array`	Specifies an array of user roles. MongoDB provides a large number of roles that can be assigned to a user. Table 12.3 lists a few of the common roles.
`pwd`	`hash` or `string`	(Optional.) Specifies a user password. When creating the user, this can be a hash or a string; however, it is stored in the database as a hash.

MongoDB provides a number of different roles that can be assigned to a user account. These roles give you the ability to implement intricate privileges and restrictions on user accounts. Table 12.3 lists some of the more common roles that can be assigned to users.

Table 12.3 **Database roles that can be assigned to user accounts**

Role	Description
`read`	Allows the user to read data from any collection within the database.
`readAnyDatabase`	Same as `read` except on the local and config databases.
`readWrite`	Provides all the functionality of `read` and allows the user to write to any collection within the database, including inserting, removing, and updating documents as well as creating, renaming, and dropping collections.
`readWriteAnyDatabase`	Same as `readWrite` except on the local and config databases.
`dbAdmin`	Allows the user to read from and write to the database, as well as clean, modify, compact, get statistics profile, and perform validations.
`dbAdminAnyDatabase`	Same as `dbAdmin` except for all databases.
`clusterAdmin`	Allows the user to generally administer MongoDB, including connections, clustering, replication listing databases, creating databases, and deleting databases.
`userAdmin`	Allows the user to create and modify user accounts on the database.
`userAdminAnyDatabase`	Same as `userAdmin` except on the local and config databases.

Note

The `readAnyDatabase`, `readWriteAnyDatabase`, `dbAdminAnyDatabase`, and `userAdminAnyDatabase` roles can only be applied to users in the admin database since they must apply to all databases.

To create a user you should switch to that database and then use the `createUser()` method to create the user object. The following MongoDB shell command illustrates creating a basic administrator user to the test database:

```
use test
db.createUser( { user: "testUser",
    pwd: "test",
    roles: [ "readWrite", "dbAdmin" ] } )
```

Now here's a more complex example. The following commands add the same user to the newDB database with only `read` rights and give them `readWrite` privileges to the `testDB2` database:

```
use newDB
db.createUser( { user: "testUser",
    roles: [ "read" ],
    otherDBRoles: { testDB2: [ "readWrite" ] } } )
```

Removing Users

Users can be removed from MongoDB using the `removeUser(<username>)` method. You need to change to the database that the user is on first. For example, to remove the `testUser` user from the `testDB` database, use the following commands from the MongoDB shell:

```
use testDB
db.removeUser("testUser")
```

Configuring Access Control

One of the first administration tasks that you will want to perform in the MongoDB shell is to add users to configure access control. MongoDB provides authentication and authorization at a database level, meaning that users exist in the context of a single database. For basic authentication purposes, MongoDB stores user credentials inside a collection called `system.users` in each database.

Initially, the admin database does not have any users assigned to it. When no users are defined in the admin database, MongoDB allows connections on the local host to have full administrative access to the database. Therefore, your first step in setting up a new MongoDB instance is to create User Administrator and Database Administrator accounts. The User Administrator account provides the ability to create user accounts in the admin and other databases. You also need to create a Database Administrator account that you can use as a superuser to manage databases, clustering, replication, and other aspects of MongoDB.

> **Note**
>
> The User Administrator and Database Administrator accounts are created in the admin database. If you are using authentication for your MongoDB database, you must authenticate to the admin database as one of those users to administer users or databases. You should also create user accounts for each database for access purposes as described in the previous section.

Creating a User Administrator Account

The first step in configuring access control is implementing a User Administrator account. The User Administrator should only have rights to create users and not manage the database or perform any other administration functions at all. This keeps a clean separation between database administration and user account administration.

Creating a User Administrator account is done by executing the following two commands in the MongoDB shell to access the admin database and then add a user with `userAdminAnyDatabase` rights.

```
use admin
db.createUser( { user: "<username>",
    pwd: "<password>",
    roles: [ "userAdminAnyDatabase" ] } )
```

The User Administrator account should be created with `userAdminAnyDatabase` as the only role. This gives the User Administrator the ability to create new user accounts but not to manipulate the database beyond that. For example, create a User Administrator account with the username `useradmin` and a password of `test` as shown in Figure 12.4:

```
use admin
db.createUser( { user: "useradmin",
    pwd: "test",
    roles: [ "userAdminAnyDatabase" ] } )
```

```
> show users
> use admin
switched to db admin
> db.addUser( { user: "useradmin",
...         pwd: "test",
...         roles: [ "userAdminAnyDatabase" ] } )
{
        "user" : "useradmin",
        "pwd" : "0b4568ab22a52a6b494fd54e64fcee9f",
        "roles" : [
                "userAdminAnyDatabase"
        ],
        "_id" : ObjectId("52a0ba533120fa0d0e424dd3")
}
>
> show users
{
        "_id" : ObjectId("52a0ba533120fa0d0e424dd3"),
        "user" : "useradmin",
        "pwd" : "0b4568ab22a52a6b494fd54e64fcee9f",
        "roles" : [
                "userAdminAnyDatabase"
        ]
}
> _
```

Figure 12.4 Creating the User Administrator account

Turning on Authentication

Once the User Administrator account has been created, restart the MongoDB database using the `--auth` parameter. For example:

```
mongod -dbpath <mongo_data_location>/data/db --auth
```

Clients will now have to use a username and password to access the database. Also, when you access MongoDB from the shell, you need to execute the following commands to authenticate to the admin database so that you can add users with rights to the database:

```
use admin
db.auth("useradmin", "test")
```

You can also authenticate to the admin database when starting the MongoDB shell using the `--username` and `--password` options, for example:

```
mongo --username "useradmin" --password "test"
```

Creating a Database Administrator Account

Creating a Database Administrator account is done by executing the `createuser` method in the MongoDB shell to access the admin database and then adding a user with `readWriteAnyDatabase`, `dbAdminAnyDatabase`, and `clusterAdmin` rights. This gives the user the ability to access all databases in the system, create new databases, and manage MongoDB clusters and replicas. The following example shows creating a Database Administrator named `dbadmin`:

```
use admin
db.createUser( { user: "dbadmin",
    pwd: "test",
    roles: [ "readWriteAnyDatabase", "dbAdminAnyDatabase", "clusterAdmin" ] } )
```

You can then use that user in the MongoDB shell to administer databases. Once you have created the new administrator account, you can authenticate as that user using the following commands:

```
use admin
db.auth("dbadmin", "test")
```

You can also authenticate to the admin database as the Database Administrator when starting the MongoDB shell using the `--username` and `--password` options, for example:

```
mongo --username "dbadmin" --password "test"
```

Administering Databases

When administering databases in the MongoDB shell, you need to use a user account that has `clusterAdmin` privileges—for example, the Database Administrator account described earlier in this chapter. Once you have a Database Administrator account created, you can authenticate as that user and perform the tasks described in the following sections.

Displaying a List of Databases

Often you may need to just see a list of databases that have been created, especially if you have created a large number of databases or are not the only one administering the system. To see a list of databases in the system, use the following `show dbs` command, which displays a list of databases that have been created:

```
show dbs
```

Changing the Current Database

Database operations are performed using the handle db, which is built into MongoDB. Many operations can only be applied on one database, and therefore to perform operations on other databases, you need to change the db handle to point to the new database.

To switch the current database, you can use the db.getSiblingDB(database) method or the use <database> method. For example, both of the following methods switch the current database handle to testDB. Either one is acceptable and sets the value of db to the database specified. You can then use db to manage the new current database:

```
db = db.getSiblingDB('testDB')
use testDB
```

Creating Databases

MongoDB doesn't provide a command in the shell to explicitly create databases. Instead you can simply use the use <new_database_name> to create a new database handle. Keep in mind that the new database is not actually saved until you add a collection to it. For example, the following commands create a new database named newDB and then add a collection named newCollection to it:

```
use newDB
db.createCollection("newCollection")
```

To verify that the new database exists, you can then use show dbs as shown in Figure 12.5.

```
> show dbs
admin    0.203125GB
local    0.078125GB
test     0.203125GB
> use newDB
switched to db newDB
> db.createCollection("newCollection")
{ "ok" : 1 }
> show dbs
admin    0.203125GB
local    0.078125GB
newDB    0.203125GB
test     0.203125GB
> _
```

Figure 12.5 Creating a new database in the MongoDB console shell

Deleting Databases

Once a database has been created, it exists in MongoDB until it is deleted by the administrator. Deleting a database is a common task on some systems. Especially when databases are created to contain temporary data, it is sometimes easier to delete databases when they become stale and simply create new ones as needed instead of trying to clean up the entries in a database.

To delete a database from the MongoDB shell, use the `dropDatabase()` method. For example, to delete the `newDB` database, use the following commands to change to the `newDB` database and then delete it:

```
use newDB
db.dropDatabase()
```

Be aware that `dropDatabase()` removes the current database, but it does not change the current database handle. That means that if you drop a database and then create a collection using the handle without changing the current database first, the dropped database is re-created.

Figure 12.6 shows an example of deleting the `newDB` from MongoDB:

```
> show dbs
admin   0.203125GB
local   0.078125GB
newDB   0.203125GB
test    0.203125GB
> use newDB
switched to db newDB
> db.dropDatabase()
{ "dropped" : "newDB", "ok" : 1 }
> show dbs
admin   0.203125GB
local   0.078125GB
test    0.203125GB
> _
```

Figure 12.6 Deleting a database in the MongoDB console shell

Copying Databases

Another common task with databases is copying them. Copying a database creates an exact duplicate of the database, only with a different name. You might want to create a copy of a database for various reasons, such as to have a backup while you perform heavy changes or to use as an archive.

To create a copy of a database, you switch to that database and then use `copyDatabase(origin, destination, [hostname])` to create a copy. The `origin` parameter is a string specifying the name of the database to copy. The `destination` parameter specifies the name of the database to create on this MongoDB server. The optional `hostname` parameter specifies a hostname of the origin database MongoDB server if you are copying a database from a different host. For example:

```
db.copyDatabase('customers', 'customers_archive')
```

Managing Collections

As a database admin, you may also find yourself administering collections within a database. MongoDB provides the functionality in the MongoDB shell to create, view, and manipulate collections in a database. The following sections cover the basics that you need to know to use the MongoDB shell to list collections, create new ones, and access the documents contained within them.

Displaying a List of Collections in a Database

Often you may need to just see a list of collections contained in a database—for example, to verify that a collection exists or to find the name of a collection that you cannot remember. To see a list of collections in a database, you need to switch to that database and then use `show collections` to get the list of collections contained in the database. For example, the following commands list the collections in the test database:

```
use test
show collections
```

Creating Collections

You must create a collection in MongoDB database before you can begin storing documents. To create a collection, you need to call `createCollection(name, [options])` on the database handle. The `name` parameter is the name of the new database. The optional `options` parameter is an object that can have the properties listed in Table 12.4 that define the behavior of the collection.

Table 12.4 **Options that can be specified when creating collections**

Role	Description
`capped`	A Boolean; when `true`, the collection is a capped collection that does not grow bigger than the maximum size specified by the `size` attribute. Default: `false`.
`autoIndexID`	A Boolean; when `true`, an `_id` field is automatically created for each document added to the collection and an index on that field is implemented. This should be `false` for capped collections. Default: `true`.
`size`	Specifies the size in bytes for the `capped` collection. The oldest document is removed to make room for new documents.
`max`	Specifies the maximum number of documents allowed in a `capped` collection. The oldest document is removed to make room for new documents.
`validator`	Allows users to specify validation rules or expressions for the collection.

Role	Description
`validationLevel`	Determines the strictness MongoDB applies to the validation rules on documents during updates.
`validationAction`	Determines whether an invalid document is errored or warned but still can be inserted.
`indexOptionDefaults`	Allows users to specify a default index configuration when a collection is created.

For example, the following lines of code create a new collection called `newCollection` in the `testDB` database as shown in Figure 12.7:

```
db.createCollection("newCollection")
```

```
> use testDB
switched to db testDB
> show collections
> db.createCollection("newCollection", {capped:false})
{ "ok" : 1 }
> show collections
newCollection
system.indexes
> _
```

Figure 12.7 Creating a new collection in the MongoDB console shell

Deleting Collections

Occasionally you also want to remove old collections when they are no longer needed. Removing old collections frees up disk space and eliminates any overhead such as indexing associated with the collection.

To delete a collection in the MongoDB shell, you need to switch to the correct database, get the collection object, and then call the `drop()` function on that object. For example, the following code deletes the `newCollection` collection from the `testDB` database as shown in Figure 12.8:

```
use testDB
show collections
coll = db.getCollection("newCollection")
coll.drop()
show collections
```

```
> use testDB
switched to db testDB
> show collections
newCollection
system.indexes
> coll = db.getCollection("newCollection")
testDB.newCollection
> coll.drop()
true
> show collections
system.indexes
> _
```

Figure 12.8 Deleting a collection in the MongoDB console shell

Finding Documents in a Collection

Most of the time you use a library such as the native MongoDB driver or Mongoose to access documents in a collection. However, sometimes you might need to look at documents inside the MongoDB shell.

The MongoDB shell provides full querying functionality to find documents in collections using the `find(query)` method on the collection object. The optional `query` parameter specifies a query document with fields and values to match documents against in the collection. The documents that match the query are removed from the collection. Using the `find()` method with no query parameter returns all documents in the collection.

For example, the following lines of code first query every item in the collection and then retrieve the documents whose `speed` field is equal to `120mph`. The results are shown in Figure 12.9.

```
use testDB
coll = db.getCollection("newCollection")
coll.find()
coll.find({speed:"120mph"})
```

```
> use testDB
switched to db testDB
> coll = db.getCollection("newCollection")
testDB.newCollection
> coll.find()
{ "_id" : ObjectId("52a0c65b3120fa0d0e424dd8"), "vehicle" : "plane", "speed" : "480mph" }
{ "_id" : ObjectId("52a0c65b3120fa0d0e424dd9"), "vehicle" : "car", "speed" : "120mph" }
{ "_id" : ObjectId("52a0c65b3120fa0d0e424dda"), "vehicle" : "train", "speed" : "120mph" }
> coll.find({speed:"120mph"})
{ "_id" : ObjectId("52a0c65b3120fa0d0e424dd9"), "vehicle" : "car", "speed" : "120mph" }
{ "_id" : ObjectId("52a0c65b3120fa0d0e424dda"), "vehicle" : "train", "speed" : "120mph" }
> _
```

Figure 12.9 Finding documents in a collection

Adding Documents to a Collection

Typically, insertion of documents in a collection should be done through your Node.js application. However, at times you may need to manually insert a document from an administrative point of view to preload a database, to fix a database, or for testing purposes.

To add documents to a collection, you need to get the collection object and then call the `insert(document)` or `save(document)` method on that object. The `document` parameter is a well-formatted JavaScript object that is converted to BSON and stored in the collection. As an example, the following commands create three new objects inside a collection as shown in Figure 12.10:

```
use testDB
coll = db.getCollection("newCollection")
coll.find()
coll.insert({ vehicle: "plane", speed: "480mph" })
coll.insert({ vehicle: "car", speed: "120mph" })
coll.insert({ vehicle: "train", speed: "120mph" })
coll.find()
```

```
> use testDB
switched to db testDB
> coll = db.getCollection("newCollection")
testDB.newCollection
> coll.find()
> coll.insert({ vehicle: "plane", speed: "480mph" })
> coll.insert({ vehicle: "car", speed: "120mph" })
> coll.insert({ vehicle: "train", speed: "120mph" })
> coll.find()
{ "_id" : ObjectId("52a0d2743120fa0d0e424dde"), "vehicle" : "plane", "speed" : "480mph" }
{ "_id" : ObjectId("52a0d2743120fa0d0e424ddf"), "vehicle" : "car", "speed" : "120mph" }
{ "_id" : ObjectId("52a0d2743120fa0d0e424de0"), "vehicle" : "train", "speed" : "120mph" }
>
```

Figure 12.10 Creating documents in a collection

Deleting Documents in a Collection

Deletion of documents in a collection also is typically done through your Node.js application. However, at times you may need to manually remove a document from an administrative point of view to fix a database or for testing purposes.

To remove documents from a collection, you need to get the collection object and then call the `remove(query)` method on that object. The optional `query` parameter specifies a query document with fields and values to match documents against in the collection. The documents that match the query are removed from the collection. Using the `remove()` method with no query parameter removes all documents in the collection. As an example, the following commands first remove documents where the vehicle is plane and then all documents from the collection, as shown in Figure 12.11:

```
use testDB
coll = db.getCollection("newCollection")
coll.find()
```

```
coll.remove({vehicle: "plane"})
coll.find()
coll.remove()
coll.find()
```

```
> use testDB
switched to db testDB
> coll = db.getCollection("newCollection")
testDB.newCollection
> coll.find()
{ "_id" : ObjectId("52a0d2743120fa0d0e424dde"), "vehicle" : "plane", "speed" : "480mph" }
{ "_id" : ObjectId("52a0d2743120fa0d0e424ddf"), "vehicle" : "car", "speed" : "120mph" }
{ "_id" : ObjectId("52a0d2743120fa0d0e424de0"), "vehicle" : "train", "speed" : "120mph" }
> coll.remove({vehicle: "plane"})
> coll.find()
{ "_id" : ObjectId("52a0d2743120fa0d0e424ddf"), "vehicle" : "car", "speed" : "120mph" }
{ "_id" : ObjectId("52a0d2743120fa0d0e424de0"), "vehicle" : "train", "speed" : "120mph" }
> coll.remove()
> coll.find()
> _
```

Figure 12.11 Deleting documents from a collection

Updating Documents in a Collection

Updates of documents in a collection should also be done through your Node.js application. However, at times you may need to manually update a document from an administrative point of view to fix a database or for testing purposes.

To update documents in a collection, you need to get the collection. Then you can use a couple of different methods: The `save(object)` method saves changes that you have made to an object, and the `update(query, update, options)` method queries for documents in the collection and then updates them as they are found.

When using the `update()` method, the `query` parameter specifies a query document with fields and values to match documents against in the collection. The `update` parameter is an object that specifies the update operator to use when making the update. For example, `$inc` increments the value of the field, `$set` sets the value of the field, `$push` pushes an item onto an array, and so on. For example, the following update object increments one field, sets another, and then renames a third:

```
{ $inc: {count: 1}, $set: {name: "New Name"}, $rename: {"nickname": "alias"} }
```

The `options` parameter of `update()` is an object that has two properties—`multi` and `upsert`—that are both Boolean values. If `upsert` is `true`, a new document is created if none are found. If `multi` is `true`, all documents that match the query are updated; otherwise, only the first document is updated.

For example, the following commands update documents with a `speed` of `120mph` by setting the `speed` to `150` and adding a new field called `updated`. Also the `save()` method is used to save changes to the `plane` document. The console output is shown in Figure 12.12:

```
use testDB
coll = db.getCollection("newCollection")
coll.find()
coll.update({ speed: "120mph" },
```

```
            { $set: { speed: "150mph" , updated: true } },
            { upsert: false, multi: true })
coll.save({ "_id" : ObjectId("52a0caf33120fa0d0e424ddb"),
            "vehicle" : "plane", "speed" : "500mph" })
coll.find()
```

```
> use testDB
switched to db testDB
> coll = db.getCollection("newCollection")
testDB.newCollection
> coll.find()
{ "_id" : ObjectId("52a0caf33120fa0d0e424ddb"), "vehicle" : "plane", "speed" : "470mph" }
{ "_id" : ObjectId("52a0caf33120fa0d0e424ddc"), "vehicle" : "car", "speed" : "120mph" }
{ "_id" : ObjectId("52a0caf33120fa0d0e424ddd"), "vehicle" : "train", "speed" : "120mph" }
> coll.update({ speed: "120mph" },
...             { $set: { speed: "150mph" , updated: true } },
...             { upsert: false, multi: true })
> coll.save({ "_id" : ObjectId("52a0caf33120fa0d0e424ddb"),
...             "vehicle" : "plane", "speed" : "500mph" })
> coll.find()
{ "_id" : ObjectId("52a0caf33120fa0d0e424ddb"), "vehicle" : "plane", "speed" : "500mph" }
{ "_id" : ObjectId("52a0caf33120fa0d0e424ddc"), "speed" : "150mph", "updated" : true, "vehicle" : "car" }
{ "_id" : ObjectId("52a0caf33120fa0d0e424ddd"), "speed" : "150mph", "updated" : true, "vehicle" : "train" }
> _
```

Figure 12.12 Updating documents from a collection

Summary

From a development perspective, most of the interaction that you have with MongoDB is from a library, such as the native MongoDB driver for Node.js. However, before you can begin implementing MongoDB in your applications, you need to install the MongoDB server and configure it to run. You should also create administrative and database accounts and then turn on authentication to ensure security even in your development environment.

This chapter discussed the process of installing MongoDB and accessing the MongoDB shell. You learned how to interact with the shell to create user accounts, databases, collections, and documents.

Next

In the next chapter, you implement MongoDB in your Node.js applications using the native MongoDB driver for the Node.js module. You learn how to include the `mongodb` module in your applications and connect to MongoDB to perform database operations.

13

Getting Started with MongoDB and Node.js

You can use several modules to access MongoDB from your Node.js applications. The MongoDB group adopted the MongoDB Node.js driver as the standard method. This driver provides all the functionality and is similar to the native commands available in the MongoDB shell client.

This chapter focuses on getting you started accessing MongoDB from your Node.js applications. You learn how to install the MongoDB Node.js driver and use it to connect to the MongoDB databases. Several sections also cover the processes of creating, accessing, and manipulating databases and collections from your Node.js applications.

Adding the MongoDB Driver to Node.js

The first step in implementing MongoDB access from your Node.js applications is to add the MongoDB driver to your application project. The MongoDB Node.js driver is the officially supported native Node.js driver for MongoDB. It has by far the best implementation and is sponsored by MongoDB.

This book cannot cover all the details about the driver. For additional information, go to http://mongodb.github.io/node-mongodb-native/ to read the documentation for the MongoDB Node.js driver. The documentation is reasonably organized although a bit rough around the edges.

Thanks to the Node.js modular framework, adding the MongoDB Node.js driver to your project is a simple `npm` command. From your project root directory, execute the following command using a console prompt:

```
npm install mongodb
```

A `node_modules` directory is created if it is not already there, and the `mongodb` driver module is installed under it. Once that is done, your Node.js application files can use the `require('mongodb')` command to access the `mongodb` module functionality.

Connecting to MongoDB from Node.js

Once you have installed the `mongodb` module using the `npm` command, you can begin accessing MongoDB from your Node.js applications by opening up a connection to the MongoDB server. The connection acts as your interface to create, update, and access data in the MongoDB database.

Accessing MongoDB is best done through the `MongoClient` class in the `mongodb` module. This class provides two main methods to create connections to MongoDB. One is to create an instance of the `MongoClient` object and then use that object to create and manage the MongoDB connection. The other method uses a connection string to connect. Either of these options works well.

Understanding the Write Concern

Before connecting to and updating data on a MongoDB server, you need to decide what level of write concern you want to implement on your connection. *Write concern* describes the guarantee that the MongoDB connection provides when reporting on the success of a write operation. The strength of the write concern determines the level of guarantee.

A stronger write concern tells MongoDB to wait until the write has successfully been written to disk completely before responding back, whereas a weaker write concern may only wait until MongoDB has successfully scheduled the change to be written before responding back. The downside of stronger write concerns is speed. The stronger a write concern, the longer MongoDB waits to respond to the client connection, thus making write requests slower.

From a MongoDB driver connection perspective, the write concern can be set to one of the levels listed in Table 13.1. This level is set on the server connection and applies to all connections to the server. If a write error is detected, then an error is returned in the callback function of the write request.

Table 13.1 **Write concern levels for MongoDB connections**

Level	Description
`-1`	Ignores network errors.
`0`	No write acknowledgement is required.
`1`	Write acknowledgement is requested.
`2`	Write acknowledgement is requested across primary and one secondary server in the replica set.
`majority`	Write acknowledgement is requested across a majority of servers in the replica set.

Connecting to MongoDB from Node.js Using the `MongoClient` Object

Using a `MongoClient` object to connect to MongoDB involves creating an instance of the client, opening a connection to the database, authenticating to the database if necessary, and then handling logout and closure as needed.

To connect to MongoDB via a `MongoClient` object, first create an instance of the `MongoClient` object using the following syntax:

```
var client = new MongoClient();
```

After you have created the `MongoClient`, you still need to open a connection to the MongoDB server database using the `connect(url, options, callback)` method. The `url` is composed of several components listed in Table 13.2. The following syntax is used for these options:

```
mongodb://[username:password@]host[:port][/[database][?options]]
```

For example, to connect to a MongoDB database named `MyDB` on a host named `MyDBServer` on port `8088`, you would use the following URL:

```
client.connect('mongodb://MyDBServer:8088/MyDB');
```

Table 13.2 **`MongoClient` connection `url` components**

Option	Description
`mongodb://`	Specifies that this string is using a MongoDB connection format.
`username`	(Optional) Specifies the user name to use when authenticating.
`password`	(Optional) Specifies the password to use when authenticating.
`host`	Specifies the host name or address of the MongoDB server. You can specify multiple `host:port` combinations to connect to multiple MongoDB servers by separating them by a comma. For example: `mongodb://host1:270017,host2:27017,host3:27017/testDB`
`port`	Specifies the port to use when connecting to the MongoDB server. Default is `27017`.
`database`	Specifies the database name to connect to. Default is `admin`.
`options`	Specifies the `key/value` pairs of options to use when connecting. These same options can be specified in the `dbOpt` and `serverOpt` parameters.

In addition to the connection `url` information, you can also provide an `options` object that specifies how the `MongoClient` object creates and manages the connection to MongoDB. This `options` object is the second parameter to the `connect()` method.

For example, the following code shows connecting to MongoDB with a reconnect interval of 500 and a connection timeout of 1000 milliseconds:

```
client.connect ('mongodb://MyDBServer:8088/MyDB',
                { connectTimeoutMS: 1000,
                  reconnectInterval: 500 },
                function(err, db){ . . . });
```

Table 13.3 lists the most important settings in the `options` object that you can set when defining the `MongoClient` object. The `callback` method is called back with an `error` as the first parameter if the connection fails or with a `MongoClient` object as the second parameter if the connection is successful.

Table 13.3 **Options used to create the server object for the `MongoClient`**

Option	Description
`readPreference`	Specifies which read preference to use when reading objects from a replica set. Setting the read preference allows you to optimize read operations. For example, read only from secondary servers to free up primary. ▪ `ReadPreference.PRIMARY` ▪ `ReadPreference.PRIMARY_PREFERRED` ▪ `ReadPreference.SECONDARY` ▪ `ReadPreference.SECONDARY_PREFERRED` ▪ `ReadPreference.NEAREST`
`ssl`	A Boolean that, when true, specifies that the connection uses SSL. The `mongod` also needs to be configured with SSL. If you are using `ssl`, you can also specify the `sslCA`, `sslCert`, `sslKey`, and `sslPass` options to set the SSL certificate authority, certificate, key, and password.
`poolSize`	Specifies the number of connections to use in the connection pool for the server. Default is `5`, meaning there can be up to five connections to the database shared by the `MongoClient`.
`ReconnectInterval`	Specifies the amount of time in milliseconds that the server waits between retries.
`auto_reconnect`	A Boolean that, when `true`, specifies whether the client will try to re-create the connection when an error is encountered.
`readConcern`	Sets the read concern for the collection.
`W`	Sets the write concern. (See Table 13.1.)
`wTimeOut`	Sets the timeout value of the write concern.
`reconnectTries`	Sets the number of times the server attempts to reconnect.
`nodelay`	A Boolean that specifies a no-delay socket.
`keepAlive`	Specifies the keepalive amount for the socket.
`connectionTimeOut`	Specifies the amount of time in milliseconds for the connection to wait before timing out.
`socketTimeOut`	Specifies the amount of time in milliseconds for a socket send to wait before timing out.

The callback function accepts an `error` as the first parameter, and a `Db` object instance as the second parameter. If an error occurs, the `Db` object instance will be `null`; otherwise, you can use it to access the database because the connection will already be created and authenticated.

While in the callback function, you can access the MongoDB database using the `Db` object passed in as the second parameter. When you are finished with the connection, call `close()` on the `Db` object to close the connection.

Listing 13.1 shows an example of using the connection `url` method. The connection is specified on line 4. Notice that the `callback` function is passed a `Db` object that is already authenticated, so no authentication is necessary.

Listing 13.1 `db_connect_url.js`: Connecting to MongoDB using a connection `url`

```
01 var MongoClient = require('mongodb').MongoClient,
02     Server = require('mongodb').Server;
03 var client = new MongoClient();
04 client.connect('mongodb://dbadmin:test@localhost:27017/testDB',
05                { poolSize: 5, reconnectInterval: 500 },
06 function(err, db) {
07   if (err){
08     console.log("Connection Failed Via Client Object.");
09   } else {
10     console.log("Connected Via Client Object . . .");
11     db.logout(function(err, result) {
12       if(!err){
13         console.log("Logged out Via Client Object . . .");
14       }
15       db.close();
16           console.log("Connection closed . . .");
17     });
18   }
```

Listing 13.1 Output `db_connect_url.js`: Connecting to MongoDB using a connection `url`

```
Connected Via Client Object ...
Logged out Via Client Object ...
Connection closed ...
```

Alternatively, you can create the connection and use the `db` object to authenticate using the `username` and `password` parameters. This allows you to connect to MongoDB without including all parameters in the `url`. In Listing 13.2, this is shown on line 4, where we connect to the database without the `username`, `password`, and `database` specified in the `url`. Then on line 10 we connect to the `testDB` database, and on line 13 we authenticate using the `username` and `password`.

Listing 13.2 `db_connect_object.js`: **Authenticating using the `db` object**

```
var MongoClient = require('mongodb').MongoClient,
    Server = require('mongodb').Server;
var client = new MongoClient();
client.connect('mongodb://localhost:27017'),
          { poolSize: 5, reconnectInterval: 500, },
function(err, db) {
   if (err){
     console.log("Connection Failed Via Client Object.");
   } else {
     var db = db.db("testDB");
   } if (db){
       console.log("Connected Via Client Object . . .");
       db.authenticate("dbadmin", "test", function(err, results){
         if (err){
           console.log("Authentication failed . . .");
           db.close();
           console.log("Connection closed . . .");
         } else {
           console.log("Authenticated Via Client Object . . .");
           db.logout(function(err, result) {
             if(!err){
               console.log("Logged out Via Client Object . . .");
             }
             db.close();
             console.log("Connection closed . . .");
           });
         }
       });
    }
 }
```

Listing 13.2 Output `db_connect_object.js`: **Authenticating using the `db` object**

```
Connected Via Client Object . . .
Authenticated Via Client Object . . .
Logged out Via Client Object . . .
Connection closed . . .
```

Understanding the Objects Used in the MongoDB Node.js Driver

The MongoDB Node.js driver works heavily from structured objects to interact with the database. You have already seen how the `MongoClient` object provides interactions to connect to the database. Other objects represent interactions with the database, collection, administrative functions, and cursors.

The following sections discuss each of these objects and provide the fundamentals that you need to use to implement database functionality in your Node.js applications. You get more exposure to these objects and methods in the next few chapters as well.

Understanding the `Db` Object

The `Db` object inside the MongoDB driver provides access to databases. It acts as a representation of the database allowing you to do things like connect, add users, and access collections. You use `Db` objects heavily to gain and maintain access to databases that you are interacting with in MongoDB.

A `Db` object is typically created when you connect to the database as described in the previous section. Table 13.4 lists the methods that can be called once you have a `Db` object.

Table 13.4 **Methods on the `Db` object**

Method	Description
`open(callback)`	Connects to the database. The `callback` function is executed once the connection has been made. The first parameter to the `callback` is an error if one occurs, and the second is the `Db` object. For example: `function(error, db){}`
`db(dbName)`	Creates a new instance of the `Db` object. The connections sockets are shared with the original.
`close([forceClose], callback)`	Closes the connection to the database. The `forceClose` parameter is a Boolean that, when `true`, forces closure of the sockets. The `callback` function is executed when the database is closed and accepts an `error` object and a `results` object: `function(error, results){}`
`admin()`	Returns an instance of an `Admin` object for MongoDB. (See Table 13.5.)
`collectionInfo([name], callback)`	Retrieves a `Cursor` object that points to collection information for the database. If `name` is specified, then only that collection is returned in the cursor. The `callback` function accepts `error` and `cursor` parameters. `function(err, cursor){}`
`collectionNames(callback)`	Returns a list of the collection names for this database. The `callback` function accepts an `error` and `names` parameters, where `names` is an array of collection names: `function(err, names){}`

Method	Description
`collection(name, [options], callback)`	Retrieves information about a collection and creates an instance of a `Collection` object. The `options` parameter is an object that has properties that define the access to the collection. The `callback` function accepts an `error` and `Collection` object as parameters: `function(err, collection){}`
`collections(callback)`	Retrieves information about all collections in this database and creates an instance of a `Collection` object for each of them. The `callback` function accepts an `error` and `collections` as parameters, where `collections` is an array of `Collection` objects: `function(err, collections){}`
`logout(callback)`	Logs the user out from the database. The `callback` accepts an `error` object and a `results` object: `function(error, results){}`
`authenticate(username, password, callback)`	Authenticates as a user to this database. You can use this to switch between users while accessing the database. The `callback` function accepts an `error` object and a `results` object: `function(error, results){}`
`addUser(username, password, callback)`	Adds a user to this database. The currently authenticated user needs user administration rights to add the user. The `callback` function accepts an `error` object and a `results` object: `function(error, results){}`
`removeUser(username, callback)`	Removes a user from the database. The callback function accepts an `error` object and a `results` object: `function(error, results){}`
`createCollection (collectionName, callback )`	Creates a new collection in the database. The `callback` function accepts an `error` object and a `results` object: `function(error, results){}`
`dropCollection (collectionName, callback )`	Deletes the collection specified by collection name from the database. The `callback` function accepts an `error` object and a `results` object: `function(error, results){}`
`renameCollection (oldName, newName, callback)`	Renames a collection in the database. The `callback` function accepts an `error` object and a `results` object: `function(error, results){}`
`dropDatabase(dbName, callback)`	Deletes this database from MongoDB. The `callback` function accepts an `error` object and a `results` object: `function(error, results){}`

Understanding the `Admin` Object

The `Admin` object is used to perform certain administrative functions on a MongoDB database. The `Admin` object represents a connection specifically to the admin database and provides functionality not included in the `Db` object.

The `Admin` object can be created using the `admin()` method on an instance of the `Db` object or by passing a `Db` object into the constructor. For example, both of the following work fine:

```
var adminDb = db.admin()
var adminDb = new Admin(db)
```

Table 13.5 lists the important administration methods that can be called from an `Admin` object. These methods allow you to perform tasks such as ping the MongoDB server, add and remove users from the admin database, and list databases.

Table 13.5 **Methods on the `Admin` object**

Method	Description
`serverStatus(callback)`	Retrieves status information from the MongoDB server. The `callback` function accepts an `error` object and a `status` object: `function(error, status){}`
`ping(callback)`	Pings the MongoDB server. This is useful since you can use your Node.js apps to monitor the server connection to MongoDB. The `callback` function accepts an `error` object and a `results` object: `function(error, results){}`
`listDatabases (callback)`	Retrieves a list of databases from the server. The callback function accepts an `error` object and a `results` object: `function(error, results){}`
`authenticate(username, password, callback)`	Same as for `Db` in Table 13.4 except for the `admin` database.
`logout(callback)`	Same as for `Db` in Table 13.4 except for the `admin` database.
`addUser(username, password, [options], callback)`	Same as for `Db` in Table 13.4 except for the `admin` database.
`removeUser(username, callback)`	Same as for `Db` in Table 13.4 except for the `admin` database.

Understanding the Collection Object

The `Collection` object represents a collection in the MongoDB database. You use the collection object to access items in the collection, add documents, query documents, and much more.

A `Collection` object can be created using the `collection()` method on an instance of the `Db` object or by passing a `Db` object and collection name into the constructor. The collection should already be created on the MongoDB server previously or using the `createCollection()` method on the `Db` object. For example, both of the following work fine:

```
var collection = db.collection()
var collection = new Collection(db, "myCollection")
db.createCollection("newCollection", function(err, collection){ }
```

Table 13.6 lists the basic methods that can be called from a `Collection` object. These methods allow you to add and modify documents in the collection, find documents, and delete the collection.

Table 13.6 **Basic methods on the `Collection` object**

Method	Description
`insert(docs, [callback])`	Inserts one or more documents into the collection. The `docs` parameter is an object describing the documents. The `callback` function must be included when using a write concern. The `callback` function accepts an `error` object and a `results` object: `function(error, results){}`
`remove([query], [options], [callback])`	Deletes documents from the collection. The `query` is an object used to identify the documents to remove. If no `query` is supplied, all documents are deleted. If a `query` object is supplied, the documents that match the query are deleted. The `options` allow you to specify the write concern using `w`, `wtimeout`, `upsert`, and `options` when modifying documents. The `callback` function must be included when using a write concern. The `callback` function accepts an `error` object and a `results` object: `function(error, results){}`
`rename(newName, callback)`	Renames the collection to `newName`. The `callback` function accepts an `error` object and a `results` object: `function(error, results){}`
`save([doc],[options], [callback])`	Saves the document specified in the `doc` parameter to the database. This is useful if you are making ad-hoc changes to objects and then needing to save them, but is not as efficient as `update()` or `findAndModify`. The `options` allow you to specify the write concern using `w`, `wtimeout`, `upsert`, and `new` options when modifying documents. The `callback` function must be included when using a write concern. The `callback` function accepts an `error` object and a `results` object: `function(error, results){}`

Method	Description
`update(query, update, [options], [callback])`	Updates the documents that match the `query` in the database with the information specified in the `document` parameter. The `options` allow you to specify the write concern using `w`, `wtimeout`, `upsert`, and `new` options when modifying documents. The `callback` function must be included when using a write concern. The `callback` function accepts an `error` object and a `results` object: `function(error, results){}`
`find(query, [options], callback)`	Creates a `Cursor` object that points to a set of documents that match the query. The `options` parameter is an object that allows you to specify the limit, sort, and many more options when building the cursor on the server side. The `callback` function accepts an `error` as the first parameter and the `Cursor` object as the second: `function(error, cursor){}`
`findOne(query, [options], callback)`	Same as `find()` except that only the first document found is included in the `Cursor`.
`findAndModify(query, sort, update, [options], callback)`	Performs modifications on documents that match the `query` parameter. The `sort` parameter determines which objects are modified first. The `doc` parameter specifies the changes to make on the documents. The `options` allow you to specify the write concern using `w`, `wtimeout`, `upsert`, and `new` options when modifying documents. The `callback` function accepts an `error` object and a `results` object: `function(error, results){}`
`findAndRemove(query, sort, [options], callback)`	Removes documents that match the `query` parameter. The `sort` parameter determines which objects are modified first. The `options` allow you to specify the write concern using `w`, `wtimeout`, `upsert`, and new options when deleting documents. The `callback` function accepts an `error` object and a `results` object: `function(error, results){}`
`distinct(key, [query], callback)`	Creates a list of distinct values for a specific document `key` in the collection. If a `query` is specified, only those documents that match the query are included. The `callback` function accepts `error` and `values` parameters, where `values` is an array of distinct values for the specified `key`: `function(error, values){}`
`count([query], callback)`	Counts the number of documents in a collection. If a `query` parameter is used, only documents that match the query are included. The `callback` function accepts an `error` object and a `count` parameter, where `count` is the number of matching documents: `function(error, count){}`

Method	Description
`drop(callback)`	Drops the current collection. The `callback` function accepts an `error` object and a `results` object: `function(error, results){}`
`stats(callback)`	Retrieves the `stats` for the collection. The stats include the `count` of items, `size` on disk, `average` object size, and much more. The `callback` function accepts an `error` object and a `stats` object: `function(error, stats){}`

Understanding the `Cursor` Object

When you perform certain operations on MongoDB using the MongoDB Node.js driver, the results come back as a `Cursor` object. The `Cursor` object acts as a pointer that can be iterated on to access a set of objects in the database. For example, when you use `find()`, the actual documents are not returned in the callback function but a `Cursor` object instead. You can then use the `Cursor` object to read the items in the results.

Because the `Cursor` object can be iterated on, an index to the current location is kept internally. That way you can read items one at a time. Keep in mind that some operations only affect the current item in the `Cursor` and increment the index. Other operations affect all items at the current index forward.

To give you an overview, Table 13.7 lists the basic methods that can be called on the `Cursor` object. These methods allow you to add and modify documents in the collection, find documents, and delete the collection.

Table 13.7 **Basic methods on the `Cursor` Object**

Method	Description
`each(callback)`	Iterates on each item in the `Cursor` from the current cursor index and calls the `callback` each time. This allows you to perform the `callback` function on each item represented by the cursor. The `callback` function accepts an `error` object and the `item` object: `function(err, item){}`
`toArray(callback)`	Iterates through the items in the `Cursor` from the current index forward and returns an array of objects to the callback function. The `callback` function accepts an `error` object and the `items` array: `function(err, items){}`
`nextObject(callback)`	Returns the next object in the `Cursor` to the `callback` function and increments the index. The `callback` function accepts an error object and the item object: `function(err, item){}`

Method	Description
`rewind()`	Resets the `Cursor` to the initial state. This is useful if you encounter an error and need to reset the cursor and begin processing again.
`count(callback)`	Determines the number of items represented by the cursor. The `callback` function accepts an `error` object and the `count` value: `function(err, count){}`
`sort(keyOrList, direction, callback)`	Sorts the items represented by the `Cursor`. The `keyOrList` parameter is a `String` or `Array` of field keys that specifies the field(s) to sort on. The `direction` parameter is a number, where `1` is ascending and `-1` is descending. The `callback` function accepts an `error` as the first parameter and the `sortedCursor` object as the second: `function(err, sortedCursor){}`
`close(callback)`	Closes the `Cursor`, which frees up memory on the client and on the MongoDB server.
`isClosed()`	Returns `true` if the `Cursor` has been closed; otherwise, returns `false`.

Accessing and Manipulating Databases

A great feature of the MongoDB Node.js driver is that it provides the ability to create and manage databases from your Node.js applications. For most installations, you design and implement your databases once and then do not touch them again. However, sometimes it is handy to be able to dynamically create and delete databases.

Listing Databases

To list the databases in your system, you use the `listDatabases()` method on an `Admin` object. That means that you need to create an instance of an `Admin` object first. The list of databases is returned as the second parameter to the callback function and is a simple array of database objects.

The following code shows an example of creating an `Admin` object and then using it to get a list of the databases on the MongoDB server:

```
MongoClient.connect("mongodb://localhost/admin", function(err, db) {
  var adminDB = db.admin();
  adminDB.listDatabases(function(err, databases){
    console.log("Before Add Database List: ");
    console.log(databases);
  });
});
```

Creating a Database

Just as with the MongoDB shell, there is no explicit method for creation of databases. Databases are created automatically whenever a collection or document is added to them. Therefore, to create a new database all you need to do is to use the `db()` method on the `Db` object provided by the `MongoClient` connection to create a new `Db` object instance. Then call `createCollection()` on the new `Db` object instance to create the database.

The following code shows an example of creating a new database named `newDB` after connecting to the server:

```
var MongoClient = require('mongodb').MongoClient;
MongoClient.connect("mongodb://localhost/", function(err, db) {
  var newDB = db.db("newDB");
  newDB.createCollection("newCollection", function(err, collection){
    if(!err){
      console.log("New Database and Collection Created");
    }
  });
});
```

Deleting a Database

To delete a database from MongoDB, you need to get a `Db` object instance that points to that database. Then call the `dropDatabase()` method on that object. It may take a while for MongoDB to finalize the deletion. If you need to verify that the deletion occurred, you can use a timeout to wait for the database delete to occur. For example:

```
newDB.dropDatabase(function(err, results){
  <handle database delete here>
});
```

Creating, Listing, and Deleting Databases Example

To help solidify your understanding of database operations, Listing 13.3 illustrates the full process of creating, listing, and deleting databases. A connection is made to the MongoDB server, and then in lines 4–7 a listing of the current databases is shown. Then in lines 8 and 9, a new database is created by calling `createCollection()`. Inside the `createCollection()` callback handler, the databases are listed again to verify creation.

In lines 15–32 the database is deleted using `dropDatabase()`. Notice that inside the `dropDatabase()` callback a `setTimeout()` timer is implemented to wait for a number of seconds before checking the list of databases to verify that the database was deleted.

Listing 13.3 `db_create_list_delete.js`: **Creating, listing, and deleting databases using the MongoDB Node.js driver**

```
var MongoClient = require('mongodb').MongoClient;
MongoClient.connect("mongodb://localhost/", function(err, db) {
  var adminDB = db.admin();
  adminDB.listDatabases(function(err, databases){
    console.log("Before Add Database List: ");
    console.log(databases);
  });
  var newDB = db.db("newDB");
  newDB.createCollection("newCollection", function(err, collection){
    if(!err){
      console.log("New Database and Collection Created");
      adminDB.listDatabases(function(err, databases){
        console.log("After Add Database List: ");
        console.log(databases);
        db.db("newDB").dropDatabase(function(err, results){
          if(!err){
            console.log("Database dropped.");
            setTimeout(function() {
              adminDB.listDatabases(function(err, results){
                var found = false;
                for(var i = 0; i < results.databases.length; i++) {
                  if(results.databases[i].name == "newDB") found = true;
                }
                if (!found){
                  console.log("After Delete Database List: ");
                  console.log(results);
                }
                db.close();
              });
            }, 15000);
          }
        });
      });
    }
  });
});
```

Listing 13.3 Output `db_create_list_delete.js`: **Creating, listing, and deleting databases using the MongoDB Node.js driver**

```
New Database and Collection Created
After Add Database List:
{ databases:
   [ { name: 'admin', sizeOnDisk: 155648, empty: false },
     { name: 'astro', sizeOnDisk: 73728, empty: false },
```

```
    { name: 'local', sizeOnDisk: 73728, empty: false },
    { name: 'newDB', sizeOnDisk: 8192, empty: false },
    { name: 'testDB', sizeOnDisk: 8192, empty: false },
    { name: 'words', sizeOnDisk: 565248, empty: false } ],
  totalSize: 884736,
  ok: 1 }
After Delete Database List:
{ databases:
   [ { name: 'admin', sizeOnDisk: 155648, empty: false },
     { name: 'astro', sizeOnDisk: 73728, empty: false },
     { name: 'local', sizeOnDisk: 73728, empty: false },
     { name: 'testDB', sizeOnDisk: 8192, empty: false },
     { name: 'words', sizeOnDisk: 565248, empty: false } ],
  totalSize: 876544,
  ok: 1 }
Database dropped.
```

Getting the Status of the MongoDB Server

Another great feature of the `Admin` object is the ability to get status information about the MongoDB server. This information includes the host name, `version`, `uptime`, open cursors, and much more. You can use this information to determine the health and status of the MongoDB server and then make adjustments in your code to handle problem situations.

To display the status of the MongoDB server, you use the `serverStatus()` method on the `Admin` object. Listing 13.4 illustrates creating the `Admin` object and then calling `serverStatus()` and displaying the results.

Listing 13.4 `db_status.js`: **Retrieving and displaying the MongoDB server status**

```
var MongoClient = require('mongodb').MongoClient;
MongoClient.connect("mongodb://localhost/test", function(err, db) {
  var adminDB = db.admin();
  adminDB.serverStatus(function(err, status){
    console.log(status);
    db.close();
  });
});
```

Listing 13.4 Output `db_status.js`: **Retrieving and displaying the MongoDB server status**

```
  version: '3.4.2',
  process: 'mongod',
  pid: 2612,
  uptime: 44775,
```

```
uptimeMillis: 44774694,
uptimeEstimate: 44774,
localTime: 2017-08-11T19:02:25.086Z,
asserts: { regular: 0, warning: 0, msg: 0, user: 0, rollovers: 0 },
connections: { current: 1, available: 999999, totalCreated: 8 },
extra_info:
```

Accessing and Manipulating Collections

A common task for heavily used Node.js installations is the dynamic manipulation of collections. For example, some larger installations give each large customer a separate collection, so as customers sign on or leave, the collections need to be added and deleted. The MongoDB Node.js driver provides easy-to-use methods on the `Db` and `Collection` objects that allow you to manipulate the collections on a database.

Listing Collections

To list the collections in a database, you need to start with a `Db` object that points to the database you want to use. Then you call the `collections()` method on the `Db` object. For example:

```
var newDB = db.db("newDB");
newDB.collections(function(err, collections){})
```

The `collections()` method returns an array of objects that contains the names of the collections, for example:

```
[ { name: 'newDB.system.indexes' },
  { name: 'newDB.newCollection',
    options: { create: 'newCollection' } } ]
```

The resulting value of the `collectionList` parameter would be an array of `Collection` objects.

Creating Collections

You have already seen the process of creating a collection. You simply use the `createCollection()` method on the `Db` object. For example:

```
var newDB = db.db("newDB");
newDB.createCollection("newCollection", function(err, collection){ })
```

The value of the `collection` parameter of the callback is a `Collection` object. You can then use this object to perform tasks such as manipulate the collection or add documents.

Deleting Collections

You can delete a collection in two ways: First, you can call `dropCollection(name)` on the `Db` object, and second, you can call the `drop()` method on the collection object, which is sometimes more convenient; for instance, when you are iterating through a list of `Collection` objects.

The following shows both methods:

```
var myDB = db.db("myDB ");
myDB.dropCollection("collectionA", function(err, results){ })
myDB.collection("collectionB", function(err, collB){
  collB.drop();
})
```

Collection Creation, Listing, and Deleting Example

To illustrate the process of creating, listing, and deleting collections, Listing 13.5 makes a series of chained callbacks that list the collections, create a new collection, and then delete it. The code is basic and easy to follow.

Listing 13.5 `collection_create_list_delete.js`: **Creating, retrieving, and deleting collections on a MongoDB database**

```
var MongoClient = require('mongodb').MongoClient;
MongoClient.connect("mongodb://localhost/", function(err, db) {
  var newDB = db.db("newDB");
  newDB.collections(function(err, collectionNames){
    console.log("Initial collections: ");
    console.log(collectionNames);
    newDB.createCollection("newCollection", function(err, collection){
      newDB.collections(function(err, collectionNames){
        console.log("Collections after creation: ");
        console.log(collectionNames);
        newDB.dropCollection("newCollection", function(err, results){
          newDB.collections(function(err, collectionNames){
            console.log("Collections after deletion: ");
            console.log(collectionNames);
            db.close();
          });
        });
      });
    });
  });
});
```

Listing 13.5 Output `collection_create_list_delete.js`: **Creating, retrieving, and deleting collections on a MongoDB database**

```
Initial collections:
[]
Collections after creation:
[ Collection {
    s:
     { pkFactory: [Object],
       db: [Object],
       topology: [Object],
       dbName: 'newDB',
       options: [Object],
       namespace: 'newDB.newCollection',
       readPreference: [Object],
       slaveOk: true,
       serializeFunctions: undefined,
       raw: undefined,
       promoteLongs: undefined,
       promoteValues: undefined,
       promoteBuffers: undefined,
       internalHint: null,
       collectionHint: null,
       name: 'newCollection',
       promiseLibrary: [Function: Promise],
       readConcern: undefined } } ]
Collections after deletion:
[]
```

Getting Collection Information

Another useful feature of the `Collection` object is the ability to get the statistics for a particular collection. The statistics can give you an idea of how big the collection is, both in number of documents as well as size on disk. You may want to add code that periodically checks the statistics of your collections to determine whether they need to be cleaned up.

Listing 13.6 shows how to access the statistics for a collection by calling the `stats()` method on the `Collection` object.

Listing 13.6 `collection_stat.js`: **Retrieving and displaying the stats for a collection**

```
var MongoClient = require('mongodb').MongoClient;
MongoClient.connect("mongodb://localhost/", function(err, db) {
  var newDB = db.db("newDB");
  newDB.createCollection("newCollection", function(err, collection){
    collection.stats(function(err, stats){
```

```
      console.log(stats);
      db.close();
    });
  });
});
```

Listing 13.6 Output `collection_stat.js`: **Retrieving and displaying the stats for a collection**

```
{ ns: 'newDB.newCollection',
  size: 0,
  count: 0,
  storageSize: 4096,
  capped: false,
  wiredTiger:
   { metadata: { formatVersion: 1 },
     creationString:
     type: 'file',
     uri: 'statistics:table:collection-4-8106062778677821448',
```

Summary

The MongoDB Node.js driver is the officially supported native method for accessing MongoDB from Node.js applications. It is simple to install and easy to incorporate into your Node.js applications. In this chapter you see the various methods and options to connect to a MongoDB database using the `MongoClient` class. You also got to see and work with the `Db`, `Admin`, `Collection`, and `Cursor` classes.

The examples in this chapter took you through creating, viewing, and deleting databases dynamically from your Node.js applications. You also learned how to create, access, and delete collections.

Next

In the next chapter, you work with MongoDB documents. You learn the methods to insert documents into a collection and how to access them. You also learn how to manipulate and delete documents using several different methods.

14

Manipulating MongoDB Documents from Node.js

In Chapter 13, "Getting Started with MongoDB and Node.js," you learned the fundamentals of using the MongoDB Node.js driver to manage and manipulate databases and collections. This chapter expands on those concepts to include manipulation of documents within collections. The MongoDB Node.js driver provides a lot of functionality in the `Collection` class, described in Chapter 13, that allows you to insert, access, modify, and remove documents from collections.

This chapter is broken down into sections that describe the basic document management tasks that you perform on collections, including inserts and deletes. This chapter introduces you to the options that control the behavior of write requests to the database. You also learn about the update structure that MongoDB uses to update documents rather than the long, complex query strings you may have seen in SQL.

Understanding Database Change Options

Several methods discussed in this chapter modify the MongoDB database. When you make changes to the database, the MongoDB Node.js driver needs to know how to handle the connection during the change process. For that reason, each method that changes the database allows you to pass in an optional `options` parameter that can specify some or all of the properties defined in Table 14.1.

Table 14.1 **Options that can be specified in the `options` parameter of database changing requests to define behavior**

Option	Description
`w`	Specifies the write concern level for database connections. See Table 13.1 for the available values.
`wtimeout`	Specifies the amount of time in milliseconds to wait for the write concern to finish. This value is added to the normal connection timeout value.

Option	Description
`fsync`	A Boolean that, when `true`, indicates that write requests wait for `fsync` to finish before returning.
`journal`	A Boolean that, when `true`, indicates that write requests wait for the journal sync to complete before returning.
`serializeFunctions`	A Boolean that, when `true`, indicates that functions attached to objects will be serialized when stored in the document.
`forceServerObjectId`	A Boolean that, when `true`, indicates that any object ID (`_id`) value set by the client is overridden by the server during insert.
`checkKeys`	A Boolean that, when `true`, causes the document keys to be checked when being inserted into the database. The default is `true`. (Warning: Setting this to `false` can open MongoDB up for injection attacks.)
`upsert`	A Boolean that, when `true`, specifies that if no documents match the update request, a new document is created.
`multi`	A Boolean that, when `true`, specifies that if multiple documents match the query in an update request, all documents are updated. When `false`, only the first document found is updated.
`new`	A Boolean that, when `true`, specifies that the newly modified object is returned by the `findAndModify()` method instead of the pre-modified version. The default is `false`.

Understanding Database Update Operators

When performing updates on objects in MongoDB, you need to specify exactly what fields need to be changed and how they need to be changed. Unlike SQL where you create long query strings that define the update, MongoDB allows you to implement an `update` object with operators that define exactly how to change the data in the documents.

You can include as many operators in the `update` object as you need. The format of the `update` object is shown here:

```
{
  <operator>: {<field_operation>, <field_operation>, . . .},
  <operator>: {<field_operation>, <field_operation>, . . .}
  . . .
}
```

For example, consider the following object:

```
{
  name: "myName",
  countA: 0,
  countB: 0,
```

```
  days: ["Monday", "Wednesday"],
  scores: [ {id:"test1", score:94}, {id:"test2", score:85}, {id:"test3", score:97}]
}
```

If you want to increment the `countA` field by `5`, increment `countB` by `1`, set name to "`New Name`", add `Friday` to the `days` array, and sort the `scores` array by the `score` field, you would use the following `update` object:

```
{
  $inc:{countA:5, countB:1},
  $set:{name:"New Name"},
  $push{days:"Friday"},
  $sort:{score:1}
}
```

Table 14.2 lists the operators that can be used in the `update` object when updating documents.

Table 14.2 **Operators that can be specified in the `update` object when performing update operations**

Operator	Description
`$inc`	Increments the value of the field by the specified amount. Operation format: `field:inc_value`
`$rename`	Renames a field. Operation format: `field:new_name`
`$setOnInsert`	Sets the value of a field when a new document is created in the update operation. Operation format: `field:value`
`$set`	Sets the value of a field in an existing document. Operation format: `field:new_value`
`$unset`	Removes the specified field from an existing document. Operation format: `field:""`
`$`	Acts as a placeholder to update the first element that matches the query condition in an update.
`$addToSet`	Adds elements to an existing array only if they do not already exist in the set. Operation format: `array_field:new_value`
`$pop`	Removes the first or last item of an array. If the `pop_value` is `-1`, the first element is removed. If the `pop_value` is `1`, the last element is removed. Operation format: `array_field:pop_value`
`$pullAll`	Removes multiple values from an array. The values are passed in as an array to the field name. Operation format: `array_field:[value1, value2, ...]`

Operator	Description
$pull	Removes items from an array that match a query statement. The query statement is a basic query object with field names and values to match. Operation format: array_field: [<query>]
$push	Adds an item to an array. Simple array format: array_field:new_value Object array format: array_field:{field:value}
$each	Modifies the $push and $addToSet operators to append multiple items for array updates. Operation format: array_field:{$each:[value1, ...]}
$slice	Modifies the $push operator to limit the size of updated arrays.
$sort	Modifies the $push operator to reorder documents stored in an array. Operation format: array_field:{$slice:<num>}
$bit	Performs bitwise AND and OR updates of integer values. Operation format: integer_field:{and:<integer>} integer_field:{or:<integer>}

Adding Documents to a Collection

Another common task when interacting with MongoDB databases is inserting documents into collections. To insert a document, you first create a JavaScript object that represents the document that you want to store. You create a JavaScript object because the BSON format that MongoDB uses is based on JavaScript notation.

Once you have a JavaScript version of your new document, you can store it in the MongoDB database using the insert() method on an instance of the Collection object connected to the database. The following shows the syntax for the insert() method:

```
insert(docs, [options], callback)
```

The docs parameter can be a single document object or an array of document objects. The options parameter specifies the database change options described previously in Table 14.1. The callback function is required if you are implementing a write concern in the options. The first parameter of the callback function is an error, and the second parameter is an array of the documents inserted into the collection.

Listing 14.1 illustrates a basic example of inserting documents. Lines 2–9 show a function that accepts the Collection object and an object to insert. The insert() method is called, and the resulting array of inserted objects (one at time in this case) is displayed on the console. Lines 10–13 open up the connection to the MongoDB server, clear out the nebulae collection, and then re-create it to provide a clean slate. Then lines 14–19 call addObject() for a series of JavaScript objects describing nebulae.

Listing 14.1 `doc_insert.js`: **Inserting documents into a collection**

```
var MongoClient = require('mongodb').MongoClient;
function addObject(collection, object){
  collection.insert(object, function(err, result){
    if(!err){
      console.log("Inserted : ");
      console.log(result);
    }
  });
}
MongoClient.connect("mongodb://localhost/", function(err, db) {
  var myDB = db.db("astro");
  myDB.dropCollection("nebulae");
  myDB.createCollection("nebulae", function(err, nebulae){
    addObject(nebulae, {ngc:"NGC 7293", name:"Helix",
      type:"planetary",location:"Aquila"});
    addObject(nebulae, {ngc:"NGC 6543", name:"Cat's Eye",
      type:"planetary",location:"Draco"});
    addObject(nebulae, {ngc:"NGC 1952", name: "Crab",
      type:"supernova",location:"Taurus"});
  });
});
```

Listing 14.1 Output `doc_insert.js`: **Inserting documents into a collection**

```
Inserted :
{ result: { ok: 1, n: 1 },
  ops:
   [ { ngc: 'NGC 7293',
       name: 'Helix',
       type: 'planetary',
       location: 'Aquila',
       _id: 598e04b98e397c0f8464bb99 } ],
  insertedCount: 1,
  insertedIds: [ 598e04b98e397c0f8464bb99 ] }
Inserted :
{ result: { ok: 1, n: 1 },
  ops:
   [ { ngc: 'NGC 6543',
       name: 'Cat\'s Eye',
       type: 'planetary',
       location: 'Draco',
       _id: 598e04b98e397c0f8464bb9a } ],
  insertedCount: 1,
  insertedIds: [ 598e04b98e397c0f8464bb9a ] }
```

```
Inserted :
{ result: { ok: 1, n: 1 },
  ops:
   [ { ngc: 'NGC 1952',
       name: 'Crab',
       type: 'supernova',
       location: 'Taurus',
       _id: 598e04b98e397c0f8464bb9b } ],
  insertedCount: 1,
  insertedIds: [ 598e04b98e397c0f8464bb9b ] }
```

Getting Documents from a Collection

A common task that you perform on data stored in a MongoDB is retrieving one or more documents. For example, consider product information for products on a commercial website. The information is stored once but retrieved many times.

The retrieval of data sounds simple; however, it can become complex as you filter, sort, limit, and aggregate the results. In fact, Chapter 15, "Accessing MongoDB from Node.js," is entirely devoted to the complexities of retrieving data.

This section introduces you to the simple basics of the `find()` and `findOne()` methods of the `Collection` object to make it easier to understand the code examples in this chapter. The syntax for `find()` and `findOne()` are shown here:

```
find(query, [options], callback)
findOne(query, [options], callback)
```

Both `find()` and `findOne()` accept a `query` object as the first parameter. The `query` object contains properties that are matched against fields in the documents. Documents that match the `query` are included in the list. The `options` parameter is an object that specifies everything else about the search for documents, such as the limit, sort, and what to return.

The `callback` function is where `find()` and `findOne()` differ. The `find()` method returns a `Cursor` object that can be iterated on to retrieve documents, whereas the `findOne()` method returns a single object.

Listing 14.2 illustrates the basic use of handling the results of `find()` and `findOne()`. The code in lines 5–10 implements `find()`. Notice that the result is a `Cursor` object. To display the results, the `toArray()` method is called, which iterates through the `Cursor` object and builds a basic JavaScript array of objects. This allows you to operate on the documents as you would a normal set of JavaScript objects.

Lines 11–18 also use the `find()` method; however, the `each()` method is used to iterate through the `Cursor` object one document at a time. For each iteration, a single document is retrieved from MongoDB and passed in as the second parameter to the `callback` function.

Lines 19–22 implement the `findOne()` method. Notice the simple query on the `type` field. The `callback` function receives the object and outputs it to the screen.

Listing 14.2 `doc_find.js`: **Finding documents in a MongoDB collection**

```
var MongoClient = require('mongodb').MongoClient;
MongoClient.connect("mongodb://localhost/", function(err, db) {
  var myDB = db.db("astro");
  myDB.collection("nebulae", function(err, nebulae){
    nebulae.find(function(err, items){
      items.toArray(function(err, itemArr){
        console.log("Document Array: ");
        console.log(itemArr);
      });
    });
    nebulae.find(function(err, items){
      items.each(function(err, item){
        if(item){
          console.log("Singular Document: ");
          console.log(item);
        }
      });
    });
    nebulae.findOne({type:'planetary'}, function(err, item){
      console.log("Found One: ");
      console.log(item);
    });
  });
});
```

Listing 14.2 Output `doc_find.js`: **Finding documents in a MongoDB collection**

```
Document Array:
[ { _id: 598e04b98e397c0f8464bb99,
    ngc: 'NGC 7293',
    name: 'Helix',
    type: 'planetary',
    location: 'Aquila' },
  { _id: 598e04b98e397c0f8464bb9b,
    ngc: 'NGC 1952',
    name: 'Crab',
    type: 'supernova',
    location: 'Taurus' },
  { _id: 598e04b98e397c0f8464bb9a,
    ngc: 'NGC 6543',
    name: 'Cat\'s Eye',
    type: 'planetary',
    location: 'Draco' } ]
Singular Document:
{ _id: 598e04b98e397c0f8464bb99,
```

```
  ngc: 'NGC 7293',
  name: 'Helix',
  type: 'planetary',
  location: 'Aquila' }
Singular Document:
{ _id: 598e04b98e397c0f8464bb9b,
  ngc: 'NGC 1952',
  name: 'Crab',
  type: 'supernova',
  location: 'Taurus' }
Singular Document:
{ _id: 598e04b98e397c0f8464bb9a,
  ngc: 'NGC 6543',
  name: 'Cat\'s Eye',
  type: 'planetary',
  location: 'Draco' }
Found One:
{ _id: 598e04b98e397c0f8464bb99,
  ngc: 'NGC 7293',
  name: 'Helix',
  type: 'planetary',
  location: 'Aquila' }
```

Updating Documents in a Collection

Once objects have been inserted into a collection you often need to update them from time to time as the data changes. The MongoDB Node.js driver provides several methods for updating documents. The most commonly used is the `update()` method, which is versatile and easy to implement. The following shows the syntax for the `update()` method:

```
update(query, update, [options], [callback])
```

The `query` parameter is a document used to identify which document(s) you want to change. The request matches the properties and values in the query with the fields and values of the object, and only those matching the query are updated. The `update` parameter is an object that specifies the changes to make to the documents that match the query. Table 14.2 lists the operators that can be used.

The `options` parameter specifies the database change options described previously in Table 14.1. The `callback` function is required if you are implementing a write concern in the `options`. The first parameter of the `callback` function is an `error`, and the second parameter is an array of the `documents` inserted into the collection.

When updating multiple documents with the `update()` call, you can isolate writes to protect the documents from other writes using the `$isolate:1` property in the `query`. This doesn't provide an all or nothing atomic write; it simply inhibits other write processes from updating the same objects you are writing to. For example:

```
update({type:"Planetary", $isolated:1}, {updated:true}, {multi:true})
```

Listing 14.3 illustrates updating multiple objects using the `update()` method. Lines 9–19 implement the `update()` method and callback to change the type `planetary` to `Planetary` and add a new field named `updated`. Notice that the `$set` operator is used to set values. Also notice that `upsert` is `false` so that new documents will not be created, `multi` is `true` so that multiple documents will get updated, and `w` is `1` so that the request will wait for the write operation before returning.

Listing 14.3 `doc_update.js`: **Updating multiple documents in the database**

```
01 var MongoClient = require('mongodb').MongoClient;
02 MongoClient.connect("mongodb://localhost/", function(err, db) {
03   var myDB = db.db("astro");
04   myDB.collection("nebulae", function(err, nebulae){
05     nebulae.find({type:"planetary"}, function(err, items){
06       items.toArray(function(err, itemArr){
07         console.log("Before Update: ");
08         console.log(itemArr);
09         nebulae.update({type:"planetary", $isolated:1},
10                        {$set:{type:"Planetary", updated:true}},
11                        {upsert:false, multi:true, w:1},
12                        function(err, results){
13           nebulae.find({type:"Planetary"}, function(err, items){
14             items.toArray(function(err, itemArr){
15               console.log("After Update: ");
16               console.log(itemArr);
17               db.close();
18             });
19           });
20         });
21       });
22     });
23   });
24 });
```

Listing 14.3 Output `doc_update.js`: **Updating multiple documents in the database**

```
Before Update:
[ { _id: 598e04b98e397c0f8464bb99,
    ngc: 'NGC 7293',
    name: 'Helix',
    type: 'planetary',
    location: 'Aquila' },
```

```
  { _id: 598e04b98e397c0f8464bb9a,
    ngc: 'NGC 6543',
    name: 'Cat\'s Eye',
    type: 'planetary',
    location: 'Draco' } ]
After Update:
[ { _id: 598e04b98e397c0f8464bb99,
    ngc: 'NGC 7293',
    name: 'Helix',
    type: 'Planetary',
    location: 'Aquila',
    updated: true },
  { _id: 598e04b98e397c0f8464bb9a,
    ngc: 'NGC 6543',
    name: 'Cat\'s Eye',
    type: 'Planetary',
    location: 'Draco',
    updated: true } ]
```

Atomically Modifying Documents in a Collection

The `Collection` object provides the `findAndModify()` function that performs an atomic write on a single document in the collection. This is useful if you need to ensure that no other processes can write to your document at the same time. The following shows the syntax for the `findAndModify()` method:

```
findAndModify(query, sort, update, [options], callback)
```

The `query` parameter is a document used to identify which document you want to modify. The request matches the properties and values in the query with the fields and values of the object, and only those matching the query are modified.

The `sort` parameter is an array of `[field, sort_order]` pairs that specify which fields to sort on when finding the item to modify. The `sort_order` value is `1` for ascending, `-1` for descending. The `update` parameter is an object that specifies the changes to make to the documents that match the query. Table 14.2 lists the operators that can be used.

The `options` parameter specifies the database change options described previously in Table 14.1.The `callback` function is required if you are implementing a write concern in the options. The first parameter of the `callback` function is an `error`, and the second parameter is the `object` being modified. If `new` is set to `true` in the `options`, then the newly modified object is returned. If `new` is set to `false`, the pre-modified object is returned. Getting back the pre-modified object can be useful if you need to verify changes or store the original somewhere else.

Listing 14.4 illustrates performing an atomic write on a single object in the MongoDB database. Lines 9–15 implement the `findAndModify()` operation. Notice that the `sort` value is `[['name', 1]]`, which means sort on `name` in ascending order. Also notice that `w` is `1` to enable the write concern, and `new` is set to `true` so that the modified object is returned in the `callback` function and displayed on the console.

Listing 14.4 `doc_modify.js`: **Atomically modifying a document using** `findAndModify()`

```
var MongoClient = require('mongodb').MongoClient;
MongoClient.connect("mongodb://localhost/", function(err, db) {
  var myDB = db.db("astro");
  myDB.collection("nebulae", function(err, nebulae){
    nebulae.find({type:"supernova"}, function(err, items){
      items.toArray(function(err, itemArr){
        console.log("Before Modify: ");
        console.log(itemArr);
        nebulae.findAndModify({type:"supernova"}, [['name', 1]],
            {$set: {type:"Super Nova", "updated":true}},
            {w:1, new:true}, function(err, doc){
          console.log("After Modify: ");
          console.log(doc);
          db.close();
        });
      });
    });
  });
});
```

Listing 14.4 Output `doc_modify.js`: **Atomically modifying a document using** `findAndModify()`

```
Before Modify:
[ { _id: 598e04b98e397c0f8464bb9b,
    ngc: 'NGC 1952',
    name: 'Crab',
    type: 'supernova',
    location: 'Taurus' } ]
After Modify:
{ lastErrorObject: { updatedExisting: true, n: 1 },
  value:
   { _id: 598e04b98e397c0f8464bb9b,
     ngc: 'NGC 1952',
     name: 'Crab',
     type: 'Super Nova',
     location: 'Taurus',
     updated: true },
  ok: 1 }
```

Saving Documents in a Collection

The `save()` method on `Collection` objects is interesting. It can be used to insert or update a document in the database. The `save()` method is not as efficient as `insert()` or `update()` but can be easier to implement in some circumstances. For example, when you are making ad-hoc changes to objects already retrieved from MongoDB, you can use `save()` without having to implement the `query` and `update` objects of the `update()` method.

The following shows the syntax of the `save()` method:

```
save(doc, [options], [callback])
```

The `doc` parameter is the document object you want to save to the collection. The `options` parameter specifies the database change options described previously in Table 14.1. The `callback` function is required if you are implementing a write concern in the options. The first parameter of the `callback` function is an `error`, and the second parameter is the `object` that was just saved to the collection.

Typically when using `save()`, the `document` object either is a completely new JavaScript object that you want to add to the collection, or it is an object you have already gotten back from the collection, made changes to, and now you want to save those changes back to the database.

Listing 14.5 illustrates retrieving an object from the database, modifying it, and saving it back to the database using the `save()` method. The `save()` method and `callback` are implemented in lines 9–15. Notice that the `save()` method is much simpler to use than the `update()` and `findAndModify()` methods. Also notice that the `savedItem` is returned to the callback function and displayed on the console.

Listing 14.5 `doc_save.js`: **Updating and saving an existing document using** `save()`

```
01 var MongoClient = require('mongodb').MongoClient;
02 MongoClient.connect("mongodb://localhost/", function(err, db) {
03   var myDB = db.db("astro");
04   myDB.collection("nebulae", function(err, nebulae){
05     nebulae.findOne({type:"supernova"}, function(err, item){
06       console.log("Before Save: ");
07       console.log(item);
08       item.info = "Some New Info";
09       nebulae.save(item, {w:1}, function(err, results){
10         nebulae.findOne({_id:item._id}, function(err, savedItem){
11           console.log("After Save: ");
12           console.log(savedItem);
13           db.close();
14         });
15       });
16     });
17   });
18 });
```

Listing 14.5 Output `doc_save.js`: **Updating and saving an existing document using** `save()`

```
Before Save:
{ _id: 598e06c4efe25f1c0cf4932e,
  ngc: 'NGC 1952',
  name: 'Crab',
  type: 'supernova',
  location: 'Taurus' }
After Save:
{ _id: 598e06c4efe25f1c0cf4932e,
  ngc: 'NGC 1952',
  name: 'Crab',
  type: 'supernova',
  location: 'Taurus',
  info: 'Some New Info' }
```

Upserting Documents in Collection

Another type of update that you can perform on documents is the `upsert`, which is the combination of updating the object if it exists or inserting it if it does not. Normal updates do not automatically insert objects because they incur a cost to determine whether the object exists. If you know that an object does exist, a normal `update()` is much more efficient, as is an `insert()` if you know the document does not already exist.

To implement an `upsert`, all you need to do is include the `upsert:true` option in the `update()` method's `options` object. This tells the request to try to update the object if it exists; otherwise, the object specified will be inserted.

Listing 14.6 illustrates using `upsert` with the `update()` method. The `update()` in lines 9–12 creates the object because it does not exist. Then in line 18 the `_id` value of the inserted document is retrieved and used in the query of the `update()` in lines 19–22 to ensure an existing document will be found and updated. Notice that initially there are no documents matching the descriptor, and then after the first update the document is inserted and then modified after the second update.

Listing 14.6 `doc_upsert.js`: **Using** `upsert` **to insert new documents or update existing ones**

```
01 var MongoClient = require('mongodb').MongoClient;
02 MongoClient.connect("mongodb://localhost/", function(err, db) {
03   var myDB = db.db("astro");
04   myDB.collection("nebulae", function(err, nebulae){
05     nebulae.find({type:"diffuse"}, function(err, items){
06       items.toArray(function(err, itemArr){
07         console.log("Before Upsert: ");
```

```
    console.log(itemArr);
    nebulae.update({type:"diffuse"},
      {$set: {ngc:"NGC 3372", name:"Carina",
          type:"diffuse",location:"Carina"}},
      {upsert:true, w:1,forceServerObjectId:false},
      function(err, results){
     nebulae.find({type:"diffuse"}, function(err, items){
      items.toArray(function(err, itemArr){
       console.log("After Upsert 1: ");
       console.log(itemArr);
       var itemID = itemArr[0]._id;
       nebulae.update({_id:itemID},
         {$set: {ngc:"NGC 3372", name:"Carina",
             type:"Diffuse",location:"Carina"}},
         {upsert:true, w:1}, function(err, results){
        nebulae.findOne({_id:itemID}, function(err, item){
         console.log("After Upsert 2: ");
         console.log(item);
         db.close();
        });
       });
      });
     });
    });
   });
  });
 });
});
```

Listing 14.6 Output `doc_upsert.js`: **Using** `upsert` **to insert new documents or update existing ones**

```
Before Upsert:
[]
After Upsert 1:
[ { _id: 598e070aac7bf01c2a209601,
    type: 'diffuse',
    ngc: 'NGC 3372',
    name: 'Carina',
    location: 'Carina' } ]
After Upsert 2:
{ _id: 598e070aac7bf01c2a209601,
  type: 'Diffuse',
  ngc: 'NGC 3372',
  name: 'Carina',
  location: 'Carina' }
```

Deleting Documents from a Collection

At times, you need to delete documents from your MongoDB collection to keep space consumption down, improve performance, and keep things clean. The `remove()` method on `Collection` objects makes it simple to delete documents from a collection. The syntax for the `remove()` method is shown here:

```
remove([query], [options], [callback])
```

The `query` parameter is a document used to identify which document(s) you want to delete. The request matches the properties and values in the `query` with the fields and values of the object, and only those matching the query are deleted. If no `query` is provided, all the documents in the collection are deleted.

The `options` parameter specifies the database change options described previously in Table 14.1. The `callback` function is required if you are implementing a write concern in the options. The first parameter of the `callback` function is an `error`, and the second parameter is a `count` of the documents deleted.

Listing 14.7 illustrates using the `remove()` method to delete objects from the collection. The `remove()` and `callback` implemented in lines 9–18 query the collection for documents that have type `planetary` and delete them from the collection. Notice that the `results` parameter of the `callback` is the `count` of documents deleted. Listing 14.7 Output shows the output of Listing 14.7 with the before delete and after delete documents in the collection.

Listing 14.7 `doc_delete.js`: Deleting documents from a collection

```
01 var MongoClient = require('mongodb').MongoClient;
02 MongoClient.connect("mongodb://localhost/", function(err, db) {
03   var myDB = db.db("astro");
04   myDB.collection("nebulae", function(err, nebulae){
05     nebulae.find(function(err, items){
06       items.toArray(function(err, itemArr){
07         console.log("Before Delete: ");
08         console.log(itemArr);
09         nebulae.remove({type:"planetary"}, function(err, results){
10           console.log("Deleted " + results + " documents.");
11           nebulae.find(function(err, items){
12             items.toArray(function(err, itemArr){
13               console.log("After Delete: ");
14               console.log(itemArr);
15               db.close();
16             });
17           });
18         });
19       });
20     });
21   });
22 });
```

Listing 14.7 Output `doc_delete.js`: **Deleting documents from a collection**

```
Before Delete:
[ { _id: 598e06c4efe25f1c0cf4932c,
    ngc: 'NGC 7293',
    name: 'Helix',
    type: 'planetary',
    location: 'Aquila' },
  { _id: 598e06c4efe25f1c0cf4932d,
    ngc: 'NGC 6543',
    name: 'Cat\'s Eye',
    type: 'planetary',
    location: 'Draco' },
  { _id: 598e06c4efe25f1c0cf4932e,
    ngc: 'NGC 1952',
    name: 'Crab',
    type: 'supernova',
    location: 'Taurus',
    info: 'Some New Info' },
  { _id: 598e070aac7bf01c2a209601,
    type: 'Diffuse',
    ngc: 'NGC 3372',
    name: 'Carina',
    location: 'Carina' } ]
Delete:
 {"n":0,"ok":1}
After Delete:
[ { _id: 598e06c4efe25f1c0cf4932c,
    ngc: 'NGC 7293',
    name: 'Helix',
    type: 'planetary',
    location: 'Aquila' },
  { _id: 598e06c4efe25f1c0cf4932d,
    ngc: 'NGC 6543',
    name: 'Cat\'s Eye',
    type: 'planetary',
    location: 'Draco' },
  { _id: 598e06c4efe25f1c0cf4932e,
    ngc: 'NGC 1952',
    name: 'Crab',
    type: 'supernova',
    location: 'Taurus',
    info: 'Some New Info' },
  { _id: 598e070aac7bf01c2a209601,
    type: 'Diffuse',
    ngc: 'NGC 3372',
    name: 'Carina',
    location: 'Carina' } ]
```

Removing a Single Document from a Collection

You can also delete documents from the database using the `findAndRemove()` method. This is similar to the `findAndModify()` method in its syntax and application. The following shows the syntax for the `findAndRemove()` method:

```
findAndRemove(query, sort, [options], callback)
```

The `query` parameter is a document used to identify which document you want to remove. The request matches the properties and values in the `query` with the fields and values of the object, and only those matching the `query` are removed.

The `sort` parameter is an array of `[field, sort_order]` pairs that specify which fields to sort on when finding the item to remove. The `sort_order` is a value of `1` for ascending and `-1` for descending. The `options` parameter specifies the database change options described previously in Table 14.1. The first parameter of the `callback` function is an `error`, and the second parameter is the `results` of the document deletion.

Listing 14.8 illustrates deleting a document using the `findAndRemove()` method. The `findAndRemove()` and callback are implemented in lines 9–18. The items of type `planetary` are searched on. The sort order `[['name', 1]]` specifies to sort the items by `name` in ascending order. Listing 14.8 Output shows that the `Cat's Eye` entry was deleted and not the `Helix` because of the sort order.

Listing 14.8 `doc_delete_one.js`: **Deleting single documents using** `findAndRemove()`

```
01 var MongoClient = require('mongodb').MongoClient;
02 MongoClient.connect("mongodb://localhost/", function(err, db) {
03   var myDB = db.db("astro");
04   myDB.collection("nebulae", function(err, nebulae){
05     nebulae.find(function(err, items){
06       items.toArray(function(err, itemArr){
07         console.log("Before Delete: ");
08         console.log(itemArr);
09         nebulae.findAndRemove({type:"planetary"}, [['name', 1]],
10                               {w:1}, function(err, results){
11           console.log("Deleted " + results + " documents.");
12           nebulae.find(function(err, items){
13             items.toArray(function(err, itemArr){
14               console.log("After Delete: ");
15               console.log(itemArr);
16               db.close();
17             });
18           });
19         });
20       });
21     });
22   });
23 });
```

Listing 14.8 Output `doc_delete_one.js`: **Deleting single documents using** `findAndRemove()`

```
Before Delete:
[ { _id: 598e06c4efe25f1c0cf4932c,
    ngc: 'NGC 7293',
    name: 'Helix',
    type: 'planetary',
    location: 'Aquila' },
  { _id: 598e06c4efe25f1c0cf4932d,
    ngc: 'NGC 6543',
    name: 'Cat\'s Eye',
    type: 'planetary',
    location: 'Draco' },
  { _id: 598e06c4efe25f1c0cf4932e,
    ngc: 'NGC 1952',
    name: 'Crab',
    type: 'supernova',
    location: 'Taurus',
    info: 'Some New Info' },
  { _id: 598e070aac7bf01c2a209601,
    type: 'Diffuse',
    ngc: 'NGC 3372',
    name: 'Carina',
    location: 'Carina' } ]
Deleted [object Object] documents.
After Delete:
[ { _id: 598e06c4efe25f1c0cf4932c,
    ngc: 'NGC 7293',
    name: 'Helix',
    type: 'planetary',
    location: 'Aquila' },
  { _id: 598e06c4efe25f1c0cf4932e,
    ngc: 'NGC 1952',
    name: 'Crab',
    type: 'supernova',
    location: 'Taurus',
    info: 'Some New Info' },
  { _id: 598e070aac7bf01c2a209601,
    type: 'Diffuse',
    ngc: 'NGC 3372',
    name: 'Carina',
    location: 'Carina' } ]
```

Summary

The MongoDB Node.js driver provides several methods to insert, access, modify, and remove documents from collections. `insert()`, `save()`, and even `update()` with `upsert` can be used to insert documents into the database. The `update()`, `save()`, and `findAndModify()` methods can be used to update existing documents. The `remove()` and `findAndRemove()` methods can be used to delete documents.

The methods used to update documents in the database include options that allow you to define the write concern, journaling, and other settings that control the behavior of the write request and response. Also the update structure that MongoDB uses to update documents is much easier to implement and maintain than the long, complex query strings you may have seen in SQL.

Next

Chapter 15 expands on the concept of finding objects in the database. This chapter introduced you to `find()` and `findOne()`, but Chapter 15 includes more complex examples of how to filter, sort, and limit the results returned when finding objects in a collection.

15

Accessing MongoDB from Node.js

In Chapter 14, "Manipulating MongoDB Documents from Node.js," you learned how to create and manipulate documents and got a brief glimpse into finding them using the `find()` method. This chapter takes a deeper look at accessing documents in a MongoDB collection using the MongoDB Node.js driver module.

There is much more to accessing documents than just returning everything in a collection. This chapter covers using the `query` object to limit which documents are returned as well as methods to limit the fields and number of documents in the query results. You also see how to count the number of documents that match query criteria without actually retrieving them from the server. This chapter also covers some advanced aggregation techniques to group the results and even generate a new fully aggregated set of documents.

Introducing the Data Set

For the purpose of introducing you to the various methods of accessing data, all the data used for examples in this chapter comes from the same data set. The data set is a collection that contains various information about 5,000 words. This provides a large enough data set to implement the necessary examples.

The structure of objects in this data set is as follows and should be fairly intuitive (which is why it was selected). This document structure gives us fields that are strings, integers, arrays, subdocuments, and arrays of subdocuments:

```
{
  word: <word>,
  first: <first_letter>,
  last: <last_letter>,
  size: <character_count>,
  letters: [<array_of_characters_in_word_no_repeats>],
```

```
  stats: {
    vowels:<vowel_count>, consonants:<consonant_count>},
  charsets: [
    {
      "type": <consonants_vowels_other>,
      "chars": [<array_of_characters_of_type_in_word>]},
    . . .
  ],
}
```

Understanding Query Objects

Throughout this chapter the various methods of data all use a `query` object of some sort to define which documents to retrieve from a MongoDB collection. The `query` object is just a standard JavaScript object with special property names that are understood by the MongoDB Node.js driver. These property names match closely the native queries that you can perform inside the MongoDB client, which makes it nice to be able to transfer back and forth.

The properties of the `query` object are called *operators* because they operate on the data to determine whether a document should be included in the result set. These operators are used to match the values of fields in the document against specific criteria.

For example, to find all documents with a `count` value greater than `10` and `name` value equal to `test`, the `query` object would be

```
{count:{$gt:10}, name:'test'}
```

The operator `$gt` specifies documents with a `count` field larger than `10`. The standard colon syntax of `name:'test'` is also an operator that specifies that the `name` field must equal `test`. Notice that the `query` object has multiple operators. You can include several different operators in the same query.

When specifying field names in a `query` object, you can use dot notation to specify subdocument fields. For example, consider the following object format:

```
{
  name:"test",
  stats: { height:74, eyes:'blue' }
}
```

You can query users that have blue eyes using the following `query` object:

```
{stats.eyes:'blue'}
```

Table 15.1 lists the more commonly used operators.

Table 15.1 **`query` object operators that define the result set returned by MongoDB requests**

Operator	Description
`$eq`	Matches documents with fields that have a value equal to the value specified.
`$gt`	Matches values that are greater than the value specified in the query. For example: `{size:{$gt:5}}`
`$gte`	Matches values that are equal to or greater than the value specified in the query. For example: `{size:{$gte:5}}`
`$in`	Matches any of the values that exist in an array specified in the query. For example: `{name:{$in:['item1', 'item2']}}`
`$lt`	Matches values that are less than the value specified in the query. For example: `{size:{$lt:5}}`
`$lte`	Matches values that are less than or equal to the value specified in the query. For example: `{size:{$lte:5}}`
`$ne`	Matches all values that are not equal to the value specified in the query. For example: `{name:{$ne:"badName"}}`
`$nin`	Matches values that do not exist in an array specified to the query. For example: `{name:{$nin:['item1', 'item2']}}`
`$or`	Joins query clauses with a logical OR; returns all documents that match the conditions of either clause. For example: `{$or:[{size:{$lt:5}}, {size:{$gt:10}}]}`
`$and`	Joins query clauses with a logical AND; returns all documents that match the conditions of both clauses. For example: `{$and:[{size:{$gt:5}}, {size:{$lt:10}}]}`
`$not`	Inverts the effect of a query expression and returns documents that do not match the query expression. For example: `{$not:{size:{$lt:5}}}`
`$nor`	Joins query clauses with a logical NOR; returns all documents that fail to match both clauses. For example: `{$nor:{size:{$lt:5}},{name:"myName"}}`
`$exists`	Matches documents that have the specified field. For example: `{specialField:{$exists:true}}`
`$type`	Selects documents if a field is of the specified BSON type number. Table 11.1 lists the different BSON type numbers. For example: `{specialField: {$type:<BSONtype>}}`
`$mod`	Performs a modulo operation on the value of a field and selects documents with a specified result. The value for the modulo operation is specified as an array with the first number being the number to divide by and the second being the remainder. For example: `{number:{$mod: [2,0]}}`

Operator	Description
$regex	Selects documents where values match a specified regular expression. For example: {myString:{$regex:'some.*exp'}}
$all	Matches arrays that contain all elements specified in the query. For example: {myArr:{$all:['one','two','three']}}
$elemMatch	Selects documents if an element in the array of subdocuments has fields that match all the specified $elemMatch conditions. For example: {myArr:{$elemMatch:{value:{$gt:5},size:{$lt:3}}}}
$size	Selects documents if the array field is a specified size. For example: {myArr:{$size:5}}

Understanding Query Options Objects

In addition to the query object, most of the methods of retrieving documents using the MongoDB Node.js driver also include an options object. The options object allows you to define the behavior of the request when retrieving documents. These options allow you to limit the result set, sort items while creating the result set, and much more.

Table 15.2 lists the options that can be set on methods that retrieve documents from the MongoDB server. Not all of these methods are available on every request. For example, when counting items that match the query it doesn't make sense to specify a limit on the result.

Table 15.2 **Options that can be specified in the options object when querying documents**

Option	Description
limit	Specifies the maximum number of documents to return.
sort	Specifies the sort order of documents as an array of [field, <sort_order>] elements where sort order is 1 for ascending and -1 for descending. For example: sort:[['name':1],['value':-1]]
fields	Specifies an object whose fields match fields that should be included or excluded from the returned documents. A value of 1 means include, a value of 0 means exclude. You can only include or exclude, not both. For example: fields:{name:1,value:1}
skip	Specifies the number of documents from the query results to skip before returning a document. Typically used when paginating result sets.
hint	Forces the query to use specific indexes when building the result set. For example: hint:{'_id':1}
explain	Returns an explanation of what will happen when performing the query on the server instead of actually running the query. This is essential when trying to debug/optimize complex queries.

Option	Description
`snapshot`	{Boolean, default:false}; specifies whether to use a snapshot query.
`timeout`	A Boolean; when true, the cursor is allowed to timeout.
`maxScan`	Specifies the maximum number of documents to scan when performing a query before returning. This is useful if you have a collection that has millions of objects and you don't want queries to run on forever.
`comment`	Specifies a string that is printed out in the MongoDB logs. This can help when troubleshooting because you can identify queries more easily.
`readPreference`	Specifies whether you want to read from a primary or secondary replica or just the nearest MongoDB server in the replica set to perform the query.
`numberOfRetries`	Specifies the number of timeout retries to perform on the query before failing. The default is 5.
`partial`	A Boolean that, when `true`, indicates the cursor will return partial results when querying against data shared between sharded systems.

Finding Specific Sets of Documents

You were introduced to the `find()` method of the `Collection` object in Chapter 14. This method returns a `Cursor` object to the callback function providing access to the documents. If no query is specified, all documents are returned, which is rarely the case. Instead, you need a subset of documents that match a set of criteria.

To limit the resulting documents included in the `find()` method, you apply a `query` object that limits the documents returned in the `Cursor`. Listing 15.1 illustrates using `query` objects in a `find` statement.

Listing 15.1 performs a bunch of different queries against the word collection described earlier in this chapter. You should already recognize all the connection code as well as the code used in `displayWords()` to iterate through the cursor and display only the word names in the documents.

In line 20, the following query is used to find words starting with a, b, or c:

```
{first:{$in: ['a', 'b', 'c']}}
```

In line 23, the following query is used to find words longer than 12 letters:

```
{size:{$gt: 12}}
```

In line 26, the following query is used to find words with an even number of letters:

```
{size:{$mod: [2,0]}}
```

In line 29, the following query is used to find words with exactly 12 letters:

```
{letters:{$size: 12}}
```

In lines 32 and 33, the following query is used to find words that both begin and end with a vowel:

```
{$and: [{first:{$in: ['a', 'e', 'i', 'o', 'u']}},
        {last:{$in: ['a', 'e', 'i', 'o', 'u']}}]}
```

In line 37, the following query is used to find words that contain more than 6 vowels:

```
{"stats.vowels":{$gt:6}}
```

In line 40, the following query is used to find words that contain all of the vowels:

```
{letters:{$all: ['a','e','i','o','u']}}
```

In line 44, the following query is used to find words with non-alphabet characters:

```
{otherChars: {$exists:true}}
```

In line 47, a bit more challenging query is used. The `$elemMatch` operator is used to match the `charsets` subdocuments. The `$and` operator forces the `type` field to equal `other` and the `chars` array field to be exactly `2`:

```
{charsets:{$elemMatch:{$and:[{type:'other'},{chars:{$size:2}}]}}}
```

Listing 15.1 `doc_query.js`: **Finding a specific set of documents in a MongoDB collection**

```
01 var MongoClient = require('mongodb').MongoClient;
02 MongoClient.connect("mongodb://localhost/", function(err, db) {
03   var myDB = db.db("words");
04   myDB.collection("word_stats", findItems);
05   setTimeout(function(){
06     db.close();
07   }, 3000);
08 });
09 function displayWords(msg, cursor, pretty){
10   cursor.toArray(function(err, itemArr){
11     console.log("\n"+msg);
12     var wordList = [];
13     for(var i=0; i<itemArr.length; i++){
14       wordList.push(itemArr[i].word);
15     }
16     console.log(JSON.stringify(wordList, null, pretty));
17   });
18 }
19 function findItems(err, words){
20   words.find({first:{$in: ['a', 'b', 'c']}}, function(err, cursor){
21     displayWords("Words starting with a, b or c: ", cursor);
22   });
23   words.find({size:{$gt: 12}}, function(err, cursor){
```

```
    displayWords("Words longer than 12 characters: ", cursor);
  });
  words.find({size:{$mod: [2,0]}}, function(err, cursor){
    displayWords("Words with even Lengths: ", cursor);
  });
  words.find({letters:{$size: 12}}, function(err, cursor){
    displayWords("Words with 12 Distinct characters: ", cursor);
  });
  words.find({$and: [{first:{$in: ['a', 'e', 'i', 'o', 'u']}},
                     {last:{$in: ['a', 'e', 'i', 'o', 'u']}}]},
             function(err, cursor){
    displayWords("Words that start and end with a vowel: ", cursor);
  });
  words.find({"stats.vowels":{$gt:6}}, function(err, cursor){
    displayWords("Words containing 7 or more vowels: ", cursor);
  });
  words.find({letters:{$all: ['a','e','i','o','u']}},
             function(err, cursor){
    displayWords("Words with all 5 vowels: ", cursor);
  });
  words.find({otherChars: {$exists:true}}, function(err, cursor){
    displayWords("Words with non-alphabet characters: ", cursor);
  });
  words.find({charsets:{$elemMatch:{$and:[{type:'other'},
                                          {chars:{$size:2}}]}}}},
             function(err, cursor){
    displayWords("Words with 2 non-alphabet characters: ", cursor);
  });
}
```

Listing 15.1 Output doc_query.js: **Finding a specific set of documents in a MongoDB collection**

```
Words longer than 12 characters:
["international","administration","environmental","responsibility","investigation",
"communication","understanding","significantly","representative"…]
Words with 12 Distinct characters:
["uncomfortable","accomplishment","considerably"]
Words with non-alphabet characters:
["don't","won't","can't","shouldn't","e-mail","long-term","so-called","mm-hmm",
"t-shirt","and/or","health-care","full-time","o'clock","self-esteem"…]
Words starting with a, b or c:
["and","a","at","as","all","about","also","any","after","ask","another","american",
"against","again","always","area","around","away","among"…]
Words containing 7 or more vowels:
["identification","questionnaire","organizational","rehabilitation"]
Words that start and end with a vowel:
["a","also","area","ago","able","age","agree","available","anyone","article","argue",
"arrive","above","audience","assume","alone","achieve","attitude"…]
```

```
Words with all 5 vowels:
["education","educational","regulation","evaluation","reputation","communicate",
"dialogue","questionnaire","simultaneously","equation","automobile"…]
Words with 2 non-alphabet characters:
["two-third's","middle-class'"]
Words with even Lengths:
["be","of","in","to","have","it","that","he","with","on","do","this","they","at","we",
"from","by","or","as","what","go","if","my","make","know","will","up"…]
```

Counting Documents

When accessing document sets in MongoDB, you may want to only get a count first before deciding to retrieve a set of documents. There are several reasons to count specific document sets. Performing a count is much less intensive on the MongoDB side because when retrieving documents using the `find()` and other methods, temporary objects such as cursors must be created and maintained by the server.

Also, when performing operations on the resulting set of documents from a `find()`, you should be aware of how many documents you are going to be dealing with, especially in larger environments. Sometimes all you want is a count. For example, if you need to know how many users are configured in your application, you could just count the number of documents in the `users` collection.

The `count()` method on the `Collection` object allows you to get a simple count of documents that match the `query` object criteria. The `count()` method is formatted exactly the same way as the `find()` method, as shown below, and performs the query and options parameters in exactly the same manner.

```
count([query], [options], callback)
```

If no `query` is specified, the `count()` returns a count of all the documents in the database. The `callback` function should accept an `error` as the first argument and the `count` as an integer as the second.

Listing 15.2 illustrates using the `count()` method with the same queries performed with `find()` in Listing 15.1. The output in Listing 15.2 Output shows that instead of a `Cursor` a simple integer is returned and displayed.

Listing 15.2 `doc_count.js`: **Counting specific sets of documents in a MongoDB collection**

```
var MongoClient = require('mongodb').MongoClient;
MongoClient.connect("mongodb://localhost/", function(err, db) {
  var myDB = db.db("words");
  myDB.collection("word_stats", countItems);
  setTimeout(function(){
    db.close();
  }, 3000);
});
function countItems(err, words){
```

```
  words.count({first:{$in: ['a', 'b', 'c']}}, function(err, count){
    console.log("Words starting with a, b or c: " + count);
  });
  words.count({size:{$gt: 12}}, function(err, count){
    console.log("Words longer than 12 characters: " + count);
  });
  words.count({size:{$mod: [2,0]}}, function(err, count){
    console.log("Words with even Lengths: " + count);
  });
  words.count({letters:{$size: 12}}, function(err, count){
    console.log("Words with 12 Distinct characters: " + count);
  });
  words.count({$and: [{first:{$in: ['a', 'e', 'i', 'o', 'u']}},
                      {last:{$in: ['a', 'e', 'i', 'o', 'u']}}]},
              function(err, count){
    console.log("Words that start and end with a vowel: " + count);
  });
  words.count({"stats.vowels":{$gt:6}}, function(err, count){
    console.log("Words containing 7 or more vowels: " + count);
  });
  words.count({letters:{$all: ['a','e','i','o','u']}},
              function(err, count){
    console.log("Words with all 5 vowels: " + count);
  });
  words.count({otherChars: {$exists:true}}, function(err, count){
    console.log("Words with non-alphabet characters: " + count);
  });
  words.count({charsets:{$elemMatch:{$and:[{type:'other'},
              {chars:{$size:2}}]}}},
              function(err, count){
    console.log("Words with 2 non-alphabet characters: " + count);
  });
}
```

Listing 15.2 Output `doc_count.js`: **Counting specific sets of documents in a MongoDB collection**

```
Words starting with a, b or c: 964
Words longer than 12 characters: 64
Words that start and end with a vowel: 227
Words with even Lengths: 2233
Words with 12 Distinct characters: 3
Words containing 7 or more vowels: 4
Words with non-alphabet characters: 24
Words with all 5 vowels: 16
Words with 2 non-alphabet characters: 2
```

Limiting Result Sets

When finding complex documents on larger systems, you often want to limit what is being returned to reduce the impact on the network, including the memory on both the server and client. You can limit the result sets that match a specific query in three ways: You can simply only accept a limited number of documents, you can limit the fields returned, or you can page the results and get them in chunks.

Limiting Results by Size

The simplest method to limit the amount of data returned in a `find()` or other query request is to use the `limit` option in the `options` parameter when performing the request. The `limit` parameter, shown below, allows only a fixed number of items to be returned with the `Cursor` object. This can save you from accidentally retrieving more objects than your application can handle:

```
limit:<maximum_documents_to_return>
```

Listing 15.3 illustrates limiting the results of a `find()` request by using the `limit:5` option in the `options` object. The output in Listing 15.3 Output shows that when `limit` is used only five words are retrieved.

Listing 15.3 `doc_limit.js`: **Limiting the specific set of documents in a MongoDB collection**

```
var MongoClient = require('mongodb').MongoClient;
MongoClient.connect("mongodb://localhost/", function(err, db) {
  var myDB = db.db("words");
  myDB.collection("word_stats", limitFind);
  setTimeout(function(){
    db.close();
  }, 3000);
});
function displayWords(msg, cursor, pretty){
  cursor.toArray(function(err, itemArr){
    console.log("\n"+msg);
    var wordList = [];
    for(var i=0; i<itemArr.length; i++){
      wordList.push(itemArr[i].word);
    }
    console.log(JSON.stringify(wordList, null, pretty));
  });
}
function limitFind(err, words){
  words.count({first:'p'}, function(err, count){
    console.log("Count of words starting with p : " + count);
  });
  words.find({first:'p'}, function(err, cursor){
```

```
    displayWords("Words starting with p : ", cursor);
  });
  words.find({first:'p'}, {limit:5}, function(err, cursor){
    displayWords("Limiting words starting with p : ", cursor);
  });
}
```

Listing 15.3 Output `doc_limit.js`: **Limiting the specific set of documents in a MongoDB collection**

```
Count of words starting with p : 353

Limiting words starting with p :
["people","put","problem","part","place"]
Words starting with p :
["people","put","problem","part","place","program","play","point","provide","power",
"political","pay"…]
```

Limiting Fields Returned in Objects

Another effective method of limiting the resulting data when retrieving documents is to limit which fields are returned. Documents may have many different fields that are useful in some circumstance but not in others. You should consider which fields should be included when retrieving documents from the MongoDB server and only request the ones necessary.

To limit the fields returned from the server, use the `fields` option of the `options` object. The `fields` option enables you to either include or exclude fields by setting the value of the document field to `0` for exclude or `1` for include. You cannot mix includes and excludes in the same expression.

For example, to exclude the fields `stats`, `value`, and `comments` when returning a document, you would use the following `fields` option:

```
{fields:{stats:0, value:0, comments:0}}
```

Often it is easier to just include a few fields; for example, if you want to include only the `name` and `value` fields of documents, you would use

```
{fields:{name:1, value:1}}
```

Listing 15.4 illustrates using the `fields` option to reduce the amount of data returned from the server by excluding fields or specifying fields to include.

Listing 15.4 `doc_fields.js`: **Limiting the fields returned with a set of documents**

```
var MongoClient = require('mongodb').MongoClient;
MongoClient.connect("mongodb://localhost/", function(err, db) {
  var myDB = db.db("words");
  myDB.collection("word_stats", limitFields);
```

```
  setTimeout(function(){
    db.close();
  }, 3000);
});
function limitFields(err, words){
  words.findOne({word:'the'}, {fields:{charsets:0}},
                function(err, item){
    console.log("Excluding fields object: ");
    console.log(JSON.stringify(item, null, 2));
  });
  words.findOne({word:'the'}, {fields:{word:1,size:1,stats:1}},
                function(err, item){
    console.log("Including fields object: ");
    console.log(JSON.stringify(item, null, 2));
  });
}
```

Listing 15.4 Output `doc_fields.js`: **Limiting the fields returned with a set of documents**

```
Excluding fields object:
{
  "_id": "58f04c8c6ec5050becd012c5",
  "word": "the",
  "first": "t",
  "last": "e",
  "size": 3,
  "letters": [
    "t",
    "h",
    "e"
  ],
  "stats": {
    "vowels": 1,
    "consonants": 2
  }
}
Including fields object:
{
  "_id": "58f04c8c6ec5050becd012c5",
  "word": "the",
  "size": 3,
  "stats": {
    "vowels": 1,
    "consonants": 2
  }
}
```

Paging Results

Paging is a common method of reducing the number of documents returned. Paging involves specifying a number of documents to skip in the matching set as well as a limit on the documents returned. Then the skip value is incremented each time by the number returned the previous time.

To implement paging on a set of documents, you need to implement the `limit` and `skip` options on the `options` object. The `skip` option specifies a number of documents to skip before returning documents. By moving the `skip` value each time, you get another set of documents you can effectively page through in the data set. Also, always include a `sort` option when paging data to ensure the order is always the same. For example, the following statements find documents 1–10, then 11–20, and 21–30:

```
collection.find({},{sort:[['_id':1]], skip:0, limit:10},
                function(err, cursor){});
collection.find({},{sort:[['_id':1]], skip:10, limit:10}, function(err, cursor){});
collection.find({},{sort:[['_id':1]], skip:20, limit:10}, function(err, cursor){});
```

Listing 15.5 illustrates using `limit` and `skip` to page through a specific set of documents. Each time a new `find()` request is implemented, which more closely mimics what would happen when handling paging requests from a webpage. Listing 15.5 Output shows the output of Listing 15.5. Notice that words are retrieved 10 at a time.

> **Warning**
>
> If the data on the system changes in such a way that it affects the results of the query, the skip may miss some items or include items again in a subsequent paged request.

Listing 15.5 `doc_paging.js`: **Paging results from a specific set of documents in a MongoDB collection**

```
var util = require('util');
var MongoClient = require('mongodb').MongoClient;
MongoClient.connect("mongodb://localhost/", function(err, db) {
  var myDB = db.db("words");
  myDB.collection("word_stats", function(err, collection){
    pagedResults(err, collection, 0, 10);
  });
});
function displayWords(msg, cursor, pretty){
  cursor.toArray(function(err, itemArr){
    console.log("\n"+msg);
    var wordList = [];
    for(var i=0; i<itemArr.length; i++){
      wordList.push(itemArr[i].word);
    }
    console.log(JSON.stringify(wordList, null, pretty));
```

```
  });
}
function pagedResults(err, words, startIndex, pageSize){
  words.find({first:'v'},
             {limit:pageSize, skip:startIndex, sort:[['word',1]]},
             function(err, cursor){
    cursor.count(true, function(err, cursorCount){
      displayWords("Page Starting at " + startIndex, cursor);
      if (cursorCount === pageSize){
        pagedResults(err, words, startIndex+pageSize, pageSize);
      } else {
        cursor.db.close();
      }
    });
  });
}
```

Listing 15.5 Output `doc_paging.js`: **Paging results from a specific set of documents in a MongoDB collection**

```
Page Starting at 0
["vacation","vaccine","vacuum","valid","validity","valley","valuable","value",
"van","vanish"]

Page Starting at 10
["variable","variation","variety","various","vary","vast","vegetable","vehicle",
"vendor","venture"]

Page Starting at 20
["verbal","verdict","version","versus","vertical","very","vessel","veteran","via",
"victim"]

Page Starting at 30
["victory","video","view","viewer","village","violate","violation","violence",
"violent","virtual"]

Page Starting at 40
["virtually","virtue","virus","visible","vision","visit","visitor","visual",
"vital","vitamin"]

Page Starting at 50
["vocal","voice","volume","voluntary","volunteer","vote","voter","voting","vs",
"vulnerable"]

Page Starting at 60
[]
```

Sorting Result Sets

An important aspect of retrieving documents from a MongoDB database is the ability to get it in a sorted format. This is especially helpful if you are only retrieving a certain number, such as the top 10, or if you are paging the requests. The `options` object provides the `sort` option that allows you to specify the sort order and direction of one or more fields in the document.

The `sort` option is specified using an array of `[field,<sort_order>]` pairs, where `sort_order` is `1` for ascending and `-1` for descending. For example, to sort on the `name` field descending first and then the `value` field ascending you would use the following:

```
sort:[['value':-1]['name':1]]
```

Listing 15.6 illustrates using the `sort` option to find and sort lists of words in different ways. Notice that in line 29 the words are sorted by size first and then by last letter, whereas in line 33 they are sorted by last letter first and then by size. The two different sort orders result in different lists of words returned.

Listing 15.6 `doc_sort.js`**: Sorting results of a** `find()` **request for a set of documents in a MongoDB collection**

```
01 var MongoClient = require('mongodb').MongoClient;
02 MongoClient.connect("mongodb://localhost/", function(err, db) {
03   var myDB = db.db("words");
04   myDB.collection("word_stats", sortItems);
05   setTimeout(function(){
06     db.close();
07   }, 3000);
08 });
09 function displayWords(msg, cursor, pretty){
10   cursor.toArray(function(err, itemArr){
11     console.log("\n"+msg);
12     var wordList = [];
13     for(var i=0; i<itemArr.length; i++){
14       wordList.push(itemArr[i].word);
15     }
16     console.log(JSON.stringify(wordList, null, pretty));
17   });
18 }
19 function sortItems(err, words){
20   words.find({last:'w'}, function(err, cursor){
21     displayWords("Words ending in w: ", cursor);
22   });
23   words.find({last:'w'}, {sort:{word:1}}, function(err, cursor){
24     displayWords("Words ending in w sorted ascending: ", cursor);
25   });
26   words.find({last:'w'}, {sort:{word:-1}}, function(err, cursor){
27     displayWords("Words ending in w sorted, descending: ", cursor);
28   });
```

```
  words.find({first:'b'}, {sort:[['size',-1],['last',1]]},
             function(err, cursor){
    displayWords("B words sorted by size then by last letter: ", cursor);
  });
  words.find({first:'b'}, {sort:[['last',1],['size',-1]]},
             function(err, cursor){
    displayWords("B words sorted by last letter then by size: ", cursor);
  });
}
```

Listing 15.6 Output `doc_sort.js`: **Sorting results of a `find()` request for a set of documents in a MongoDB collection**

```
Words ending in w:
["know","now","how","new","show","few","law","follow","allow","grow","low","view",
"draw","window","throw","interview","tomorrow"…
Words ending in w sorted ascending:
["allow","arrow","below","blow","borrow","bow","chew","cow","crew","draw","elbow",
"eyebrow","fellow","few","flow"…
Words ending in w sorted, descending:
["yellow","wow","withdraw","window","widow","view","tomorrow","throw","swallow",
"straw","somehow","snow"…
B words sorted by size then by last letter:
["businessman","background","basketball","biological","behavioral","boyfriend",
"beginning"…
B words sorted by last letter then by size:
["bacteria","banana","bomb","bulb","basic","background","boyfriend","backyard",
"balanced","behind","beyond"…
```

Finding Distinct Field Values

A useful query against a MongoDB collection is to get a list of the distinct values for a single field in a set of documents. *Distinct* means that even though there are thousands of documents, you only want to know the unique values that exist.

The `distinct()` method on `Collection` objects allows you to find a list of distinct values for a specific field. The syntax for the `distinct()` method is shown below:

```
distinct(key, [query], [options],callback)
```

The `key` parameter is the string value of the field name you want to get values for. You can specify subdocuments using the dot syntax such as `stats.count`. The `query` parameter is an object with standard query options defined in Table 15.1. The `options` parameter is an `options` object that allows you to define the `readPreference` option defined in Table 15.2. The `callback` function should accept an `error` as the first parameter, and the `results` parameter, which is an array of distinct values for the field specified in the `key` parameter, as the second.

Listing 15.7 illustrates finding the distinct values in the words collection. Notice that a query in line 14 limits the words to those starting with u. In line 18, to access the `stats.vowels` field, the dot syntax is used.

Listing 15.7 `doc_distinct.js`: **Finding distinct field values in a specific set of documents in a MongoDB collection**

```
01 var MongoClient = require('mongodb').MongoClient;
02 MongoClient.connect("mongodb://localhost/", function(err, db) {
03   var myDB = db.db("words");
04   myDB.collection("word_stats", distinctValues);
05   setTimeout(function(){
06     db.close();
07   }, 3000);
08 });
09 function distinctValues(err, words){
10   words.distinct('size', function(err, values){
11     console.log("\nSizes of words: ");
12     console.log(values);
13   });
14   words.distinct('first', {last:'u'}, function(err, values){
15     console.log("\nFirst letters of words ending in u: ");
16     console.log(values);
17   });
18   words.distinct('stats.vowels', function(err, values){
19     console.log("\nNumbers of vowels contained in words: ");
20     console.log(values);
21   });
22 }
```

Listing 15.7 Output `doc_distinct.js`: **Finding distinct field values in a specific set of documents in a MongoDB collection**

```
Sizes of words:
[ 3, 2, 1, 4, 5, 9, 6, 7, 8, 10, 11, 12, 13, 14 ]

First letters of words ending in u:
[ 'y', 'm', 'b' ]

Numbers of vowels contained in words:
[ 1, 2, 0, 3, 4, 5, 6, 7 ]
```

Grouping Results

When performing operations on large data sets, it is often useful to group the results based on the distinct values of one or more fields in a document. This could be done in code after retrieving the documents; however, it is much more efficient to have MongoDB do it for you as part of a single request that is already iterating through the documents.

To group the results of a query together, you can use the `group()` method on the `Collection` object. The group request first collects all the documents that match a `query`, and then adds a group object to an array based on distinct values of a set of `keys`, performs operations on the group objects, and returns the array of group objects. The syntax for the `group()` method is shown below:

```
group(keys, query, initial, reduce, finalize, command, [options], callback)
```

The parameters of the `group()` method are described in the following list:

- **`keys`:** This can be an object, array, or function expressing the keys to group by. The simplest method is to specify the key(s) in an object such as `{field1:true, field2:true}` or an array such as

  `['first', 'last']`.

- **`query`:** Query object that defines which documents to be included in the initial set. See Table 15.1 for a list of query options.
- **`initial`:** Specifies an initial group object to use when aggregating data while grouping. An initial object is created for each distinct set of `keys`. The most common use is a counter that tracks a count of items that match the keys. For example:

  `{"count":0}`

- **`reduce`:** This is a `function(obj, prev)` with two parameters, `obj` and `prev`. This function is executed on each document that matches the query. The `obj` parameter is the current document, and the `prev` parameter is the object created by the `initial` parameter. You can then use the `obj` object to update the `prev` object with new values such as counts or sums. For example, to increment the count value you would use:

  `function(obj, prev) { prev.count++; }`

- **`finalize`:** This is a `function(obj)` that accepts one parameter, `obj`, which is the final object resulting from the `initial` parameter and updated as `prev` in the `reduce` function. This function is called on the resulting object for each distinct `key` before returning the array in the response.
- **`command`:** A Boolean that, when `true`, specifies the command will run using the internal group command instead of `eval()`. The default is `true`.
- **`options`:** This object allows you to define the `readPreference` option.
- **`callback`:** This accepts an `error` as the first parameter and an array of the `results` objects as the second.

Listing 15.8 illustrates implementing grouping of words based on various key sets. Lines 10–18 implement a basic grouping of words by first and last letter. The query in line 11 limits the words to those beginning with o and ending with a vowel. The initial object for each has a count property only, which is updated for each matching document in the function on line 13.

Lines 19–28 add the concept of summing the total vowels in the documents while grouping them together by incrementing the `prev.totalVowels` with the `obj.stats.vowels` value in line 23. Then lines 29–40 show the use of a finalize function that adds a new `obj.total` property to the group objects that is a sum of the `obj.vowels` and `obj.consonants` properties of the object.

Listing 15.8 `doc_group.js`: **Grouping a set of documents by specific fields in a MongoDB collection**

```
01 var MongoClient = require('mongodb').MongoClient;
02 MongoClient.connect("mongodb://localhost/", function(err, db) {
03   var myDB = db.db("words");
04   myDB.collection("word_stats", groupItems);
05   setTimeout(function(){
06     db.close();
07   }, 3000);
08 });
09 function groupItems(err, words){
10   words.group(['first','last'],
11               {first:'o',last:{$in:['a','e','i','o','u']}},
12               {"count":0},
13               function (obj, prev) { prev.count++; }, true,
14               function(err, results){
15         console.log("\n'O' words grouped by first and last" +
16                     " letter that end with a vowel: ");
17         console.log(results);
18   });
19   words.group(['first'],
20               {size:{$gt:13}},
21               {"count":0, "totalVowels":0},
22               function (obj, prev) {
23                 prev.count++; prev.totalVowels += obj.stats.vowels;
24               }, {}, true,
25               function(err, results){
26     console.log("\nWords grouped by first letter larger than 13: ");
27     console.log(results);
28   });
29   words.group(['first'],{}, {"count":0, "vowels":0, "consonants":0},
30               function (obj, prev) {
31                 prev.count++;
32                 prev.vowels += obj.stats.vowels;
33                 prev.consonants += obj.stats.consonants;
34               },function(obj){
35                 obj.total = obj.vowels + obj.consonants;
```

```
          }, true,
          function(err, results){
      console.log("\nWords grouped by first letter with totals: ");
      console.log(results);
  });
}
```

Listing 15.8 Output `doc_group.js`: **Grouping a set of documents by specific fields in a MongoDB collection**

```
'O' words grouped by first and last letter that end with a vowel:
[ { first: 'o', last: 'e', count: 21 },
  { first: 'o', last: 'o', count: 1 },
  { first: 'o', last: 'a', count: 1 } ]

Words grouped by first letter larger than 13:
[ { first: 'a', count: 4, totalVowels: 22 },
  { first: 'r', count: 5, totalVowels: 30 },
  { first: 'c', count: 2, totalVowels: 11 },
  { first: 't', count: 2, totalVowels: 10 },
  { first: 'i', count: 4, totalVowels: 24 },
  { first: 'd', count: 2, totalVowels: 11 },
  { first: 's', count: 1, totalVowels: 6 },
  { first: 'o', count: 1, totalVowels: 7 } ]

Words grouped by first letter with totals:
[ { first: 't',
    count: 250,
    vowels: 545,
    consonants: 1017,
    total: 1562 },
  { first: 'b',
    count: 218,
    vowels: 417,
    consonants: 769,
    total: 1186 },
  { first: 'a',
    count: 295,
    vowels: 913,
    consonants: 1194,
    total: 2107 },
  { first: 'o',
    count: 118,
    vowels: 356,
    consonants: 435,
```

```
  total: 791 },
{ first: 'i',
  count: 189,
  vowels: 655,
  consonants: 902,
  total: 1557 },
{ first: 'h',
  count: 139,
  vowels: 289,
  consonants: 511,
  total: 800 },
{ first: 'f',
  count: 203,
  vowels: 439,
  consonants: 774,
  total: 1213 },
{ first: 'y', count: 16, vowels: 31, consonants: 50, total: 81 },
{ first: 'w',
  count: 132,
  vowels: 255,
  consonants: 480,
  total: 735 },
{ first: 'd',
  count: 257,
  vowels: 675,
  consonants: 1102,
  total: 1777 },
{ first: 'c',
  count: 451,
  vowels: 1237,
  consonants: 2108,
  total: 3345 },
{ first: 's',
  count: 509,
  vowels: 1109,
  consonants: 2129,
  total: 3238 },
{ first: 'n', count: 82, vowels: 205, consonants: 314, total: 519 },
{ first: 'g',
  count: 112,
  vowels: 236,
  consonants: 414,
  total: 650 },
{ first: 'm',
  count: 200,
```

```
    vowels: 488,
    consonants: 778,
    total: 1266 },
  { first: 'k', count: 21, vowels: 33, consonants: 70, total: 103 },
  { first: 'u', count: 58, vowels: 173, consonants: 233, total: 406 },
  { first: 'p',
    count: 353,
    vowels: 902,
    consonants: 1575,
    total: 2477 },
  { first: 'j', count: 33, vowels: 72, consonants: 114, total: 186 },
  { first: 'l',
    count: 142,
    vowels: 307,
    consonants: 503,
    total: 810 },
  { first: 'v', count: 60, vowels: 163, consonants: 218, total: 381 },
  { first: 'e',
    count: 239,
    vowels: 788,
    consonants: 1009,
    total: 1797 },
  { first: 'r',
    count: 254,
    vowels: 716,
    consonants: 1011,
    total: 1727 },
  { first: 'q', count: 16, vowels: 50, consonants: 59, total: 109 },
  { first: 'z', count: 1, vowels: 2, consonants: 2, total: 4 } ]
```

Applying MapReduce by Aggregating Results

One benefit of MongoDB is the ability to MapReduce the results of database queries into a completely different structure than the original collections. MapReduce is the process of mapping the values on a DB lookup into a completely different form and then reducing it to make it more consumable.

MongoDB has a MapReduce framework but has also added a framework that simplifies the process of piping one MapReduce operation into another in a series to produce some extraordinary results with the data. Aggregation is the concept of applying a series of operations to documents on the MongoDB server as they are being compiled into a result set. This is much more efficient than retrieving them and processing them in your Node.js application because the MongoDB server can operate on chunks of data locally.

Understanding the aggregate() Method

The Collection object provides the aggregate() method to perform aggregation operations on data. The syntax for the aggregate() method is shown below:

```
aggregate(operators, [options], callback)
```

The operators parameter is an array of aggregation operators, shown in Table 15.3, that allow you to define what aggregation operation to perform on the data. The options parameter is an object that allows you to set the readPreference property that defines where to read the data from. The callback parameter should be a function that accepts an error as the first parameter and a results array as the second. The results array is the fully aggregated object set returned by the aggregation.

Using Aggregation Framework Operators

The aggregation framework provided by MongoDB is powerful in that it allows you to pipe the results of one aggregation operator into another multiple times. To illustrate this, look at the following data set:

```
{o_id:"A", value:50, type:"X"}
{o_id:"A", value:75, type:"X"}
{o_id:"B", value:80, type:"X"}
{o_id:"C", value:45, type:"Y"}
```

The following aggregation operator set would pipeline the results of the $match into the $group operator and then return the grouped set in the results parameter of the callback function. Notice that when referencing the values of fields in documents that the field name is prefixed by a dollar sign, for example $o_id and $value. This syntax tells the aggregate framework to treat it as a field value instead of a string.

```
aggregate([{$match:{type:"X"}},
           {$group:{set_id:"$o_id", total: {$sum: "$value"}}},
           function(err, results){}]);
```

After the $match operator completes, the documents that would be applied to $group would be:

```
{o_id:"A", value:50, type:"X"}
{o_id:"A", value:75, type:"X"}
{o_id:"B", value:80, type:"X"}
```

Then after the $group operator is applied, a new array of objects is sent to the callback function with set_id and total fields as shown below:

```
{set_id:"A", total:"125"}
{set_id:"B", total:"80"}
```

Table 15.3 defines the types of aggregation commands that you can include in the `operators` parameter to the `aggregate()` method:

Table 15.3 **Aggregation operators that can be used in the `aggregate()` method**

Operator	Description
`$project`	Reshapes the documents by renaming, adding, or removing fields. You can also recompute values and add subdocuments. For example, the following includes `title` and excludes `name`: `{$project{title:1, name:0}}` The following is an example of renaming `name` to `title`: `{$project{title:"$name"}}` The following is an example of adding a new field total and computing its value from `price` and `tax` fields: `{$project{total:{$add:["$price", "$tax"]}}}`
`$match`	Filters the document set using the query operators defined in Table 15.1. For example: `{$match:{value:{$gt:50}}}`
`$limit`	Restricts the number of documents that can be passed to the next pipe in the aggregation. For example: `{$limit:5}`
`$skip`	Specifies a number of documents to skip before processing the next pipe in the aggregation. For example: `{$skip:10}`
`$unwind`	Specifies an array field that splits, with a separate document created for each value. For example: `{$unwind:"$myArr"}`
`$group`	Groups the documents together into a new set of documents for the next level in the pipe. The fields of the new object must be defined in the `$group` object. You can also apply group expression operators, listed in Table 15.4, to the multiple documents in the group. For example, to sum the `value` field: `{$group:{set_id:"$o_id", total: {$sum: "$value"}}}`
`$sort`	Sorts the documents before passing them on to the next pipe in the aggregation. The sort specifies an object with `field:<sort_order>` properties where `<sort_order>` is `1` for ascending and `-1` for descending. For example: `{$sort: {name:1, age:-1}}`
`$collStatus`	Returns a collection's or view's statistics.
`$redact`	Restricts each document in the stream based on stored values in the documents. Can implement field level redaction. Every one input document outputs one or zero documents.

Operator	Description
`$sample`	Selects a specific number of random documents from its input.
`$geoNear`	Returns an ordered stream of documents based on proximity to a geospatial point. An additional distance field and a location identifier field can be included in the output documents.
`$lookup`	Used to perform an equality match between a field in the input documents with field documents in a joined collection.
`$out`	Writes the resulting documents of the aggregation pipeline to a collection. The `$out` stage must be used in the last stage of the pipeline.
`$indexStats`	Returns statistics of the use of each index for the collection.
`$facet`	Processes multiple aggregation pipelines in a single stage on the same input documents. Allows the creation of multifaceted aggregations that can characterize data across multiple dimensions or facets in a single stage.
`$bucket`	Categorizes incoming documents into groups called buckets, based on certain expressions and bucket boundaries.
`$bucketAuto`	Categorizes incoming documents into a specific number of groups called buckets, based on certain expressions. The bucket boundaries are automatically determined to try and evenly distribute documents into the specified number of buckets.
`$sortByCount`	Sorts incoming documents by the value of a specified expression and then determines the number of documents in each specific group.
`$addFields`	Adds new fields to documents.
`$replaceRoot`	Replaces a document with a specified embedded document, replacing all fields in the input document.
`$count`	Returns a count of all documents at this point of the aggregation pipeline.
`$graphLookup`	Searches a collection and adds a new `array` field on each output document that contains the traversal results of the search for that document.

Implementing Aggregation Expression Operators

When you implement the aggregation operators, you are building a new document that will be passed to the next level in the aggregation pipeline. The MongoDB aggregation framework provides a number of expression operators that help when computing values for new fields or for comparison of existing fields in the documents.

When operating on a `$group` aggregation pipe, multiple documents match the defined fields in the new documents created. MongoDB provides a set of operators that you can apply to those documents and use to compute values for fields in the new group document based on values of fields in the original set of documents. Table 15.4 lists the `$group` expression operators.

Table 15.4 **Aggregation `$group` expression operators**

Operator	Description
`$addToSet`	Returns an array of all the unique values for the selected field among all the documents in that group. For example: `colors: {$addToSet: "$color"}`
`$first`	Returns the first value for a field in a group of documents. For example: `firstValue:{$first: "$value"}`
`$last`	Returns the last value for a field in a group of documents. For example: `lastValue:{$last: "$value"}`
`$max`	Returns the highest value for a field in a group of documents. For example: `maxValue:{$max: "$value"}`
`$min`	Returns the lowest value for a field in a group of documents. For example: `minValue:{$min: "$value"}`
`$avg`	Returns an average of all the values for a field in a group of documents. For example: `avgValue:{$avg: "$value"}`
`$push`	Returns an array of all values for the selected field among all the documents in that group of documents. For example: `username:{$push: "$username"}`
`$sum`	Returns the sum of all the values for a field in a group of documents. For example: `total:{$sum: "$value"}`

Several string and arithmetic operators also can be applied when computing new field values. Table 15.5 lists some of the more common operators that you can apply when computing new field values in the aggregation operators:

Table 15.5 **String and arithmetic operators used in aggregation expressions**

Operator	Description
`$add`	Computes the sum of an array of numbers. For example: `valuePlus5:{$add:["$value", 5]}`
`$divide`	Takes two numbers and divides the first number by the second. For example: `valueDividedBy5:{$divide:["$value", 5]}`

Operator	Description
`$mod`	Takes two numbers and calculates the modulo of the first number divided by the second. For example: `valueMod5:{$mod:["$value", 5]}`
`$multiply`	Computes the product of an array of numbers. For example: `valueTimes5:{$multiply:["$value", 5]}`
`$subtract`	Takes two numbers and subtracts the second number from the first. For example: `valueMinus5:{$minus:["$value", 5]}`
`$concat`	Concatenates two strings. For example: `title:{$concat:["$title", " ", "$name"]}`
`$strcasecmp`	Compares two strings and returns an integer that reflects the comparison. For example: `isTest:{$strcasecmp:["$value", "test"]}`
`$substr`	Takes a string and returns a portion of that string. For example: `hasTest:{$substr:["$value", "test"]}`
`$toLower`	Converts a string to lowercase. For example: `titleLower:{$toLower:"$title"}`
`$toUpper`	Converts a string to uppercase. For example: `titleUpper:{$toUpper:"$title"}`

Aggregation Examples

Listing 15.9 illustrates three examples of implementing aggregation against the words collection.

The first example, in lines10–20, implements a `$match` to get words beginning in vowels and then a `$group` to calculate the largest and smallest sizes. The results are then sorted using `$sort` and displayed in Listing 15.9 Output.

The second example, in lines 21–27, uses `$match` to limit the words to size 4. Then `$limit` is used to only process five documents in the `$project` operator. The third example, in lines 28–34, uses a `$group` to get the `average` size of the words and set the `_id` value to the word. Then the words are sorted in descending order by `average` and displayed in Listing 15.9 Output.

Listing 15.9 `doc_aggregate.js`: **Grouping a set of documents by specific fields in a MongoDB collection**

```
var MongoClient = require('mongodb').MongoClient;
MongoClient.connect("mongodb://localhost/", function(err, db) {
  var myDB = db.db("words");
  myDB.collection("word_stats", aggregateItems);
  setTimeout(function(){
    db.close();
  }, 3000);
});
function aggregateItems(err, words){
  words.aggregate([{$match: {first:{$in:['a','e','i','o','u']}}},
                   {$group: {_id:"$first",
                             largest:{$max:"$size"},
                             smallest:{$min:"$size"},
                             total:{$sum:1}}},
                   {$sort: {_id:1}}],
              function(err, results){
    console.log("Largest and smallest word sizes for " +
                "words beginning with a vowel: ");
    console.log(results);
  });
  words.aggregate([{$match: {size:4}},
                   {$limit: 5},
                   {$project: {_id:"$word", stats:1}}],
              function(err, results){
    console.log("Stats for 5 four letter words: ");
    console.log(results);
  });
  words.aggregate([{$group: {_id:"$first", average:{$avg:"$size"}}},
                   {$sort: {average:-1}},
                   {$limit: 5}],
              function(err, results){
    console.log("Letters with largest average word size: ");
    console.log(results);
  });
}
```

Listing 15.9 Output `doc_aggregate.js`: **Grouping a set of documents by specific fields in a MongoDB collection**

```
Stats for 5 four letter words:
[ { stats: { vowels: 2, consonants: 2 }, _id: 'have' },
  { stats: { vowels: 1, consonants: 3 }, _id: 'that' },
  { stats: { vowels: 1, consonants: 3 }, _id: 'with' },
  { stats: { vowels: 1, consonants: 3 }, _id: 'this' },
  { stats: { vowels: 1, consonants: 3 }, _id: 'they' } ]
```

```
Largest and smallest word sizes for words beginning with a vowel:
[ { _id: 'a', largest: 14, smallest: 1, total: 295 },
  { _id: 'e', largest: 13, smallest: 3, total: 239 },
  { _id: 'i', largest: 14, smallest: 1, total: 189 },
  { _id: 'o', largest: 14, smallest: 2, total: 118 },
  { _id: 'u', largest: 13, smallest: 2, total: 58 } ]
Letters with largest average word size:
[ { _id: 'i', average: 8.238095238095237 },
  { _id: 'e', average: 7.523012552301255 },
  { _id: 'c', average: 7.419068736141907 },
  { _id: 'a', average: 7.145762711864407 },
  { _id: 'p', average: 7.01699716713881 } ]
```

Summary

In this chapter you looked at the `query` and `options` objects used by `Collection` methods to access documents in the database. The `query` object allows you to limit which documents are considered for operations. The `options` object allows you to control the interaction of the requests to limit the number of documents returned, which document to start on, and what fields should be returned.

The `distinct()`, `group()`, and `aggregate()` methods allow you to group documents based on field values. The MongoDB aggregation framework is a powerful feature that allows you to process documents on the server before returning them to the client. The aggregation framework allows you to pipe documents from one aggregation operation to the next, each time mapping and reducing to a more defined set of data.

Next

In the next chapter, you use the `mongoose` module to implement an Object Document Model (ODM), which provides a more structured approach to data modeling from Node.js.

16

Using Mongoose for Structured Schema and Validation

Now that you understand the native driver, it won't be hard to make the jump to using Mongoose. Mongoose is an Object Document Model (ODM) library that provides additional functionality to the MongoDB Node.js native driver. For the most part, it is used as a way to apply a structured schema to a MongoDB collection. This provides the benefits of validation and type casting.

Mongoose also attempts to simplify some of the complexities of making database calls by implementing builder objects that allow you to pipe additional commands into find, update, save, remove, aggregate, and other database operations. This can make it easier to implement your code.

This chapter discusses the Mongoose module and how to use it to implement a structured schema and validation on your collections. You are introduced to new objects and a new way of implementing MongoDB in your Node.js applications. Mongoose doesn't replace the MongoDB Node.js native driver; instead, it enhances it with additional functionality.

Understanding Mongoose

Mongoose is an Object Document Model (ODM) library that wraps around the MongoDB Node.js driver. The main purpose is to provide a schema-based solution to model data stored in the MongoDB database.

The chief benefits of using Mongoose are:

- You can create a schema structure for your documents.
- Objects/documents in the model can be validated.
- Application data can be typecast into the object model.

- Business logic hooks can be applied using middleware.
- Mongoose is in some ways easier to use than the MongoDB Node.js native driver.

However, there are some downsides to using Mongoose as well. Those drawbacks are:

- You are required to provide a schema, which isn't always the best option when MongoDB doesn't require it.
- It doesn't perform certain operations, such as storing data, as well as the native driver does.

Additional Objects

Mongoose sits on top of the MongoDB Node.js native driver and extends the functionality in a couple of different ways. It adds some new objects—`Schema`, `Model`, and `Document`—that provide the functionality necessary to implement the ODM and validation.

The `Schema` object defines the structured schema for documents in a collection. It allows you to define the fields and types to include, uniqueness, indexes, and validation. The `Model` object acts as a representation of all documents in the collection. The `Document` object acts as a representation of the individual document in a collection.

Mongoose also wraps the standard functionality used for implementing query and aggregation parameters into new objects, `Query` and `Aggregate`, which allow you to apply the parameters of database operations in a series of method calls before finally executing them. This can make it simpler to implement code as well as reuse instances of those object to perform multiple database operations.

Connecting to a MongoDB Database Using Mongoose

Connecting to the MongoDB database using Mongoose is similar to using the connection string method discussed in Chapter 13, "Getting Started with MongoDB and Node.js." It uses the same connection string format and options syntax shown below:

```
connect(uri, options, [callback])
```

The `connect()` method is exported at the root level of the `mongoose` module. For example, the following code connects to the `words` database on the `localhost`:

```
var mongoose = require('mongoose');
mongoose.connect('mongodb://localhost/words');
```

The connection can be closed using the `disconnect()` method of the `mongoose` module, for example:

```
mongoose.disconnect();
```

Once created, the underlying `Connection` object can be accessed in the `connection` attribute of the `mongoose` module. The `Connection` object provides access to the connection, underlying

Db object, and Model object that represents the collection. This gives you access to all the Db object functionality described in Chapter 13. For example, to list the collections on the database you could use the following code:

```
mongoose.connection.db.collectionNames(function(err, names){
  console.log(names);
});
```

The Connection object emits the open event that can be used to wait for the connection to open before trying to access the database. To illustrate the basic life cycle of a MongoDB connection via Mongoose, Listing 16.1 imports the mongoose module, connects to the MongoDB database, waits for the open event, and then displays the collections in the database and disconnects.

Listing 16.1 `mongoose_connect.js`: **Connecting to a MongoDB database by using Mongoose**

```
var mongoose = require('mongoose');
mongoose.connect('mongodb://localhost/words');
mongoose.connection.on('open', function(){
  console.log(mongoose.connection.collection);
  mongoose.connection.db.collectionNames(function(err, names){
    console.log(names);
    mongoose.disconnect();
  });
});
```

Listing 16.1 Output `mongoose_connect.js`: **Connecting to a MongoDB database by using Mongoose**

```
[Function]
[ Collection {
    s:
     { pkFactory: [Object],
       db: [Object],
       topology: [Object],
       dbName: 'words',
       options: [Object],
       namespace: 'words.word_stats',
       readPreference: null,
       slaveOk: false,
       serializeFunctions: undefined,
       raw: undefined,
       promoteLongs: undefined,
       promoteValues: undefined,
       promoteBuffers: undefined,
       internalHint: null,
```

```
    collectionHint: null,
    name: 'word_stats',
    promiseLibrary: [Function: Promise],
    readConcern: undefined } } ]
```

Defining a Schema

A fundamental requirement of using Mongoose is to implement a schema. The schema defines the fields and field types for documents in a collection. This can be useful if your data is structured in a way that supports a schema because you can validate and typecast objects to match the requirements of the schema.

For each field in the schema, you need to define a specific value type. The value types supported are:

- `String`
- `Number`
- `Boolean` or `Bool`
- `Array`
- `Buffer`
- `Date`
- `ObjectId` or `Oid`
- `Mixed`

A schema must be defined for each different document type that you plan to use. Also, you should only store one document type in each collection.

Understanding Paths

Mongoose uses the term `path` to define access paths to fields in the main document as well as subdocuments. For example, if a document has a field named `name`, which is a subdocument with `title`, `first`, and `last` properties, the following are all paths:

```
name
name.title
name.first
name.last
```

Creating a Schema Definition

To define a schema for a model, you need to create a new instance of a `Schema` object. The `Schema` object `definition` accepts an object describing the schema as the first parameter and an `options` object as the second parameter:

```
new Schema(definition, options)
```

The options object defines the interaction with the collection on the MongoDB server. The most commonly used options that can be specified are shown in Table 16.1.

Table 16.1 **Options that can be specified when defining a Schema object**

Option	Description
autoIndex	A Boolean that, when true, indicates that the autoindex feature for the collection is turned off. The default is true.
bufferCommands	A Boolean that, when true, indicates that commands that cannot be completed due to connection issues are buffered. The default is true.
capped	Specifies the maximum number of documents supported in a capped collection.
collection	Specifies the collection name to use for this Schema model. Mongoose automatically connects to this collection when compiling the schema model.
id	A Boolean that, when true, indicates that the documents in the model will have an id getter that corresponds to the _id value of the object. The default is true.
_id	A Boolean that, when true, indicates that Mongoose automatically assigns an _id field to your documents. The default is true.
[illegible]	Specifies the replica read preferences. Value can be primary, primaryPreferred, secondary, secondaryPreferred, or nearest.
[illegible]	A Boolean; when true, Mongoose applies a write concern to requests that update the database. The default is true.
[illegible]	A Boolean that, when true, indicates that attributes passed in the object that do not appear in the defined schema are not saved to the database. The default is true.

For example, to create a schema for a collection called students, with a name field that is a String type, an average field that is a Number type, and a scores field that is an Array of Number types, you use:

```
var schema = new Schema({
  name: String,
  average: Number,
  scores: [Number]
}, {collection:'students'});
```

Adding Indexes to a Schema

You might want to assign indexes to specific field that you frequently use to find documents. You can apply indexes to a schema object when defining the schema or using the index(fields) command. For example, both of the following commands add an index to the name field in ascending order:

```
var schema = new Schema({
  name: {type: String, index: 1}
});
//or
var schema = new Schema({name: String});
schema.index({name:1});
```

You can get a list of indexed fields on a schema object using the indexes() method. For example:

```
schema.indexes()
```

Implementing Unique Fields

You can also specify that the value of a field must be unique in the collection, meaning no other documents can have the same value for that field. This is done by adding the unique property to the Schema object definition. For example, to add an index and make the name field unique in the collection, you use:

```
var schema = new Schema({
  name: {type: String, index: 1, unique: true}
});
```

Forcing Required Fields

You can also specify that a field must be included when creating a new instance of a Document object for the model. By default, if you do not specify a field when creating a Document instance, the object is created without one. For fields that must exist in your model, add the required property when defining the Schema. For example, to add an index, ensure uniqueness, and force including the name field in the collection, you use:

```
var schema = new Schema({
  name: {type: String, index: 1, unique: true, required: true}
});
```

You can get a list of required fields on a schema object using the requiredPaths() method. For example:

```
schema.requiredPaths()
```

Adding Methods to the Schema Model

Mongoose schemas enables you to add methods to the Schema object that are automatically available on document objects in the model. This allows you to call the methods using the Document object.

Methods are added to the Schema object by assigning a function to the Schema.methods property. The function is just a standard JavaScript function assigned to the Document object.

The Document object can be accessed using the this keyword. For example, the following assigns a function named fullName to a model that returns a combination of the first and last name.

```
var schema = new Schema({
  first: String,
  last: String
});
schema.methods.fullName = function(){
  return this.first + " " + this.last;
};
```

Implementing the Schema on the Words Database

Listing 16.2 implements a schema on the word_stats collection defined in Chapter 15, "Accessing MongoDB from Node.js." This schema is used in other examples in this chapter, so it is exported in the final line of code. Notice that the word and first fields have an index assigned to them and that the word field is both unique and required.

For the stats subdocument the document is defined as normal but with types specified in lines 9–11. Also notice that for the charsets field, which is an array of subdocuments, the syntax defines an array and defines the single subdocument type for the model. In lines 13–15 a startsWith() method is implemented that is available on Document objects in the model. Listing 16.2 Output shows the required paths and indexes.

Listing 16.2 word_schema.js: **Defining the schema for the word_stats collection**

```
01 var mongoose = require('mongoose');
02 var Schema = mongoose.Schema;
03 var wordSchema = new Schema({
04   word: {type: String, index: 1, required:true, unique: true},
05   first: {type: String, index: 1},
06   last: String,
07   size: Number,
08   letters: [String],
09   stats: {
10     vowels:Number, consonants:Number},
11     charsets: [Schema.Types.Mixed]
12 }, {collection: 'word_stats'});
13 wordSchema.methods.startsWith = function(letter){
14   return this.first === letter;
15 };
16 exports.wordSchema = wordSchema;
17 console.log("Required Paths: ");
18 console.log(wordSchema.requiredPaths());
19 console.log("Indexes: ");
20 console.log(wordSchema.indexes());
```

Listing 16.2 Output `word_schema.js`: **Defining the schema for the `word_stats` collection**

```
Required Paths:
[ 'word' ]
Indexes:
[ [ { word: 1 }, { background: true } ],
[ { first: 1 }, {background: true } ] ]
```

Compiling a Model

Once you have defined the `Schema` object for your model, you need to compile it into a `Model` object. When Mongoose compiles the model, it uses the connection to the MongoDB established by `mongoose.connect()` and ensures that the collection is created and has the appropriate indexes, as well as required and unique settings when applying changes.

The compiled `Model` object acts in much the same way as the `Collection` object defined in Chapter 13. It provides the functionality to access, update, and remove objects in the model and subsequently in the MongoDB collection.

To compile the model, you use the `model()` method in the `mongoose` module. The `model()` method uses the following syntax:

```
model(name, [schema], [collection], [skipInit])
```

The `name` parameter is a string that can be used to find the model later using `model(name)`. The `schema` parameter is the `Schema` object discussed in the previous section. The `collection` parameter is the name of the collection to connect to if one is not specified in the `Schema` object. The `skipInit` option is a Boolean that defaults to `false`. When `true`, the initialization process is skipped and a simple `Model` object with no connection to the database is created.

The following shows an example of compiling the model for the `Schema` object defined in Listing 16.2:

```
var Words = mongoose.model('Words', wordSchema);
```

You can then access the compiled `Model` object at any time using the following:

```
mongoose.model('Words')
```

Understanding the Query Object

Once you have the `Schema` object compiled into a `Model` object, you are completely ready to begin accessing, adding, updating, and deleting documents in the model, which makes the changes to the underlying MongoDB database. However, before you jump in, you need to understand the nature of the `Query` object provided with Mongoose.

Many of the methods in the Model object match those in the Collection object defined in Chapter 13. For example, there are find(), remove(), update(), count(), distinct(), and aggregate() methods. The parameters for these methods are for the most part exactly the same as for the Collection object with a major difference: the callback parameter.

Using the Mongoose Model object, you can either pass in the callback function or omit it from the parameters of the method. If the callback function is passed in, the methods behave as you would expect them to. The request is made to MongoDB, and the results returned in the callback function.

However, if you do not pass in a callback function, the actual MongoDB request is not sent. Instead, a Query object is returned that allows you to add additional functionality to the request before executing it. Then, when you are ready to execute the database call, you use the exec(callback) method on the Query object.

The simplest way to explain this is to look at an example of a find() request; using the same syntax as in the native driver is perfectly acceptable in Mongoose:

```
model.find({value:{$gt:5}},{sort:{[['value',-1]]}, fields:{name:1, title:1, value:1}},
         function(err, results){});
```

However, using Mongoose, all the query options can also be defined separately using the following code:

```
var query = model.find({});
query.where('value').lt(5);
query.sort('-value');
query.select('name title value');
query.exec(function(err, results){});
```

The model.find() call returns a Query object instead of performing the find() because no callback is specified. Notice that the query properties and options properties are broken out in subsequent method calls on the query object. Then, once the query object is fully built, the exec() method is called and the callback function is passed into that.

You can also string the query object methods together, for example:

```
model.find({}).where('value').lt(5).sort('-value').select('name title value')
.exec(function(err, results){});
```

When exec() is called, the Mongoose library builds the necessary query and options parameters and then makes the native call to MongoDB. The results are returned in the callback function.

Setting the Query Database Operation

Each Query object must have a database operation associated with it. The database operation determines what action to take when connecting to the database, from finding documents to storing them. There are two ways to assign a database operation to a query object. One way is to call the operation from the `Model` object and not specify a callback. The `query` object returned has that operation assigned to it. For example:

```
var query =  model.find();
```

Once you already have a `Query` object, you can change the operation that is applied by calling the method on the `Query` object. For example, the following code creates a `Query` object with the `count()` operation and then switches to a `find()` operation:

```
var query =  model.count();
query.where('value').lt(5);
query.exec(function(){});
query.find();
query.exec(function(){});
```

This allows you to dynamically reuse the same `Query` object to perform multiple database operations. Table 16.2 lists the operation methods that you can call on the `Query` object. This is also the list of methods on a compiled `Model` object that can return a `Query` object by omitting the `callback` function. Keep in mind that if you pass in a `callback` function to any of these methods, the operation is executed and the callback called when finished.

Table 16.2 **Methods available on the `Query` and `Model` objects to set the database operation**

Method	Description
`create(objects, [callback])`	Inserts the objects specified in the `objects` parameter to the MongoDB database. The `objects` parameter can be a single JavaScript object or an array of JavaScript objects. A `Document` object instance for the model is created for each object. The `callback` function receives an `error` object as the first parameter and the saved `documents` as additional objects. For example: `function(err, doc1, doc2, doc3, …)`
`count([query], [callback])`	Sets the operation to `count`. When the callback is executed, the `results` returned are the number of items matching the `Query`.
`distinct([query], [field], [callback])`	Sets the operation to `distinct`, which limits the results to an array of the distinct `values` of the `field` specified when the `callback` is executed.
`find([query], [options], [callback])`	Sets the operation to a `find`, which returns an array of the `Document` objects that match the `Query`.
`findOne([query], [options], [callback])`	Sets the operation to a `findOne`, which returns the first `Document` object that matches the `Query`.
`findOneAndRemove([query], [options], [callback])`	Sets the operation to a `findAndRemove`, which deletes the first document in the collection that matches the `Query`.

Method	Description
`findOneAndUpdate([query], [update], [options], [callback])`	Sets the operation to a `findAndUpdate`, which updates the first document in the collection that matches the `Query`. The update operation is specified in the `update` parameter. See Table 14.2 for the `update` operators that can be used.
`remove([query], [options], [callback])`	Sets the operation to a `remove`, which deletes all the documents in the collection that match the `Query`.
`update([query], [update], [options], [callback])`	Sets the operation to `update`, which updates all documents in the collection that match the `Query`. The update operation is specified in the `update` parameter. See Table 14.2 for the update operators that can be used.
`aggregate(operators, [callback])`	Applies one or more aggregate `operators` to the collection. The `callback` function accepts an `error` as the first parameter and an array of JavaScript `objects` representing the aggregated results as the second parameter.

Setting the Query Database Operation Options

The `Query` object also has methods that allow you to set the options such as `limit`, `skip`, and `select` that define how the request is processed on the server. These can be set in the `options` parameter of the methods listed in Table 16.2 or by calling the methods on the `Query` object listed in Table 16.3.

Table 16.3 **Methods available on the `Query` and `Model` objects to set the database operation options**

Method	Description
`setOptions(options)`	Sets the options used to interact with MongoDB when performing the database request. See Table 15.2 for a description of the options that can be set.
`limit(number)`	Sets the maximum `number` of documents to include in the results.

`select(fields)`	Specifies the fields that should be included in each document of the result set. The `fields` parameter can be either a space-separated string or an object. When using the string method, adding a + to the beginning of the field name forces inclusion even if the field doesn't exist in the document, and adding a - excludes the field. For example:
	`select('name +title -value');`
	`select({name:1, title:1, value:0);`

Method	Description

`sort(fields)`	Specifies the `fields` to sort on in string form or object form. For example:
	`sort('name -value');`
	`sort({name:1, value:-1})`

`skip(number)`	Specifies the `number` of documents to skip at the beginning of the result set.
`read(preference)`	Enables you to set the read `preference` to primary, `primaryPreferred`, `secondary`, `secondaryPreferred`, or `nearest`.
`snapshot(Boolean)`	Sets the query to a snapshot query when `true`.
`safe(Boolean)`	When set to `true`, the database request uses a write concern for update operations.
`hint(hints)`	Specifies the indexes to use or exclude when finding documents. Use a value of `1` for include and `-1` for exclude. For example: `hint(name:1, title:-1);`
`comment(string)`	Adds the `string` to the MongoDB log with the query. This is useful to identify queries in the log files.

Setting the Query Operators

The `Query` object also allows you to set the operators and values used to find the document that you want to apply the database operations to. These operators define this like "field values greater than a certain amount." The operators all work off a path to the field. That path can be specified by the `where()` method, or included in the operator method. If no operator method is specified, the last path passed to a `where()` method is used.

For example, the `gt()` operator below compares against the value field:

```
query.where('value').gt(5)
```

However, in the following statement, the `lt()` operator compares against the score field:

```
query.where('value').gt(5).lt('score', 10);
```

Table 16.4 lists the most common methods that can be applied to the `Query` object.

Table 16.4 **Methods available on `Query` objects to define the query operators**

Method	Description
`where(path, [value])`	Sets the current field `path` for the operators. If a `value` is also included, only documents where that field equals the `value` are included. For example: `where('name', "myName")`

Method	Description
gt([path], value)	Matches values that are greater than the value specified in the query. For example: gt('value', 5) gt(5)
gte([path], value)	Matches fields that are equal to or greater than the value specified in the query.
lt([path], value)	Matches values that are less than the value specified in the query.
lte([path], value)	Matches fields that are less than or equal to the value specified in the query.
ne([path], value)	Matches all fields that are not equal to the value specified in the query.
in([path], array)	Matches any of the values that exist in an array specified in the query. For example: in('name', ['item1', 'item2']) in(['item1', 'item2'])
nin([path], array)	Matches values that do not exist in an array specified in the query.
or(conditions)	Joins query clauses with a logical OR and returns all documents that match the conditions of either clause. For example: or([{size:{$lt:5}},{size:{$gt:10}}])
and(conditions)	Joins query clauses with a logical AND and returns all documents that match the conditions of both clauses. For example: and([{size:{$lt:10}},{size:{$gt:5}}])
nor(conditions)	Joins query clauses with a logical NOR and returns all documents that fail to match both conditions. For example: nor([{size:{$lt:5}},{name:"myName"}])
exists([path], Boolean)	Matches documents that have the specified field. For example: exists('name', true} exists('title', false}
mod([path], value, remainder)	Performs a modulo operation on the value of a field and selects documents that have the matching remainder. For example: mod('size', 2,0)
regex([path], expression)	Selects documents where values match a specified regular expression. For example: regex('myField', 'some.*exp')

Method	Description
`all([path], array)`	Matches array fields that contain all elements specified in the array `parameter`. For example: `all('myArr', ['one','two','three'])`
`elemMatch([path], criteria)`	Selects documents if an element in the array of subdocuments has fields that match all the specified `$elemMatch` `criteria`. The `criteria` can be an object or a function. For example: `elemMatch('item', {{value:5},size:{$lt:3}})` `elemMatch('item', function(elem){ elem.where('value', 5); elem.where('size').gt(3); })`
`size([path], value)`	Selects documents if the array field is a specified size. For example: `size('myArr', 5)`

Understanding the Document Object

When you use the `Model` object to retrieve documents from the database, the documents are presented in the callback function as Mongoose `Document` objects. `Document` objects inherit from the `Model` class and represent the actual document in the collection. The `Document` object allows you to interact with the document from the perspective of your schema model by providing a number of methods and extra properties that support validation and modifications.

Table 16.5 lists the most useful methods and properties on the `Document` object.

Table 16.5 **Methods and properties available on `document` objects**

Method/Property	Description
`equals(doc)`	Returns `true` if this `Document` object matches the document specified by the `doc` parameter.
`id`	Contains the `_id` value of the document.
`get(path, [type])`	Returns the value of the specified `path`. The `type` parameter allows you to typecast the type of value to return.
`set(path, value, [type])`	Sets the `value` of the field at the specified `path`. The `type` parameter allows you to typecast the type of value to set.
`update(update, [options], [callback])`	Updates the document in the MongoDB database. The `update` parameter specifies the update operators to apply to the document. See Table 14.2 for the `update` operators that can be used.

Method/Property	Description
`save([callback])`	Saves changes that have been made to the `Document` object to the MongoDB database. The `callback` function accepts an `error` object as the only parameter.
`remove([callback])`	Removes the `Document` object from the MongoDB database. The `callback` function accepts an `error` object as the only parameter.
`isNew`	A Boolean that, if `true`, indicates this is a new object to the model that has not been stored in MongoDB.
`isInit(path)`	Returns `true` if the field at this path has been initialized.
`isSelected(path)`	Returns `true` if the field at this path was selected in the result set returned from MongoDB.
`isModified(path)`	Returns `true` if the field at this path has been modified but not yet saved to MongoDB.
`markModified(path)`	Marks the `path` as being modified so that it will be saved/updated to MongoDB.
`modifiedPaths()`	Returns an array of paths in the object that have been modified.
`toJSON()`	Returns a JSON string representation of the `Document` object.
`toObject()`	Returns a normal JavaScript object without the extra properties and methods of the `Document` object.
`toString()`	Returns a string representation of the `Document` object.
`validate(callback)`	Performs a validation on the `Document`. The `callback` function accepts only an `error` parameter.
`invalidate(path, msg, value)`	Marks the `path` as invalid causing the validation to fail. The `msg` and `value` parameters specify the error message and `value`.
`errors`	Contains a list of errors in the document.
`schema`	Links to the `Schema` object that defines the `Document` object's model.

Finding Documents Using Mongoose

Finding documents using the `mongoose` module is similar in some ways to using the MongoDB Node.js native driver and yet different in other ways. The concepts of logic operators, limit, skip, and distinct are all the same. However, there are two big differences.

The first major difference is that when using Mongoose, the statements used to build the request can be piped together and reused because of the `Query` object discussed earlier in this chapter. This allows Mongoose code to be much more dynamic and flexible when defining what documents to return and how to return them.

For example, all three of the following queries are identical, just built in different ways:

```
var query1 = model.find({name:'test'}, {limit:10, skip:5, fields:{name:1,value:1}});
var query2 = model.find().where('name','test').limit(10).skip(5).
select({name:1,value:1});
var query3 = model.find().
query3.where('name','test')
query3.limit(10).skip(5);
query3.select({name:1,value:1});
```

A good rule to follow when building your query object using Mongoose is to only add things as you need them in your code.

The second major difference is that MongoDB operations such as `find()` and `findOne()` return `Document` objects instead of JavaScript objects. Specifically, `find()` returns an array of `Document` objects instead of a `Cursor` object, and `findOne()` returns a single `Document` object. The `Document` objects allow you to perform the operations listed in Table 16.5.

Listing 16.3 illustrates several examples of implementing the Mongoose way of retrieving objects from the database. Lines 9–14 count the number of words that begin and end with a vowel. Then in line 15 the same query object is changed to a `find()` operation, and a `limit()` and `sort()` are added before executing it in line 16.

Lines 22–32 use `mod()` to find words with an even length and greater than six characters. Also the output is limited to ten documents, and each document returns only the `word` and `size` fields.

Listing 16.3 `mongoose_find.js`: **Finding documents in a collection by using Mongoose**

```
01 var mongoose = require('mongoose');
02 var db = mongoose.connect('mongodb://localhost/words');
03 var wordSchema = require('./word_schema.js').wordSchema;
04 var Words = mongoose.model('Words', wordSchema);
05 setTimeout(function(){
06   mongoose.disconnect();
07 }, 3000);
08 mongoose.connection.once('open', function(){
09   var query = Words.count().where('first').in(['a', 'e', 'i', 'o', 'u']);
10   query.where('last').in(['a', 'e', 'i', 'o', 'u']);
11   query.exec(function(err, count){
12     console.log("\nThere are " + count +
13                 " words that start and end with a vowel");
14   });
15   query.find().limit(5).sort({size:-1});
16   query.exec(function(err, docs){
17     console.log("\nLongest 5 words that start and end with a vowel: ");
18     for (var i in docs){
19       console.log(docs[i].word);
20     }
21   });
```

```
  query = Words.find();
  query.mod('size',2,0);
  query.where('size').gt(6);
  query.limit(10);
  query.select({word:1, size:1});
  query.exec(function(err, docs){
    console.log("\nWords with even lengths and longer than 5 letters: ");
    for (var i in docs){
      console.log(JSON.stringify(docs[i]));
    }
  });
});
```

Listing 16.3 Output `mongoose_find.js`: **Finding documents in a collection by using Mongoose**

```
There are 5 words that start and end with a vowel

Words with even lengths and longer than 5 letters:
{"_id":"598e0ebd0850b51290642f8e","word":"american","size":8}
{"_id":"598e0ebd0850b51290642f9e","word":"question","size":8}
{"_id":"598e0ebd0850b51290642fa1","word":"government","size":10}
{"_id":"598e0ebd0850b51290642fbe","word":"national","size":8}
{"_id":"598e0ebd0850b51290642fcc","word":"business","size":8}
{"_id":"598e0ebd0850b51290642ff9","word":"continue","size":8}
{"_id":"598e0ebd0850b51290643012","word":"understand","size":10}
{"_id":"598e0ebd0850b51290643015","word":"together","size":8}
{"_id":"598e0ebd0850b5129064301a","word":"anything","size":8}
{"_id":"598e0ebd0850b51290643037","word":"research","size":8}

Longest 5 words that start and end with a vowel:
administrative
infrastructure
intelligence
independence
architecture
```

Adding Documents Using Mongoose

Documents can be added to the MongoDB library using either the `create()` method on the `Model` object or the `save()` method on a newly created `Document` object. The `create()` method accepts an array of JavaScript objects and creates a `Document` instance for each JavaScript object, which applies validation and a middleware framework to them. Then the `Document` objects are saved to the database.

The syntax of the `create()` method is shown below:

```
create(objects, [callback])
```

The `callback` function of the `create` method receives an `error` for the first parameter if it occurs and then additional parameters, one for each document. Lines 27–32 of Listing 16.4 illustrate using the `create()` method and handling the saved documents coming back. Notice that the `create()` method is called on the `Model` object `Words` and that the arguments are iterated on to display the created documents, as shown in Listing 16.4 Output.

The `save()` method is called on a `Document` object that has already been created. It can be called even if the document has not yet been created in the MongoDB database, in which case the new document is inserted. The syntax for the `save()` method is

```
save([callback])
```

Listing 16.4 also illustrates the `save()` method of adding documents to a collection using Mongoose. Notice that a new `Document` instance is created in lines 6–11 and that the `save()` method is called on that document instance.

Listing 16.4 `mongoose_create.js`: **Creating new documents in a collection by using Mongoose**

```
01 var mongoose = require('mongoose');
02 var db = mongoose.connect('mongodb://localhost/words');
03 var wordSchema = require('./word_schema.js').wordSchema;
04 var Words = mongoose.model('Words', wordSchema);
05 mongoose.connection.once('open', function(){
06   var newWord1 = new Words({
07     word:'gratifaction',
08     first:'g', last:'n', size:12,
09     letters: ['g','r','a','t','i','f','c','o','n'],
10     stats: {vowels:5, consonants:7}
11   });
12   console.log("Is Document New? " + newWord1.isNew);
13   newWord1.save(function(err, doc){
14     console.log("\nSaved document: " + doc);
15   });
16   var newWord2 = { word:'googled',
17     first:'g', last:'d', size:7,
18     letters: ['g','o','l','e','d'],
19     stats: {vowels:3, consonants:4}
20   };
21   var newWord3 = {
22     word:'selfie',
23     first:'s', last:'e', size:6,
24     letters: ['s','e','l','f','i'],
25     stats: {vowels:3, consonants:3}
26   };
27   Words.create([newWord2, newWord3], function(err){
```

```
    for(var i=1; i<arguments.length; i++){
      console.log("\nCreated document: " + arguments[i]);
    }
    mongoose.disconnect();
  });
});
```

Listing 16.4 Output `mongoose_create.js`: **Creating new documents in a collection by using Mongoose**

```
Is Document New? True
Saved document: { __v: 0,
  word: 'gratifaction',
  first: 'g',
  last: 'n',
  size: 12,
  _id: 598e10192e335a163443ec13,
  charsets: [],
  stats: { vowels: 5, consonants: 7 },
  letters: [ 'g', 'r', 'a', 't', 'i', 'f', 'c', 'o', 'n' ] }

Created document: { __v: 0,
  word: 'googled',
  first: 'g',
  last: 'd',
  size: 7,
  _id: 598e10192e335a163443ec14,
  charsets: [],
  stats: { vowels: 3, consonants: 4 },
  letters: [ 'g', 'o', 'l', 'e', 'd' ] },{ __v: 0,
  word: 'selfie',
  first: 's',
  last: 'e',
  size: 6,
  _id: 598e10192e335a163443ec15,
  charsets: [],
  stats: { vowels: 3, consonants: 3 },
  letters: [ 's', 'e', 'l', 'f', 'i' ] }
```

Updating Documents Using Mongoose

There are several methods for updating documents when using Mongoose. Which one you use depends on the nature of your application. One method is simply to call the `save()` function described in the previous section. The `save()` method can be called on objects already created in the database.

The other way is to use the `update()` method on either the `Document` object for a single update or on the `Model` object to update multiple documents in the model. The advantages of the `update()` method are that it can be applied to multiple objects and provides better performance. The following sections describe these methods.

Saving Document Changes

You have already seen how to use the `save()` method to add a new document to the database. You can also use it to update an existing object. Often the `save()` method is the most convenient to use when working with MongoDB because you already have an instance of the `Document` object.

The `save()` method detects whether the object is new, determines which fields have changed, and then builds a database request that updates those fields in the database. Listing 16.5 illustrates implementing a `save()` request. The word `book` is retrieved from the database, and the first letter is capitalized, changing the word and first fields.

Notice that `doc.isNew` in line 8 reports that the document is not new. Also, in line 14 the modified fields are reported to the console using `doc.modifiedFields()`. These are the fields that are updated.

Listing 16.5 `mongoose_save.js`: **Saving documents in a collection by using Mongoose**

```
01 var mongoose = require('mongoose');
02 var db = mongoose.connect('mongodb://localhost/words');
03 var wordSchema = require('./word_schema.js').wordSchema;
04 var Words = mongoose.model('Words', wordSchema);
05 mongoose.connection.once('open', function(){
06   var query = Words.findOne().where('word', 'book');
07   query.exec(function(err, doc){
08     console.log("Is Document New? " + doc.isNew);
09     console.log("\nBefore Save: ");
10     console.log(doc.toJSON());
11     doc.set('word','Book');
12     doc.set('first','B');
13     console.log("\nModified Fields: ");
14     console.log(doc.modifiedPaths());
15     doc.save(function(err){
16       Words.findOne({word:'Book'}, function(err, doc){
17         console.log("\nAfter Save: ");
18         console.log(doc.toJSON());
19         mongoose.disconnect();
20       });
21     });
22   });
23 });
```

Listing 16.5 Output mongoose_save.js: **Saving documents in a collection by using Mongoose**

```
Is Document New? false

Before Save:
{ _id: 598e0ebd0850b51290642fc7,
  word: 'book',
  first: 'b',
  last: 'k',
  size: 4,
  charsets:
   [ { chars: [Object], type: 'consonants' },
     { chars: [Object], type: 'vowels' } ],
  stats: { vowels: 2, consonants: 2 },
  letters: [ 'b', 'o', 'k' ] }

Modified Fields:
[ 'word', 'first' ]

After Save:
{ _id: 598e0ebd0850b51290642fc7,
  word: 'Book',
  first: 'B',
  last: 'k',
  size: 4,
  charsets:
   [ { chars: [Object], type: 'consonants' },
     { chars: [Object], type: 'vowels' } ],
  stats: { vowels: 2, consonants: 2 },
  letters: [ 'b', 'o', 'k' ] }
```

Updating a Single Document

The `Document` object also provides the `Update()` method that enables you to update a single document using the update operators described in Table 14.2. The syntax for the `update()` method on `Document` objects is shown below:

```
update(update, [options], [callback])
```

The `update` parameter is an object that defines the update operation to perform on the document. The `options` parameter specifies the write preferences, and the callback function accepts an `error` as the first argument and the `number` of documents updated as the second.

Listing 16.6 shows an example of using the `update()` method to update the word `gratifaction` to `gratifactions` by setting the `word`, `size`, and `last` fields using a `$set` operator as well as pushing the letter `s` on the end of `letters` using the `$push` operator.

Listing 16.6 `mongoose_update_one.js`: **Updating a single document in a collection by using Mongoose**

```
var mongoose = require('mongoose');
var db = mongoose.connect('mongodb://localhost/words');
var wordSchema = require('./word_schema.js').wordSchema;
var Words = mongoose.model('Words', wordSchema);
mongoose.connection.once('open', function(){
  var query = Words.findOne().where('word', 'gratifaction');
  query.exec(function(err, doc){
    console.log("Before Update: ");
    console.log(doc.toString());
    var query = doc.update({$set:{word:'gratifactions',
                                  size:13, last:'s'},
                            $push:{letters:'s'}});
    query.exec(function(err, results){
      console.log("\n%d Documents updated", results);
      Words.findOne({word:'gratifactions'}, function(err, doc){
        console.log("\nAfter Update: ");
        console.log(doc.toString());
        mongoose.disconnect();
      });
    });
  });
});
```

Listing 16.6 Output `mongoose_update_one.js`: **Updating a single document in a collection by using Mongoose**

```
Before Update:
{ _id: 598e10192e335a163443ec13,
  word: 'gratifaction',
  first: 'g',
  last: 'n',
  size: 12,
  __v: 0,
  charsets: [],
  stats: { vowels: 5, consonants: 7 },
  letters: [ 'g', 'r', 'a', 't', 'i', 'f', 'c', 'o', 'n' ] }

NaN Documents updated

After Update:
{ _id: 598e10192e335a163443ec13,
  word: 'gratifactions',
  first: 'g',
  last: 's',
```

```
  size: 13,
  __v: 0,
  charsets: [],
  stats: { vowels: 5, consonants: 7 },
  letters: [ 'g', 'r', 'a', 't', 'i', 'f', 'c', 'o', 'n', 's' ] }
```

Updating Multiple Documents

The `Model` object also provides an `Update()` method that allows you to update multiple documents in a collection using the `update` operators described in Table 14.2. The syntax for the `update()` method on `Model` objects is slightly different, as shown below:

```
update(query, update, [options], [callback])
```

The `query` parameter defines the query used to identify which objects to update. The `update` parameter is an object that defines the update operation to perform on the document. The `options` parameter specifies the write preferences, and the `callback` function accepts an `error` as the first argument and the `number` of documents updated as the second.

A nice thing about updating at the `Model` level is that you can use the `Query` object to define which objects should be updated. Listing 16.7 shows an example of using the `update()` method to update the `size` field of words that match the regex `/grati.*/` to `0`. Notice that an `update` object is defined in line 11; however, multiple query options are piped onto the `Query` object before executing it in line 14. Then another `find()` request is made, this time using the regex `/grat.*/` to show that only those matching the update query actually change.

Listing 16.7 `mongoose_update_many.js`: **Updating multiple documents in a collection by using Mongoose**

```
01 var mongoose = require('mongoose');
02 var db = mongoose.connect('mongodb://localhost/words');
03 var wordSchema = require('./word_schema.js').wordSchema;
04 var Words = mongoose.model('Words', wordSchema);
05 mongoose.connection.once('open', function(){
06   Words.find({word:/grati.*/}, function(err, docs){
07     console.log("Before update: ");
08     for (var i in docs){
09       console.log(docs[i].word + " : " + docs[i].size);
10     }
11     var query = Words.update({}, {$set: {size: 0}});
12     query.setOptions({multi: true});
13     query.where('word').regex(/grati.*/);
14     query.exec(function(err, results){
15       Words.find({word:/grat.*/}, function(err, docs){
16         console.log("\nAfter update: ");
17         for (var i in docs){
18           console.log(docs[i].word + " : " + docs[i].size);
```

```
        }
        mongoose.disconnect();
      });
    });
  });
});
```

Listing 16.7 Output `mongoose_update_many.js`: **Updating multiple documents in a collection by using Mongoose**

```
Before update:
gratifactions : 13
immigration : 11
integration : 11
migration : 9

After update:
grateful : 8
gratifactions : 0
immigration : 0
integrate : 9
integrated : 10
integration : 0
migration : 0
```

Removing Documents Using Mongoose

There are two main ways to remove objects from a collection using Mongoose. You can use the `remove()` method on either the `Document` object for a single deletion or on the `Model` object to delete multiple documents in the model. Deleting a single object is often convenient if you already have a `Document` instance. However, it is often much more efficient to delete multiple documents at the same time at the `Model` level. The following sections describe these methods.

Removing a Single Document

The `Document` object provides the `remove()` method that allows you to delete a single document from the model. The syntax for the `remove()` method on `Document` objects is shown below. The `callback` function accepts an `error` as the only argument if an error occurs or the deleted `document` as the second if the delete is successful:

```
remove([callback])
```

Listing 16.8 shows an example of using the `remove()` method to remove the word `unhappy`.

Listing 16.8 `mongoose_remove_one.js`: **Deleting a document from a collection by using Mongoose**

```
var mongoose = require('mongoose');
var db = mongoose.connect('mongodb://localhost/words');
var wordSchema = require('./word_schema.js').wordSchema;
var Words = mongoose.model('Words', wordSchema);
mongoose.connection.once('open', function(){
  var query = Words.findOne().where('word', 'unhappy');
  query.exec(function(err, doc){
    console.log("Before Delete: ");
    console.log(doc);
    doc.remove(function(err, deletedDoc){
      Words.findOne({word:'unhappy'}, function(err, doc){
        console.log("\nAfter Delete: ");
        console.log(doc);
        mongoose.disconnect();
      });
    });
  });
});
```

Listing 16.8 Output `mongoose_remove_one.js`: **Deleting a document from a collection by using Mongoose**

```
Before Delete:
{ _id: 598e0ebd0850b51290643f21,
  word: 'unhappy',
  first: 'u',
  last: 'y',
  size: 7,
  charsets:
   [ { chars: [Object], type: 'consonants' },
     { chars: [Object], type: 'vowels' } ],
  stats: { vowels: 2, consonants: 5 },
  letters: [ 'u', 'n', 'h', 'a', 'p', 'y' ] }

After Delete:
null
```

Removing Multiple Documents

The `Model` object also provides a `remove()` method that allows you to delete multiple documents in a collection using a single call to the database. The syntax for the `remove()` method on `Model` objects is slightly different, as shown below:

```
update(query, [options], [callback])
```

The `query` parameter defines the query used to identify which objects to delete. The `options` parameter specifies the write preferences, and the `callback` function accepts an `error` as the first argument and the `number` of documents deleted as the second.

A nice thing about deleting at the `Model` level is that you delete multiple documents in the same operation, saving the overhead of multiple requests. Also, you can use the `Query` object to define which objects should be updated.

Listing 16.9 shows an example of using the `remove()` method to delete words that match the regex `/grati.*/` expression. Notice that multiple query options are piped onto the `Query` object before executing it in line 13. The number of documents removed is displayed, and then another `find()` request is made, this time using the regex `/grat.*/` to show that only those matching the `remove` query actually are deleted.

Listing 16.9 `mongoose_remove_many.js`: **Deleting multiple documents in a collection by using Mongoose**

```
01 var mongoose = require('mongoose');
02 var db = mongoose.connect('mongodb://localhost/words');
03 var wordSchema = require('./word_schema.js').wordSchema;
04 var Words = mongoose.model('Words', wordSchema);
05 mongoose.connection.once('open', function(){
06   Words.find({word:/grat.*/}, function(err, docs){
07     console.log("Before delete: ");
08     for (var i in docs){
09       console.log(docs[i].word);
10     }
11     var query = Words.remove();
12     query.where('word').regex(/grati.*/);
13     query.exec(function(err, results){
14       console.log("\n%d Documents Deleted.", results);
15       Words.find({word:/grat.*/}, function(err, docs){
16         console.log("\nAfter delete: ");
17         for (var i in docs){
18           console.log(docs[i].word);
19         }
20         mongoose.disconnect();
21       });
22     });
23   });
24 });
```

Listing 16.9 Output `mongoose_remove_many.js`: **Deleting multiple documents in a collection by using Mongoose**

```
Before delete:
grateful
gratifactions
immigration
integrate
integrated
integration
migration

NaN Documents Deleted.

After delete:
grateful
integrate
integrated
```

Aggregating Documents Using Mongoose

The `Model` object provides an `aggregate()` method that allows you to implement the MongoDB aggregation pipeline discussed in Chapter 15. If you haven't read the aggregation section in Chapter 15 yet, you should do so before reading this section. Aggregation in Mongoose works similarly to the way it works in the MongoDB Node.js native driver. In fact, you can use the exact same syntax if you want. You also have the option of using the Mongoose `Aggregate` object to build and then execute the aggregation pipeline.

The `Aggregate` object works similarly to the `Query` object in that if you pass in a `callback` function, `aggregate()` is executed immediately. If not, an `Aggregate` object is returned, and you can apply a pipeline method.

For example, the following calls the `aggregate()` method immediately:

```
model.aggregate([{$match:{value:15}}, {$group:{_id:"$name"}}],
                 function(err, results) {});
```

You can also pipeline aggregation operations using an instance of the `Aggregate` object. For example:

```
var aggregate = model.aggregate();
aggregate.match({value:15});
aggregate.group({_id:"$name"});
aggregate.exec();
```

Table 16.6 describes the methods that can be called on the `Aggregate` object.

Table 16.6 **Pipeline methods for the `Aggregate` object in Mongoose**

Method	Description
`exec(callback)`	Executes the `Aggregate` object pipeline in the order they are added. The `callback` function receives an `error` object as the first parameter and an array of JavaScript `objects` as the second, representing the aggregated results.
`append(operations)`	Appends additional `operations` to the `Aggregation` object pipeline. You can apply multiple `operations`, for example: `append({match:{size:1}}, {$group{_id:"$title"}}, {$limit:2})`
`group(operators)`	Appends a `group` operation defined by the group `operators`. For example: `group({_id:"$title", largest:{$max:"$size"}})`
`limit(number)`	Appends a `limit` operation that limits the aggregated results to a specific `number`.
`match(operators)`	Appends a `match` operation defined by the `operators` parameter. For example: `match({value:{$gt:7, $lt:14}, title:"new"})`
`project(operators)`	Appends a project operation defined by the `operators` parameter. For example: `project({_id:"$name", value:"$score", largest:{$max:"$size"}})`
`read(preference)`	Specifies the replica `read preference` use for aggregation. Value can be `primary`, `primaryPreferred`, `secondary`, `secondary-Preferred`, or `nearest`.
`skip(number)`	Appends a `skip` operation that skips the first `number` documents when applying the next operation in the aggregation pipeline.
`sort(fields)`	Appends a `sort` operation to the aggregation pipeline. The `fields` are specified in an object where a value of `1` is include, and a value of `-1` is exclude. For example: `sort({name:1, value:-1})`
`unwind(arrFields)`	Appends an `unwind` operation to the aggregation pipeline, which unwinds the `arrFields` by creating a new document in the aggregation set for each value in the array. For example: `unwind("arrField1", "arrField2", "arrField3")`

Listing 16.10 illustrates implementing aggregation in Mongoose using three examples. The first example, in lines 9–19, implements aggregation in the native driver way, but by using the `Model` object. The aggregated result set is the largest and smallest word sizes for words beginning with a vowel.

The next example, in lines 20–27, implements aggregation by creating an `Aggregate` object and appending operations to it using the `match()`, `append()`, and `limit()` methods. The results are stats for the five four-letter words.

The final example, in lines 28–35, uses the `group()`, `sort()`, and `limit()` methods to build the aggregation pipeline that results in the top five letters with the largest average word size.

Listing 16.10 `mongoose_aggregate.js`: **Aggregating data from documents in a collection by using Mongoose**

```
01 var mongoose = require('mongoose');
02 var db = mongoose.connect('mongodb://localhost/words');
03 var wordSchema = require('./word_schema.js').wordSchema;
04 var Words = mongoose.model('Words', wordSchema);
05 setTimeout(function(){
06   mongoose.disconnect();
07 }, 3000);
08 mongoose.connection.once('open', function(){
09   Words.aggregate([{$match: {first:{$in:['a','e','i','o','u']}}},
10                          {$group: {_id:"$first",
11                            largest:{$max:"$size"},
12                            smallest:{$min:"$size"},
13                            total:{$sum:1}}},
14                    {$sort: {_id:1}}],
15               function(err, results){
16     console.log("\nLargest and smallest word sizes for " +
17                 "words beginning with a vowel: ");
18     console.log(results);
19   });
20   var aggregate = Words.aggregate();
21   aggregate.match({size:4});
22   aggregate.limit(5);
23   aggregate.append({$project: {_id:"$word", stats:1}});
24   aggregate.exec(function(err, results){
25     console.log("\nStats for 5 four letter words: ");
26     console.log(results);
27   });
28   var aggregate = Words.aggregate();
29   aggregate.group({_id:"$first", average:{$avg:"$size"}});
30   aggregate.sort('-average');
31   aggregate.limit(5);
32   aggregate.exec( function(err, results){
33     console.log("\nLetters with largest average word size: ");
34     console.log(results);
35   });
36 });
```

Listing 16.10 Output `mongoose_aggregate.js`: **Aggregating data from documents in a collection by using Mongoose**

```
Stats for 5 four letter words:
[ { stats: { vowels: 2, consonants: 2 }, _id: 'have' },
  { stats: { vowels: 1, consonants: 3 }, _id: 'that' },
  { stats: { vowels: 1, consonants: 3 }, _id: 'with' },
  { stats: { vowels: 1, consonants: 3 }, _id: 'this' },
  { stats: { vowels: 1, consonants: 3 }, _id: 'they' } ]

Largest and smallest word sizes for words beginning with a vowel:
[ { _id: 'a', largest: 14, smallest: 1, total: 295 },
  { _id: 'e', largest: 13, smallest: 3, total: 239 },
  { _id: 'i', largest: 14, smallest: 1, total: 187 },
  { _id: 'o', largest: 14, smallest: 2, total: 118 },
  { _id: 'u', largest: 13, smallest: 2, total: 57 } ]

Letters with largest average word size:
[ { _id: 'i', average: 8.20855614973262 },
  { _id: 'e', average: 7.523012552301255 },
  { _id: 'c', average: 7.419068736141907 },
  { _id: 'a', average: 7.145762711864407 },
  { _id: 'p', average: 7.01699716713881 } ]
```

Using the Validation Framework

One of the most important aspects of the `mongoose` module is that of validation against a defined model. Mongoose provides a built-in validation framework that only requires you to define validation functions to perform on specific fields that need to be validated. When you try to create a new instance of a `Document`, read a `Document` from the database, or save a `Document`, the validation framework calls your custom validation methods and returns an error if the validation fails.

The validation framework is actually simple to implement. You call the `validate()` method on the specific path in the `Model` object that you want to apply validation to and pass in a `validation` function. The `validation` function should accept the value of the field and then use that value to return `true` or `false` depending on whether the value is valid. The second parameter to the `validate()` method is an `error` string that is applied to the error object if validation fails. For example:

```
Words.schema.path('word').validate(function(value){
  return value.length < 20;
}, "Word is Too Big");
```

The error object thrown by validation has the following fields:

- **`error.errors.<field>.message`:** String defined when adding the validate function
- **`error.errors.<field>.type`:** Type of validation error

- **error.errors.<field>.path:** Path in the object that failed validation
- **error.errors.<field>.value:** Value that failed validation
- **error.name:** Error type name
- **err.message:** Error Message

Listing 16.11 shows a simple example of adding validation to the word model, where a word of length 0 or greater than 20 is invalid. Notice that when the `newWord` is saved in line 18, an error is passed to the `save()` function. The output in lines 12–26 shows the various values of different parts of the error, as shown in Listing 16.11 Output. You can use these values to determine how to handle validation failures in the code.

Listing 16.11 `mongoose_validation.js`: **Implementing validation of documents in the model by using Mongoose**

```
01 var mongoose = require('mongoose');
02 var db = mongoose.connect('mongodb://localhost/words');
03 var wordSchema = require('./word_schema.js').wordSchema;
04 var Words = mongoose.model('Words', wordSchema);
05 Words.schema.path('word').validate(function(value){
06   return value.length < 0;
07 }, "Word is Too Small");
08 Words.schema.path('word').validate(function(value){
09   return value.length > 20;
10 }, "Word is Too Big");
11 mongoose.connection.once('open', function(){
12   var newWord = new Words({
13     word:'supercalifragilisticexpialidocious',
14     first:'s',
15     last:'s',
16     size:'supercalifragilisticexpialidocious'.length,
17   });
18   newWord.save(function (err) {
19     console.log(err.errors.word.message);
20     console.log(String(err.errors.word));
21     console.log(err.errors.word.type);
22     console.log(err.errors.word.path);
23     console.log(err.errors.word.value);
24     console.log(err.name);
25     console.log(err.message);
26     mongoose.disconnect();
27   });
28 });
```

Listing 16.11 Output `mongoose_validation.js`: **Implementing validation of documents in the model by using Mongoose**

```
Word is Too Small
Word is Too Small
undefined
word
supercalifragilisticexpialidocious
ValidationError
Words validation failed
```

Implementing Middleware Functions

Mongoose provides a middleware framework where `pre` and `post` functions are called before and after the `init()`, `validate()`, `save()`, and `remove()` methods on a `Document` object. A middleware framework allows you to implement functionality that should be applied before or after a specific step in the process. For example, when creating word documents using the model defined earlier in this chapter, you may want to automatically set the size to the length of the word field as shown below in the following `pre save()` middleware function:

```
Words.schema.pre('save', function (next) {
  console.log('%s is about to be saved', this.word);
  console.log('Setting size to %d', this.word.length);
  this.size = this.word.length;
  next();
});
```

There are two types of middleware functions—the `pre` and the `post` functions—and they are handled a bit differently. The `pre` functions receive a `next` parameter, which is the next middleware function to execute. The `pre` functions can be called asynchronously or synchronously. In the case of the asynchronous method, an additional `done` parameter is passed to the `pre` function allowing you to notify the asynchronous framework that you are finished. If you are applying operations that should be done in order in the middleware, you use the synchronous method.

To apply the middleware synchronously, you simply call `next()` in the middleware function. For example:

```
schema.pre('save', function(next){
  next();
});
```

To apply the middleware asynchronously, add a `true` parameter to the `pre()` method to denote asynchronous behavior and then call `doAsync(done)` inside the middleware function. For example:

```
schema.pre('save', true, function(next, done){
  next();
  doAsync(done);
});
```

The `post` middleware functions are called after the `init`, `validate`, `save`, or `remove` operation has been processed. This allows you to do any cleanup work necessary when applying the operation. For example, the following implements a simple `post save` method that logs that the object has been saved:

```
schema.post('save', function(doc){
  console.log("Document Saved: " + doc.toString());
});
```

Listing 16.12 illustrates the process of implementing middleware for each stage of the `Document` life cycle. Notice that the `validate` and `save` middleware functions are executed when saving the document. The `init` middleware functions are executed when retrieving the document from MongoDB using `findOne()`. The `remove` middleware functions are executed when using `remove()` to delete the document from MongoDB.

Also notice that the `this` keyword can be used in all the middleware functions except `pre init` to access the `Document` object. In the case of `pre init`, we do not have a document from the database yet to use.

Listing 16.12 `mongoose_middleware.js`: **Applying a middleware framework to a model by using Mongoose**

```
var mongoose = require('mongoose');
var db = mongoose.connect('mongodb://localhost/words');
var wordSchema = require('./word_schema.js').wordSchema;
var Words = mongoose.model('Words', wordSchema);
Words.schema.pre('init', function (next) {
  console.log('a new word is about to be initialized from the db');
  next();
});
Words.schema.pre('validate', function (next) {
  console.log('%s is about to be validated', this.word);
  next();
});
Words.schema.pre('save', function (next) {
  console.log('%s is about to be saved', this.word);
  console.log('Setting size to %d', this.word.length);
  this.size = this.word.length;
  next();
});
Words.schema.pre('remove', function (next) {
  console.log('%s is about to be removed', this.word);
  next();
});
Words.schema.post('init', function (doc) {
  console.log('%s has been initialized from the db', doc.word);
});
Words.schema.post('validate', function (doc) {
```

```
  console.log('%s has been validated', doc.word);
});
Words.schema.post('save', function (doc) {
  console.log('%s has been saved', doc.word);
});
Words.schema.post('remove', function (doc) {
  console.log('%s has been removed', doc.word);
});
mongoose.connection.once('open', function(){
  var newWord = new Words({
    word:'newword',
    first:'t',
    last:'d',
    size:'newword'.length,
  });
  console.log("\nSaving: ");
  newWord.save(function (err){
    console.log("\nFinding: ");
    Words.findOne({word:'newword'}, function(err, doc){
      console.log("\nRemoving: ");
      newWord.remove(function(err){
        mongoose.disconnect();
      });
    });
  });
});
```

Listing 16.12 Output `mongoose_middleware.js`: **Applying a middleware framework to a model by using Mongoose**

```
Saving:
newword is about to be validated
newword has been validated
newword is about to be saved
Setting size to 7
newword has been saved

Finding:
a new word is about to be initialized from the db
newword has been initialized from the db

Removing:
newword is about to be removed
newword has been removed
```

Summary

This chapter introduced you to Mongoose, which provides a structured schema to a MongoDB collection that provides the benefits of validation and typecasting. You learned about the new `Schema`, `Model`, `Query`, and `Aggregation` objects and how to use them to implement an ODM. You also got a chance to use the sometimes more friendly Mongoose methods to build a `Query` object before executing database commands.

You were also introduced to the validation and middleware frameworks. The validation framework allows you to validate specific fields in the model before trying to save them to the database. The middleware framework allows you to implement functionality that happens before and/or after each `init`, `validate`, `save`, or `remove` operation.

Next

In the next chapter, you delve into some more advanced MongoDB topics, such as indexes, replication, and sharding.

17

Advanced MongoDB Concepts

There is much more to MongoDB than can be fully covered in this book. This chapter covers some additional fundamentals beyond the normal database create, access, and delete operations. Designing and implementing indexes allows you to improve database performance. Also, implementing replica sets and sharding provide additional performance improvements and high availability.

Adding Indexes

MongoDB allows you to index fields in your collections that make it faster to find documents. When an index is added in MongoDB, a special data structure is created in the background that stores a small portion of a collection's data and then optimizes the structure of that data to make it faster to find specific documents.

For example, applying an `_id` index basically creates a sorted array of `_id` values. Once the index has been created, the following benefits occur:

- When looking up an object by `_id`, an optimized search can be performed on the ordered index to find the object in question.
- Say that you want objects back sorted by `_id`, and the sort has already been performed on the index so it doesn't need to be done again. MongoDB just needs to read the documents in the order the `_id` appears in the index.
- Say that you want documents 10–20 sorted by `_id`, the operation is just a matter of slicing that chunk out of the index to get the `_id` values to look up objects.
- If all you need is a list of sorted `_id` values, MongoDB does not even need to read the documents at all. It can just return the values directly from the index.

Keep in mind, however, that those benefits come at a cost. The following are some of costs associated with indexes:

- Indexes take up space on disk and in memory.
- Indexes take up processing time when inserting and updating documents. That means that database writes to collections with a large number of indexes can suffer performance hits.
- The larger the collection, the greater the cost in resources and performance. Extremely large collections may make it impractical to apply some indexes.

Several different types of indexes can be applied to fields in a collection to support various design requirements. Table 17.1 lists the different index types.

Table 17.1 **Types of Indexes Supported by MongoDB**

Option	Description
Default `_id`	All MongoDB collections have an index on the `_id` by default. If applications do not specify a value for `_id`, the driver or the `mongod` create an `_id` field with an `ObjectID` value. The `_id` index is unique, and prevents clients from inserting two documents with the same value for `_id`.
Single field	The most basic type of index is one on a single field. This is similar to the `_id` index but on any field that you need. The index can be sorted in ascending or descending order. The values of the fields do not necessarily need to be unique. For example: `{name: 1}`
Compound	Specifies an index on multiple fields. The index is sorted on the first field value, then the second, and so on. You can also mix the sort direction. For example, you can have one field sorting ascending and another sorted descending. `{name: 1, value: -1}`
Multikey	If you add a field that stores an array of items, a separate index for every element in the array also is created. This allows you to find documents more quickly by values contained in the index. For example, consider an array of objects named `myObjs` where each object has a `score` field: `{myObjs.score: 1}`
Geospatial	MongoDB allows you to create a geospatial index based on `2d` or `2sphere` coordinates. This allows you to more effectively store and retrieve data that has a reference to a geospatial location. For example: `{"locs":"2d"}`
Text	MongoDB also supports adding a text index that supports faster lookup of string elements by words that are contained inside. The index does not store words like *the*, *a*, *and*, etc. For example: `{comment: "text"}`

Option	Description
Hashed	When using hashed base sharding, MongoDB allows you to use a hashed index, which only indexes hashed values that match those stored in that particular server. This reduces the overhead of keeping hashes around for items on other servers. For example: `{key: "hashed"}`

Indexes can also have special properties that define how MongoDB handles the index. These properties are

- **`unique`**: This forces the index to only include a single instance of each field value and thus MongoDB rejects adding a document that has a duplicate value to one that is already in the index.
- **`sparse`**: This ensures that the index only contains entries for documents that have the indexed field. The index skips documents that do not have the indexed field.
- **`TTL`**: TTL or Time To Live indexes apply the concept of only allowing documents to exist in the index for a certain amount of time—for example, log entries or event data that should be cleaned up after a certain amount of time. The index keeps track of insertion time and removes the earliest items after they have expired.

The `unique` and `sparse` properties can be combined such that the index rejects documents that have a duplicate value for the index field and rejects documents that do not include the indexed field.

Indexes can be created from the MongoDB shell, MongoDB Node.js native client, or Mongoose. To create an index from the MongoDB shell, you use the `ensureIndex(index, properties)` method. For example:

```
db.myCollection.ensureIndex({name:1}, {background:true, unique:true, sparse: true})
```

The background option specifies whether the index created should take place in the foreground of the shell or the background. Running in the foreground completes faster but takes up more system resources, so it's not a good idea on a production system during peak times.

To create an index from the MongoDB Node.js native driver, you can call the `ensureIndex(collection, index, options, callback)` method on an instance of the `Db` object. For example:

```
var MongoClient = require('mongodb').MongoClient;
MongoClient.connect("mongodb://localhost/", function(err, db) {
  db.ensureIndex('myCollection', {name: 1},
                 {background: true, unique: true, sparse: true},
                 function(err){
    if(!err) console.log("Index Created");
  });
});
```

To create an index using the `Schema` object in Mongoose, you set the index options on the field in the schema for example:

```
var s = new Schema({ name: { type: String, index: true, unique: true, sparse: true});
```

You can also add the index to the `Schema` object later using the `index()` method, for example:

```
s.schema.path.('some.path').index({unique: true, sparse: true});
```

Using Capped Collections

Capped collections are fixed-size collections that insert, retrieve, and delete documents based on insertion order. This allows the capped collection to support high throughput operations. Capped collections work similarly to circular buffers in that once a collection fills its allocated space, it makes room for new documents by overwriting the oldest documents in the collection.

Capped collections can also be limited based on a maximum number of documents. This is useful in reducing the indexing overhead that can occur when storing large numbers of documents in a collection.

Capped collections are useful for rotating event logs or caching data because you do not need to worry about expending the overhead and effort of implementing code in your application to clean up the collection.

To create a capped collection from the MongoDB shell, you use the `createCollection()` method on the `db` object, specify the capped property, and set the size in bites as well as the optional maximum number of documents. For example:

```
db.createCollection("log", { capped : true, size : 5242880, max : 5000 } )
```

From the MongoDB Node.js native driver, you can also specify a capped collection in the `db.createCollection()` method described in Chapter 13, "Getting Started with MongoDB and Node.js." For example:

```
db.createCollection("newCollection", { capped : true, size : 5242880, max : 5000 }
                    function(err, collection){ });
```

From Mongoose, you can define the collection as capped in the schema options. For example:

```
var s = new Schema({ name:String, value:Number},
                   { capped : true, size : 5242880, max : 5000});
```

Applying Replication

Replication is one of the most critical aspects of high-performance databases. *Replication* is the process of defining multiple MongoDB servers that have the same data. The MongoDB servers in the replica set will be one of three types, as illustrated in Figure 17.1:

- **Primary:** The primary server is the only server in a replica set that can be written to and ensures the data integrity during write operations. A replica set can only have one primary server.

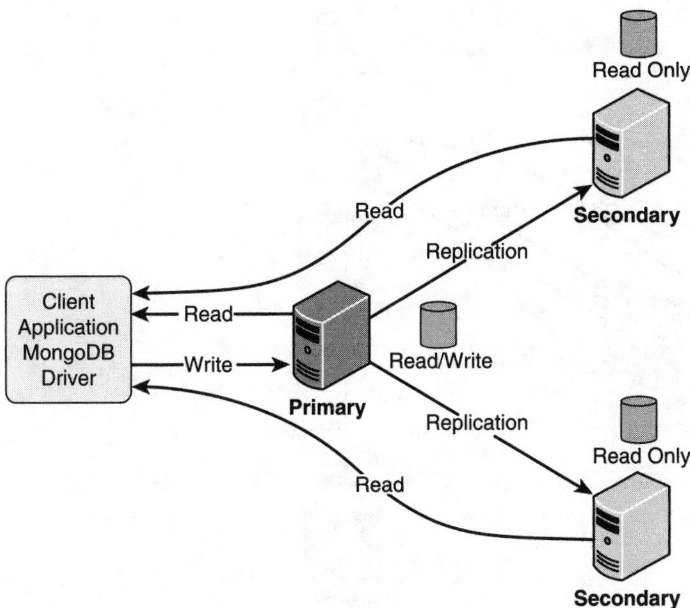

Figure 17.1 Implementing a replica set in MongoDB

- **Secondary:** Secondary servers contain a duplicate of the data on the primary server. To ensure the data is accurate, the replica servers apply the operations log, or oplog, from the primary server, ensuring that every write operation on the primary server also happens on the secondary servers in the same order. Clients can read from secondary servers but not write to them.
- **Arbiter:** The arbiter server is kind of interesting. It does not contain a replica of the data but can be used when electing a new primary if the primary server experiences a problem. When the primary server fails, the failure is detected, and other servers in the replica set elect a new primary using a heartbeat protocol between the primary, secondary, and arbiter servers. Figure 17.2 shows an example of the configuration using an arbiter server.

Replication provides two benefits: performance and high availability. Replica sets provide better performance because although clients cannot write to secondary servers they can read from them, which allows you to provide multiple read sources for your applications.

Replica sets provide high availability because if the primary server happens to fail, other servers that have a copy of the data can take over. The replica set uses a heartbeat protocol to communicate between the servers and determine whether the primary server has failed, at which point a new master is elected.

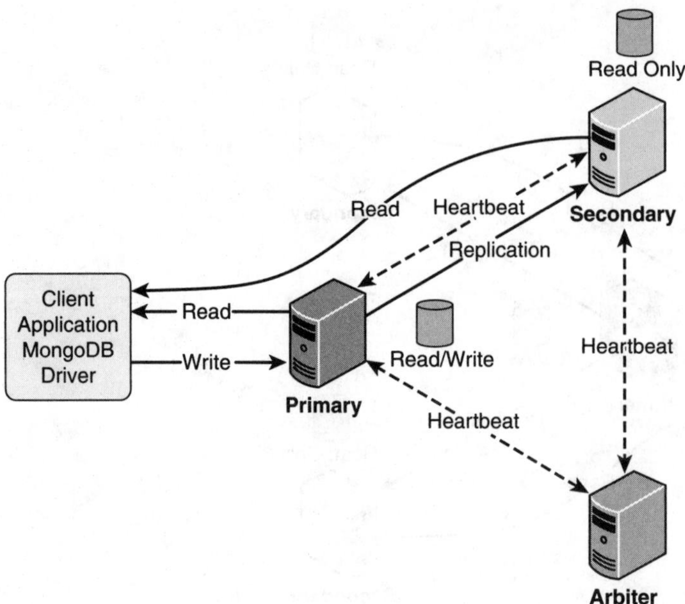

Figure 17.2 Implementing an arbiter server in a MongoDB replica set to ensure an odd number of servers

You should have at least three servers in the replica set, and you should also try and have an odd number. This makes it easier for the servers to elect a primary. This is where arbiter servers come in handy. They require few resources but can save time when electing a new primary. Figure 17.2 shows the replica set configuration with an arbiter. Notice that the arbiter does not have a replica; it only participates in the heartbeat protocol.

Replication Strategy

There are a few concepts to apply when you are determining how to deploy a MongoDB replica set. The following sections discuss a few of the different things you should consider before implementing a MongoDB replica set.

Number of Servers

The first question is how many servers should be included in the replica set. This depends on the nature of data interaction from clients. If the data from clients is mostly writes, you are not going to get a big benefit from a large number of servers. However, if your data is mostly static and you have a high number of read requests, more secondary servers will definitely make a difference.

Number of Replica Sets

Also consider the data. In some instances, it makes more sense to break up the data into multiple replica sets, each containing a different segment of the data. This allows you to fine-tune the servers in each set to meet the data and performance needs. Only consider this if there is no correlation between the data, so clients accessing the data would rarely need to connect to both replica sets at the same time.

Fault Tolerance

How important is the fault tolerance to your application? It will likely be a rare occurrence for your primary server to go down. If it doesn't really affect your application too much and the data can easily be rebuilt, you may not need replication. However, if you promise your customer Seven Nines availability, any outage is bad, and an extended outage is unacceptable. In those cases, it makes sense to add additional servers to the replica set to ensure availability.

Another thing to consider is placing one of the secondary servers in an alternative data center to support instances when your entire data center fails. However, for the sake of performance, you should keep the majority of secondary servers in your primary data center.

If you are concerned about fault tolerance, you should also enable journaling as described in Chapter 12, "Getting Started with MongoDB." Enabling journaling allows transactions to be replayed even if the power fails in your data center.

Deploying a Replica Set

Implementing a replica set is simple in MongoDB. The following steps take you through the process of prepping and deploying the replica set.

1. First ensure that each member in the replica set is accessible to each other using DNS or hostnames. Adding a virtual private network for the replica servers to communicate on will enhance the performance of the system because the replication process will not be affected by other traffic on the network. If the servers are not behind a firewall so the data communications are safe, you should also configure an `auth` and `kwFile` for the servers to communicate on for security.

2. Configure the `replSet` value, which is a unique name for the replica set, either in the `mongodb.conf` file or on your command line for each server in the replica set, for example:

   ```
   mongod --port 27017 --dbpath /srv/mongodb/db0 --replSet rs0
   ```

3. Start the MongoDB client using the `mongo` command and execute the following command on each server in the replica set to initiate the replica set operations:

   ```
   rs.initiate()
   ```

4. Use the MongoDB shell to connect to the MongoDB server that acts as the primary and execute the following command for each secondary host:

   ```
   rs.add(<secondary_host_name_or_dns>)
   ```

5. Use the following command to view the configuration on each server:

```
rs.conf()
```

6. Inside your application, define the read preference for reading data from the replica set. The previous chapters already described how to do this by setting the preference to `primary`, `primaryPreferred`, `secondary`, `secondaryPreferred`, or `nearest`.

Implementing Sharding

A serious problem that many large-scale applications encounter is that the data stored in the MongoDB is so enormous that it severely impacts performance. When a single collection of data becomes too large, indexing can cause a severe performance hit, the amount of data on disk can cause a system performance hit, and the number of requests from clients can quickly overwhelm the server. The application gets slower and slower at an accelerated rate when reading from and writing to the database.

MongoDB solves this problem through sharding. *Sharding* is the process of storing documents across multiple MongoDB servers running on different machines. This allows the MongoDB database to scale horizontally. The more MongoDB servers you add, the larger the number of documents that can be supported by your application. Figure 17.3 illustrates the concept of sharding. From the application's perspective there is a single collection; however, there are actually four MongoDB shard servers, and each contains a portion of the documents in the collections.

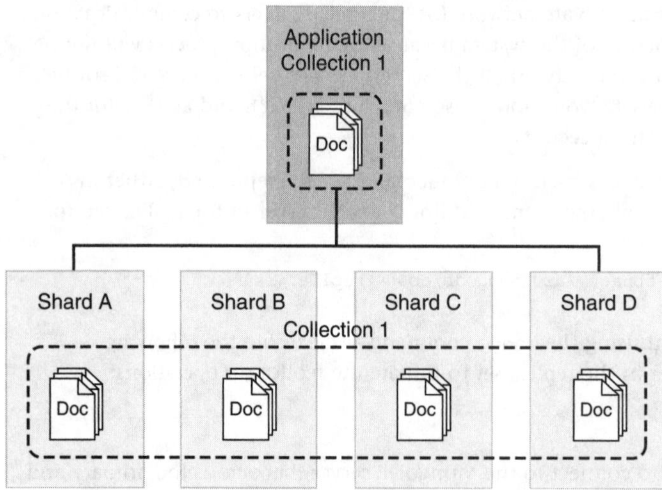

Figure 17.3 From the application's perspective there is only a single collection to access; however, the documents for that collection are split across multiple MongoDB shard servers

Sharding Server Types

Three types of MongoDB servers are involved when sharding your data. These servers each play a specific role to present a unified view to the applications. The following list describes each of the server types, and the diagram in Figure 17.4 illustrates the interaction between the different types of sharding servers.

- **Shard:** A shard actually stores the documents that make up the collection. The shard can be an individual server; however, to provide high availability and data consistency in production, consider using a replica set that provides primary and secondary copies of the shard.
- **Query router:** The query router runs an instance of `mongos`. The query router provides the interface for client applications to interact with the collection and obfuscates the fact that the data is in fact sharded. The query router processes the request, sends targeted operations to the shards, and then combines the shard responses into a single response to the client. A sharded cluster can contain more than one query router, which is a good way to load balance large numbers of client requests.
- **Config:** Config servers store the metadata about the sharded cluster that contains a mapping of the cluster's data set to the shards. The query router uses this metadata when targeting operations to specific shards. Production sharded clusters should have exactly three config servers.

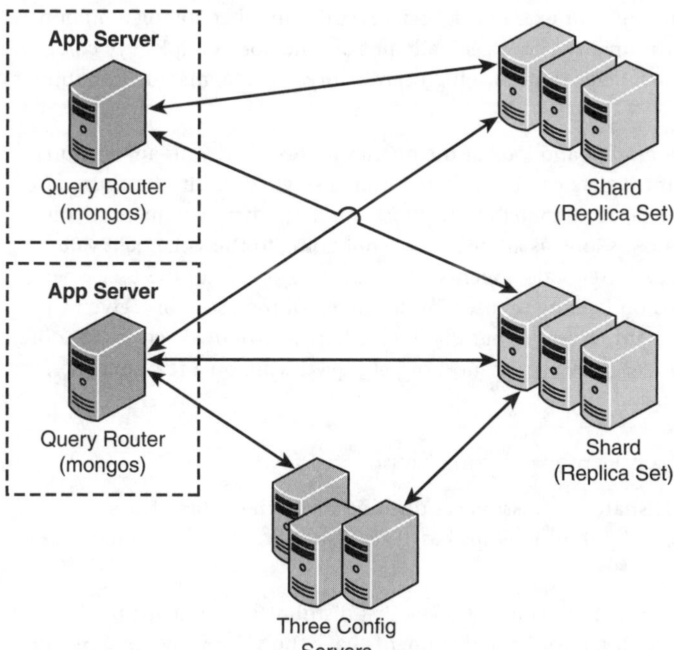

Figure 17.4 The router servers accept requests from the MongoDB clients and then communicate with the individual shard servers to read or write data

Choosing a Shard Key

The first step in sharding a large collection is to decide on a shard key that is used to determine which documents should be stored in which shard. The shard key is an indexed field or an indexed compound field that must be included in every document in the collection. MongoDB uses the value of the shard key to split the collection between the shards in the cluster.

Selecting a good shard key can be critical to achieving the performance that you need from MongoDB. A bad key can seriously impact the performance of the system, whereas a good key can improve performance and ensure future scalability. If a good key does not exist in your documents, you may want to consider adding a field specifically to be a sharding key.

When selecting a shard key, keep in mind the following considerations:

- **Easily divided:** The shard key needs to be easily divided into chunks.
- **Randomness:** When using range-based sharding, random keys can ensure that documents are more evenly distributed, so no one server is overloaded.
- **Compound keys:** It is best to shard using a single field when possible; however, if a good single field key doesn't exist, you can still get better performance from a good compound field than a bad single field key.
- **Cardinality:** Cardinality defines the uniqueness of the values of the field. A field has high cardinality if it is unique, for example, a Social Security number among a million people. A field has low cardinality if it is generally not unique, for example, eye color in a million people. Typically, fields that have high cardinality provide much better options for sharding.
- **Query targeting:** Take a minute and look at the queries necessary in your applications. Queries perform better if the data can be collected from a single shard in the cluster. If you can arrange for the shard key to match the most common query parameters, you will get better performance as long as all queries are not going to the same field value. Consider the example of arranging documents based on the zip code of the user when all your queries are based on looking up users by zip code. All the users for a given zip code exist on the same shard server. If your queries are fairly distributed across zip codes, a zip code key is a good idea. However, if most of your queries are on a few zip codes, a zip code key is actually a bad idea.

To illustrate shard keys better consider the following keys:

- **`{ "zipcode": 1}`**: This shard key distributes documents by the value of the `zipcode` field. That means that all lookups based on a specific `zipcode` go to a single shard server.
- **`{ "zipcode": 1, "city": 1 }`**: This shard key first distributes documents by the value of the `zipcode` field. If a number of documents have the same value for `zipcode`, they can be split off to other shards based on the `city` field value. That means you are

no longer guaranteed that a query on a single `zipcode` will hit only one shard. However, queries based on `zipcode` and `city` will go to the same shard.

- **`{ "_id": "hashed" }`**: This shard key distributes documents by a hash of the value of the `_id` field. This ensures a more even distribution across all shards in the cluster. However, it makes it impossible to target queries so that they will hit only a single shard server.

Selecting a Partitioning Method

The next step in sharding a large collection is to decide how to partition the documents based on the shard key. You can use two methods to distribute the documents into different shards based on the shard key value. Which method you use depends on the type of shard key you select:

- **Range-based sharding:** Divides the data set into specific ranges based on the value of the shard key. This method works well for shard keys that are numeric. For example, if you have a collection of products and each product is given a specific product ID from 1 to 1,000,000, you could shard the products in ranges of 1–250,000; 250,001–500,000, and so on.
- **Hash-based sharding:** Uses a hash function that computes a field value to create chunks. The hash function ensures that shard keys that have a close value end up in different shards to ensure a good distribution.

It is vital that you select a shard key and distribution method that distributes documents as evenly as possible across the shards; otherwise, one server ends up overloaded while another is relatively unused.

The advantage of range-based sharding is that it is often easy to define and implement. Also if your queries are often range-based as well, it is more performant than hash-based sharding. However, it is difficult to get an even distribution with range-based sharding unless you have all the data up front and the shard key values will not change going forward.

Hash-based sharding takes more understanding of the data but typically provides the best overall approach to sharding because it ensures a much more evenly spaced distribution.

The index used when enabling sharding on the collection determines which partitioning method is used. If you have an index based on a value, MongoDB uses range-based sharding. For example, the following implements a range-based shard on the `zip` and `name` fields of the document:

```
db.myDB.myCollection.ensureIndex({"zip": 1, "name":1})
```

To shard using the hash-based method, you need to define the index using the hash method, for example:

```
db.myDB.myCollection.ensureIndex({"name":"hash"})
```

Deploying a Sharded MongoDB Cluster

The process of deploying a sharded MongoDB cluster involves several steps to set the different types of servers and then configuring the databases and collections. To deploy a sharded MongoDB cluster, you need to

1. Create the config server database instances.
2. Start query router servers.
3. Add shards to the cluster.
4. Enable sharding on a database.
5. Enable sharding on a collection.

The following sections describe each of these steps in more detail.

> **Warning**
> All members of a sharded cluster must be able to connect to all other members of a sharded cluster, including all shards and all config servers. Make sure that the network and security systems, including all interfaces and firewalls, allow these connections.

Creating the Config Server Database Instances

The config server processes are simply `mongod` instances that store the cluster's metadata instead of the collections. Each config server stores a complete copy of the cluster's metadata. In production deployments, you must deploy exactly three config server instances, each running on different servers to ensure high availability and data integrity.

To implement the config servers, perform the following steps on each:

1. Create a data directory to store the config database.
2. Start the config server instances passing the path to the data directory created in step 1, and also include the `--configsvr` option to denote that this is a config server. For example:

   ```
   mongod --configsvr --dbpath <path> --port <port>
   ```

3. Once the `mongod` instance starts up, the config server is ready.

> **Note**
> The default port for config servers is `27019`.

Starting Query Router Servers (`mongos`)

The query router (`mongos`) servers do not require database directories because the configuration is stored on the config servers and the data is stored on the shard server. The `mongos` servers are lightweight, and therefore it is acceptable to have a mongos instance on the same system that runs your application server.

You can create multiple instances of the mongos servers to route requests to the sharded cluster. However, these instances shouldn't be running on the same system to ensure high availability.

To start an instance of the mongos server, you need to pass in the --configdb parameter with a list of the DNS names/hostnames of the config servers you want to use for the cluster. For example:

```
mongos --configdb c1.test.net:27019,c2.test.net:27019,c3.test.net:27019
```

By default, a mongos instance runs on port 27017. However, you can also configure a different port address using the --port <port> command line option.

> **Tip**
>
> To avoid downtime, give each config server a logical DNS name (unrelated to the server's physical or virtual hostname). Without logical DNS names, moving or renaming a config server requires shutting down every mongod and mongos instance in the sharded cluster.

Adding Shards to the Cluster

The shard servers in a cluster are just standard MongoDB servers. They can be a standalone server or a replica set. To add the MongoDB servers as shards in the cluster, all you need to do is access the mongos server from the MongoDB shell and use the sh.addShard() command.

The syntax for the sh.addShard() command is:

```
sh.addShard(<replica_set_or_server_address>)
```

For example, to add a replica set named rs1 on a server named mgo1.test.net as a shard in the cluster server, execute the following command from the MongoDB shell on the mongos server:

```
sh.addShard( "rs1/mgo1.test.net:27017" )
```

For example, to add a server named mgo1.test.net as a shard in the cluster server, execute the following command from the MongoDB shell on the mongos server:

```
sh.addShard( "mgo1.test.net:27017" )
```

Once you have added all the shards to the replica set, the cluster will be communicating and sharding the data, although for predefined data it takes some time for the chunks to be fully distributed.

Enabling Sharding on a Database

Prior to sharding a collection you need to enable the database it resides in to handle sharding. Enabling sharding doesn't automatically redistribute the data, but instead just assigns a primary shard for the database and makes other configuration adjustments that make it possible to enable the collections for sharding.

To enable the database for sharding, you need to connect to a mongos instance using the MongoDB shell and issue the sh.enableSharding(database) command. For example, to enable a database named bigWords you would use:

```
sh.enableSharding("bigWords");
```

Enabling Sharding on a Collection

Once the database has been enabled for sharding, you are ready to enable sharding at the collection level. You do not need to enable sharding for all collections in the database, just the one that it makes sense on.

Use the following steps to enable sharding on a collection:

1. Determine which field(s) will be used for the shard key as described above.
2. Create a unique index on the key field(s) using ensureIndex() described earlier in this chapter.

   ```
   db.myDB.myCollection.ensureIndex( { _id : "hashed" } )
   ```

3. Enable sharding on the collection using sh.shardCollection(<database>.<collection>, shard_key). The shard_key is the pattern used to create the index. For example:

   ```
   sh.shardCollection("myDB.myCollection", { "_id": "hashed" } )
   ```

Set Up Shard Tag Ranges

Once you have enabled sharding on a collection, you might want to add tags to target specific ranges of the shard key values. A really good example of this is where the collection is sharded by zip codes. To improve performance, tags can be added for specific city codes, such as NYC and SFO, and the zip code ranges for those cities specified. This ensures that documents for a specific city are stored on a single shard in the cluster, which can improve performance for queries based on multiple zip codes for the same city.

To set up shard tags, you simply need to add the tag to the shard using the sh.addShardTag(shard_server, tag_name) command from a mongos instance. For example:

```
sh.addShardTag("shard0001", "NYC")
sh.addShardTag("shard0002", "SFO")
```

Then to specify range for a tag, in this case the zip code ranges for each city tag, you use the sh.addTagRange(collection_path, startValue, endValue, tag_name) command from the mongos instance. For example:

```
sh.addTagRange("records.users", { zipcode: "10001" }, { zipcode: "10281" }, "NYC")
sh.addTagRange("records.users", { zipcode: "11201" }, { zipcode: "11240" }, "NYC")
sh.addTagRange("records.users", { zipcode: "94102" }, { zipcode: "94135" }, "SFO")
```

Notice that multiple ranges are added for NYC. This allows you to specify multiple ranges within the same tag that is assigned to a single shard.

If you need to remove a shard tag later, you can do so using the `sh.removeShardTag(shard_server, tag_name)` method. For example:

```
sh.removeShardTag("shard0002", "SFO")
```

Repairing a MongoDB Database

There are a couple of reasons to run a repair on the MongoDB database—for example, if the system crashes, or there is a data integrity problem manifested in the application, or even just to reclaim some unused disk space.

You can initiate a repair of a MongoDB database from the MongoDB shell or from the `mongod` command line. To execute a repair from the command line, use `--repair` and `--repairpath <repair_path>` syntax. The `<repair_path>` specifies the location to store temporary repair files. For example:

```
mongod --repair --repairpath /tmp/mongdb/data
```

To execute a repair from the MongoDB client, use the `db.repairDatabase(options)` command, for example:

```
db.repairDatabase({ repairDatabase: 1,
  preserveClonedFilesOnFailure: <boolean>,
  backupOriginalFiles: <boolean> })
```

When a repair is initiated, all collections in the database are compacted, which reduces the size on disk. Also any invalid records in the database are deleted. Therefore, it may be better to restore from backup rather than run a repair.

The time it takes to run the repair depends on the size of the data. A repair impacts the performance on the systems and should be run during off peak hours.

> **Warning**
>
> If you are trying to repair a member of a replica set and you have access to an intact copy of your data on another replica, you should restore from that intact copy because repairDatabase will delete the corrupt data and it will be lost.

Backing Up MongoDB

The best backup strategy for MongoDB is to implement high availability using a replica set. This ensures that the data is as up-to-date as possible and ensures that it is always available. However, also consider the following if your data is critical and cannot be replaced:

- **What if the data center fails?** In this case you can back up the data periodically and store it off-site, or you can add a replica somewhere off-site.
- **What if something happens to corrupt the actual application data that gets replicated?** This is always a concern. In this instance, the only option is to have a backup from a previous point.

If you decide that you need to implement periodic backups of data, also consider the impact that backups will have on the system and decide on a strategy. For example:

- **Production impact:** Backups are often intensive and need to be performed at a time when they have the least impact on your environment.
- **Requirements:** If you plan on implementing something like a block-level snapshot to back up the database, you need to make sure the system infrastructure supports it.
- **Sharding:** If you are sharding the data, all shards must be consistent. You cannot back up one without backing up all. Also you must stop the writes to the cluster to generate the point-in-time backup.
- **Relevant data:** You can also reduce the impact that backups have on your system by only backing up data that is critical to your system. For example, if a database will never change, it only needs to be backed up once, or if data in a database can easily be regenerated but is very large, it may be worth accepting the cost of regeneration rather than frequent backups.

There are two main approaches to backing up MongoDB. The first is to perform a binary dump of the data using the `mongodump` command. The binary data can be stored off-site for later use. For example, to dump the database for a replica set named `rset1` on `host mg1.test.net` and on a standalone system named `mg2.test.net` to a folder called `/opt/backup/current`, use the following command:

```
mongodump --host rset1/mg1.test.net:27018,mg2.test.net --out /opt/backup/current
```

The second method for backing up MongoDB databases is to use a file system snapshot. The snapshots are quick to complete; however, they are also much larger. You need to have journaling enabled, and the system has to support the block-level backups. If you are interested in implementing a snapshot method for backups, check out the guide at the following location: http://docs.mongodb.org/manual/tutorial/back-up-databases-with-filesystem-snapshots/.

Summary

This chapter finished off the MongoDB introduction by adding some more advanced concepts. You learned how to define different types of indexes to improve the speed for queries. You learned how to deploy a MongoDB replica set to ensure high availability and improve read performance. The replica set has read/write master and read-only replicas.

You were introduced to the concept of partitioning data in large collections into shards that exist on separate partitions to allow your implementation to scale horizontally. You also looked at different backup strategies and options to protect the most critical data in your MongoDB databases.

Next

In the next chapter you get back to the Node.js world with the `express` module. The `express` module allows you to more easily implement a webserver running on Node.js by supporting routes and other functionality.

18

Implementing Express in Node.js

Express is a lightweight module that wraps the functionality of the Node.js `http` module in a simple to use interface. Express also extends the functionality of the `http` module to make it easy for you to handle server routes, responses, cookies, and statuses of HTTP requests. This chapter gets you started implementing Express as the webserver for your Node.js applications. You learn how to configure the Express server, design routes, and use the `Request` and `Response` objects to send and receive HTTP requests. You also get a look at how to implement template engines in Express.

Getting Started with Express

It is simple to start using Express in your Node.js projects. All you need to do is add the `express` module using the following command from the root of your project:

```
npm install express
```

You can also add express to your `package.json` module to ensure that express is installed when you deploy your application.

Once you have installed express, you need to create an instance of the `express` class to act as the HTTP server for your Node.js application. The following lines of code import the `express` module and create an instance of `express` that you can use:

```
var express = require('express');
var app = express();
```

Configuring Express Settings

Express provides several application settings that control the behavior of the Express server. These settings define the environment as well as how Express handles JSON parsing, routing, and views. Table 18.1 lists the different settings that can be defined on an `express` object.

The `express` object provides the `set(setting, value)` and `enable(setting)` and `disable(setting)` methods to set the value of the application settings. For example, the following lines of code enable the `trust proxy` setting and set the `view engine` to `pug`:

```
app.enable('trust proxy');
app.disable('strict routing');
app.set('view engine', 'pug');
```

To get the value of a setting, you can use the `get(setting)`, `enabled(setting)`, and `disabled(setting)` methods. For example:

```
app.enabled('trust proxy');  \\true
app.disabled('strict routing'); \\true
app.get('view engine'); \\pug
```

Table 18.1 **Express application settings**

Setting	Description
`env`	Defines the environment mode string, such as `development`, `testing`, and `production`. The default is the value of `process.env.NODE_ENV`.
`trust proxy`	Enables/disables reverse proxy support. The default is disabled.
`jsonp callback name`	Defines the default callback name of JSONP requests. The default is `?callback=`.
`json replacer`	Defines the JSON replacer callback function. The default is `null`.
`json spaces`	Specifies the number of spaces to use when formatting JSON response. The default is `2` in development, `0` in production.
`case sensitive routing`	Enables/disables case sensitivity. For example, `/home` is not the same as `/Home`. The default is disabled.
`strict routing`	Enables/disables strict routing. For example, `/home` is not the same as `/home/`. The default is disabled.
`view cache`	Enables/disables view template compilation caching, which keeps the cached version of a compiled template. The default is enabled.
`view engine`	Specifies the default template engine extension that is used when rendering templates if a file extension is omitted from the view.
`views`	Specifies the path for the template engine to look for view templates. The default is `./views`.

Starting the Express Server

To begin implementing Express as the HTTP server for your Node.js application, you need to create an instance and begin listening on a port. The following three lines of code start a rudimentary Express server listening on port 8080:

```
var express = require('express');
var app = express();
app.listen(8080);
```

The `app.listen(port)` call binds the underlying HTTP connection to the `port` and begins listening on it. The underlying HTTP connection is the same connection produced using the `listen()` method on a `Server` object created using the `http` library discussed earlier in this book.

In fact, the value returned by `express()` is actually a callback function that maps to the callback function that is passed into the `http.createServer()` and `https.createServer()` methods.

To illustrate this, Listing 18.1 illustrates implementing a basic HTTP and HTTPS server using Node.js. Notice that the app variable returned from `express()` is passed into the `createServer()` methods. Also, notice that an `options` object is defined to set the `host`, `key`, and `cert` used to create the HTTPS server. Lines 13–15 implement a simple get route that handles the / path.

Listing 18.1 `express_http_https.js`: **Implementing HTTP and HTTPS servers using Express**

```
01 var express = require('express');
02 var https = require('https');
03 var http = require('http');
04 var fs = require('fs');
05 var app = express();
06 var options = {
07     host: '127.0.0.1',
08     key: fs.readFileSync('ssl/server.key'),
09     cert: fs.readFileSync('ssl/server.crt')
10   };
11 http.createServer(app).listen(80);
12 https.createServer(options, app).listen(443);
13 app.get('/', function(req, res){
14   res.send('Hello from Express');
15 });
```

Configuring Routes

The previous section discussed how to start the Express HTTP server. However, before the server can begin accepting requests, you need to define routes. A *route* is simply a definition that describes how to handle the path portion of the URI in the HTTP request to the Express server.

Implementing Routes

There are two parts when defining the route. First is the HTTP request method (typically `GET` or `POST`). Each of these methods often needs to be handled completely differently. Second, is the path specified in the URL—for example, / for the root of the website, `/login` for the login page, and `/cart` to display a shopping cart.

The `express` module provides a series of functions that allow you to implement routes for the Express server. These functions all use the following syntax:

```
app.<method>(path, [callback . . .], callback)
```

The `<method>` portion of the syntax actually refers to the HTTP request method, such as `GET` or `POST`. For example:

```
app.get(path, [middleware, ...], callback)
app.post(path, [middleware, ...], callback)
```

The `path` refers to the path portion of the URL that you want to be handled by the `callback` function. The `middleware` parameters are `0` or more middleware functions that are applied before executing the `callback` function. The `callback` function is the request handler that handles the request and sends the response back to the client. The `callback` function accepts a `Request` object as the first parameter and a `Response` object as the second.

For example, the following code implements some basic `GET` and `POST` routes:

```
app.get('/', function(req, res){
  res.send("Server Root");
});
app.get('/login', function(req, res){
  res.send("Login Page");
});
app.post('/save', function(req, res){
  res.send("Save Page");
});
```

When the Express server receives an HTTP request, it looks for a route that has been defined for the appropriate HTTP method and path. If one is found, a `Request` and `Response` object is created to manage the request and is passed into the callback function(s) for the route.

Express also provides the `app.all()` method that works exactly the same as the `app.post()` and `app.get()` methods. The only difference is that the callback function for `app.all()` is called on every request for the specified path regardless of HTTP method. Also, the `app.all()` method can accept the `*` character as a wildcard in the path. This is a great feature for implementing request logging or other special functionality to handle requests. For example:

```
app.all('*', function(req, res){
  // global handler for all paths
});
app.all('/user/*', function(req, res){
  // global handler for /user path
});
```

Applying Parameters in Routes

As you begin implementing routes, you will quickly see that for complex systems the number of routes can get out of hand. To reduce the number of routes, you can implement parameters within the URL. Parameters allow you to use the same route for similar requests by providing unique values for different requests that define how your application handles the request and builds the response.

For example, you would never have a separate route for every user or product in your system. Instead you would pass in a user ID or product ID as a parameter to one route, and the server code would use that ID to determine which user or product to use. There are four main methods for implementing parameters in a route:

- **Query string:** Uses the standard `?key=value&key=value...` HTTP query string after the path in the URL. This is the most common method for implementing parameters, but the URLs can become long and convoluted.
- **`POST` params:** When implementing a web form or other `POST` request, you can pass parameters in the body of the request.
- **regex:** Defines a regular expression as the path portion of the route. Express uses the regex to parse the path of the URL and store matching expressions as an array of parameters.
- **Defined parameter:** Defines a parameter by name using `:<param_name>` in the path portion of the route. Express automatically assigns that parameter a name when parsing the path.

The following sections discuss these methods with the exception of `POST` params, which is covered in the next chapter.

Applying Route Parameters Using Query Strings

The simplest method to add parameters to a route is to pass them using the normal HTTP query string format of `?key=value&key=value...` Then you can use the `url.parse()` method discussed earlier in the book to parse the `url` attribute of the `Request` object to get the parameters.

The following code implements a basic `GET` route to `/find?author=<author>&title=<title>` that accepts `author` and `title` parameters. To actually get the value of author and title, the `url.parse()` method is used to build a query object:

```
app.get('/find', function(req, res){
  var url_parts = url.parse(req.url, true);
  var query = url_parts.query;
  res.send('Finding Book: Author: ' + query.author +
           ' Title: ' + query.title);
});
```

For example, consider the following URL:

```
/find?author=Brad&title=Node
```

The `res.send()` method returns:

```
Finding Book: Author: Brad Title: Node
```

Applying Route Parameters Using Regex

One way to implement parameters in routes is to use a regex expression to match patterns. This allows you to implement patterns that do not follow a standard / formatting for the path.

The following code implements a regex parser to generate route parameters for GET requests at the URL `/book/<chapter>:<page>` path. Notice that the values of the parameters are not named; instead, `req.params` is an array of matching items in the URL path.

```
app.get(/^\/book\/(\w+)\:(\w+)?$/, function(req, res){
  res.send('Get Book: Chapter: ' + req.params[0] +
           ' Page: ' + req.params[1]);
});
```

For example, consider the following URL:

```
/book/12:15
```

The `res.send()` method returns

```
Get Book: Chapter: 12 Page: 15
```

Applying Route Parameters Using Defined Parameters

If your data is more structured, a defined parameter is a better method to use than regex. Using a defined parameter allows you to define your parameters by name within the route path. You define parameters in the path of the route using `:<param_name>`. When using defined parameters, `req.param` is a function instead of an array, where calling `req.param(param_name)` returns the value of the parameter.

The following code implements a basic `:userid` parameter expecting a URL with a `/user/<user_id>` format:

```
app.get('/user/:userid', function (req, res) {
  res.send("Get User: " + req.param("userid"));
});
```

For example, consider the following URL:

```
/user/4983
```

The `res.send()` method returns

```
Get User: 4983
```

Applying Callback Functions for Defined Parameters

A major advantage of using defined parameters is that you can specify callback functions that are executed if the defined parameter is found in a URL. When parsing the URL, if Express finds a parameter that has a callback registered, it calls the parameter's callback function before calling the route handler. You can register more than one callback function for a route.

To register a callback function, you use the `app.param()` method. The `app.param()` method accepts the defined parameter as the first argument, and then a callback function that receives the `Request`, `Response`, `next`, and `value` parameters.

```
app.param(param, function(req, res, next, value){} );
```

The `Request` and `Response` objects are the same as are passed to the route `callback`. The `next` parameter is a callback function for the next `app.param()` callback registered, if any. You must call `next()` somewhere in your `callback` function or the callback chain will be broken. The `value` parameter is the value of the parameter parsed from the URL path.

For example, the following code logs every request received that has the `userid` parameter specified in the route. Notice that `next()` is called before leaving the `callback` function:

```
app.param('userid', function(req, res, next, value){
  console.log("Request with userid: " + value);
  next();
});
```

To see how the preceding code works, consider the following URL:

```
/user/4983
```

The `userid` of `4983` is parsed from the URL and the `consol.log()` statement displays

```
Request with userid: 4983
```

Applying Route Parameters Example

To clarify the example, Listing 18.2 implements query strings, regex, and defined parameters to Express routes. The `POST` method is covered in the next chapter. Lines 8–16 implement the query string method. Lines 17–23 implement the regex method. Lines 24–33 implement a defined parameter along with a callback function that is executed whenever the `userid` parameter is specified in the request parameters. Figure 18.1 shows the console output from the code in Listing 18.2.

Listing 18.2 `express_routes.js`: Implementing route parameters in Express

```
01 var express = require('express');
02 var url = require('url');
03 var app = express();
04 app.listen(80);
05 app.get('/', function (req, res) {
06   res.send("Get Index");
07 });
08 app.get('/find', function(req, res){
09   var url_parts = url.parse(req.url, true);
10   var query = url_parts.query;
11   var response = 'Finding Book: Author: ' + query.author +
```

```
                 ' Title: ' + query.title;
  console.log('\nQuery URL: ' + req.originalUrl);
  console.log(response);
  res.send(response);
});
app.get(/^\/book\/(\w+)\:(\w+)?$/, function(req, res){
  var response = 'Get Book: Chapter: ' + req.params[0] +
              ' Page: ' + req.params[1];
  console.log('\nRegex URL: ' + req.originalUrl);
  console.log(response);
  res.send(response);
});
app.get('/user/:userid', function (req, res) {
  var response = 'Get User: ' + req.param('userid');
  console.log('\nParam URL: ' + req.originalUrl);
  console.log(response);
  res.send(response);
});
app.param('userid', function(req, res, next, value){
  console.log("\nRequest received with userid: " + value);
  next();
});
```

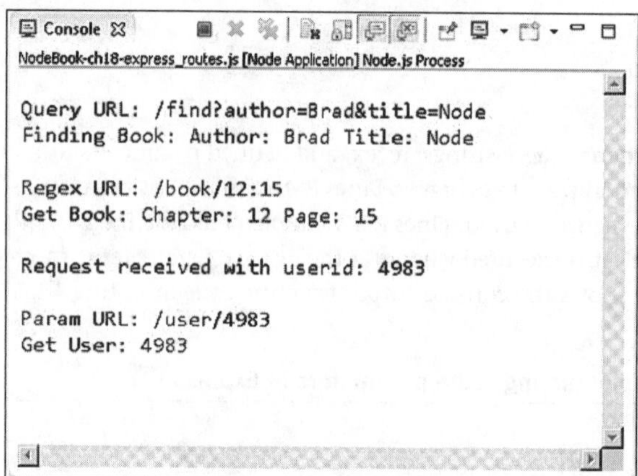

Console
NodeBook-ch18-express_routes.js [Node Application] Node.js Process
Query URL: /find?author=Brad&title=Node
Finding Book: Author: Brad Title: Node
Regex URL: /book/12:15
Get Book: Chapter: 12 Page: 15
Request received with userid: 4983
Param URL: /user/4983
Get User: 4983

Figure 18.1 Implementing route parameters using query strings, regex, and defined parameters

Using Requests Objects

The route handlers are passed a `Request` object as the first parameter. The `Request` object provides the data and metadata about the request, including the URL, headers, query string, and much more. This allows you to handle the request appropriately in your code.

Table 18.2 lists some of the more commonly used properties available in the `Request` object.

Table 18.2 **Properties and methods of the HTTP `Request` object**

Setting	Description
`originalUrl`	The original URL string of the request.
`protocol`	The protocol string, for example, `http` or `https`.
`ip`	IP address of the request.
`path`	Path portion of the request URL.
`hostname`	Hostname of the request.
`method`	HTTP method. `GET`, `POST`, etc.
`query`	Query string portion of the request URL.
`fresh`	A Boolean that is `true` when last-modified matches the current.
`stale`	A Boolean that is `false` when last-modified matches.
`secure`	A Boolean that is `true` when a TLS connection is established.
`acceptsCharset(charset)`	Returns `true` if the character set specified by `charset` is supported.
`get(header)`	Returns the value of the `header`.

Listing 18.3 illustrates accessing the various parts of the `Request` object. The output in Figure 18.2 shows the actual values associated with a GET request.

Listing 18.3 `express_request.js`: **Accessing properties of the `Request` object in Express**

```
var express = require('express');
var app = express();
app.listen(80);
app.get('/user/:userid', function (req, res) {
  console.log("URL:\t   " + req.originalUrl);
  console.log("Protocol:  " + req.protocol);
  console.log("IP:\t   " + req.ip);
  console.log("Path:\t   " + req.path);
  console.log("Host:\t   " + req.host);
  console.log("Method:\t   " + req.method);
  console.log("Query:\t   " + JSON.stringify(req.query));
  console.log("Fresh:\t   " + req.fresh);
  console.log("Stale:\t   " + req.stale);
  console.log("Secure:\t   " + req.secure);
```

```
  console.log("UTF8:\t    " + req.acceptsCharset('utf8'));
  console.log("Connection: " + req.get('connection'));
  console.log("Headers: " + JSON.stringify(req.headers,null,2));
  res.send("User Request");
});
```

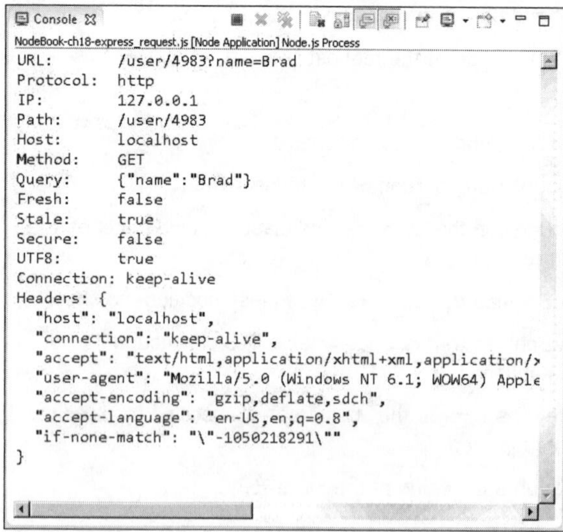

Figure 18.2 Accessing properties of the `Request` object

Using `Response` Objects

The `Response` object passed to the route handler provides the necessary functionality to build and send a proper HTTP response. The following sections discuss using the `Response` object to set headers, set the status, and send data back to the client.

Setting Headers

An important part of formulating a proper HTTP response is to set the headers. For example, setting the `Content-Type` header determines how the browser handles the response. The `Response` object provides several helper methods to get and set the header values that are sent with the HTTP response.

The most commonly used methods are `get(header)` and `set(header, value)`, which gets and sets any header value. For example, the following code first gets `the Content-Type` header and then sets it:

```
var oldType = res.get('Content-Type');
res.set('Content-Type', 'text/plain');
```

Table 18.3 describes the helper methods to get and set header values.

Table 18.3 **Methods to get and set header values on the Response object**

Setting	Description
`get(header)`	Returns the value of the `header` specified.
`set(header, value)`	Sets the value of the `header`.
`set(headerObj)`	Accepts an object that contains multiple `'header':'value'` properties. Each of the headers in the `headerObj` is set in the `Response` object.
`location(path)`	Sets the location header to the `path` specified. The path can be a URL path such as `/login`, a full URL such as `http://server.net/`, a relative path such as `../users`, or a browser action such as `back`.
`type(type_string)`	Sets the `Content-Type` header based on the `type_string` parameter. The `type_string` parameter can be a normal content type such as `application/json`, a partial type such as `png`, or it can be a file extension such as `.html`.
`attachment([filepath])`	Sets the `Content-Disposition` header to attachment, and if a `filepath` is specified the `Content-Type` header is set based on the file extension.

Setting the Status

You also need to set the HTTP status for the response if it is something other than 200. It is important to send the correct status response so that the browser or other applications can handle the HTTP response correctly. To set the status response, use the `status(number)` method where the number parameter is the HTTP response status defined in the HTTP spec.

For example, the following lines set different statuses:

```
res.status(200); // OK
res.status(300); // Redirection
res.status(400); // Bad Request
res.status(401); // Unauthorized
res.status(403); // Forbidden
res.status(500); // Server Error
```

Sending Response

You already saw the `send()` method in action when sending simple responses in some earlier examples in this chapter. The `send()` method can use one of the following formats, where status is the HTTP status code and body is a `String` or `Buffer` object:

```
res.send(status, [body])
res.send([body])
```

If you specify a `Buffer` object, the `Content-Type` is automatically set to `application/octet-stream` unless you explicitly set it to something else. For example:

```
res.set('Content-Type', 'text/html');
res.send(new Buffer('<html><body>HTML String</body></html>'));
```

The `send()` method can really handle all the responses necessary as long as you set the appropriate headers and status for the response. Once the `send()` method completes, it sets the value of the `res.finished` and `res.headerSent` properties. You can use these to verify the response was sent as well as how much data was transferred. The following shows an example value of the `res.headerSent` property:

```
HTTP/1.1 200 OK
X-Powered-By: Express
Content-Type: text/html
Content-Length: 92
Date: Tue, 17 Dec 2013 18:52:23 GMT
Connection: keep-alive
```

Listing 18.4 illustrates some of the basics of setting the status and headers, and sending a response. Notice that in lines 18–21 the route for `/error` sets the status to 400 before sending the response. Figure 18.3 shows the `res.headerSent` data in the console output on the Express server.

Listing 18.4 `express_send.js`: **Sending status, headers, and response data using the** `Response` **object**

```
01 var express = require('express');
02 var url = require('url');
03 var app = express();
04 app.listen(80);
05 app.get('/', function (req, res) {
06   var response = '<html><head><title>Simple Send</title></head>' +
07                  '<body><h1>Hello from Express</h1></body></html>';
08   res.status(200);
09   res.set({
10     'Content-Type': 'text/html',
11     'Content-Length': response.length
12   });
13   res.send(response);
14   console.log('Response Finished? ' + res.finished);
15   console.log('\nHeaders Sent: ');
16   console.log(res.headerSent);
17 });
18 app.get('/error', function (req, res) {
19   res.status(400);
20   res.send("This is a bad request.");
21 });
```

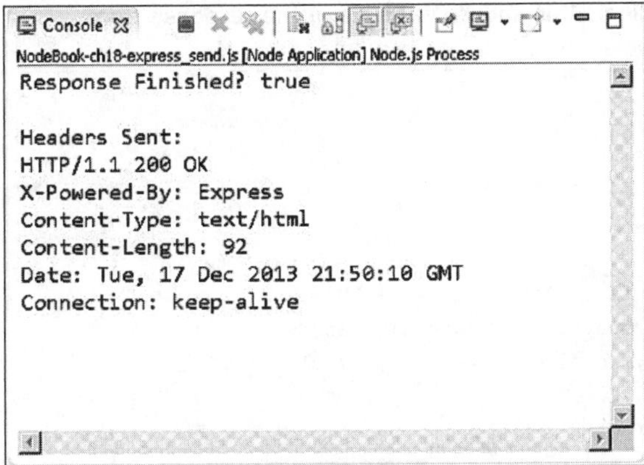

Figure 18.3 The res.headerSent output after a response has been sent

Sending JSON Responses

A growing trend has been to use JSON data to transfer information from the server to the client and then having the client dynamically populate the HTML elements on the page, rather than the server building HTML documents or parts of HTML documents and sending the HTML to the client. Express facilitates sending JSON by providing the json() and jsonp() methods on the Response object. These methods use a similar syntax as send() except that the body is a JSON stringifiable JavaScript object:

```
res.json(status, [object])
res.json([body])
res.jsonp(status, [object])
res.jsonp([object])
```

The JavaScript object is converted to a JSON string and sent back to the client. In the case of jsonp(), the URL of the request object includes a ?callback=<method> parameter and then the JSON string is wrapped in a function with the method name that can be called from the browser client to support the JSONP design.

Listing 18.5 implements both json() and jsonp() to illustrate sending JSON data back to the server. Notice that in line 6 the json spaces application setting is set to 4, and in line 7 a basic JavaScript object is passed into the json() call. On line 12 an error code is set in the response, and the response object is a JSON object.

In lines 14–19 the jsonp() method is implemented. Notice that the jsonp callback name is set to cb in line 15. That means that instead of passing ?callback=<function> in the URL, the client needs to pass ?cb=<function> in the URL. Figure 18.4 shows the output to the browser for each of these calls.

Listing 18.5 `express_json.js`: **Sending JSON and JSONP data in the response from Express**

```
var express = require('express');
var url = require('url');
var app = express();
app.listen(80);
app.get('/json', function (req, res) {
  app.set('json spaces', 4);
  res.json({name:"Smithsonian", built:'1846', items:'137M',
            centers: ['art', 'astrophysics', 'natural history',
                      'planetary', 'biology', 'space', 'zoo']});
});
app.get('/error', function (req, res) {
  res.json(500, {status:false, message:"Internal Server Error"});
});
app.get('/jsonp', function (req, res) {
  app.set('jsonp callback name', 'cb');
  res.jsonp({name:"Smithsonian", built:'1846', items:'137M',
            centers: ['art', 'astrophysics', 'natural history',
                      'planetary', 'biology', 'space', 'zoo']});
});
```

Sending Files

A great helper method in Express is the `sendfile(filepath)` method on the `Response` object. The `sendfile()` method does everything that needs to be done to send files to the client in a single function call. Specifically, the `sendfile()` method does the following:

- Sets the `Content-Type` header to the type based on file extension
- Sets other appropriate headers such as `Content-Length`
- Sets the status of the response
- Sends the contents of the file to the client using the connection inside the `Response` object

The `sendfile()` method uses the following syntax:

```
res.sendfile(path, [options], [callback])
```

The `path` should point to the file that you want to send to the client. The `options` parameter is an object that contains a `maxAge` property that defines the maximum age for the content and a `root` property that is a root path to support relative paths in the `path` parameter. The `callback` function is called when the file transfer is complete and should accept an `error` object as the only parameter.

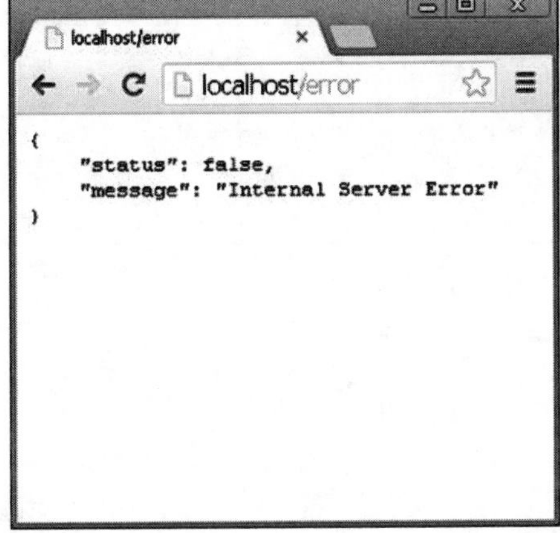

Figure 18.4 Sending JSON and JSONP data to the browser

Listing 18.6 illustrates how easy it is to send the contents of a file using the `sendfile()` command. Notice that a `root` path is specified in line 8, so only the filename is required in line 6. Also notice that the `callback` function has code to handle the error. Figure 18.5 shows the image displayed in the browser.

Listing 18.6 `express_send_file.js`: **Sending files in an HTTP request from Express**

```
01 var express = require('express');
02 var url = require('url');
03 var app = express();
04 app.listen(80);
05 app.get('/image', function (req, res) {
06   res.sendfile('arch.jpg',
07                { maxAge: 1,//24*60*60*1000,
08                  root: './views/'},
09                function(err){
10     if (err){
11       console.log("Error");
12     } else {
13       console.log("Success");
14     }
15   });
16 });
```

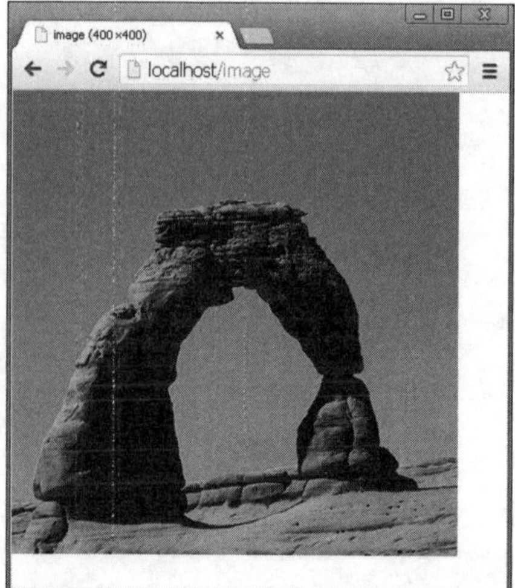

Figure 18.5 Image file sent in an HTTP response to the client

Sending a Download Response

Express also includes a `res.download()` method that works similarly to the `res.sendfile()` method with only a few differences. The `res.download()` method sends the file in the HTTP response as an attachment, which means the `Content-Disposition` header will be set. The `res.download()` method uses the following syntax:

```
res.download(path, [filename], [callback])
```

The `path` points to the file to send to the client. The `filename` parameter can specify a different filename that should be sent in the `Content-Disposition` header. The `callback` function is executed once the file download has completed.

Redirecting the Response

A common need when implementing a webserver is the ability to redirect a request from the client to a different location on the same server or on a completely different server. The `res.redirect(path)` method handles redirection of the request to a new location.

Listing 18.7 illustrates the various redirection addressing that you can use. In line 6 a redirect is done to a completely new domain address. In line 9 a redirect is made to a different path on the same server, and in line 15 a redirect is made to a relative path on the same server.

Listing 18.7 `express_redirect.js`: **Redirecting requests on an Express server**

```
01 var express = require('express');
02 var url = require('url');
03 var app = express();
04 app.listen(80);
05 app.get('/google', function (req, res) {
06   res.redirect('http://google.com');
07 });
08 app.get('/first', function (req, res) {
09   res.redirect('/second');
10 });
11 app.get('/second', function (req, res) {
12   res.send("Response from Second");
13 });
14 app.get('/level/A', function (req, res) {
15   res.redirect("../B");
16 });
17 app.get('/level/B', function (req, res) {
18   res.send("Response from Level B");
19 });
```

Implementing a Template Engine

A growing trend in the industry is to use a template engine to generate HTML using a template file and application data rather than trying to build HTML files from scratch or use static files. The template engines use the template object to build HTML based on values provided by the application. Template engines provide two benefits:

- **Simplicity:** Templates try to make it easy to generate the HTML either by a shorthand notation or by allowing JavaScript to be embedded in the HTML document directly.
- **Speed:** Template engines optimize the process of building the HTML documents. Many compile a template and store the compiled version in a cache that makes it faster to generate the HTML response.

The following sections discuss implementing template engines in Express. Several template engines are available for use in Express, and in this section, you learn about Pug (formerly Jade) and Embedded JavaScript (EJS). These two work in different ways and together give you an idea of what is available. Pug uses a shorthand notation of HTML in the template, so the template files do not look anything like HTML. The advantage is that the template files are small and easy to follow. The disadvantage is that you need to learn yet another language.

EJS, on the other hand, uses special notation to embed JavaScript in normal HTML documents. This makes it much easier to transition from normal HTML. The downside is that the HTML documents are even more complex than the originals and not as tidy as Pug templates.

To run the example for this section, you need to install both the Pug and EJS modules in your application using the following commands:

```
npm install Pug
npm install EJS
```

Defining the Engine

The first step in implementing a template engine is to define a default template engine for the Express application. This is done by setting the `view engine` setting on the `express()` application object. You also need to set the `views` setting to the location where your template files are stored. For example, the following sets the `./views` directory as the root for template documents and `pug` as the view engine:

```
var app = express();
app.set('views', './views');
app.set('view engine', 'pug');
```

Then you need to register the template engines for the template extensions that you want them to handle using the `app.engine(ext, callback)` method. The `ext` parameter is the file extension used for the template files, and the `callback` is a function that supports Express's rendering functionality.

Many engines provide the callback functionality in an `__express` function. For example:

```
app.engine('pug', require('pug').__express)
```

The `__express` functionality often only works on the default extension name. In that case, you can use a different function. For example, EJS provides the `renderFile` function for that purpose. You can use the following to register EJS for `ejs` extensions:

```
app.engine('ejs', require('ejs').__express)
```

However, if you want to register EJS for HTML extensions, you use

```
app.engine('html', require('ejs').renderFile)
```

Once the extension is registered, the engine callback function is be called to render any templates with that extension. If you choose a different engine besides Pug or EJS, you need to figure out how they expect to register with Express.

Adding Locals

When rendering a template, you often want to include dynamic data—for example, to render a user page for user data just read from the database. In this case you can generate a `locals` object that contains properties that map to variable names defined in the templates. The `express()` app object provides the `app.locals` property to store local variables.

To assign a local template variable directly, you can use dot syntax. For example, the following code defines the local variables `title` and `version`:

```
app.locals.title = 'My App';
app.locals.version = 10;
```

Creating Templates

You also need to create template files. When creating template files, keep in mind these considerations:

- **Reusability:** Try to make your templates reusable in other parts of your application and in other applications. Most template engines cache the templates to speed up performance. The more templates you have requires more caching time. Try to organize your templates so that they can be used for multiple purposes. For example, if you have several tables of a data displayed in your app, only make a single template for all of them that can not only dynamically add the data, but can also set column headers, titles, and such.
- **Size:** As template sizes grow, they tend to become more and more unwieldy. Try to keep your templates compartmentalized to the type of data they are presenting. For example, a page that has a menu bar, form, and table could be split into three separate templates.
- **Hierarchy:** Most websites and applications are built on some sort of hierarchy. For example, the `<head>` section as well as a banner and menu may be the same throughout the site. Use a separate template for components that show up in multiple locations, and just include those subtemplates when building your final page.

Listing 18.8 shows a basic EJS template that applies a set of local variables in a list to display user information. The EJS code is basic and only uses the <%= variable %> to pull values from the Express local variables.

Listing 18.8 `user_ejs.html`: **Simple EJS template for displaying a user**

```
<!DOCTYPE html>
<html lang="en">
<head>
<title>EJS Template</title>
</head>
<body>
  <h1>User using EJS Template</h1>
    <ul>
        <li>Name: <%= uname %></li>
        <li>Vehicle: <%= vehicle %></li>
        <li>Terrain: <%= terrain %></li>
        <li>Climate: <%= climate %></li>
        <li>Location: <%= location %></li>
    </ul>
</body>
</html>
```

Listing 18.9 and Listing 18.10 show using Pug to implement a main template and then consume it in a subtemplate. The main template in Listing 18.9 is basic, only implementing the `doctype`, `html`, `head`, and `title` elements. It also defines the `block content` element defined in Listing 18.10.

Notice that line 1 in Listing 18.10 extends `main_pug` to include those elements first and then adds the `h1`, `ul`, and `li` elements, which get values from the `local` variables.

Listing 18.9 `main_pug.pug`: **Simple Pug template that defines the main webpage**

```
doctype 5
html(lang="en")
  head
    title="Pug Template"
  body
    block content
```

Listing 18.10 `user_pug.pug`: **Simple Pug template that includes the main_pug.pug template and adds elements for displaying a user**

```
1 extends main_pug
2 block content
3   h1 User using Pug Template
```

```
  ul
    li Name: #{uname}
    li Vehicle: #{vehicle}
    li Terrain: #{terrain}
    li Climate: #{climate}
    li Location: #{location}
```

Rendering Templates in a Response

Once you have the template engine defined and configured and have created your templates, you can send a rendered template using the Express `app` object or using the `Response` object. To render a template in the Express `app` you use the `app.render()` method:

```
app.render(view, [locals], callback)
```

The `view` parameter specifies the view filename in the views directory. If no extension is included on the file, the default extensions such as `.pug` and `.ejs` are tried. The `locals` parameter allows you to pass in a `locals` object if one has not been defined in `app.locals` already. The `callback` function is executed after the template has been rendered and accepts an `error` object for the first parameter and the string form of the rendered template as the second.

To render a template directly into the response, you can also use the `res.render()` function, which works exactly the same as `app.render()`, except that no callback is needed. The rendered results automatically are sent in the response.

The `app.render()` and `res.render()` methods both work well. If you do not need to do anything with the data before sending it, the `res.render()` method saves the extra code to call `res.send()` to send the data.

Listing 18.11 puts all the template rendering concepts together in a couple of basic examples. Lines 5–8 set up the `views` directory and `view engine` and register `pug` and `ejs`. Then in lines 10–13 user information is defined in `app.locals`.

Lines 14–16 handle the `/pug` route, which directly renders the `user_pug.pug` template from Listing 18.10 with the defined locals in the client response.

Lines 17–21 handle the `/ejs` route by first calling `app.render()` to render the `users_ejs.html` template defined in Listing 18.8 into a string, `renderedData`. Then that data is sent using the `res.send()` command. Figure 18.6 shows the rendered webpages from both functions.

Listing 18.11 `express_templates.js`: **Implementing Pug and EJS templates in Express**

```
01 var express = require('express'),
02     pug = require('pug'),
03     ejs = require('ejs');
04 var app = express();
05 app.set('views', './views');
```

```
app.set('view engine', 'pug');
app.engine('pug', pug.__express);
app.engine('html', ejs.renderFile);
app.listen(80);
app.locals.uname = 'Caleb';
app.locals.vehicle = 'TARDIS';
app.locals.terrain = 'time and space';
app.locals.location = 'anywhere anytime';
app.get('/pug', function (req, res) {
  res.render('user_pug');
});
app.get('/ejs', function (req, res) {
  app.render('user_ejs.html', function(err, renderedData){
    res.send(renderedData);
  });
});
```

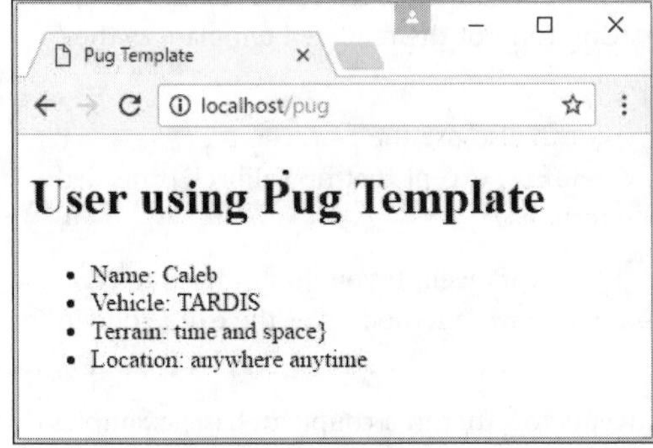

Figure 18.6 Webpages generated by rendering Pug and EJS templates

Summary

This chapter focused on the basics of getting Express installed, configured, and running for your Node.js applications. You learned how to configure routes to handle HTTP requests and how to use the `Request` object to get information about the request. You also learned how to configure the headers and status for the response and then send HTML strings, files, and rendered templates.

Next

In the next chapter, you implement some of the middleware that Express provides to extend functionality. Middleware allows you to handle cookies, sessions, and authentication as well as control the cache.

19

Implementing Express Middleware

Much of the functionality that Express brings to the table is through middleware functions that get executed between the point when the request is received by Node.js and the time that the response is sent. Express uses the `connect` module to provide a middleware framework that allows you to easily insert middleware functionality on a global or path level or for a single route.

The middleware provided with Express allows you to quickly support serving static files, implement cookies, support sessions, process `POST` data, and much more. You can even create your own custom middleware functions that can be used to preprocess the requests and provide your own functionality.

This chapter focuses on the basics of implementing Express middleware. It also provides some examples of using middleware to handle `POST` requests, serve static files, and implement sessions, cookies, and authentication.

Understanding Middleware

Express provides a simple but effective middleware framework that allows you to provide additional functionality between the point when a request is received and when you actually handle the request and send the response. Middleware allows you to apply authentication, cookies, and sessions and otherwise manipulate the request before it is passed to the handler.

Express is built on top of the `connect` NPM module, which provides the underlying middleware support. The following list describes some of the built-in middleware components that come with Express. Additional Express middleware components are available as NPMs if you query the NPM repository, and you can also create your own custom middleware:

- **`logger`**: Implements a formatted request logger to track requests to the server
- **`static`**: Allows the Express server to stream static file get requests
- **`favicon`**: Provides functionality to support sending the favicon to the browser

- **basicAuth**: Provides support for basic HTTP authentication
- **cookieParser**: Allows you to read cookies from the request and set cookies in the response
- **cookieSession**: Provides cookie-based session support
- **session**: Provides a fairly robust session implementation
- **bodyParser**: Parses the body data of `POST` requests into the `req.body` property
- **query**: Converts the query string to a JavaScript object and stores it as `req.query`
- **compress**: Provides Gzip compress support for large responses to the client
- **csrf**: Provides cross-site request forgery protection

Middleware can be applied either globally to all routes under a specific path or to specific routes. The following sections describe each of these methods.

Assigning Middleware Globally to a Path

To assign middleware to all routes, you can implement the `use()` method on the Express `application` object. The `use()` method uses the following syntax:

```
use([path], middleware)
```

The `path` variable is optional and defaults to /, which mean all paths. The `middleware` is a function that has the following syntax, where `req` is the `Request` object, `res` is the `Response` object, and `next` is the next middleware function to execute:

```
function(req, res, next)
```

Each of the built-in middleware components has a constructor that returns the appropriate middleware function. For example, to apply the `logger` middleware to all paths with default parameters, you use the following statements:

```
var express = require('express');
var app = express();
app.use('/', express.logger());
```

Assigning Middleware to a Single Route

You can also apply `logger` to a single route by passing it after the `path` parameter. For example, in the following code, requests to the `/loggedRoute` are logged; however, requests to the `/otherRoute` are not logged.

```
app.get('/loggedRoute', express.logger(), function(req, res) {
  res.send('This request was logged.');
});
app.get('/otherRoute', function(req, res) {
  res.send('This request was not logged.');
});
```

Adding Multiple Middleware Functions

You can assign as many middleware functions globally and to routes as you want. For example, the following code assigns the `query`, `logger`, and `bodyParser` middleware modules:

```
app.use('/', express.logger()).
use('/', express.query()).
use('/', express.bodyParser());
```

Keep in mind that the order you assign the functions is the order that they will be applied during a request. Some middleware functions need to be added before others.

Using the `query` Middleware

One of the most useful and simple middleware components is the `query` middleware. The `query` middleware converts the query string in the URL into a JavaScript object and stores it as the `query` property on the `Request` object.

The following code shows the basics of implementing the `query` middleware. The query string for the request looks like `?id=10,score=95`. Notice that `JSON.stringify` can be called on `req.query` because it is a JavaScript object.

```
var express = require('express');
var app = express();
app.use('/', express.query());
app.get('/', function(req, res) {
  var id = req.query.id;
  var score = req.query.score;
  console.log(JSON.stringify(req.query));
  res.send("done");
});
```

Serving Static Files

A commonly used Express middleware is the `static` middleware, which allows you to serve static files directly from disk to the client. You can use `static` middleware to support things like JavaScript files, CSS files, image files, and HTML documents that do not change. The `static` module is easy to implement and uses the following syntax:

```
express.static(path, [options])
```

The `path` is the root path to where the static files are referenced from in the requests. The `options` parameter allows you to set the following properties:

- **`maxAge`:** Sets the browser cache `maxAge` in milliseconds. The default is `0`.
- **`hidden`:** A Boolean that, when `true`, indicates that transfer of hidden files is enabled. The default is `false`.

- **`redirect`:** A Boolean that, when `true`, indicates that if the request path is a directory, the request is redirected to the path with a trailing /. The default is `true`.
- **`index`:** Specifies the default filename for the root path. The default is `index.html`.

Listings 19.1 through 19.3 show the Express code, HTML, and CSS that illustrate implementing the `static` middleware to support serving a static HTML, CSS, and image file. Notice that two `static` paths are implemented: one for the route / that maps to a subdirectory named `static` and the second for route `/images` that maps to a peer directory named `images`. Figure 19.1 shows the statically served HTML document in a web browser.

Listing 19.1 `express_static.js`: **Express code that implements two static routes**

```
var express = require('express');
var app = express();
app.use('/', express.static('./static'), {maxAge:60*60*1000});
app.use('/images', express.static( '../images'));
app.listen(80);
```

Listing 19.2 `./static/index.html`: **Static HTML file that requests the CSS and image files from the server**

```
<html>
<head>
  <title>Static File</title>
  <link rel="stylesheet" type="text/css" href="css/static.css">
</head>
<body>
    <img src="/images/arch.jpg" height="200px"/>
    <img src="/images/flower.jpg" height="200px" />
    <img src="/images/bison.jpg" height="200px" />
</body>
</html>
```

Listing 19.3 `./static/css/static.css`: **CSS file that formats the images**

```
img
{
    display:inline;
    margin:3px;
    border:5px solid #000000;
}
```

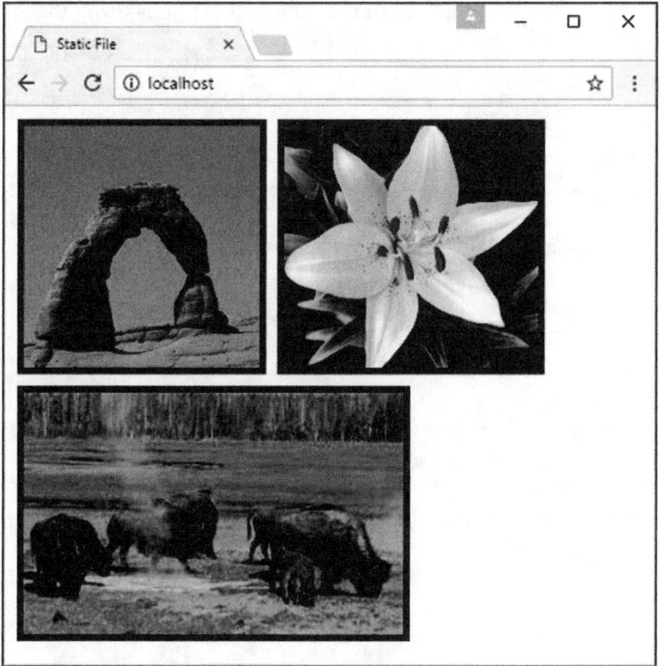

Figure 19.1 HTML, CSS, and image files served statically to a browser

Handling POST Body Data

Another common use for Express middleware is to handle body data inside a `POST` request. The data inside a request body can be in various formats such as `POST` parameter strings, JSON strings, or raw data. Express provides the `bodyParser` middleware that attempts to parse the data in the body of requests and properly format them as the `req.body` property of the `Request` object.

For example, if `POST` parameters or JSON data is received they are converted to a JavaScript object and stored as the `req.body` property of the `Request` object. Listing 19.4 illustrates using the `bodyParser` middleware to support reading form data posted to the server.

Lines 4–9 handle the `GET` request and respond with a basic form. It is not well formatted HTML; however, it is adequate to illustrate the use of the `bodyParser` middleware.

Lines 11–20 implement a `POST` request handler. Notice that in line 16, the first name entered in the form field is accessed using `req.body.first` to help build the hello message in the response. That really is it. You can handle any kind of form data in the body in this manner. Figure 19.2 shows the web form usage in the browser.

Listing 19.4 `express_post.js`: **Handling `POST` parameters in the request body using the `bodyParser` middleware**

```
var express = require('express');
var app = express();
app.use(express.bodyParser());
app.get('/', function (req, res) {
  var response = '<form method="POST">' +
        'First: <input type="text" name="first"><br>' +
        'Last: <input type="text" name="last"><br>' +
        '<input type="submit" value="Submit"></form>';
  res.send(response);
});
app.post('/',function(req, res){
  var response = '<form method="POST">' +
        'First: <input type="text" name="first"><br>' +
        'Last: <input type="text" name="last"><br>' +
        '<input type="submit" value="Submit"></form>' +
        '<h1>Hello ' + req.body.first + '</h1>';
  res.type('html');
  res.end(response);
  console.log(req.body);
});
app.listen(80);
```

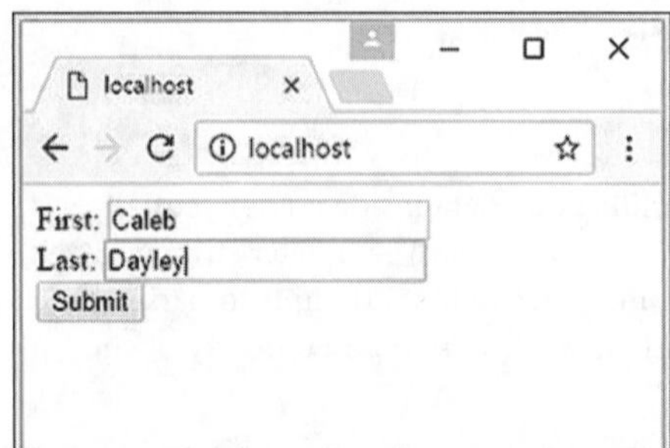

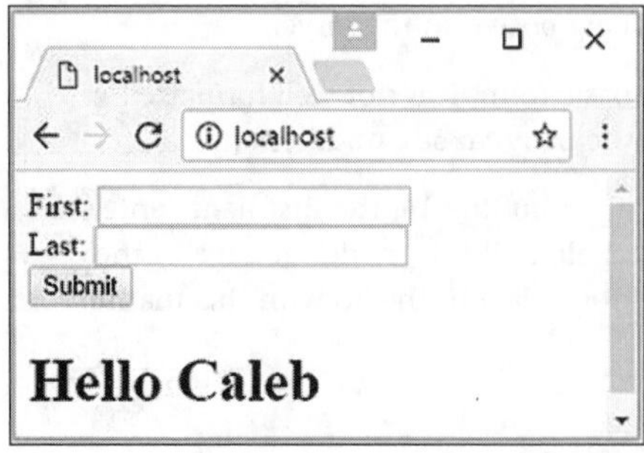

Figure 19.2 Handling `POST` parameters in the request body using the `bodyParser` middleware

Sending and Receiving Cookies

The `cookieParser` middleware provided in Express makes handling cookies simple. The `cookieParser` middleware parses the cookies from the request and stores them in the `req.cookies` property as a JavaScript object. The `cookieParser` middleware uses the following syntax:

```
express.cookieParser([secret])
```

The optional `secret` string parameter prevents cookie tampering by internally signing the cookies using the secret string.

To set a cookie in a response, you can use the `res.cookie()` method shown below:

```
res.cookie(name, value, [options])
```

A cookie with the `name` and `value` specified is added to the response. The `options` property allows you to set the following properties for the cookie:

- **`maxAge`:** Specifies the amount of time in milliseconds for the cookie to live before it expires.
- **`httpOnly`:** A Boolean that, when `true`, indicates that this cookie should only be accessed by the server and by not client-side JavaScript.
- **`signed`:** A Boolean that, when `true`, indicates that the cookie will be signed and you need to access it using the `req.signedCookie` object instead of the `req.cookie` object.
- **`path`:** Specifies the path that the cookie applies to.

For example, the following sets a `hasVisited` cookie:

```
res.cookie('hasVisited', '1',
           { maxAge: 60*60*1000,
             httpOnly: true,
             path:'/'});
```

Cookies can be removed from the client using the `res.clearCookie()` method. For example:

```
res.clearCookie('hasVisited');
```

Listing 19.5 illustrates a simple implementation of getting a cookie named `req.cookies.hasVisited` from the request, and if it hasn't been set, setting it.

Listing 19.5 `express_cookies.js`: **Sending and receiving cookies using Express**

```
var express = require('express');
var app = express();
app.use(express.cookies());
app.get('/', function(req, res) {
  console.log(req.cookies);
  if (!req.cookies.hasVisited){
    res.cookie('hasVisited', '1',
               { maxAge: 60*60*1000,
                 httpOnly: true,
```

```
                   path:'/'});
  }
  res.send("Sending Cookie");
});
app.listen(80);
```

Implementing Sessions

You can also use Express middleware to provide session support for your applications. For complex session management, you may want to implement it yourself; however, for basic session support, the `cookieSession` middleware works relatively well.

The `cookieSession` middleware utilizes the `cookieParser` middleware underneath, so you need to add `cookieParser` prior to adding `cookieSession`. The following shows the syntax for adding the `cookieSession` middleware:

```
res.cookie([options])
```

The `options` property allows you to set the following properties for the cookie:

- **`key`:** Name of the cookie that identifies the session.
- **`secret`:** String used to sign the session cookie to prevent cookie tampering.
- **`cookie`:** An object that defines the cookie settings, including `maxAge`, `path`, `httpOnly`, and `signed`. The default is `{ path:'/', httpOnly:true, maxAge:null }`
- **`proxy`:** A Boolean that, when `true`, causes Express to trust the reverse proxy when setting secure cookies via `x-forwarded-proto`.

When `cookieSession` is implemented, the session is stored as an object in `req.session`. Any changes you make to `req.session` flow across multiple requests from the same browser.

Listing 19.6 shows an example of implementing a basic `cookieSession` session. Notice that `cookieParser` is added first in line 3 and then `cookieSession` is added in line 4 with a secret string. There are two routes in the example. When `/restricted` route is accessed, the `restrictedCount` value is incremented in the session and the response is redirected to `/library`. Then in `library`, if the `restrictedCount` is not `undefined`, the value is displayed; otherwise, a welcome message is displayed. Figure 19.3 shows the different outputs in the web browser.

Listing 19.6 `express_session.js`: Implementing a basic cookie session using Express

```
01 var express = require('express');
02 var app = express();
03 app.use(express.cookieParser());
04 app.use(express.cookieSession({secret: 'MAGICALEXPRESSKEY'}));
05 app.get('/library', function(req, res) {
06   console.log(req.cookies);
07   if(req.session.restricted) {
```

```
    res.send('You have been in the restricted section ' +
             req.session.restrictedCount + ' times.');
  }else {
    res.send('Welcome to the library.');
  }
});
app.get('/restricted', function(req, res) {
  req.session.restricted = true;
  if(!req.session.restrictedCount){
    req.session.restrictedCount = 1;
  } else {
    req.session.restrictedCount += 1;
  }
  res.redirect('/library');
});
app.listen(80);
```

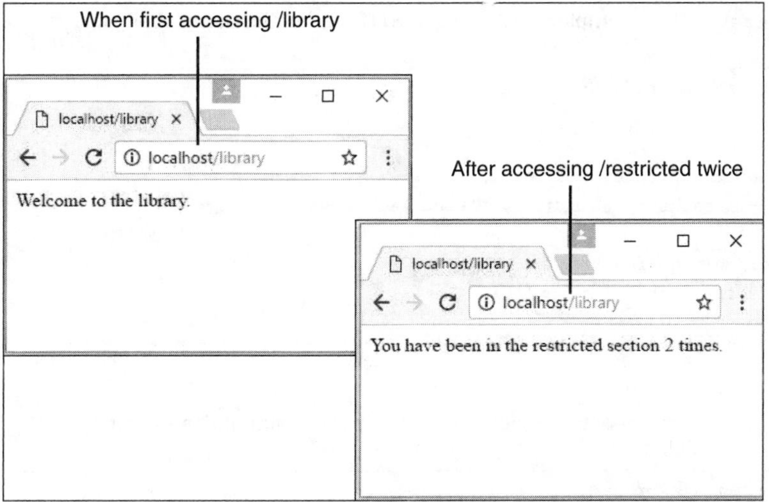

Figure 19.3 Using basic session handling to track improper access to a route

Applying Basic HTTP Authentication

Express middleware also is commonly used to apply basic HTTP authentication. HTTP authentication uses the `Authorization` header to send the encoded username and password from the browser to the server. If no authorization information is stored in the browser for the URL, the browser launches a basic login dialog box to allow the user to enter the username and password. Basic HTTP authentication works well for basic sites that require a minimal authentication method, and is easy to implement.

The `basicAuth` middleware function in Express provides the support to handle basic HTTP authentication. The `basicAuth` middleware uses the following syntax:

```
express.basicAuth(function(user, pass){})
```

The function passed to `basicAuth` accepts the `user` and `password` and then returns `true` if they are correct or `false` if they are not. For example:

```
app.use(express.basicAuth(function(user, password) {
  return (user === 'testuser' && pass === 'test');
}));
```

Typically, you store the `user` and `password` in the database and inside the authentication function retrieve the user object to validate against.

Listing 19.7 and Listing 19.8 illustrate how easy it is to implement the `basicAuth` middleware. Listing 19.7 implements a global authentication, and Listing 19.8 implements authentication against a single route. Figure 19.4 shows the browser requesting authentication and then the authenticated webpage.

Listing 19.7 `express_auth.js`: **Implementing basic HTTP authentication globally for the site**

```
var express = require('express');
var app = express();
app.listen(80);
app.use(express.basicAuth(function(user, pass) {
  return (user === 'testuser' && pass === 'test');
}));
app.get('/', function(req, res) {
  res.send('Successful Authentication!');
});
```

Listing 19.8 `express_auth_one.js`: **Implementing basic HTTP authentication for a single route**

```
var express = require('express');
var app = express();
var auth = express.basicAuth(function(user, pass) {
  return (user === 'testuser' && pass === 'test');
});
app.get('/library', function(req, res) {
  res.send('Welcome to the library.');
});
app.get('/restricted', auth, function(req, res) {
  res.send('Welcome to the restricted section.');
});
app.listen(80);
```

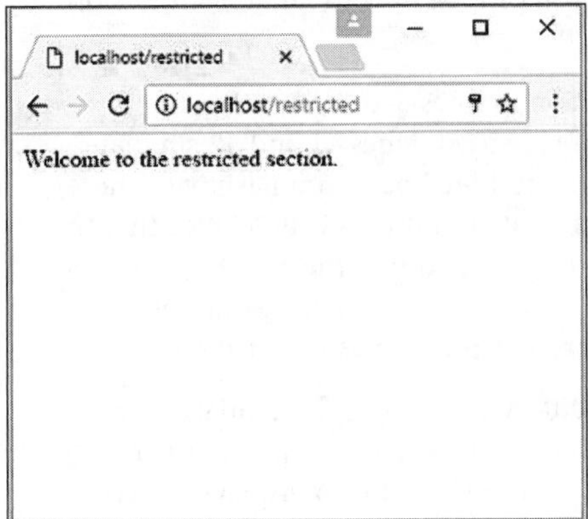

Figure 19.4 Using basic HTTP authentication

Implementing Session Authentication

A major downside to basic HTTP authentication is that the login sticks around as long as the credentials are stored and is not really all that secure. A much better route is to implement your own authentication and store the authentication in a session that you can expire whenever you want.

The `session` middleware inside Express works well for implementing session authentication. The `session` middleware attaches a `Session` object `req.session` to the `Request` object that provides the session functionality. Table 19.1 describes the methods that can be called on the `res.session` object.

Table 19.1 **Methods on the `res.session` object to manage sessions**

Option	Description
`regenerate([callback])`	Removes the `req.session` object and creates a new one enabling you to reset the session
`destroy([callback])`	Removes the `req.session` object
`save([callback])`	Saves the session data
`touch([callback])`	Resets the `maxAge` count for the session cookie
`cookie`	Specifies the cookie object linking the session to the browser

Listing 19.9 illustrates implementing session authentication using the `crypto` module to generate secure passwords. The example is rudimentary to keep it small enough for the book; however, it contains the basic functionality so you can see how to implement session authentication.

The passwords are encrypted using the `hasPW()` function in lines 3–6. Notice that the `bodyParser`, `cookieParser`, and `session` middleware are used. Lines 41 and 42 simulate getting a user object from the database and comparing the stored password hash with the password hash from the request body. The `session` is created in lines 45–49. Notice that the `regenerate()` function is used to regenerate a new `session` and that the `callback` function passed to `regenerate()` sets the `session.user` and `session.success` properties of the session. If the authentication fails, only the `session.error` property is set for the `session`.

The `/login` get route in lines 26–38 displays a rudimentary login to get credentials. If `session.error` is set, it is also displayed on the login page. The `/restricted` route in lines 11–20 checks the session to see whether it has a valid user, and if so displays a success message; otherwise, the `session.error` is set and the response is redirected to `/login`.

The `/logout` route in lines 21–25 calls `destroy()` on the `session` to remove the authentication. You could also have other code destroy the `session` based on a timeout, amount of requests, and so on. Figure 19.5 shows the browser screens forcing a login and then displaying success.

Listing 19.9 `express_auth_session.js`: **Implementing session authentication in Express**

```
01 var express = require('express');
02 var crypto = require('crypto');
03 function hashPW(pwd){
04   return crypto.createHash('sha256').update(pwd).
05          digest('base64').toString();
06 }
07 var app = express();
08 app.use(express.bodyParser());
09 app.use(express.cookieParser('MAGICString'));
10 app.use(express.session());
```

```
app.get('/restricted', function(req, res){
  if (req.session.user) {
    res.send('<h2>'+ req.session.success + '</h2>' +
             '<p>You have Entered the restricted section<p><br>' +
             ' <a href="/logout">logout</a>');
  } else {
    req.session.error = 'Access denied!';
    res.redirect('/login');
  }
});
app.get('/logout', function(req, res){
  req.session.destroy(function(){
    res.redirect('/login');
  });
});
app.get('/login', function(req, res){
  var response = '<form method="POST">' +
    'Username: <input type="text" name="username"><br>' +
    'Password: <input type="password" name="password"><br>' +
    '<input type="submit" value="Submit"></form>';
  if(req.session.user){
    res.redirect('/restricted');
  }else if(req.session.error){
    response +='<h2>' + req.session.error + '<h2>';
  }
  res.type('html');
  res.send(response);
});
app.post('/login', function(req, res){
  //user should be a lookup of req.body.username in database
  var user = {name:req.body.username, password:hashPW("myPass")};
  if (user.password === hashPW(req.body.password.toString())) {
    req.session.regenerate(function(){
      req.session.user = user;
      req.session.success = 'Authenticated as ' + user.name;
      res.redirect('/restricted');
    });
  } else {
    req.session.regenerate(function(){
      req.session.error = 'Authentication failed.';
      res.redirect('/restricted');
    });
    res.redirect('/login');
  }
});
app.listen(80);
```

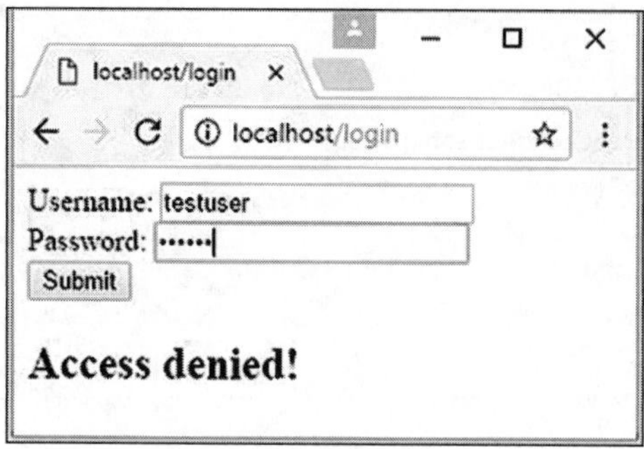

Figure 19.5 Implementing session authentication in Node.js using Express session middleware

Creating Custom Middleware

A great feature of Express middleware is the ability to create your own. All you need to do is provide a function that accepts the `Request` object as the first parameter, the `Response` object as the second parameter, and a `next` parameter as the third. The `next` parameter is a function passed by the middleware framework that points to the next middleware function to execute, so you must call `next()` prior to exiting your custom function or the handler will never be called.

To illustrate how easy it is to implement your own custom middleware functionality in Express, Listing 19.10 implements a middleware function named `queryRemover()` that strips the query string off the URL prior to sending it on to the handler.

Notice that `queryRemover()` accepts a the `Request` and `Response` objects as the first two parameters and the `next` parameter as the third. The `next()` callback function is executed prior to leaving the middleware function as required. Figure 19.6 displays the console output showing that the query string portion of the URL has been removed.

Listing 19.10 `express_middleware.js`: **Implementing custom middleware to remove the query string from the `Request` object**

```
var express = require('express');
var app = express();
function queryRemover(req, res, next){
  console.log("\nBefore URL: ");
  console.log(req.url);
  req.url = req.url.split('?')[0];
  console.log("\nAfter URL: ");
  console.log(req.url);
  next();
};
app.use(queryRemover);
app.get('/no/query', function(req, res) {
  res.send("test");
});
app.listen(80);
```

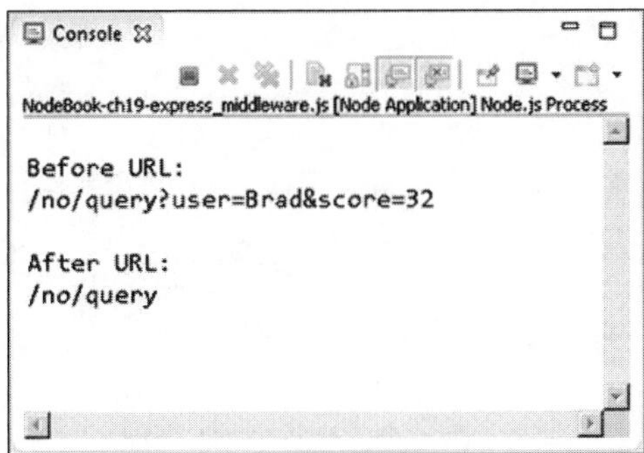

Figure 19.6 Implementing custom middleware to remove the query string from the `Request` object

Summary

This chapter introduced you to the world of Express middleware and how to implement middleware in your code. The `parseBody` middleware allows you to parse `POST` parameters or JSON data in the body of the request. The `static` middleware allows you to set routes to serve static files such as JavaScript, CSS, and images. The `cookieParser`, `cookieSession`, and `session` middleware allow you to implement cookies and sessions.

You also learned how to use the middleware framework to implement basic HTTP authentication and more advanced session authentication. A great advantage of Express middleware is that it is simple to implement your own middleware functionality.

Next

In the next chapter, you jump into the world of Angular and get an overview of the TypeScript language to prepare to build Angular components. You learn where Angular fits in the Node.js stack and how to begin implementing it in your projects.

20

Jumping into TypeScript

Angular is built on TypeScript, so it is important that you have an understanding of it in order to use Angular. This chapter will help you understand the fundamentals of TypeScript.

This chapter will familiarize you with the additions TypeScript gives to JavaScript. If you are familiar with C# and object-oriented programming, TypeScript will seem more familiar than JavaScript. This chapter will also familiarize you with the basics of programming in TypeScript; it discusses types, interfaces, classes, modules, functions, and generics. It is not intended to be a full language guide; rather, it is a primer on the language to help prepare you for using Angular.

Learning the Different Types

Like JavaScript, TypeScript uses data types to handle data, but there are some differences in syntax. TypeScript also adds in an extra type enumeration. The following list goes over the types and variables and their syntax for TypeScript:

- **String:** This data type stores character data as a string. The character data is specified by either single or double quotation marks. All the data contained in the quotes will be assigned to the string variable. Consider these examples:

  ```
  var myString: string = 'Some Text';
  var anotherString: string = "Some More Text";
  ```

- **Number:** This data type stores data as a numeric value. Numbers are useful in counting, calculations, and comparisons. Here are some examples:

  ```
  var myInteger: number = 1;
  var cost: number = 1.33;
  ```

- **Boolean:** This data type stores a single bit that is either `true` or `false`. Booleans are often used for flags. For example, you might set a variable to `false` at the beginning of some code and then check it on completion to see if the code execution hit a certain spot. The following examples define `true` and `false` variables:

  ```
  var yes: boolean = true;
  var no: boolean = false;
  ```

- **Array:** An indexed array is a series of separate distinct data items, all stored under a single variable name. Items in the array can be accessed by their zero-based index, using `array[index]`. The following are two examples of creating a simple array and then accessing the first element, which is at index `0`:

```
var arr:string[] = ["one", "two", "three"];
var firstInArr = arr[0];
var arr2:Array<number> = ["a", "second", "array"];
var firstInArr2 = arr[0];
```

- **Null:** Sometimes you do not have a value to store in a variable, either because it hasn't been created or you are no longer using it. At such a time, you can set a variable to `null`. Using `null` is better than assigning a value of `0` or an empty string (`""`) because those may be valid values for the variable. By assigning `null` to a variable, you can assign no value and check against `null` inside your code, like this:

```
var newVar = null;
```

- **Any:** In TypeScript you may not always know what type of variable you will be getting or using. In such a case, you can assign the variable type as `any` to allow any other type to be assigned to a variable. The following is an example of assigning multiple types to the same variable:

```
Var anyType: any = "String Assigned";
Var anyType = 404;
Var anyType = True;
```

- **Void:** You use void when you don't want a variable to have any type at all. In TypeScript, using `void` prohibits you from assigning or returning a value. In most cases you use `void` when declaring a function you don't want to have a return value. The following example is a function of type `void`:

```
function empty(): void { document.write("code goes here"); }
```

- **Enum:** TypeScript lets us use `enum`, which allows you to give names to enumerated values. The following is the syntax to declare `enum`:

```
Enum People {Bob, John, Alex}
```

Also, to reference the values in `enum`, you use this syntax:

```
var x = People.Bob
```

or this:

```
var y = People[0]
```

By using this syntax, you set `var x` equal to the number `0` and `var y` equal to the string `Bob`.

Understanding Interfaces

Interfaces are a fundamental part of TypeScript. They allow you to have a set structure for an application. They are powerful tools that allow you to set structures for objects, functions, arrays, and classes. You can think of interfaces as defining standards you want your interface subsets to follow.

To define an interface in TypeScript, you use the keyword `interface` followed by the structure you want your objects to follow, like this:

```
interface Person {
     hairColor: string;
     age: number;
}
```

You can also add optional items to interfaces to allow some flexibility within a program. You do this by using the syntax `attribute?: Boolean;`, as shown in the following examples:

```
interface Person {
    hairColor: string;
    age: number;
    alive?: Boolean;
}
```

You can define an interface for functions in TypeScript. This helps ensure that functions take in specific types of parameters. The following example sets `var z` equal to `variables x + y`, using an instance of the interface `AddNums`:

```
interface AddNums {
    (num1: number, num2: number)
}
var x: number = 5;
var y: number = 10;

var newNum: AddNums;
newNum = function(num1: number, num2: number){
    var result: number = num1 + num2;
    document.write(result)
    return result;
}

var z = newNum(x, y);
```

Interfaces also allow you to define how you would like arrays to look. You give arrays the index type to define the types allowed for an object's index. You then give the return type for the index. Here is an example:

```
interface Stringy {
    [index: number]: string;
}
```

```
var coolArray: Stringy;
coolArray = ["Apples", "Bananas"];
```

Finally, interfaces allow you to define class structures. As with a function interface, this allows you to set required variables and methods within each class. It's important to note that this only describes the public portion of a class and not a private section. (We talk more about classes in the next section.) In this example, the interface has a property called `name` and a method called `feed`:

```
interface PersonInterface {
    name: string;
    feed();
}
```

Implementing Classes

JavaScript is a language that is based on prototype inheritance. Thanks to ECMAScript 6 (ES6) and TypeScript, you can use class-based programming. You can describe the objects you put into a program by using the base attributes to describe classes.

To define a class in TypeScript, you use the syntax `class ClassName{ code goes here }`. The following example defines a simple class that defines a `Person` object with a `feed` function:

```
class Person {
    name: string;
    age: number;
    hungry: boolean = true;
    constructor(name: string, age?: number) {
        this.name = name;
        this.age = age;
    }
    feed() {
        this.hungry = false;
        return "Yummy!";
    }
}
var Brendan = new Person("Brendan", 21);
```

Notice that the last line uses the `new` keyword to call into the constructor and initiate a new instance of the class with the name `Brendan`. This uses the constructor method from the class, which pulls in `"Brendan"` and `21` as its parameters to build a person named Brendan.

Say that you have a method `feed` as part of your class that you would like to be able to use. Here is how you use it:

```
Brendan.feed()
```

Class Inheritance

Classes are subject to inheritance, and you can pass functionality to other classes by using methods and attributes. This example shows how you can make an extension of `Person` called `SecretAgent` and give it extra properties that `Person` doesn't have:

```
class SecretAgent extends Person {
    licenseToKill: boolean = true;
    weaponLoaded: boolean = true;
    unloadWeapon() {
        this.weaponLoaded = false;
        return "clip empty";
    }
    loadWeapon() {
        this.weaponLoaded = true;
        return "locked 'n' loaded";
    }
}

var doubleOSeven = new SecretAgent("James Bond");
let loadResult = doubleOSeven.loadWeapon();
let unloadResult = doubleOSeven.unloadWeapon();
let feedResult = doubleOSeven.feed();
```

So now you have a class `SecretAgent` that extends the `Person` class. This means you can still invoke the original `feed` method on the `Person` class, but it gives you some extra attributes and methods on the `SecretAgent` class.

Implementing Modules

Modules in TypeScript allow you to organize your code over multiple files. This helps keep your files shorter and more maintainable. Modules are able to do this by allowing you to import the functionality you need from within the module you are working on. You can do this if you `export` the class you need functionality from.

The following example splits the `Person` class into two separate modules:

```
module Person {
    export interface PersonInterface {
        name: string;
        hungry: boolean;
        feed();
    }
}

/// <reference path="Person.ts" />
module Person {
    export class Person implements PersonInterface {
    name: string;
```

```
        age: number;
        hungry: boolean = true;
        constructor(name: string, age?: number) {
            this.name = name;
            this.age = age;
        }
        feed() {
            this.hungry = false;
            return 'Yummy!';
        }
        }
}

var Brendan = newPerson("Brendan", 21);
```

In this example, the root module has the interface for `Person`. The submodule starts by using `/// <reference path="Person.ts" />` to point to the root module so it can have access to the `PersonInterface` interface. The example then proceeds to build the `Person` class in the submodule.

Understanding Functions

Functions in TypeScript are similar to functions in JavaScript, but they have added capabilities. TypeScript functions enable you to give types to the parameters and even to what will be returned by a function. While giving a function a type is optional, it's very helpful when you want to make sure that your functions don't give you back something you don't want.

TypeScript allows you to give a function a return type, much in the same way you give return types to variables. You first declare the function name and parameters, and then you can define the type of the function. Also remember that you can assign types to the parameters as well. Check out the following example:

```
function hello(x: string, y: string): string{
    Return x + ' ' + y;
}
```

Like interfaces, TypeScript functions give you the power to create optional parameters. This is helpful when you know that parameters may be circumstantial. It's important to know that optional parameters need to come after the required ones, or an error will be thrown. The following example shows a function `soldierOfGondor` which takes in a required variable `name`, and an optional variable `prefWeapon`:

```
function soldierOfGondor(name: string, prefWeapon?: string){
    Return "Welcome " + name + " to the Gondor infantry."
}
```

With TypeScript functions, you can create default parameters. A default parameter is optional, but if it isn't given, it has a default value instead of nothing. You create a default parameter by setting one of the parameters equal to the desired default value:

```
function soldierOfGondor(name: string, prefWeapon = "Sword"){
    return "hello " + name + " you can pick up your " + prefWeapon + " at the armory.";
}
```

Summary

Understanding TypeScript is critical to being able to use Angular to its full potential. This chapter goes over enough of the fundamental TypeScript properties and methods to get you through the rest of the book. You've learned how TypeScript uses its different types and how to write and use interfaces, classes, modules, and functions.

Next

In the next chapter you will learn about Angular and get an overview of its design and intention. Then you will learn how to create your own Angular application step-by-step, preparing you to jump into future chapters.

21

Getting Started with Angular

Angular is a perfect client-side framework for most web applications because it provides a very clean and structured approach. With a clean, structured front end, you will find that it is much easier to implement clean, well-structured server-side logic.

This chapter introduces you to Angular as well as the major components involved in an Angular application. It is critical that you understand these components before you try to implement an Angular application because the framework is different from more traditional JavaScript web application programming.

After you get a good grasp of the components of an Angular application, you'll learn how to construct a basic Angular application, step by step. This should prepare you to jump into the following chapters, which provide much more detail on implementing Angular.

Why Angular?

JavaScript is a powerful programming language that allows developers to use a web browser as a full application platform. Angular provides a great framework that makes it faster and easier to create client-side JavaScript applications. Developers use Angular because it provides a lot of the structure of web applications—such as data binding, dependency injection, and HTTP communications—that teams would otherwise need to develop themselves.

Understanding Angular

Angular is a JavaScript framework, which means it provides a number of APIs and structure that helps you quickly and easily create complex client-side code. Angular does a great job at providing not only features but also a basic framework and programming model to create client applications. The following sections describe the most important aspects of the Angular framework and how they contribute to make Angular a great JavaScript framework.

Modules

In general, Angular apps use a modular design. While not required, modules are highly recommended because they allow you to separate your code into separate files. This helps you keep your code files short and manageable while still allowing you to access the functionality from each one.

Unlike how you use modules with TypeScript, with Angular you import external modules at the top of a file and export the functionality you need at the bottom. You do this by using the key terms `import` and `export`, with the following syntax:

```
Import {Component} from 'angular2/core';
Export class App{}
```

Directives

Directives are JavaScript classes with metadata that defines the structure and behavior. Directives provide the majority of UI functionality for Angular applications. There are three major types of directives:

- **Components:** A component directive is a directive that incorporates an HTML template with JavaScript functionality to create a self-contained UI element that can be added to an Angular application as a custom HTML element. Components are likely to be the directives you use the most in Angular.
- **Structural:** You use structural directives when you need to manipulate the DOM. Structural directives allow you to create and destroy elements and components from a view.
- **Attribute:** An attribute directive changes the appearance and behavior of HTML elements by using HTML attributes.

Data Binding

One of the best features of Angular is the built-in *data binding*—the process of linking data from a component with what is displayed in a web page. Angular provides a very clean interface to link model data to elements in a web page.

When data is changed on a web page, the model is updated, and when data is changed in the model, the web page is automatically updated. This way, the model is always the only source for data represented to the user, and the view is just a projection of the model.

Dependency Injection

Dependency injection is a process in which a component defines dependencies on other components. When the code is initialized, the dependent component is made available for access within the component. Angular applications make heavy use of dependency injection.

A common use for dependency injection is consuming services. For example, if you are defining a component that requires access to a web server via HTTP requests, you can inject the

HTTP services into the component, and the functionality is available in the component code. In addition, one Angular component consumes the functionality of another via dependency.

Services

Services are the major workhorses in the Angular environment. Services are singleton classes that provide functionality for a web app. For example, a common task of web applications is to perform AJAX requests to a web server. Angular provides an HTTP service that houses all the functionality to access a web server.

The service functionality is completely independent of context or state, so it can be easily consumed from the components of an application. Angular provides a lot of built-in service components for basic uses, such as HTTP requests, logging, parsing, and animation. You can also create your own services and reuse them throughout your code.

Separation of Responsibilities

An extremely important part of designing Angular applications is the separation of responsibilities. The whole reason you choose a structured framework is to ensure that code is well implemented, easy to follow, maintainable, and testable. Angular provides a very structured framework to work from, but you still need to ensure that you implement Angular in the appropriate manner.

The following are a few rules to follow when implementing Angular:

- The view acts as the official presentation structure for the application. Indicate any presentation logic as directives in the HTML template of the view.
- If you need to perform any DOM manipulation, do it in a built-in or custom directive JavaScript code—and nowhere else.
- Implement any reusable tasks as services and add them to your modules by using dependency injection.
- Ensure that the metadata reflects the current state of the model and is the single source for data consumed by the view.
- Define controllers within the module namespace and not globally to ensure that your application can be packaged easily and avoid overwhelming the global namespace.

Adding Angular to Your Environment

To get started with Angular, you need to set up a few things first to get it ready to use. Here's what you need:

- Angular libraries to make Angular applications
- A web server to serve the files to the browser

- A transpiler to convert your TypeScript code back to JavaScript
- A watcher so that the transpiler knows when there has been a file change
- An editor in which to write your code

> **Note**
> We recommend that you use Visual Studio Code (https://code.visualstudio.com/); it has good TypeScript and Angular support built in, and is a lightweight editor with many available extensions.

Fortunately, the Angular team has done most of the work for you here. All you need to do is go to the Angular QuickStart website, which walks you through the process. The following Angular QuickStart website takes you through the basics of Angular: https://angular.io/docs/ts/latest/quickstart.html. This website explains the basics of Angular's command-line interface (CLI): https://angular.io/docs/ts/latest/cli-quickstart.html.

> **Note**
> We recommend that you use the CLI while learning Angular. The CLI generates all the bootstrap and configuration files for you. It also includes a lightweight server for testing your code.

Using the Angular CLI

Angular provides a powerful CLI that makes building out Angular applications a much more streamlined process. By using the CLI, you will quickly be able to generate new Angular applications, components, directives, pipes, and services. The following sections go over some of the most important tools available through the CLI.

Generating Content with the CLI

One of the most common purposes of the CLI is to generate content for applications. It automates the process of creating and bootstrapping a new Angular application, letting you get straight to the meat of the application.

From the command line, run the command `ng new [application name]` to create a new Angular application. If you navigate to that newly created application, you have access to many other useful commands. Table 21.1 lists some of the most important commands that the CLI has to offer.

Table 21.1 **Angular CLI Command Options**

Command	Alias	Purpose
`ng new`		Creates a new Angular application
`ng serve`		Builds and runs the angular application for testing
`ng eject`		Makes the webpack config files available to be edited
`ng generate component [name]`	`ng g c [name]`	Creates a new component
`ng generate directive [name]`	`ng g d [name]`	Creates a new directive
`ng generate module [name]`	`ng g m [name]`	Creates a module
`ng generate pipe [name]`	`ng g p [name]`	Creates a pipe
`ng generate service [name]`	`ng g s [name]`	Creates a service
`ng generate enum [name]`	`ng g e [name]`	Creates an enumeration
`ng generate guard [name]`	`ng g g [name]`	Creates a guard
`ng generate interface [name]`	`ng g i [name]`	Creates an interface

While an in-depth guide of everything the CLI has to offer is beyond the scope of this book, it is worth learning how to use.

Creating a Basic Angular Application

Now that you understand the basics of the Angular CLI, you are ready to get started implementing Angular code. This section walks you through a very basic Angular application that implements an Angular component with an inline template, an inline stylesheet, and the `Component` class.

For this example, it is expected that you have started working through the Angular QuickStart guide and understand the basics of the CLI. The first thing to do is to create a directory where you can place your projects.

When you have your directory set up, the next step is to generate your first Angular application. Run the following command to create the application for this example:

```
ng new first
```

Next, run the following command to launch a server that will render the application:

```
ng serve
```

The following sections describe the important steps in implementing the Angular application and the code involved in each step. Each of these steps is described in much more detail in later chapters, so don't get bogged down in them here. What is important at this point is that you understand the process of implementing the HTML, component, class, and bootstrap and generally how they interact with each other.

Figure 21.1 shows the web application you are going to create. It shows a simple message that has been printed out by an Angular component.

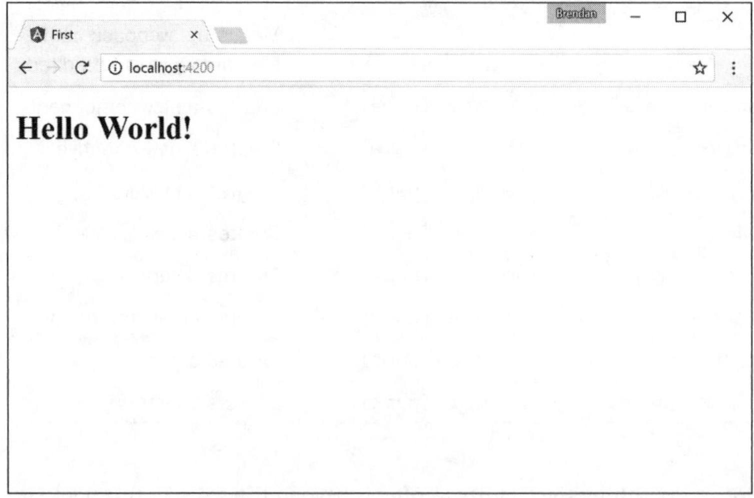

Figure 21.1 Implementing a basic Angular web application that uses a component to load an HTML template to the view

Creating Your First Angular App

Now that you've seen how Angular works, let's get into a practical example. This example doesn't change much that was generated by the CLI, but it will familiarize you with the different pieces of an Angular application.

To get started, navigate to the file `src/app/app.component.ts` in your application directory. It looks like this:

```
import {Component} from '@angular/core';
@Component({
  selector: 'message',
  template: `
    <h1>Hello World!</h1>
  `,
})
export class Chap3Component{
  title = 'My First Angular App';
}
```

Notice that line 1 imports the component module. Then the component decorator is defined and given a selector and a template. The selector is the name given to the component, and the template is the HTML that the component will generate. For this example, change the template and selector to match the ones on lines 3–6 and change the title variable as shown on line 9.

After the decorator is defined, lines 8–10 create the `export` class to make your component available to the rest of the application as well as define variables and functions that are made available to the component template.

Understanding and Using NgModule

Now that you've created your component, you need some way to tell the rest of your app about it. You do this by importing NgModule from Angular. NgModule is an Angular decorator that allows you to place all your imports, declarations, and bootstrap files for a particular module in a single location. This makes bootstrapping all the files in large applications very easy. NgModule has several metadata options that allow different things to be imported, exported, and bootstrapped:

- `providers`: This is an array of injectable objects that are available in the injector of the current module.
- `declarations`: This is an array of directives, pipes, and/or components that belong in the current module.
- `imports`: This is an array of directives, pipes, and/or components that will be available to other templates within the current module.
- `exports`: This is an array of directives, pipes, and/or modules that can be used within any component that imports the current module.
- `entryComponents`: This is an array of components that will be compiled and will have a component factory created when the current module is defined.
- `bootstrap`: This is an array of components that will be bootstrapped when the current module is bootstrapped.
- `schemas`: This is an array of elements and properties that aren't directives or components.
- `id`: This is a simple string that acts as a unique ID to identify this module.

As is often the case, it's easiest to learn this by doing, so let's get started using `NgModule`. Navigate to the file named `app.module.ts` in your `app` folder. It looks like this:

```
import { BrowserModule } from '@angular/platform-browser';
import { NgModule } from '@angular/core';
import { FormsModule } from '@angular/forms';
import { HttpModule } from '@angular/http';

import { Chap3Component } from './app.component';

```

```
@NgModule({
  declarations: [
    Chap3Component
  ],
  imports: [
    BrowserModule,
    FormsModule,
    HttpModule
  ],
  providers: [],
  bootstrap: [Chap3Component]
})
export class AppModule { }
```

First, you import `NgModule`, `BrowserModule`, and any custom components, directives, services, and so on that your app has. Second, you configure the `@NgModule` object to bootstrap everything together. Notice that when the component is imported, the bootstrap property has the component's export class name. Finally, you export the class named `AppModule`.

Creating the Angular Bootstrapper

Now that you've looked at your component and module, you need some way to tell the rest of your app about it. You do this by importing the bootstrapper through `platformBrowserDynamic` from Angular.

Navigate to the file named `main.ts` in your `app` folder, which looks like this:

```
import { enableProdMode } from '@angular/core';
import { platformBrowserDynamic } from '@angular/platform-browser-dynamic';

import { AppModule } from './app/app.module';
import { environment } from './environments/environment';

if (environment.production) {
  enableProdMode();
}

platformBrowserDynamic().bootstrapModule(AppModule);
```

The imports are `enableProdMode`, `platformBrowserDynamic`, `AppModule`, and `environment`. `enableProdMode` uses Angular's optimizations for a production application. `platformBrowserDynamic` is used to bootstrap the application together, using the application module `AppModule`, as shown in the following code:

```
platformBrowserDynamic().bootstrapModule(AppModule);
```

The environment variable determines the state of the application—whether it should be deployed in development mode or production mode.

platform is then assigned the result from the function platformBrowserDynamic. platform has the method bootstrapModule(), which consumes the module. Notice that when you import and bootstrap a component, the name you use is the same as the component's export class.

Now open the command prompt, navigate to your root directory, and run the command ng serve. This command compiles your code and opens a browser window. You may need to point your browser to the local host and port. The command lets you know the URL to navigate your browser to, as shown in the following example:

```
** NG Live Development Server is running on http://localhost:4200 **
```

Listing 21.1 shows the html index file that loads the application. Line 12 shows where the message component gets applied.

Listing 21.2 shows the Angular module that bootstraps the component. Lines 1–4 show the Angular modules BrowserModule, NgModule, FormsModule, and HttpModule each getting imported. Line 6 shows the Angular component Chap3Component getting imported. Lines 9–11 show the component being declared. Lines 12–16 show the imports array which makes the imported modules available to the application. Line 18 bootstraps the main component of the application.

> **Note**
>
> This application doesn't need the FormsModule or the HttpModule to run. However, they are included to help show the syntax of importing extra modules into the application.

Listing 21.3 shows the Angular component which has the selector message. This component displays the message Hello World! in the browser.

Listing 21.1 first.html: A Simple Angular Template That Loads the First Component

```
01 <!doctype html>
02 <html>
03 <head>
04   <meta charset="utf-8">
05   <title>First</title>
06   <base href="/">
07
08   <meta name="viewport" content="width=device-width, initial-scale=1">
09   <link rel="icon" type="image/x-icon" href="favicon.ico">
10 </head>
11 <body>
12   <message>Loading...</message>
13 </body>
14 </html>
```

Listing 21.2 `app.module.ts`: **An Angular Module that bootstraps the application**

```
import { BrowserModule } from '@angular/platform-browser';
import { NgModule } from '@angular/core';
import { FormsModule } from '@angular/forms';
import { HttpModule } from '@angular/http';

import { Chap3Component } from './app.component';

@NgModule({
  declarations: [
    Chap3Component
  ],
  imports: [
    BrowserModule,
    FormsModule,
    HttpModule
  ],
  providers: [],
  bootstrap: [Chap3Component]
})
export class AppModule { }
```

Listing 21.3 `first.component.ts`: **An Angular Component**

```
import {Component} from 'angular2/core';
@Component({
  selector: 'message',
  template: `
    <h1>Hello World!<h1>
  `,
  styles:[`
    h1 {
      font-weight: bold;
    }
  `]
})
export class Chap3component{
  title = 'Chapter 21 Example';
}
```

Listings 21.4 and 21.5 show the compiled JavaScript code from the TypeScript files in Listings 21.2 and 21.3.

Note

This is the only time we show you the compiled JavaScript files in this book because these are generated automatically for you when the application is compiled and run—and to help keep the book more readable.

Listing 21.4 `app.module.js`: **The JavaScript Version of the Angular Module that bootstraps the application**

```
"use strict";
var __decorate = (this && this.__decorate) ||
   function (decorators, target, key, desc) {
    var c = arguments.length, r = c < 3 ? target :
        desc === null ? desc = Object.getOwnPropertyDescriptor(target, key) : desc, d;
    if (typeof Reflect === "object" && typeof Reflect.decorate === "function")
        r = Reflect.decorate(decorators, target, key, desc);
    else for (var i = decorators.length - 1; i >= 0; i--)
         if (d = decorators[i]) r = (c < 3 ? d(r) : c > 3 ? d(target, key, r)
             : d(target, key)) || r;
    return c > 3 && r && Object.defineProperty(target, key, r), r;
};
exports.__esModule = true;
var platform_browser_1 = require("@angular/platform-browser");
var core_1 = require("@angular/core");
var forms_1 = require("@angular/forms");
var http_1 = require("@angular/http");
var app_component_1 = require("./app.component");
var AppModule = (function () {
    function AppModule() {
    }
    AppModule = __decorate([
        core_1.NgModule({
            declarations: [
                app_component_1.Chap3Component
            ],
            imports: [
                platform_browser_1.BrowserModule,
                forms_1.FormsModule,
                http_1.HttpModule
            ],
            providers: [],
            bootstrap: [app_component_1.Chap3Component]
        })
    ], AppModule);
    return AppModule;
}());
exports.AppModule = AppModule;
```

Listing 21.5 `first.component.js`: **The JavaScript Version of the Angular Component File**

```
"use strict";
var __decorate = (this && this.__decorate)
    || function (decorators, target, key, desc) {
    var c = arguments.length, r = c < 3
        ? target : desc === null
        ? desc = Object.getOwnPropertyDescriptor(target, key) : desc, d;
    if (typeof Reflect === "object" && typeof Reflect.decorate === "function")
        r = Reflect.decorate(decorators, target, key, desc);
    else for (var i = decorators.length - 1; i >= 0; i--)
        if (d = decorators[i]) r = (c < 3 ? d(r) : c > 3
            ? d(target, key, r) : d(target, key)) || r;
    return c > 3 && r && Object.defineProperty(target, key, r), r;
};
exports.__esModule = true;
var core_1 = require("@angular/core");
var Chap3Component = (function () {
    function Chap3Component() {
        this.title = 'Chapter 21 Example';
    }
    Chap3Component = __decorate([
        core_1.Component({
            selector: 'message',
            template: "\n    <h1>Hello World!<h1>\n  "
        })
    ], Chap3Component);
    return Chap3Component;
}());
exports.Chap3Component = Chap3Component;
```

Summary

The Angular framework provides a very structured method for creating websites and web applications. Angular structures a web application using a very clean, componentized approach. Angular uses data binding to ensure that there is only one source of data. It also takes advantage of templates with directives that extend HTML capabilities, enabling you to implement totally customized HTML components.

This chapter looks at the different components in an Angular application and how they interact with each other. At the end of this chapter, a detailed example of how to implement a basic Angular application, including a component, a module, and a bootstrapper is seen.

Next

In the next chapter, you will learn about Angular components. You will learn how to build a template using HTML and CSS. You will then go over how you can build your own components.

22

Angular Components

Angular components are the building blocks you use to create Angular applications. Angular components allow you to build self-contained UI elements for an application. Components allow you to control how your application looks and functions through TypeScript code and an HTML template. This chapter discusses how to create Angular components using a TypeScript class that defines the look and behavior of UI elements.

Component Configuration

An Angular component consists of two main parts: the definition in the decorator section and the class section, which defines the logic. The decorator section is used to configure the component, including things like the selector name and HTML template. The class section enables you to give the component its logic, data, and event handlers, as well as export it to be used in other TypeScript files.

With these two sections you can create a basic component. The following example shows what a component might look like:

```
Import {Component} from '@angular/core';
@Component({
     selector: 'my-app',
     template: '<p>My Component</p>'
})
Export class AppComponent{
    Title = 'Chapter 1 Example';
}
```

To create a component, you import `Component` from Angular and apply it to a TypeScript class that you can then use to control the look and functionality of the component. Within the `@Component` decorator are several component configuration options you need to understand. The following list includes some of the most important options available:

- `selector`: This option allows you to define the HTML tag name used to add the component to the application via HTML.

- `template`: This option allows you to add inline HTML to define the look of the component. This is for when there won't be very much code to add, and it's helpful for when you don't want extra files.
- `templateUrl`: This option allows you to import an external template file rather than inline HTML. This is helpful for separating a large amount of HTML code out of a component to help with maintainability.
- `styles`: This option allows you to add inline CSS to your component. Use it when only minor style changes are needed.
- `stylesUrls`: This option allows you to import an array of external CSS stylesheet(s). You should use this rather than styles when importing external CSS files.
- `viewProviders`: This is an array of dependency injection providers. It allows you to import and use Angular services that provide application functionality such as HTTP communications.

Defining a Selector

In a component, a selector tells Angular where to apply the component in HTML. You apply Angular to a component to HTML by giving it a selector and then using the selector name as a tag name in your HTML file. This makes the functionality of the Angular component available in HTML. The following is an example of a selector:

```
@Component({
     selector: 'angular-rules'
})
```

`You can then add the selector to HTML files by using the following syntax:`

```
<angular-rules></angular-rules>
```

> **Note**
>
> It's important to note that when defining a selector name, there can't be any white spaces. For example, you can't name a selector `angular rules`, but you can name it `angular-rules` or `angular_rules`.

Building a Template

You use a template to define how an Angular component should look. Templates are written in HTML, but they allow you to include Angular magic to do some pretty cool things. Angular allows for both inline templates and external template files.

You can add a template to the Angular `@component` decorator. For a single-line template, you can use either single or double quotes to wrap it. For a multiple-line template, you use backquotes (`); you generally find the backquote key in the upper left of your keyboard, on the same key as the tilde symbol (~). Using the backquote is very important as it will break your code if it's not correct. Here is an example of a single-line template compared to a multiple-line template:

```
@Component({
      selector: 'my-app',
      template: '<h1>Hello World!</h1>'
})
@Component({
      selector: 'my-app',
      template: `
    <h1>Hello World!</h1>
      `
})
```

> **Note**
>
> For the template and styles configuration options, you need to use the backquote (`), generally located on the same key as the tilde symbol (~).

The same principles you use for templates also apply to CSS. You use the keyword `styles` to tell a component about inline styling. The only major difference is that styles takes in an object of strings instead of just one string. The following example shows some inline styling:

```
@Component ({
    selector: 'my-app',
    template: '<p>hello world</p>',
styles: [`
        p {
            color: yellow;
            font-size: 25px;
        }
    `]
})
```

> **Note**
>
> You need to use the backquote key for a multiple-line stylesheet.

Using Inline CSS and HTML in Angular Applications

You've learned how to implement HTML and CSS in an Angular component. This section builds an example based on that knowledge.

In this exercise you will see how Angular components use and include external templates and stylesheets. The purpose of this exercise is to illustrate how this use of templates allows for more readable and manageable code.

The code in Listing 22.1 is the Angular component. Line 1 imports the component necessary to define the component. Lines 3 through 18 define the component. The component has a very simple template, as shown in lines 5 through 7, and some CSS styling in lines 8 through 13 to go with it.

Figure 22.1 shows the finished Angular component rendered.

Listing 22.1 `intro.ts`: **A Simple Angular Template and Styling to Display a `<span>` Element**

```
01 import { Component } from '@angular/core';
02
03 @Component({
04   selector: 'app-root',
05   template: `
06     <span>Hello my name is Brendan</span>
07   `,
08   styles:[`
09     span {
10       font-weight: bold;
11       border: 1px ridge blue;
12       padding: 5px;
13     }
14   `]
15 })
16 export class AppComponent {
17   title = 'Chapter 22 Intro';
18 }
```

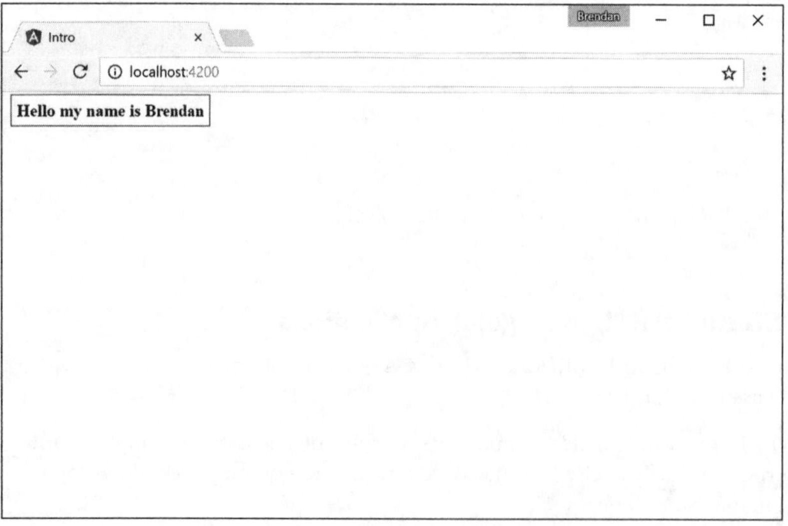

Figure 22.1 Implementing a basic Angular web application that loads an HTML template and styles to the view

Using Constructors

When you use Angular, you often need to have default values and an initial setup for your component variables. Angular uses constructors to give its components default values. This section goes over how to create and implement them.

Constructors go in the `Component` class. Their purpose is to set default values and initial configuration of variables for that class so that when those variables are used within the component, they are never uninitialized. The following is an example of constructor syntax:

```
export class constructor {
     name: string;
     constructor(){
          this.name = "Brendan";
     {
}
```

Now that you've learned what a constructor is and what it looks like, let's get into an example that uses one. This simple exercise uses a constructor to define the current date at the time the component is created.

Listing 22.2 shows an Angular component with a selector named `simple-constructor` and a simple template. Note the `{{today}}` on line 6 is a form of data binding, which is discussed in more detail in Chapter 24, "Data Binding." For now, you should focus on how the constructor works.

Figure 22.2 shows the rendered Angular component.

Listing 22.2 `constructor.component.ts`: **A Simple Component that Displays the Date**

```
01 import {Component} from '@angular/core';
02
03 @Component({
04   selector: 'simple-constructor',
05   template: `
06     <p>Hello today is {{today}}!</p>
07   `,
08 })
09 export class UsingAConstructor {
10   today: Date;
11   constructor() {
12     this.today = new Date();
13   }
14 }
```

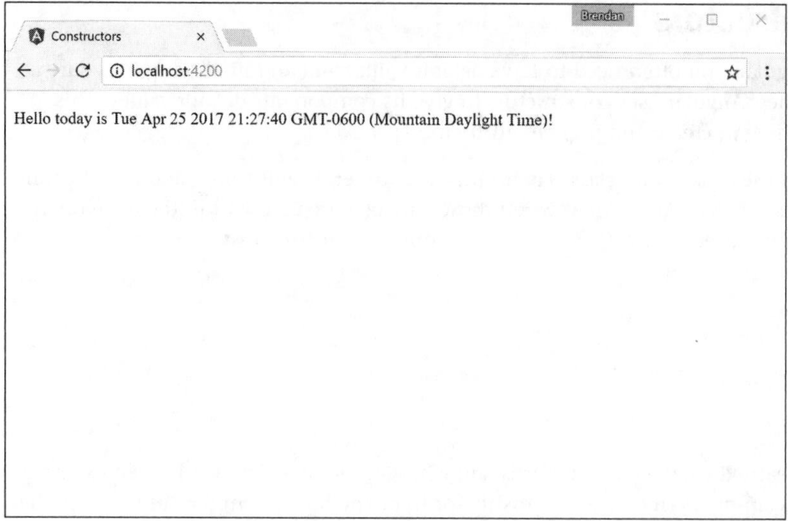

Figure 22.2 Implementing a basic Angular web application that uses a constructor to define default variables

Using External Templates

Another way to incorporate templates and stylesheets into Angular components is through a separate file. Using this method is handy because it helps you separate what the files do. It also makes the component easier to read. Under your `@Component` decorator, you place the keyword `templateUrl` followed by the path from the root of the application to your template HTML file. Here is an example.

```
@Component ({
     selector: 'my-app',
     templateUrl: "./view.example.html"
})
```

You use the keyword `styleUrls` to tell the component about external stylesheets. The difference with the external stylesheets is that you pass in an array of one or more stylesheets. The following example shows how to import external stylesheets:

```
@Component ({
    selector: 'my-app',
    templateUrl: "./view.example.html"
styleUrls: ["./styles1.css", "./styles2.css"]
})
```

Note

The `styleUrls` configuration option takes in an *array* of comma-separated strings.

Earlier in this chapter, in the "Building a Template" section, you learned how to implement external HTML and CSS files into an Angular component. The example in this section builds on that knowledge and walks you through an Angular application that incorporates external HTML and CSS files.

Listing 22.3 shows an Angular component with the selector named `external`, and `templateUrl` and `styleUrls`, which link the external files you need for this application.

Listing 22.4 shows an external template named `externalTemplate.html`. The component uses this file to render the view on the browser.

Listing 22.5 shows an external stylesheet named `external.css`. The component applies this file to the component template file.

Figure 22.3 shows the finished Angular component rendered.

Listing 22.3 `external.component.ts`: **An Angular Component with External File Dependencies**

```
import { Component } from '@angular/core';

@Component({
  selector: 'app-root',
  templateUrl: './app.component.html',
  styleUrls: ['./app.component.css']
})
export class AppComponent {
  title = 'Chapter 22 Using External templates and styles';
}
```

Listing 22.4 `externalTemplate.html`: **An HTML Template File for the Component to Pull In and Use**

```
<h1>Congratulations</h1>
<p>
  You've successfully loaded an external html file.
  <span>
    If I'm red then You managed to get the styles in there as well
  </span>
</p>
```

Listing 22.5 `external.css`: **A CSS Stylesheet for the Component to Apply to Its Template**

```
span{
  color: red;
  border: 2px solid red;
}
```

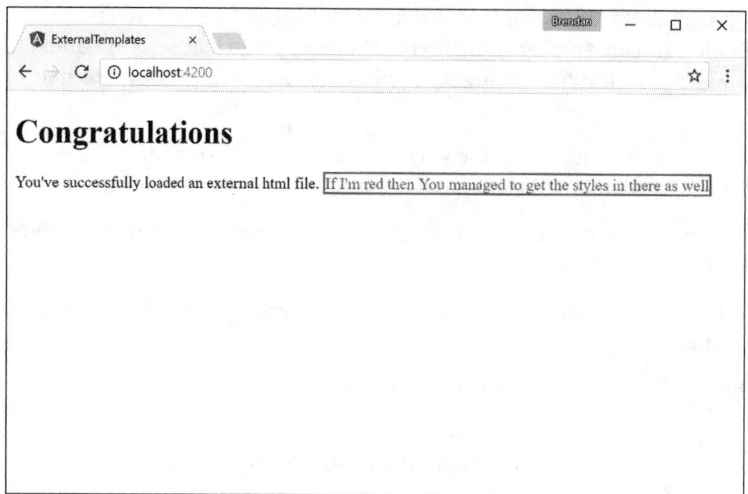

Figure 22.3 Implementing a basic Angular web application that loads an external HTML template and stylesheet to the view

Injecting Directives

Dependency injection can be a difficult concept to fully grasp. However, it is a very important part of Angular, and when you understand the basics, the Angular implementation becomes quite clear. Dependency injection is a well-known design pattern in many server-side languages, but had not been used extensively in a JavaScript framework until Angular came along.

The idea of Angular dependency injection is to define and dynamically inject a dependency object into another object, which makes available all the functionality provided by the dependency object. Angular provides dependency injection through the use of providers and an injector service.

In Angular, to use dependency injection on another directive or component, you need to add the directive's or component's class name to the `declarations` metadata in the `@NgModule` decorator within the module for the application, which takes in an array of directives imported into your application. The following is the syntax of the declarations array.

```
...
declarations: [ OuterComponent, InnerComponent ],
...
```

Building a Nested Component with Dependency Injection

You've learned what dependency injection is and how to use it for components and directives. This section shows you how to use what you've learned to create a nested component. This section walks you through an Angular application that incorporates a component that has a second component within it.

Listing 22.6 shows the `outer.component.ts` file, which loads an external template and stylesheet.

Listing 22.7 shows the `outer.html` template file that the `outer.component.ts` file loads. Notice that the HTML tag `nested` is a custom HTML tag that you use to load the inner component. You do this exactly the same way you load the outer component in the main HTML file.

Listing 22.8 shows the `outer.css` file that gives the outer component and its child components default styles. These styles are inherited by the inner component.

Listing 22.9 shows the `inner.component.ts` file. This is the inner component that the outer component has injected. Notice that the selector for this component, which was used to load this directive within the outer component, is nested.

Figure 22.4 shows the completed application in the browser window.

Listing 22.6 `outer.component.ts`: **The Outer Component for the Application**

```
import { Component } from '@angular/core';

@Component({
  selector: 'app-root',
  templateUrl: './app.component.html',
  styleUrls: ['./app.component.css']
})
export class AppComponent {
  title = 'Nested Example';
}
```

Listing 22.7 `outer.html`: **An HTML Template for the Component to Apply the View**

```
<div>
  <h1>the below text is a nested component</h1>
  <nested></nested>
</div>
```

Listing 22.8 `outer.css`: **A CSS Stylesheet for the Outer Component to Apply to Its Template**

```
div {
  color: red;
  border: 3px ridge red;
  padding: 20px;
}
nested {
  font-size: 2em;
  font-weight: bolder;
  border: 3px solid blue;
}
```

Listing 22.9 `inner.component.ts`: **The Nested Component**

```
import {Component} from '@angular/core';
@Component({
  selector: 'nested',
  template: `
    <span>Congratulations I'm a nested component</span>
  `,
  styles: [`
    span{
      color: #228b22;
    }
  `]
})
export class InnerComponent {}
```

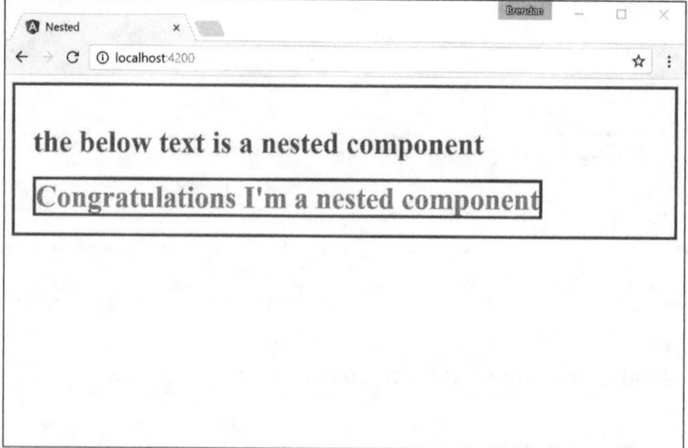

Figure 22.4 Displaying nested components

Passing in Data with Dependency Injection

Dependency injection is a powerful tool that allows you to build a reusable directive to be used within any application that imports that directive. Sometimes data needs to be passed through the application to the directive that's being injected. This is made possible through Angular inputs.

In Angular, to input data to another directive or component, you need to import the `Input` decorator from `@angular/core`. The following code shows the syntax:

```
import {Component, Input} from '@angular/core';
```

When the `Input` decorator has been imported, you can begin to define what data you would like to have input into the directive. Start by defining `@input()`, which takes in a string as a parameter. The HTML uses that string to pass in the data to the imported directive. Do this by using the following syntax:

```
@Input('name') personName: string;
```

Creating an Angular Application that Uses Inputs

Now that you have learned how to use inputs with dependency injection, it's time to get started on an example. This section walks through an Angular application that passes data to a directive from another directive.

Listing 22.10 shows the `person.component.ts` file, which is the entry point for the application that will pass data into the `input.component.ts` file.

Listing 22.11 shows the `input.component.ts` file. It is the component that will take in and handle the inputs from an external directive.

Figure 22.5 shows the completed application in the browser window.

Listing 22.10 `person.component.ts`: A Component that Imports `input.component` and Passes Data to It through the Selector

```
import { Component } from '@angular/core';
import {myInput} from './input.component';
@Component({
  selector: 'app-root',
  template: `
    <myInput name="Brendan" occupation="Student/Author"></myInput>
    <myInput name="Brad" occupation="Analyst/Author"></myInput>
    <myInput name="Caleb" occupation="Student/Author"></myInput>
    <myInput></myInput>
  `
})
export class AppComponent {
  title = 'Using Inputs in Angular';
}
```

Listing 22.11 `input.component.ts`: A Component that Takes Data through Its Selector to Modify What Is Displayed via HTML

```
import {Component, Input} from '@angular/core';
@Component ({
  selector: "myInput",
  template: `
    <div>
      Name: {{personName}}
      <br />
      Job: {{occupation}}
    </div>
  `,
```

```
  styles: [`
    div {
      margin: 10px;
      padding: 15px;
      border: 3px solid grey;
    }
  `]
})
export class myInputs {
  @Input('name') personName: string;
  @Input('occupation') occupation: string;
  constructor() {
    this.personName = "John Doe";
    this.occupation = "Anonymity"
  }
}
```

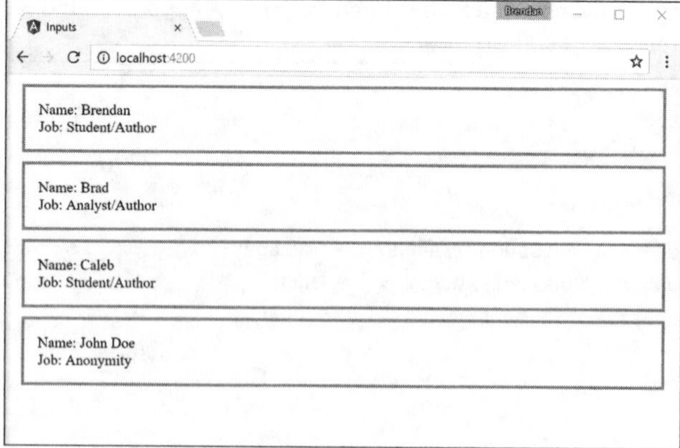

Figure 22.5 Displaying information passed down through inputs

Summary

Angular components are the main building blocks of Angular applications. This chapter shows how to build a component, from the decorator to the class. It shows different ways of including templates and stylesheets. It also shows how to use dependency injection to incorporate external directives or components within each other.

Next

In the next chapter you will learn about expressions, and how Angular evaluates them and adds them dynamically to a webpage. Then you will learn about pipes and how they are used. You will then learn how to build your very own custom pipe.

23

Expressions

A great feature of Angular is the capability to add JavaScript-like expressions inside an HTML template. Angular evaluates expressions and then can dynamically add the results to a web page. Expressions are linked to a component, and you can have an expression that utilizes values in the component, and its value can change as the model changes.

Using Expressions

Using expressions is the simplest way to represent data from a component in an Angular view. Expressions are encapsulated blocks of code inside brackets, like this:

```
{{expression}}
```

The Angular compiler compiles an expression into HTML elements so that the results of the expression are displayed. For example, look at the following expressions:

```
{{1+5}}
{{'One' + 'Two'}}
```

Based on these expressions, the web page displays the following values:

```
6
OneTwo
```

Expressions are bound to the data model, which provides two huge benefits. First, you can use the property names and functions that are defined in the component inside your expressions. Second, because the expressions are bound to the component, when data in the component changes, so do the expressions. For example, say that a component contains the following values:

```
name: string='Brad';
score: number=95;
```

You can directly reference the `name` and `score` values in the template expressions, as shown here:

```
Name: {{name}}
Score: {{score}}
Adjusted: {{score+5}}
```

Angular expressions are similar to TypeScript/JavaScript expressions in several ways, but they differ in these ways:

- **Attribute evaluation:** Property names are evaluated against the component model instead of against the global JavaScript namespace.
- **More forgiving:** Expressions do not throw exceptions when they encounter undefined or null variable types; instead, they treat them as having no value.
- **No flow control:** Expressions do not allow the following:
  - Assignments (for example, `=`, `+=`, `-=`)
  - The `new` operator
  - Conditionals
  - Loops
  - Increment and decrement operators (`++` and `--`)

  Also, you cannot throw an error inside an expression

Angular evaluates as expressions the strings used to define the values of directives. This means you can include expression-type syntax within a definition. For example, when you set the value of the `ng-click` directive in the template, you specify an expression. Inside that expression, you can reference a component variable and use other expression syntax, as shown here:

```
<span ng-click="myFunction()"></span>
<span ng-click="myFunction(var, 'stringParameter')"></span>
<span ng-click="myFunction(5*var)"></span>
```

Because the Angular template expressions have access to the component, you can also make changes to the component inside the Angular expression. For example, this `(click)` directive changes the value of `msg` inside the component model:

```
<span (click)="msg='clicked'"></span>
```

The following sections take you through some examples of using the expression capability in Angular.

Using Basic Expressions

In this section, you get a chance to see how Angular expressions handle rendering of strings and numbers. This example illustrates how Angular evaluates expressions that contain strings and numbers as well as basic mathematical operators.

Listing 23.1 shows an Angular component. This component has a template that contains several types of expressions wrapped in double curly brackets (`{{}}`). Some of the expressions are just numbers or strings, some include the `+` operation to combine strings and/or numbers, and one applies a `===` operator to compare two numbers.

Figure 23.1 shows the rendered web page. Note that numbers and strings are rendered directly to the final view. Adding strings and numbers together enables you to build text strings that are rendered to the view. Also note that using a comparison operator renders the word `true` or `false` to the view.

Listing 23.1 `basicExpressions.component.ts`: **Basic Strings and Numbers with Simple Math Operations in an Angular Template**

```
import { Component } from '@angular/core';

@Component({
  selector: 'app-root',
  template: `
    <h1>Expressions</h1>
    Number:<br>
    {{5}}<hr>
    String:<br>
    {{'My String'}}<hr>
    Adding two strings together:<br>
    {{'String1' + ' ' + 'String2'}}<hr>
    Adding two numbers together:<br>
    {{5+5}}<hr>
    Adding strings and numbers together:<br>
    {{5 + '+' + 5 + '='}}{{5+5}}<hr>
    Comparing two numbers with each other:<br>
    {{5===5}}<hr>
  `,
})
export class AppComponent {}
```

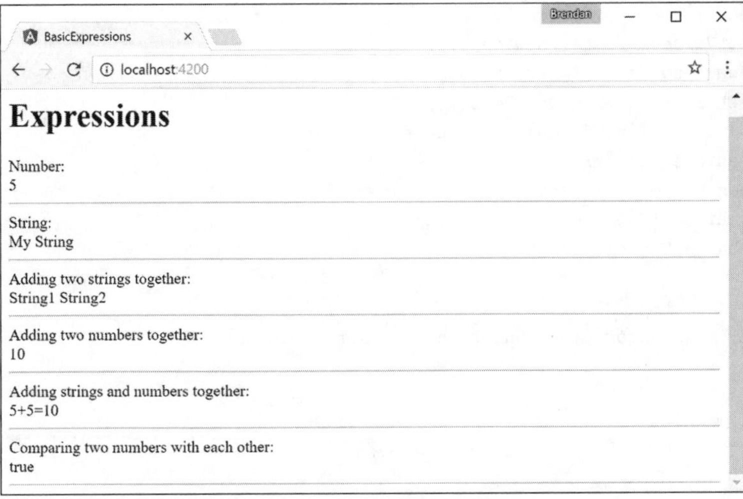

Figure 23.1 Using Angular expressions that contain strings, numbers, and basic math operations

Interacting with the `Component` Class in Expressions

Now that you have seen some basic Angular expressions, let's take a look at how to interact with the `Component` class inside Angular expressions. In the previous example, all the input for the expressions came from explicit strings or numbers. This section illustrates the true power of Angular expressions that come from interacting with the model.

Listing 23.2 shows an Angular component file that applies Angular expressions that use values from the `Component` class to render text to the screen as well as act as parameters to functions. Note that the variable names in the `Component` class can be used directly in the expressions. For example, the expression in line 9 creates a string based on the values of the `speed` and `vehicle` variables.

Figure 23.2 shows the rendered web page, based on the expressions. Note that when the links of the page are clicked, the resulting function calls adjust the `Component` class variables, which change how the previously discussed expressions are rendered.

Listing 23.2 `classExpressions.component.ts`: **An Angular Application that Uses Expressions to Interact with Data from the `Component` Class**

```
01 import { Component } from '@angular/core';
02
03 @Component({
04   selector: 'app-root',
05   template: `
06     Directly accessing variables in the component:<br>
07       {{speed}} {{vehicle}}<hr>
08     Adding variables in the component:<br>
09       {{speed + ' ' + vehicle}}<hr>
10     Calling function in the component:<br>
11       {{lower(speed)}} {{upper('Jeep')}}<hr>
12     <a (click)="setValues('Fast', newVehicle)">
13       Click to change to Fast {{newVehicle}}</a><hr>
14     <a (click)="setValues(newSpeed, 'Rocket')">
15       Click to change to {{newSpeed}} Rocket</a><hr>
16     <a (click)="vehicle='Car'">
17       Click to change the vehicle to a Car</a><hr>
18     <a (click)="vehicle='Enhanced ' + vehicle">
19       Click to Enhance Vehicle</a><hr>
20   `,
21   styles:[`
22     a{color: blue; text-decoration: underline; cursor: pointer}
23   `]
24 })
```

```
export class AppComponent {
  speed = 'Slow';
  vehicle = 'Train';
  newSpeed = 'Hypersonic';
  newVehicle = 'Plane';
  upper = function(str: any){
    str = str.toUpperCase();
    return str;
  }
  lower = function(str: any){
    return str.toLowerCase();
  }
  setValues = function(speed: any, vehicle: any){
    this.speed = speed;
    this.vehicle = vehicle;
  }
}
```

Using TypeScript in Angular Expressions

This section takes a look at some additional TypeScript interactions within the `Component` class. As described previously, much of the TypeScript functionality is supported in Angular expressions. To illustrate this better, this example shows some array manipulation and uses the TypeScript `Math` object within expressions.

Listing 23.3 implements an Angular component that uses Angular expressions that take advantage of `push()` and `shift()` to display the arrays, show the array length, and manipulate the array elements. Note that with `Math` added to the `Component` class, you are able to use TypeScript `Math` operations directly in the expressions in lines 12 and 21.

Figure 23.3 shows the Angular web page rendered. Notice that as the links are clicked, the arrays are adjusted and the expressions are reevaluated.

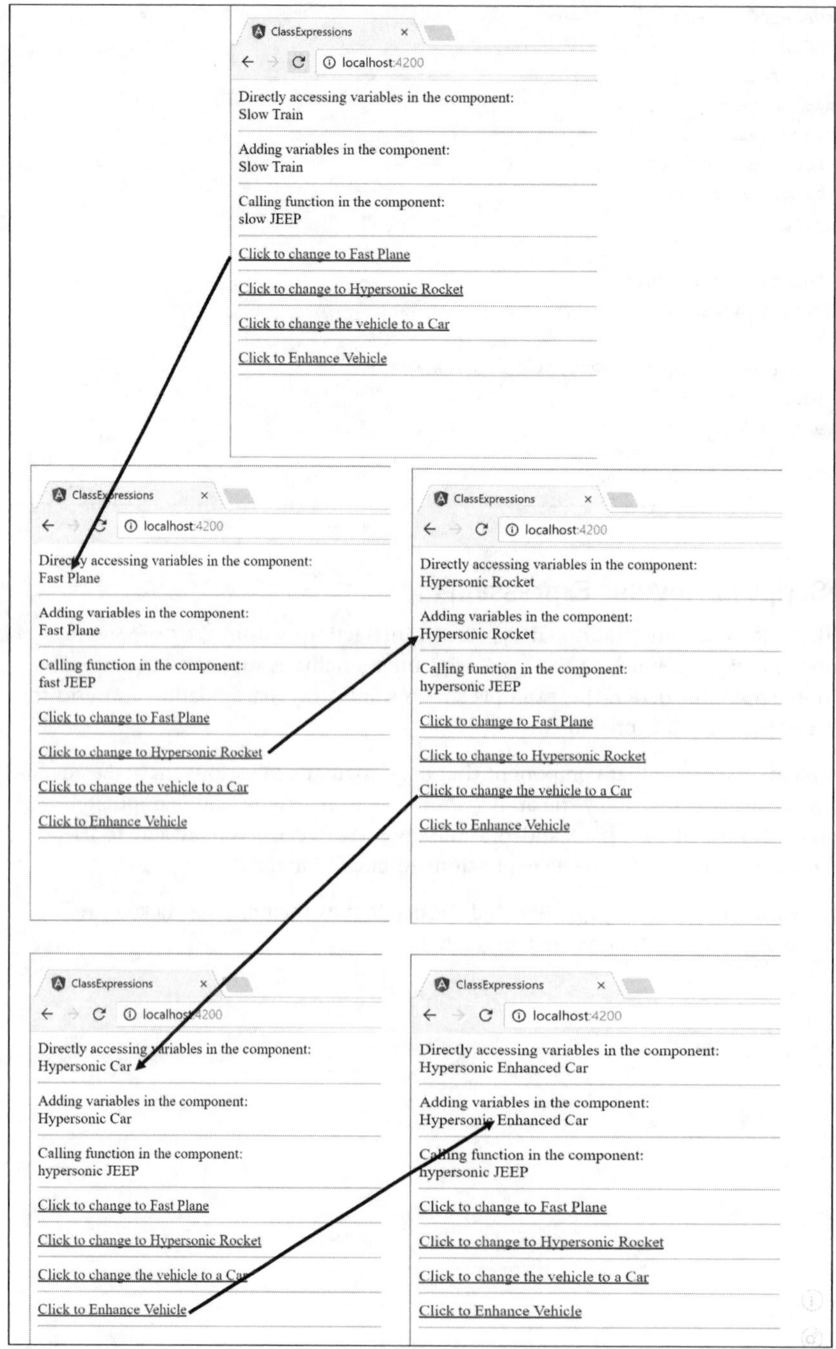

Figure 23.2 Using Angular expressions to represent and use `Component` class data in the Angular view

Listing 23.3 `typescriptExpressions.component.ts`: **An Angular Component that Uses Expressions Containing Arrays and** `Math`

```
import { Component } from '@angular/core';

@Component({
  selector: 'app-root',
  template: `
    <h1>Expressions</h1>
    Array:<br>
      {{myArr.join(', ')}}<br/>
      <hr>
    Elements removed from array:<br>
      {{removedArr.join(', ')}}<hr>
    <a (click)="myArr.push(myMath.floor(myMath.random()*100+1))">
      Click to append a value to the array
    </a><hr>
    <a (click)="removedArr.push(myArr.shift())">
      Click to remove the first value from the array
    </a><hr>
    Size of Array:<br>
      {{myArr.length}}<hr>
    Max number removed from the array:<br>
      {{myMath.max.apply(myMath, removedArr)}}<hr>
  `,
  styles: [`
    a {
      color: blue;
      cursor: pointer;
    }
  `],
})
export class AppComponent {
  myMath = Math;
  myArr: number[] = [1];
  removedArr: number[] = [0];
}
```

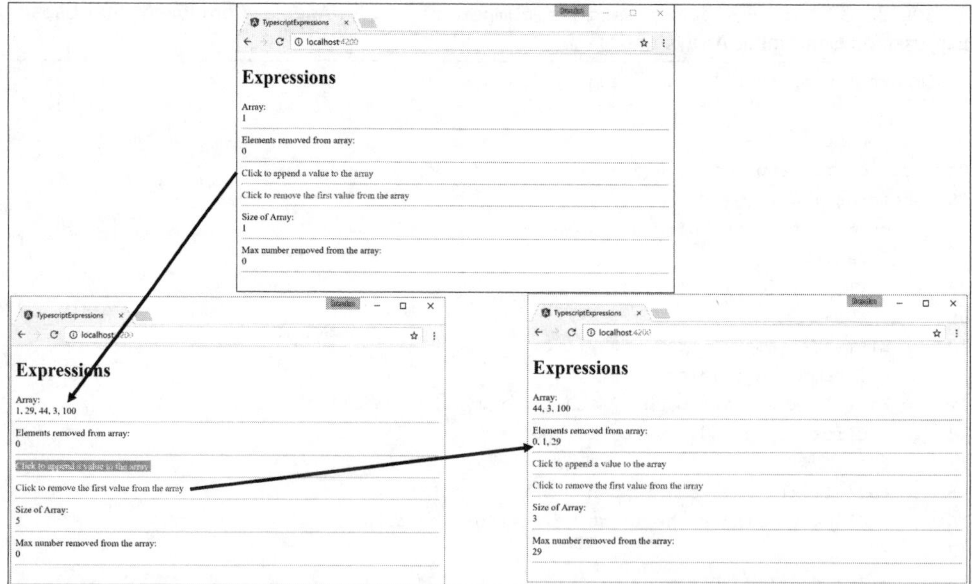

Figure 23.3 Using Angular expressions that apply TypeScript array and `Math` operations to interact with scope data

Using Pipes

A great feature of Angular is the capability to implement pipes. A *pipe* is a type of operator that hooks into the expression parser and modifies the results of the expression for display in a view—for example, to format time or currency values.

You implement pipes inside expressions, using the following syntax:

```
{{ expression | pipe}}
```

If you chain multiple pipes together, they are executed in the order in which you specify them:

```
{{ expression | pipe | pipe }}
```

Some filters allow you to provide input in the form of function parameters. You add these parameters by using the following syntax:

```
{{ expression | pipe:parameter1:parameter2 }}
```

Angular provides several types of pipes that enable you to easily format strings, objects, and arrays in component templates. Table 23.1 lists the built-in pipes provided with Angular.

Table 23.1 **Pipes That Modify Expressions in Angular Component Templates**

Filter	Description
`currency[ :currencyCode?[ :symbolDisplay?[ :digits?]]]`	Formats a number as currency, based on the `currencyCode` value provided. If no `currencyCode` value is provided, the default code for the locale is used. Here is an example: `{{123.46 | currency:"USD" }}`
`json`	Formats a TypeScript object into a JSON string. Here is an example: `{{ {'name':'Brad'} | json }}`
`slice:start:end`	Limits the data represented in the expression by the indexed amount. If the expression is a string, it is limited in the number of characters. If the result of the expression is an array, it is limited in the number of elements. Consider these examples: `{{ "Fuzzy Wuzzy" | slice:1:9 }}` `{{ ['a','b','c','d'] | slice:0:2 }}`
`lowercase`	Outputs the result of the expression as lowercase.
`uppercase`	Outputs the result of the expression as uppercase.
`number[:pre.post-postEnd]`	Formats the number as text. If a `pre` parameter is specified, the number of whole numbers is limited to that size. If `post-postEnd` is specified, the number of decimal places displayed is limited to that range or size. Consider these examples: `{{ 123.4567 | number:1.2-3 }}` `{{ 123.4567 | number:1.3 }}`
`date[:`*`format`*`]`	Formats a TypeScript date object, a timestamp, or an ISO 8601 date string, using the *`format`* parameter. Here is an example: `{{1389323623006 | date:'yyyy-MM-dd HH:mm:ss Z'}}` The *`format`* parameter uses the following date formatting characters: ▪ **yyyy:** Four-digit year ▪ **yy:** Two-digit year ▪ **MMMM:** Month in year, `January` through `December` ▪ **MMM:** Month in year, `Jan` through `Dec` ▪ **MM:** Month in year, padded, `01` through `12` ▪ **M:** Month in year, `1` through `12` ▪ **dd:** Day in month, padded, `01` through `31` ▪ **d:** Day in month, `1` through `31`

Filter	Description
	▪ **EEEE:** Day in week, `Sunday` through `Saturday` ▪ **EEE:** Day in Week, `Sun` through `Sat` ▪ **HH:** Hour in day, padded, `00` through `23` ▪ **H:** Hour in day, `0` through `23` ▪ **hh** or **jj:** Hour in a.m./p.m., padded, `01` through `12` ▪ **h** or **j:** Hour in a.m./p.m., `1` through `12` ▪ **mm:** Minute in hour, padded, `00` through `59` ▪ **m:** Minute in hour, `0` through `59` ▪ **ss:** Second in minute, padded, `00` through `59` ▪ **s:** Second in minute, `0` through `59` ▪ **.sss** or **,sss:** Millisecond in second, padded, `000-999` ▪ **a:** a.m./p.m. marker ▪ **Z:** Four-digit time zone offset, `-1200` through `+1200` The *`format`* string for `date` can also be one of the following predefined names: ▪ **medium:** Same as `'yMMMdHms'` ▪ **short:** same as `'yMdhm'` ▪ **fullDate:** same as `'yMMMMEEEEd'` ▪ **longDate:** same as `'yMMMMd'` ▪ **mediumDate:** same as `'yMMMd'` ▪ **shortDate:** same as `'yMd'` ▪ **mediumTime:** same as `'hms'` ▪ **shortTime:** same as `'hm'` The format shown here is `en_US`, but the format always matches the locale of the Angular application.
`async`	Waits for a promise and returns the most recent value received. It then updates the view.

Using Built-in Pipes

This section shows how the built-in Angular pipes handle the transformation of data in Angular expressions. The purpose of this example is to show how pipes transform the data provided.

Listing 23.4 shows the Angular component with a template that contains several examples of built-in pipes wrapped in {{}} brackets. The `Component` class contains data for some of the pipes to use.

Figure 23.4 shows the rendered application with the transformed data.

Listing 23.4 `builtInPipes.component.ts`: **An Angular Component That Contains an Example of Built-in Pipes**

```
import { Component } from '@angular/core';

@Component({
  selector: 'app-root',
  template: `
    Uppercase: {{"Brendan" | uppercase }}<br>
    Lowercase: {{"HELLO WORLD" | lowercase}}<br>
    Date: {{ today | date:'yMMMMEEEEhmsz'}}<br>
    Date: {{today | date:'mediumDate'}}<br>
    Date: {{today | date: 'shortTime'}}<br>
    Number: {{3.1415927 | number:'2.1-5'}}<br>
    Number: {{28 | number:'2.3'}}<br>
    Currency: {{125.257 | currency:'USD':true: '1.2-2'}}<br>
    Currency: {{2158.925 | currency}}<br>
    Json: {{jsonObject | json}}<br>
    PercentPipe: {{.8888 | percent: '2.2'}}<br>
    SlicePipe: {{"hello world" | slice:0:8}}<br>
    SlicePipe: {{days | slice:1:6}}<br>
    legen...  {{wait | async}} {{dairy | async}}
  `
})
export class AppComponent {
  today = Date.now();
  jsonObject = [{title: "mytitle"}, {title: "Programmer"}];
  days=['Sunday', 'Monday', 'Tuesday', 'Wednesday',
        'Thursday', 'Friday', 'Saturday'];
  wait = new Promise<string>((res, err) => {
    setTimeout(function () {
      res('wait for it...');
    },1000);
  });
  dairy = new Promise<string>((res, err) => {
    setTimeout(function() {
      res('dairy');
    },2000)
  })
}
```

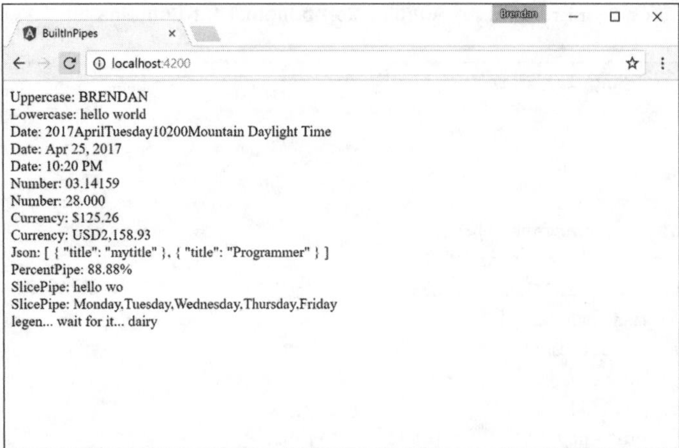

Figure 23.4 Using Angular pipes that transform data within expressions

Building a Custom Pipe

Angular enables you to create your own custom pipes and then use them within expressions and services as if they were built-in pipes. Angular provides the `@pipe` decorator to create a pipe and register it with the dependency injector server.

The `@pipe` decorator takes in metadata, just as an Angular component does. The metadata options are `name` and `pure`. The `name` metadata works like the selector of a component: It tells Angular where you want to use the pipe. The `pure` metadata tells the pipe how to handle change detection. A `pure` pipe updates when there is a change to the input value or an object reference. An `impure` pipe can update whenever there is an event, such as a keystroke, mouse click, or mouse movement. The following example demonstrates a sample pipe and its syntax:

```
@Pipe({
     name: 'example',
     Pure: true
})
```

The `pipe` class works much the same as the `Component` class, in that it is where the logic of the pipe resides. However, the logic needs to be within a `Transform` method, which tells the pipe how to transform whatever is to the left of the pipe symbol (|). Review the following example:

```
Export class customPipe{
     Transform(parameter1:string, parameter2:number) : string {
          myStr = "logic goes in here";
          return myStr;
     }
}
```

Creating a Custom Pipe

This section shows how to build a custom pipe that filters out select words from a string. The purpose of this example is to show you how to create and apply a custom pipe that can transform data.

Listing 23.5 shows an Angular pipe with the `name` metadata `censor`. The `export` class contains the `Transform` method, which replaces certain words with a different string and then returns the transformed string.

Listing 23.6 shows an Angular component which contains template that uses the custom pipe, as well as the `pipe` metadata to import the pipe. Notice that on line 6, there is the expression that you use to implement the pipe. The pipe takes in a string as an argument and replaces the word with it.

Figure 23.5 shows the rendered application, using the custom pipe.

Listing 23.5 `custom.pipe.ts`: **An Angular Pipe That Replaces Certain Words in a String**

```
import {Pipe} from '@angular/core';

@Pipe({name: 'censor'})
export class censorPipe{
  transform(input:string, replacement:string) : string {
    var cWords = ["bad", "rotten", "terrible"];
    var out = input;
    for(var i=0; i<cWords.length; i++){
      out = out.replace(cWords[i], replacement);
    }
    return out
  }
}
```

Listing 23.6 `customPipes.component.ts`: **An Angular Component That Imports and Uses a Custom Pipe**

```
01 import { Component } from '@angular/core';
02
03 @Component({
04   selector: 'app-root',
05   template: `
06     {{phrase | censor:"*****"}}
07   `
08 })
09 export class AppComponent {
10   phrase:string="This bad phrase is rotten ";
11 }
```

Figure 23.5 Using a custom Angular pipe that transforms data in an expression

Summary

Angular comes with powerful built-in expressions and pipes and provides the option to create custom pipes. This chapter discusses the available built-in expressions and pipes and how to implement them. It also discusses how to build and implement a custom pipe. Expressions are bits of TypeScript code contained within {{}}, and pipes are able to manipulate those expressions. Expressions have access to information within the `Component` class and can render class variables to the view.

Next

In the next chapter you will learn about databinding. You will learn about how it links data together and expand on the many different types of databinding.

24

Data Binding

One of the best features of Angular is the built-in data binding. *Data binding* is the process of linking data from a component with what is displayed in a web page. When data in the component changes, the UI rendered to the user is automatically updated. Angular provides a very clean interface to link the model data to elements in a web page.

Understanding Data Binding

Data binding means linking data in an application with the UI element that is rendered to the user. When data is changed in the model, the web page is automatically updated. This way, the model is always the only source for data represented to the user, and the view is just a projection of the model. The glue that puts the view and the model together is data binding.

There are many ways in Angular to use data binding to make an application look and act in different ways. The following is a list of the types of data binding available with Angular that are discussed in this chapter:

- **Interpolation:** You can use double curly braces ({{}}) to get values directly from the `Component` class.
- **Property binding:** You can use this type of binding to set the property of an HTML element.
- **Event binding:** You can use this type of binding to handle user inputs.
- **Attribute binding:** This type of binding allows the setting of attributes to an HTML element.
- **Class binding:** You can use this type of binding to set CSS class names to the element.
- **Style binding:** You can use this type of binding to create inline CSS styles for the element.
- **Two-way binding with `ngModel`:** You can use this type of binding with data entry forms to receive and display data.

Interpolation

Interpolation involves using the {{}} double curly braces to evaluate a template expression. This can be in a hard-coded form, or it can reference a property of the `Component` class.

The syntax for interpolation should look familiar from Chapter 23, "Expressions." However, you can also use interpolation to give an HTML tag property a value (for example, the `img` tag). Here is an example of the syntax to do this:

```
<img src="{{imgUrl}}"/>
```

Now let's look at an example that shows some cool things you can do with interpolation binding.

Listing 24.1 shows an Angular component. This component has a template that contains types of interpolation and expressions wrapped in {{}} brackets. The `Component` class gives values to be used within the {{}} brackets. (Be sure to change the `imageSrc` variable to the appropriate image name.)

Figure 24.1 shows the rendered web page. As you can see, interpolation can use strings from the `Component` class to populate the template.

Listing 24.1 `interpolation.component.ts`: **Interpolation with Strings and a Function**

```
import { Component } from '@angular/core';

@Component({
  selector: 'app-root',
  template: `
    {{str1 + ' ' + name}}
    <br>
    <img src="{{imageSrc}}" />
    <br>
    <p>{{str2 + getLikes(likes)}}</p>
  `,
  styles: [`
    img{
      width: 300px;
      height: auto;
    }
    p{
      font-size: 35px;
      color: darkBlue;
    }
  `]
})
export class AppComponent {
  str1: string = "Hello my name is"
  name: string = "Brendan"
  str2: string = "I like to"
```

```
  likes: string[] = ['hike', "rappel", "Jeep"]
  getLikes = function(arr: any){
    var arrString = arr.join(", ");
    return " " + arrString
  }
  imageSrc: string = "../assets/images/angelsLanding.jpg"
}
```

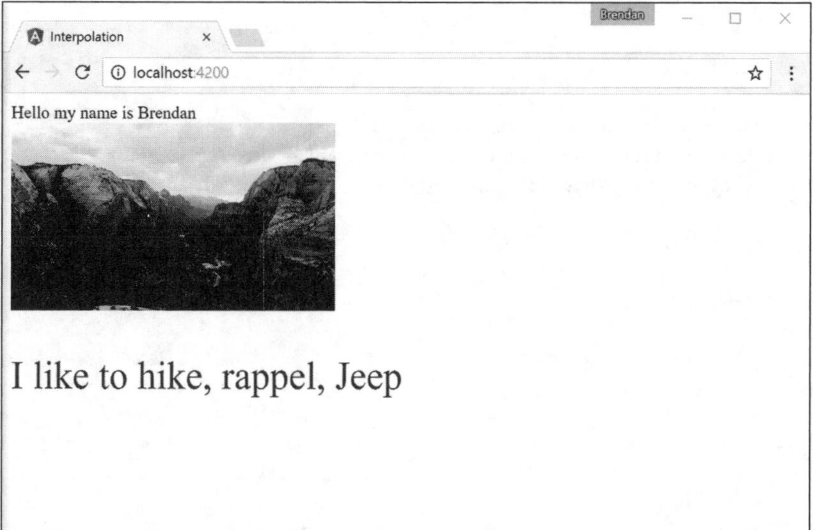

Figure 24.1 Using interpolation to combine strings, define an `imageSrc` URL, and run a function

Property Binding

You use property binding when you need to set the property of an HTML element. You do this by defining the value you want within the `Component` class. Then you bind that value to the component template, using the following syntax:

```
<img [src]="myValue">
```

> **Note**
>
> In many cases, it is possible to use interpolation to achieve the same results you get with property binding.

Now let's take a look at an example of property binding. Listing 24.2 shows an Angular component. This component has a template that contains types of property binding. It also makes a comparison between property binding and interpolation.

Figure 24.2 shows the rendered web page. As you can see, interpolation can use strings from the Component class to populate the template.

Listing 24.2 property.component.ts: **Property Binding with Logic and the Application of a Class Name**

```
import { Component } from '@angular/core';

@Component({
  selector: 'app-root',
  template: `
    <img [src]="myPic"/>
    <br>
    <button [disabled]="isEnabled">Click me</button><hr>
    <button disabled="{!isEnabled}">Click me</button><br>
    <p [ngClass]="className">This is cool stuff</p>
  `,
  styles: [`
    img {
      height: 100px;
      width auto;
    }
    .myClass {
      color: red;
      font-size: 24px;
    }
  `]
})
export class AppComponent {
  myPic: string = "../assets/images/sunset.JPG";
  isEnabled: boolean = false;
  className: string = "myClass";
}
```

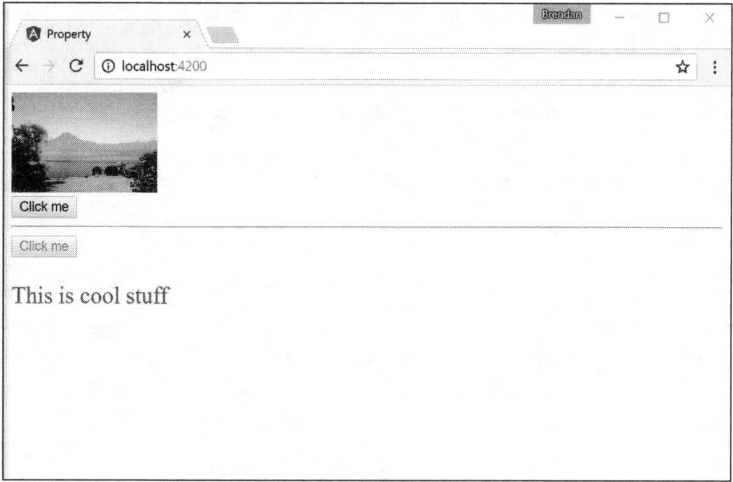

Figure 24.2 Using property binding to define an `imageSrc` URL, set a button to disabled mode, and assign a class name

Attribute Binding

Attribute binding is similar to property binding but is tied to the HTML attribute rather than the DOM property. You are not likely to use attribute binding very often, but it is important to know what it is and how to use it. You will generally only use attribute binding on attributes that do not have a corresponding DOM property (for example, `aria`, `svg`, and `table span` attributes). You define an attribute binding by using the following syntax:

```
<div [attr.aria-label] = "labelName"></div>
```

> **Note**
>
> Because attribute binding and property binding function almost the same way, we do not present an example for attribute binding in this book.

Class Binding

You use class binding to bind CSS style tags to HTML elements. It assigns the class based on the result of an expression being `true` or `false`. If the result is `true`, the class gets assigned. The following is an example of the syntax:

```
<div [class.nameHere] = "true"></div>
<div [class.anotherName] = "false"></div>
```

Now let's take a look at an example of class binding. Listing 24.3 shows an Angular component that has a template. This template contains types of class binding that show how to apply a class name using two different methods.

Figure 24.3 shows the rendered web page. As you can see, the class names take effect and allow the CSS styles to change the HTML.

Listing 24.3 `class.component.ts`: **Property Binding with Logic and the Application of a Class Name**

```
import { Component } from '@angular/core';

@Component({
  selector: 'app-root',
  template: `
    <div [class]="myCustomClass"></div>
    <span [class.redText]="isTrue">Hello my blue friend</span>
  `,
  styles: [`
    .blueBox {
      height: 150px;
      width: 150px;
      background-color: blue;
    }
    .redText{
      color: red;
      font-size: 24px;
    }
  `]
})
export class AppComponent {
  myCustomClass: string = 'blueBox';
  isTrue = true;
}
```

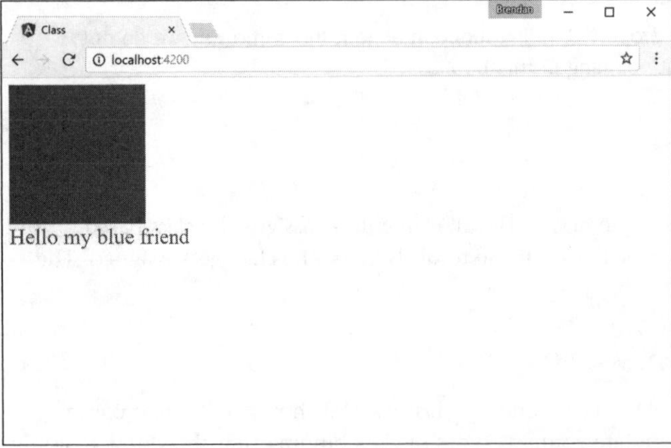

Figure 24.3 An Angular application that applies class binding to add custom classes to HTML elements

Style Binding

You use style binding to assign inline styles to an HTML element. Style binding works by defining the CSS style property in the brackets, with the assignment expression in the quotation marks. The syntax looks almost the same as for class binding but with `style` instead of `class` as the prefix:

```
<p [style.styleProperty] = "assignment"></p>
<div [style.backgroundColor] = "'green'"></div>
```

Now let's take a look at an example of style binding. Listing 24.4 shows an Angular component that has a template. This template contains types of style binding that show how to apply custom inline styles to an application.

Figure 24.4 shows the rendered web page. As you can see, the styles take effect, and the CSS styles change the HTML accordingly.

Listing 24.4 `style.component.ts`: **Style Binding to Change the Appearance of the HTML**

```
import { Component } from '@angular/core';

@Component({
  selector: 'app-root',
  template: `
    <span [style.border]="myBorder">Hey there</span>
    <div [style.color]="twoColors ? 'blue' : 'forestgreen'">
      what color am I
    </div>
    <button (click)="changeColor()">click me</button>
  `
})
export class AppComponent {
  twoColors: boolean = true;
  changeColor = function(){
    this.twoColors = !this.twoColors;
  }
  myBorder = "1px solid black";
}
```

Figure 24.4 The rendered web page with custom styles applied via a button that runs a function to adjust the value of the `twoColors` variable

Event Binding

You use event binding to handle user inputs such as clicking, keystrokes, and mouse movements. Angular event binding is similar to HTML event attributes; the major difference is that the prefix "on" is removed from the binding, and instead the event is surrounded by parentheses (`()`). For example, `onkeyup` in HTML looks like `(keyup)` in Angular.

A common purpose for event binding is to run functions from the component. The following is the syntax for click event binding:

```
<button (click)="myFunction()">button</button>
```

Let's look at an example of event binding. Listing 24.5 shows an Angular component. This component has event binding that calls a function to change the image URL once clicked.

Figure 24.5 shows the rendered web page. You can see both the initial web page and the results of clicking the button to trigger the event.

Listing 24.5 `event.component.ts`: **Event Binding to Change the Image URL That Displays on the Web Page**

```
import { Component } from '@angular/core';

@Component({
  selector: 'app-root',
  template: `
    <div (mousemove)="move($event)">
```

```
      <img [src]="imageUrl"
        (mouseenter)="mouseGoesIn()"
        (mouseleave)="mouseLeft()"
        (dblclick)="changeImg()" /><br>
        double click the picture to change it<br>
        The Mouse has {{mouse}}<hr>
      <button (click)="changeImg()">Change Picture</button><hr>
      <input (keyup)="onKeyup($event)"
        (keydown)="onKeydown($event)"
        (keypress)="keypress($event)"
        (blur)="underTheScope($event)"
        (focus)="underTheScope($event)">
        {{view}}
      <p>On key up: {{upValues}}</p>
      <p>on key down: {{downValues}}</p>
      <p>on key press: {{keypressValue}}</p>
      <p (mousemove)="move($event)">
        x coordinates: {{x}}
        <br> y coordinates: {{y}}
      </p>
    </div>
  `,
  styles: [`
    img {
      width: auto;
      height: 300px;
    }
  `]
})
export class AppComponent {
  counter = 0;
  mouse: string;
  upValues: string = '';
  downValues: string = '';
  keypressValue: string = "";
  x: string = "";
  y: string = '';
  view: string = '';

  mouseGoesIn = function(){
    this.mouse = "entered";
  };
  mouseLeft = function(){
    this.mouse = "left";
  }
  imageArray: string[] = [
    "../assets/images/flower.jpg",
    "../assets/images/lake.jpg", //extensions are case sensitive
```

```
    "../assets/images/bison.jpg",
  ]
  imageUrl: string = this.imageArray[this.counter];
  changeImg = function(){
    if(this.counter < this.imageArray.length - 1){
      this.counter++;
    }else{
      this.counter = 0;
    }
    this.imageUrl=this.imageArray[this.counter];
  }
  onKeyup(event:any){
    this.upValues = event.key;
    //this.upValues += event.target.value + ' | ';
  }
  onKeydown(event:any){
    this.downValues = event.key;
    //this.downValues += event.target.value + " | ";
  }
  keypress(event:any){
    this.keypressValue = event.key;
    //this.keypressValue += event.target.value + " | ";
  }
  move(event:any){
    this.x = event.clientX;
    this.y = event.clientY;
  }
  underTheScope(event:any){
    if(event.type == "focus"){
      this.view = "the text box is focused";
    }
    else if(event.type == "blur"){
      this.view = "the input box is blurred";
    }
    console.log(event);
  }
}
```

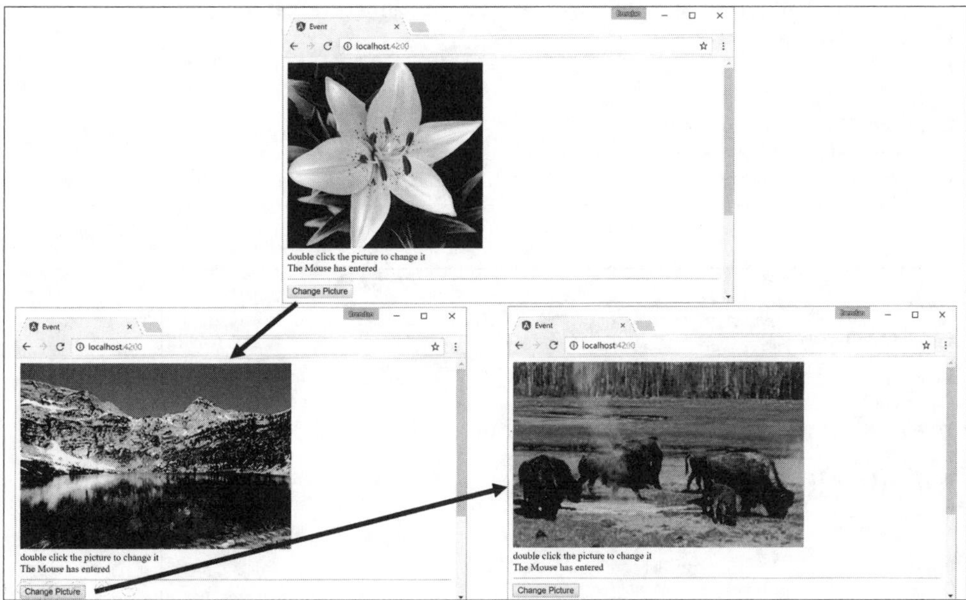

Figure 24.5 The initial result when the web page is loaded and the result from the event being triggered

Two-Way Binding

Two-way binding allows for data to be easily displayed and updated simultaneously. This makes it easy to reflect any changes the user makes to the DOM. Angular does this by using `ngModel` to watch for changes and then update the value. This is the syntax:

```
<input [(ngModel)] = "myValue">
```

Now let's take a look at an example of two-way binding. Listing 24.6 shows an Angular component that has a template. This template shows different ways to accomplish two-way data binding.

Figure 24.6 shows the rendered web page. It shows that the styles take effect and the CSS styles change the HTML accordingly.

Listing 24.6 `twoWay.component.ts`: **Different Methods to Implement Two-Way Data Binding**

```
import { Component } from '@angular/core';
@Component({
  selector: 'app-root',
  template: `
    <input [(ngModel)]="text"><br>
    <input bindon-ngModel="text"><br>
```

```
    <input [value]="text" (input)="text=$event.target.value">
    <h1>{{text}}</h1>
  `
})
export class AppComponent {
  text: string = "some text here";
}
```

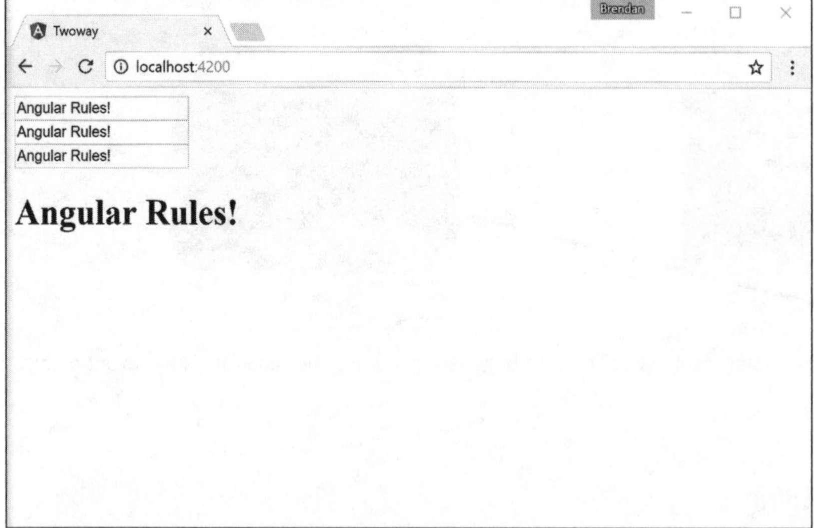

Figure 24.6 An Angular application that shows multiple ways to accomplish two-way data binding. The variable and the view are updated every time there is a change to the input field

Summary

Angular allows for powerful and very useful types of data binding. As you have seen in this chapter, you can bind data in the application model to the UI elements that are rendered to the user. This chapter goes over the available types of data binding and how to implement them. Data binding allows for data to be both displayed to the user and updated by the user in a simple and efficient manner.

Next

The next chapter talks about built in directives. You will learn about what they are, as well as how to implement them in your Angular templates.

25

Built-in Directives

One of the most powerful features Angular provides is directives. *Directives* extend the behavior of HTML, enabling you to create custom HTML elements, attributes, and classes with functionality specific to an application. Angular provides many built-in directives, which provide the capability to interact with form elements, bind data in a component to the view, and interact with browser events.

This chapter discusses the built-in directives and how to implement them in Angular templates. You will learn how to apply these directives in your Angular templates and support them in back-end controllers to quickly turn a rendered view into an interactive application.

Understanding Directives

Directives are a combination of Angular template markup and supporting TypeScript code. Angular directive markups can be HTML attributes, element names, or CSS classes. The TypeScript directive code defines the template data and behavior of the HTML elements.

The Angular compiler traverses the template DOM and compiles all directives. Then it links the directives by combining a directive with a scope to produce a new live view. The live view contains the DOM elements and functionality defined in the directive.

Using Built-in Directives

Much of the Angular functionality that you need to implement in HTML elements is provided through built-in directives. These directives provide a wide variety of support for Angular applications. The following sections describe most of the Angular directives, which fall into three categories:

- **Component:** A directive with a template
- **Structural:** A directive that manipulates elements in the DOM
- **Attribute:** A directive that manipulates the appearance and behavior of a DOM element

The following sections describe these three types of directives. You do not need to understand all the directives right away. The following sections provide tables for reference. In addition, the following sections and chapters provide sample code for using many of these directives.

Components Directives

Angular components are a form of structural directive that utilize a template. A component creates a selector that is used as an HTML tag to dynamically add HTML, CSS, and Angular logic to the DOM. Components are at the heart of Angular.

Structural Directives

Several directives dynamically update, create, and remove elements from the DOM. These directives create the layout, look, and feel of an application. Table 25.1 lists these directives and describes the behavior and usage of each.

Table 25.1 **Structural Directives**

Directive	Description
ngFor	This directive is used to create a copy of a template for each item within an iterable object. Here is an example: <div *ngFor="let person of people"></div>
ngIf	When this directive is present in an element, that element is added to the DOM if the value returns true. If the value returns false, then that element is removed from the DOM, preventing that element from using resources. Here is an example: <div *ngIf="person"></div>
ngSwitch	This directive displays a template based on the value passed in it. As with ngIf, if the value does not match the case, the element is not created. Here is an example: <div [ngSwitch]="timeOfDay"> <span [ngSwitchCase]="'morning'">Morning</span> <span [ngSwitchCase]="'afternoon'">Afternoon</span> <span [ngSwitchDefault]="'daytime'">Evening</span> The ngSwitch directive relies on two other directives to work: ngSwitchCase and ngSwitchDefault. These directives are be explained below.
ngSwitchCase	This directive evaluates the value it has stored against the value passed into ngSwitch and determines whether the HTML template it is attached to should be created.
ngSwitchDefault	This directive creates the HTML template if all the above ngSwitchCase expressions evaluate to false. This ensures that some HTML is generated no matter what.

The directives in Table 25.1 are used in a variety of different ways in various parts of the code. They allow for dynamic manipulation of the DOM, based on what data is passed to them. Structural directives dynamically manipulate the DOM by using expressions or values. Two of the most common structural directives are `ngIf` and `ngSwitch`.

`ngIf` displays a section of HTML if a value or an expression returns `true`. `ngIf` uses the `*` symbol to let Angular know it's there. The following is an example of the syntax for `ngIf`:

```
<div *ngIf="myFunction(val)" >...</div>
<div *ngIf="myValue" >{{myValue}}</div>
```

> **Note**
>
> `ngFor` is another example of a directive that uses the * symbol as a prefix to let Angular know it's there.

`ngSwitch` uses `ngSwitchCase`, which displays a section of HTML if a value or an expression returns `true`. `ngSwitch` is surrounded by `[]` as a form of one-way data binding to pass the data to each `ngSwitchCase` for evaluation. The following is an example of the syntax for `ngSwitch`:

```
<div [ngSwitch]="time">
      <span *ngSwitchCase="'night'">It's night time </span>
      <span *ngSwitchDefault>It's day time </span>
```

Listing 25.1 shows an Angular component which has a template that contains built-in structural directives. The `ngIf` directive dynamically adds and removes HTML from the DOM. `ngSwitch` does the same thing as `ngIf`, but it allows for more options, along with a default option if all the cases return `false`.

Lines 6 and 7 in Listing 25.1 use `ngIf` to determine whether the HTML should be displayed.

Line 10 shows the extended form of `ngFor` to dynamically add HTML based on the amount of data passed to it. (This example simply shows another method of using the `ngFor` directive, but the rest of the book will use the shorter form `*ngFor`.)

Line 15 uses the shorthand form of the `ngFor` directive to display data. This method is used throughout the rest of this book.

Lines 20 through 26 use `ngSwitchCase` to determine which piece of HTML should be displayed.

Figure 25.1 shows the rendered web page. As you can see, interpolation can use strings from the `Component` class to populate the template.

Listing 25.1 `structural.component.ts`: **Structural Built-in Functions**

```
01 import { Component } from '@angular/core';
02
03 @Component({
04   selector: 'app-root',
05   template: `
```

```
    <div *ngIf="condition">condition met</div>
    <div *ngIf="!condition">condition not met</div>
    <button (click)="changeCondition()">Change Condition</button>
    <hr>
    <template ngFor let-person [ngForOf]="people">
      <div>name: {{person}}</div>
    </template>
    <hr>
    <h3>Monsters and where they live</h3>
    <ul *ngFor="let monster of monsters">
        {{monster.name}}:
        {{monster.location}}
    </ul>
    <hr>
    <div [ngSwitch]="time">
      <span *ngSwitchCase="'night'">It's night time
      <button (click)="changeDay()">change to day</button>
      </span>
      <span *ngSwitchDefault>It's day time
      <button (click)="changeNight()">change to night</button></span>
    </div>
  `
})
export class AppComponent {
  condition: boolean = true;
  changeCondition = function(){
    this.condition = !this.condition;
  }
  changeDay = function(){
    this.time = 'day';
  }
  changeNight = function(){
    this.time = 'night'
  }
  people: string[] = [
    "Andrew", "Dillon", "Philipe", "Susan"
  ]
  monsters = [
    { name: "Nessie",
      location: "Loch Ness, Scotland" },
    { name: "Bigfoot",
      location: "Pacific Northwest, USA" },
    { name: "Godzilla",
      location: "Tokyo, sometimes New York" }
  ]
  time: string = 'night';
}
```

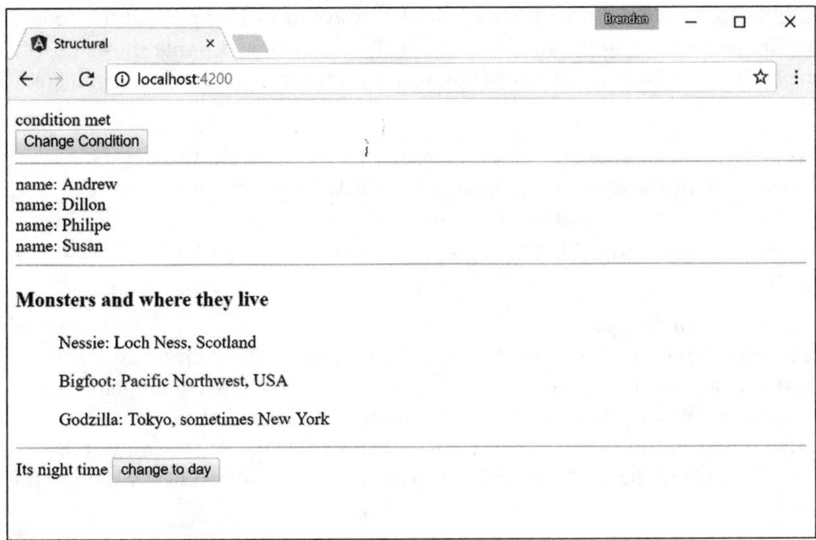

Figure 25.1 Using built-in structural directives

Attribute Directives

Angular attribute directives modify how HTML elements look and behave. They are injected straight into the HTML and dynamically modify how the user interacts with an HTML segment. Attribute directives are so named because they often look like normal HTML attributes. An example of an attribute directive that you've been using throughout the book is `ngModel`, which modifies an element by changing the display value.

Table 25.2 lists the attribute directives and describes the behavior and usage of each.

Table 25.2 **Attribute Directives**

Directive	Description
`ngModel`	This directive watches a variable for changes and then updates display values based on those changes. Consider these examples: `<input [(ngModel)]="text"> ` `<h1>{{text}}</h1>`
`ngForm`	This directive creates a form group and allows it to track the values and validation within that form group. By using `ngSubmit`, you can pass the form data as an object to the submission event. Here is an example: `<form #formName="ngForm" (ngSubmit)="onSubmit(formName)"></form>`
`ngStyle`	This directive updates the styles of an HTML element.

The directives in Table 25.2 are used in a variety of different ways in various parts of the code. They allow for manipulation of an application's behavior. The following example shows how to use some of the built-in attribute directives to build a form that submits data to a simulated database.

Listing 25.2 shows an Angular component. Lines 9 through 14 set the default values for the variables used throughout the application. Lines 15 through 17 define the enabler method, which sets the Boolean `isDisabled` to the opposite value of what it was. Lines 18 through 30 define the `addClass` method, which pushes a value from the event target to the `selectedClass` array.

Listing 25.3 shows an Angular template file that uses `ngModel`, `ngClass`, `ngStyle`, and `ngForm` to modify the look and behavior of the HTML template. Lines 7 through 12 create an HTML selection element that assigns a color to the `color` variable on the attribute component. Lines 14 through 18 create an HTML selection element that uses the `change` event to invoke the `addClass` method and pass in the `event` object. Lines 16 through 21 display the output of the component variables, using the `ngClass` and `ngStyle` directives to dynamically modify the look of the elements.

The code in Listing 25.4 is the CSS for the component that sets up the styles for the application.

Figure 25.2 shows the rendered web page. It shows that interpolation can use strings from the `Component` class to populate the template.

Listing 25.2 `attribute.component.ts`: A Component That Builds and Manages an Angular Form

```
01 import { Component } from '@angular/core';
02
03 @Component({
04   selector: 'app-root',
05   templateUrl: './attribute.component.html',
06   styleUrls: ['./attribute.component.css']
07 })
08 export class AppComponent {
09   colors: string[] = ["red", "blue", "green", "yellow"];
10   name: string;
11   color: string = 'color';
12   isDisabled: boolean = true;
13   classes:string[] = ['bold', 'italic', 'highlight'];
14   selectedClass:string[] = [];
15   enabler(){
16     this.isDisabled = !this.isDisabled;
17   }
18   addClass(event: any){
19     this.selectedClass = [];
```

```
    var values = event.target.options;
    var opt: any;

    for (var i=0, iLen = values.length; i<iLen; i++){
      opt = values[i];

      if (opt.selected){
        this.selectedClass.push(opt.text);
      }
    }
  }
}
```

Listing 25.3 `attribute.component.html`: **An Angular Template for the Attribute Component**

```
<form>
  <span>name: </span>
  <input name="name" [(ngModel)]="name">
  <br>
  <span>color:</span>
  <input type="checkbox" (click)="enabler()">
  <select #optionColor [(ngModel)]="color" name="color"
          [disabled]="isDisabled">
    <option *ngFor="let color of colors" [value]="color">
      {{color}}
    </option>
  </select><hr>
  <span>Change Class</span><br>
  <select #classOption multiple name="styles" (change)="addClass($event)">
    <option *ngFor="let class of classes" [value]="class" >
      {{class}}
    </option>
  </select><br>
  <span>
    press and hold control/command
    <br>
    to select multiple options
  </span>
</form>
<hr>
<span>Name: {{name}}</span><br>
<span [ngClass]="selectedClass"
     [ngStyle]="{'color': optionColor.value}">
color: {{optionColor.value}}
</span><br>
```

Listing 25.4 `attribute.component.css`: **A CSS File That Styles the Application**

```
.bold {
  font-weight: bold;
}
.italic {
  font-style: italic;
}
.highlight {
  background-color: lightblue;
}
```

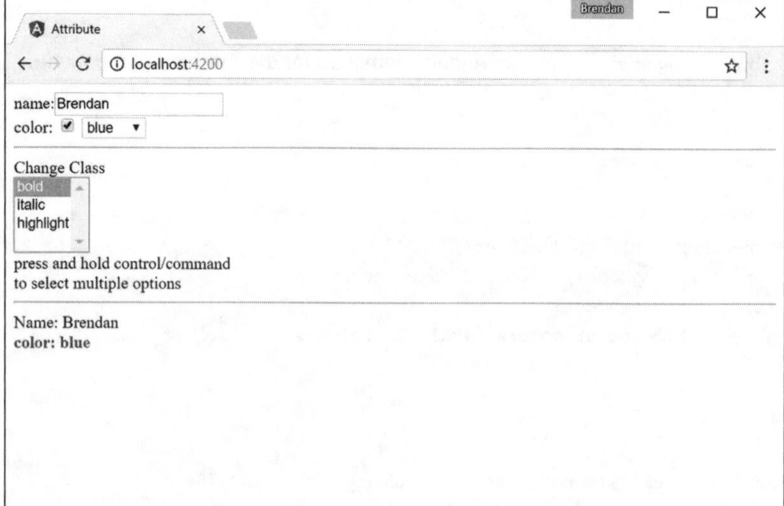

Figure 25.2 An Angular application that shows multiple ways to apply attribute directives to modify the behavior of the DOM

Summary

Angular offers many built-in directives that provide functionality to manipulate the look, feel, and behavior of an application, without requiring you to write large amounts of code. This chapter goes over some of the available built-in directives and provides examples of how to utilize Angular's built-in directives.

Next

In this chapter you learned about built-in directives. In the next Chapter you will learn about custom directives and how to make your own directives that you can implement in Angular.

26

Custom Directives

As with many other features of Angular, you can extend functionality by creating your own custom directives. Custom directives allow you to extend the functionality of HTML by implementing the behavior of elements yourself. If you have code that needs to manipulate the DOM, it should be done inside a custom directive.

You implement a custom directive by calling the @`directive` class, much the same way you define a component. The @`directive` class metadata should include the selector of the directive to be used in the HTML. The `Directive` export class is where the logic for the directive will reside. For example, the following is a basic definition for a directive:

```
import { Directive } from '@angular/core';
@Directive({
    selector: '[myDirective]'
})
export class myDirective { }
```

Creating a Custom Attribute Directive

You can define a limitless number of types of custom directives, which makes Angular incredibly extensible. Custom directives are the most complex portion of Angular to explain. The best way to get you started is to show you an example of custom directives to give you a feel for how they can be implemented and interact with each other.

This section shows how to implement a custom attribute directive. The zoom directive created in this example is designed to add custom functionality to whatever image it is applied to. With this directive applied, you can scroll over an image with the mouse wheel to make the element grow or shrink in size.

Listing 26.1 shows the zoom component, which displays a list of images. These images have the zoom directive applied to them, allowing the mouse scroll event to increase or decrease the size of each image.

Listing 26.2 shows the zoom directive. This directive has the selector `zoom`. This directive imports `Directive`, `ElementRef`, `HostListener`, `Input`, and `Renderer` from `@angular/core` to provide the functionality this directive needs.

Lines 10 through 12 of Listing 26.2 watch for the mouse cursor to enter the element, and when it does, it applies a border to the element with the `border()` function to let the user know the directive is active.

Lines 14 through 16 remove the border when the cursor leaves the element to tell the user the directive is no longer active.

Lines 17 through 26 listen for the mouse wheel to be activated. Depending on which direction the wheel is scrolled, the element's size is adjusted with the `changeSize()` function.

Lines 27 through 31 define the `border()` function. This function takes in three parameters and then applies those parameters to style the host element.

Lines 32 through 36 define the `changeSize()` function, which changes the size of the host element.

Listing 26.3 shows the HTML file for `zoom.component.ts`. It creates a row of images and applies the zoom directive to those images.

Listing 26.4 shows the styles for `zoom.component.ts`. It sets the height of the images to 200px initially so they aren't rendered huge if they have a high resolution.

The web page that results from Listings 26.1–26.4 is shown in Figure 26.1.

Listing 26.1 `zoom.component.ts`**: A Structural Directive**

```
import { Component } from '@angular/core';

@Component({
  selector: 'app-root',
  templateUrl: './app.component.html',
  styleUrls: ['./app.component.css']
})
export class AppComponent {
  images: string[] = [
    '../assets/images/jump.jpg',
    '../assets/images/flower2.jpg',
    '../assets/images/cliff.jpg'
  ]
}
```

Listing 26.2 `zoom.directive.ts`**: A Custom Attribute Directive**

```
01 import { Directive, ElementRef, HostListener, Input, Renderer }
02   from '@angular/core';
03 @Directive({
04     selector: '[zoom]'
05 })
06
```

```
export class ZoomDirective {
    constructor(private el: ElementRef, private renderer: Renderer) { }

    @HostListener('mouseenter') onMouseEnter() {
        this.border('lime', 'solid', '5px');
    }

    @HostListener('mouseleave') onMouseLeave() {
        this.border();
    }
    @HostListener('wheel', ['$event']) onWheel(event: any) {
        event.preventDefault();
        if(event.deltaY > 0){
            this.changeSize(-25);
        }
        if(event.deltaY < 0){
            this.changeSize(25);
        }
    }
    private border(
      color: string = null,
      type: string = null,
      width: string = null
      ){
        this.renderer.setElementStyle(
            this.el.nativeElement, 'border-color', color);
        this.renderer.setElementStyle(
            this.el.nativeElement, 'border-style', type);
        this.renderer.setElementStyle(
            this.el.nativeElement, 'border-width', width);
    }
    private changeSize(sizechange: any){
        let height: any = this.el.nativeElement.offsetHeight;
        let newHeight: any = height + sizechange;
        this.renderer.setElementStyle(
            this.el.nativeElement, 'height', newHeight + 'px');
    }
}
```

Listing 26.3 `app.component.html`: **An HTML File That Uses the Zoom Directive**

```
<h1>
  Attribute Directive
</h1>
<span *ngFor="let image of images">
  <img zoom src="{{image}}" />
</span>
```

Listing 26.4 `app.component.css`: **A CSS File that Sets the Image Height**

```
img {
  height: 200px;
}
```

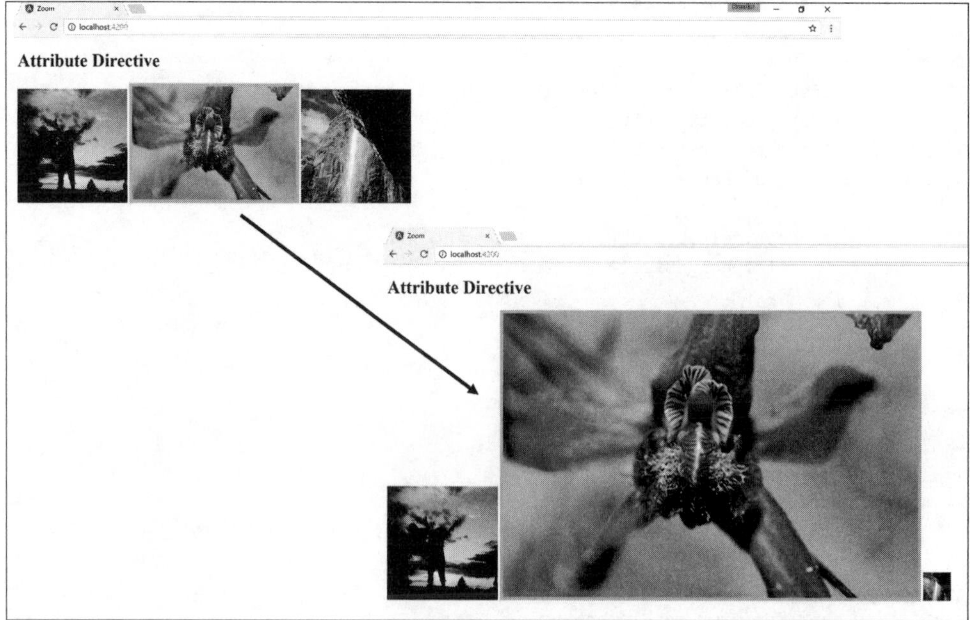

Figure 26.1 Applying a custom attribute directive

Creating a Custom Directive with a Component

Angular components are also a type of directive. What distinguishes a component from a directive is that components use an HTML template to generate a view. But because a component underneath is just a directive, it can be applied to HTML elements to add custom functionality in some really cool ways.

Angular offers a built-in directive called `ng-content`. This directive allows Angular to take existing HTML from between two element tags that use a directive and use that HTML within the components template. The syntax of `ng-content` is as follows:

```
<ng-content></ng-content>
```

The example in this section shows how to use a component as a custom directive to change how the element looks with a containing template.

This example implements a custom directive container that is designed to add a surrounding "container" HTML template to the element it is being applied to. This directive has two inputs title and description that can be used to give the host element a description and title.

Listing 26.5 shows the root component, which displays various HTML elements. These elements have the container directive applied, which adds a header with an optional title, a footer with an optional description, and borders to each element.

Listing 26.5 `app.component.ts`: **The Root Component**

```
import { Component } from '@angular/core';

@Component({
  selector: 'app-root',
  templateUrl: './app.component.html',
  styleUrls: ['./app.component.css'],
})
export class AppComponent {

  images: any = [
    {
      src: "../assets/images/angelsLanding.jpg",
      title: "Angels Landing",
      description: "A natural wonder in Zion National Park Utah, USA"
    },
    {
      src: "../assets/images/pyramid.JPG",
      title: "Tikal",
      description: "Mayan Ruins, Tikal Guatemala"
    },
    {
      src: "../assets/images/sunset.JPG"
    },
  ]
}
```

Listing 26.6 shows the HTML for the root component. The code creates several elements of different types, such as `image`, `div`, and `p`, and applies the container directive to them.

Listing 26.6 `app.component.html`: **HTML for the Root Component**

```
<span *ngFor="let image of images" container title="{{image.title}}"
  description="{{image.description}}">
  <img src="{{image.src}}"  />
</span>
<span container>
  <p>Lorem ipsum dolor sit amet, consectetur adipiscing elit,
```

```
    sed do eiusmod tempor incididunt ut labore </p>
</span>
<span container>
  <div class="diver">
  </div>
</span>
```

Listing 26.7 shows the CSS for the root component. It sets a max image height to keep the size of the image smaller. It also sets some default styling for the class `diver` so that it is visible to the user.

Listing 26.7 `app.component.css`: **CSS for the Root Component**

```
img{ height: 300px; }
p{ color: red }
.diver{
  background-color: forestgreen;
  height: 300px;
  width: 300px;
}
```

Listing 26.8 shows the container directive. This directive has the selector `container` and the inputs `title` and `description`. This directive imports `Directive`, `Input`, and `Output` from `@angular/core` to provide the functionality this directive needs.

Listing 26.8 `container.component.ts`: **A Component that Defines the Container**

```
import { Component, Input, Output } from '@angular/core';

@Component({
  selector: '[container]',
  templateUrl: './container.component.html',
  styleUrls: ['./container.component.css']
})
export class ContainerComponent {
  @Input() title: string;
  @Input() description: string;
}
```

Listing 26.9 shows the HTML for the container directive. Lines 2 through 4 create the title bar for the container. Lines 5 through 7 apply the content attribute directive. `ng-content` acts as a placeholder and will be replaced with the template from the container component shown in Listing 26.8. Lines 8 through 10 create the description bar for the container component.

Listing 26.9 `container.component.html`: **HTML for the Container Component**

```
<div class="sticky">
    <div class="title" >
        {{ title }}
    </div>
    <div class="content">
        <ng-content></ng-content>
    </div>
    <div class="description">
        {{ description }}
    </div>
</div>
```

Listing 26.10 shows the CSS for the container component. This file sets the CSS to give the container component borders, a title bar, and a description bar.

Listing 26.10 `container.component.css`: **CSS for the Container Component**

```
.title {
    color: white;
    background-color: dimgrey;
    padding: 10px;
}
.content {
    text-align: center;
    margin: 0px;
}
.description {
    color: red;
    background-color: lightgray;
    margin-top: -4px;
    padding: 10px;
}
.sticky {
    display: inline-block;
    padding: 0px;
    margin: 15px;
    border-left: dimgrey 3px solid;
    border-right: dimgrey 3px solid;
}
```

The web page that results from Listings 26.5 through 26.10 is shown in Figure 26.2.

Figure 26.2 Custom component directive

Summary

Angular directives extend the behavior of HTML. Directives can be applied to Angular templates as HTML elements, attributes, and classes. The functionality of directives is defined in the `@directive` class. Angular provides several built-in directives that interact with form elements, bind data, and interact with browser events. For example, `ngModel` binds the value of a form element directly to the component. When the component value changes, so does the value displayed by the element and vice versa.

One of the most powerful features of Angular is the ability to create your own custom directives. Implementing a custom directive in code is simple, using the `@directive` class. However, directives can also be very complex because of the myriad ways they can be implemented.

Next

In the next chapter you will learn how to use events and observables to handle change detection in your Angular components. You will also learn how to create, emit, and handle your own custom events.

27 Events and Change Detection

Angular has powerful browser events that extend HTML events by using Angular data binding to handle responses. Some of the built-in Angular events are discussed in Chapter 24, “Data Binding,” in the section “Event Binding.” This chapter goes over built-in events, custom events, and event handling with an Angular application.

Using Browser Events

Using the built-in events in Angular works like data binding. By wrapping an event name in `()`, you let Angular know what event you’re binding to. The event is followed by a statement that can be used to manipulate the data. The following is an example of the syntax for a built-in event:

```
<input type="text" (change)="myEventHandler($event)" />
```

Table 27.1 lists some of the HTML events, along with their Angular counterparts and short descriptions.

Table 27.1 **HTML Events with Angular Syntax and a Description of the Event**

HTML Event	Angular Syntax	Description
`onclick`	`(click)`	Event that is fired when the HTML element is clicked on
`onchange`	`(change)`	Event that is fired when the value of the HTML element is changed
`onfocus`	`(focus)`	Event that is fired when the HTML element is selected
`onsubmit`	`(submit)`	Event that is fired when the form is submitted

HTML Event	Angular Syntax	Description

`onkeyup,`
 `onkeydown,`
 `onkeypress`
	`(keyup),`
	 `(keydown),`
	 `(keypress)`
		Events that are fired intermittently when the keyboard keys are pressed

`onmouseover`	`(mouseover)`	Event that is fired when the cursor moves over an HTML element

Some of these events should be familiar to you as they have been used in previous chapters. Notice that the Angular syntax uses one-way data binding, which involves using `()` around each event to pass information about the event to the component.

Emitting Custom Events

A great feature of components is the capability to emit events within the component hierarchy. Events enable you to send notifications to different levels in the application to indicate that the events have occurred. An event can be anything you choose, such as a value changed or a threshold reached. This is extremely useful in many situations, such as for letting child components know that a value has changed in a parent component or vice versa.

Emitting a Custom Event to the Parent Component Hierarchy

To emit an event from a component, you use the `EventEmitter` class. This class has the `emit()` method, which sends an event upward through the parent component hierarchy. Any ancestor components that have registered for the event are notified. The `emit()` method uses the following syntax, where `name` is the event name and `args` is zero or more arguments to pass to the event handler functions:

```
@Output() name: EventEmitter<any> = new EventEmitter();
myFunction(){
  this.name.emit(args);
}
```

Handling Custom Events with a Listener

To handle an event that is emitted, you use syntax similar to that used for the built-in events Angular has to offer. The event handler method uses the following syntax, where `name` is the name of the event to listen for, and `event` is the value passed by `EventEmitter`:

```
<div (name)="handlerMethod(event)">
```

Implementing Custom Events in Nested Components

Listings 27.1, 27.2, and 27.3 illustrate the use of `EventEmitter`, `Output`, `emit`, and an event handler to send and handle events up the component hierarchy.

Listing 27.1 shows a custom event component that uses a custom event from a child component to pass data to a variable in the parent. Lines 9 through 11 implement a custom event handler, which takes in an event and applies it to the variable `text`.

In Listing 27.2, line 1 implements a custom event named `myCustomEvent`, which passes the event to the component method `eventHandler`. The `eventHandler` method takes in the emitted value and assigns the value to the variable `text`, which is outputted on line 3.

In Listing 27.3, line 1 imports `Output` and `EventEmitter` from `@angular/core` to be used within the component. Line 15 uses `Output` and `EventEmitter` to create the custom event `myCustomEvent`. Lines 19 and 24 both emit the event and pass the variable `message` to the parent component.

Figure 27.1 shows the rendered web page.

Listing 27.1 `customevent.component.ts`: A Main Component with an Event Handler

```
01 import { Component } from '@angular/core';
02
03 @Component({
04   selector: 'app-root',
05   templateUrl: 'customevent.component.html'
06 })
07 export class AppComponent {
08   text: string = '';
09   eventHandler(event: any){
10     this.text = event;
11   }
12
13 }
```

Listing 27.2 `customevent.component.html`: HTML That Implements a Custom Event

```
01 <child (myCustomEvent)="eventHandler($event)"></child>
02 <hr *ngIf="text">
03 {{text}}
```

Listing 27.3 `child.component.ts`: A Child Component That Emits an Event

```
01 import { Component, Output, EventEmitter } from '@angular/core';
02
03 @Component({
04   selector: 'child',
05   template: `
06     <button (click)="clicked()" (mouseleave)="mouseleave()">
07       Click Me
```

```
    </button>
  `,
  styleUrls: ['child.component.css']
})
export class ChildComponent {
  private message = "";

  @Output() myCustomEvent: EventEmitter<any> = new EventEmitter();

  clicked() {
    this.message = "You've made a custom event";
    this.myCustomEvent.emit(this.message);
  }

  mouseleave(){
    this.message = "";
    this.myCustomEvent.emit(this.message);
  }
}
```

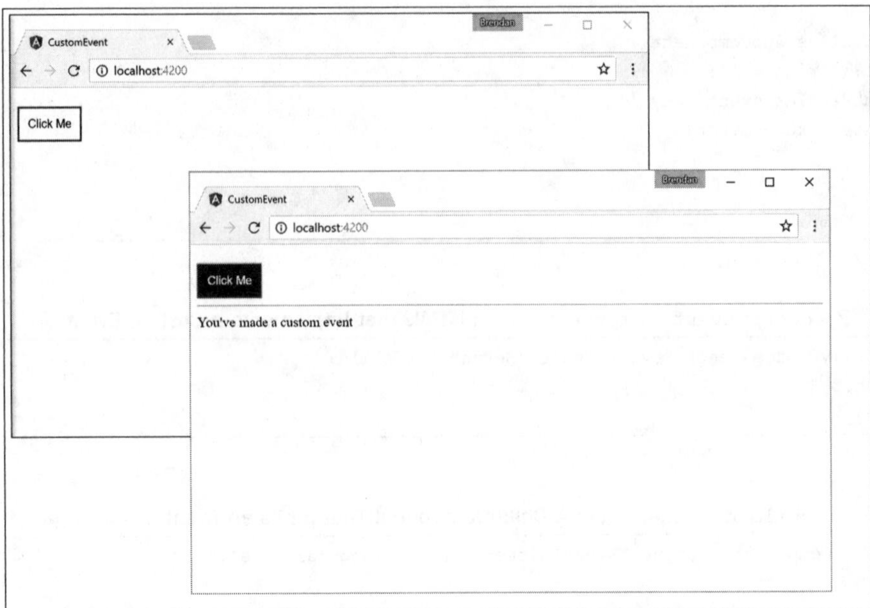

Figure 27.1 Creating a custom event

Deleting Data in a Parent Component from a Child Component

Listings 27.4 through 27.9 illustrate the use of `EventEmitter`, `input`, `Output`, `emit`, and an event handler to send and handle events up the component hierarchy.

Listing 27.4 shows a component that creates a list of characters that can be manipulated via custom events. The `selectCharacter()` function on line 21 is an event handler that changes the `character` value, which can then be passed down to the details component.

In Listing 27.5, line 9 implements a custom event called `CharacterDeleted`, which invokes the `deleteChar()` method that takes in the event. Lines 24 through 30 of Listing 27.5 implement a handler for the `CharacterDeleted` event, which removes the character name from the `names` property. In line 14 of Listing 27.7, the child component emits this event via the `emit()` method.

In Listing 27.7, line 10 creates the character input, which takes data in from the parent. Line 11 creates the `CharacterDeleted EventEmitter`, which is used on line 14 to pass the character data back up to the parent to be handled.

In Listing 27.8, line 8 invokes the `deleteChar()` method which then activates the `EventEmitter` on line 41 to send the `character` data back to the parent component.

Figure 27.2 shows the rendered web page.

Listing 27.4 `character.component.ts`: **A Main Component, Which Passes Data Down to a Nested Component**

```
01 import { Component } from '@angular/core';
02
03 @Component({
04   selector: 'app-root',
05   templateUrl: './app.component.html',
06   styleUrls: ['./app.component.css']
07 })
08 export class AppComponent {
09   character = null;
10
11   characters = [{name: 'Frodo', weapon: 'Sting',
12                            race: 'Hobbit'},
13                 {name: 'Aragorn', weapon: 'Sword',
14                              race: 'Man'},
15                 {name:'Legolas', weapon: 'Bow',
16                              race: 'Elf'},
17                 {name: 'Gimli', weapon: 'Axe',
18                            race: 'Dwarf'}
19   ]
20
21   selectCharacter(character){
22     this.character = character;
```

```
  }
  deleteChar(event){
    var index = this.characters.indexOf(event);
    if(index > -1) {
      this.characters.splice(index, 1);
    }
    this.character = null;
  }

}
```

Listing 27.5 `character.component.html`: **HTML That Implements a Custom Event**

```
<h2>Custom Events in Nested Components</h2>
<div *ngFor="let character of characters">
  <div class="char" (click)="selectCharacter(character)">
    {{character.name}}
  </div>
</div>
<app-character
  [character]="character"
  (CharacterDeleted)="deleteChar($event)">
</app-character>
```

Listing 27.6 `character.component.css`: **Styles for the Character Component**

```
.char{
    padding: 5px;
    border: 2px solid forestgreen;
    margin: 5px;
    border-radius: 10px;
    cursor: pointer;
}
.char:hover{
  background-color: lightgrey;
}
body{
  text-align: center;
}
```

Listing 27.7 `details.component.ts`: **A Details Component That Emits a Delete Event**

```
import { Component, Output, Input, EventEmitter } from '@angular/core';

@Component({
  selector: 'app-character',
```

```
  templateUrl: './characters.component.html',
  styleUrls: ['./characters.component.css']
})
export class CharacterComponent {

  @Input('character') character: any;
  @Output() CharacterDeleted  = new EventEmitter<any>();

deleteChar(){
  this.CharacterDeleted.emit(this.character);
}

}
```

Listing 27.8 `details.component.html`: **HTML that Triggers a Delete Event**

```
<div>
  <div *ngIf="character">
    <h2>Character Details</h2>
    <div class="cInfo">
      <b>Name: </b>{{character.name}}<br>
      <b>Race: </b>{{character.race}}<br>
      <b>Weapon: </b>{{character.weapon}}<br>
      <button (click)="deleteChar()">Delete</button>
    </div>
  </div>
</div>
```

Listing 27.9 `details.component.css`: **Styles for the Details Component**

```
div{
    display: block;
}
.cInfo{
    border: 1px solid blue;
    text-align: center;
    padding: 10px;
    border-radius: 10px;
}
h2{
  text-align: center;
}
button{
  cursor: pointer;
}
```

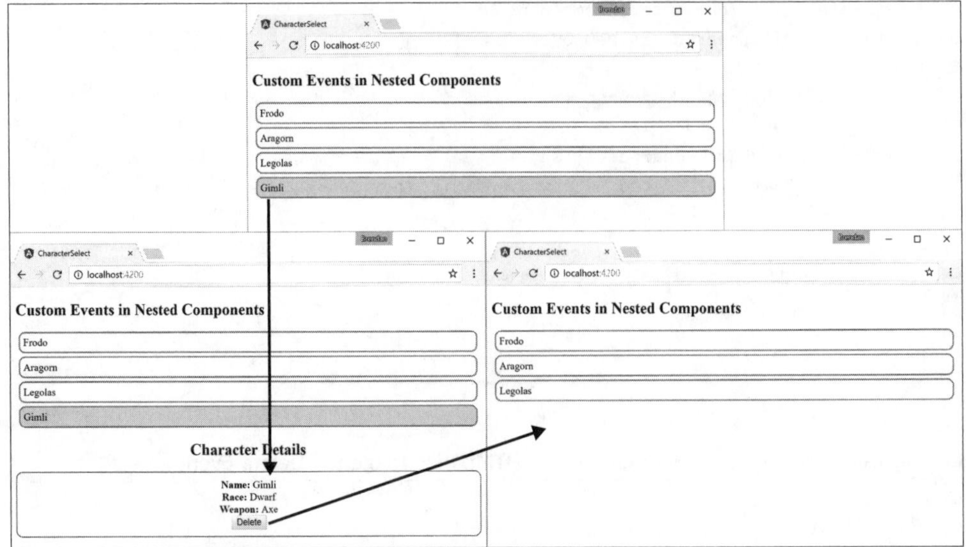

Figure 27.2 Using events to send and delete data

Using Observables

Observables offer components a way to observe data that changes asynchronously, such as data coming from a server or from user input. Basically, observables allow you to watch values for changes over time. Unlike a JavaScript promise, which returns a single value, an observable is capable of returning an array of values. This array of values doesn't have to be received all at once, either, which makes observables that much more powerful.

Creating an Observable Object

You import `Observable` from `rxjs/observable` to be used within a component. Once it is imported, you can create an observable object by using the following syntax, where `name` is the observable name:

```
private name: Observable<Array<number>>;
```

Once the observable object is created, it is available to be subscribed to and to make the observable data available to the rest of the component. This is done in two parts: implementing the observable and using the `subscribe` method. This following is a basic example of an observable:

```
private name: Observable<Array<number>>;
ngOnInit(){
  this.name = new Observable(observer => {
```

```
04     observer.next("my observable")
05     observer.complete();
06   }
07   Let subscribe = this.name.subscribe(
08     data => { console.log(data) },
09     Error => { errorHandler(Error) },
10     () => { final() }
11   );
12   subscribe.unsubscribe();
13 }
```

Lines 3 through 6 instantiate the observable `name` as `observer`, making it available to be subscribed to. Line 4 uses the method `next` on `observer`, which passes data to the observable. Line 5 uses the method `complete` on `observer` to close the connection of the observable.

The subscription to the observable occurs in lines 7 through 11. This subscription has three callback functions. The first is called when data is successfully received by the subscription. The second is the error handler, which is called when the subscription fails. The third is the final one, which runs code when the subscription completes, whether the subscription succeeds or fails.

On line 8, data is passed to the `console.log` function when the subscription successfully receives the data. Line 9 calls the function `errorHandler`. Line 10 invokes `final()`.

Watching for Data Changes with Observables

Listings 27.10 and 27.11 illustrate the use of `Observable` to watch for changes of data. The example in this section uses observables to watch for data changes and then makes that data available to be displayed on the DOM.

Listing 27.10 shows the component for the application. This component creates two `Observable` objects, `pass` and `run`. These observables have a function that goes and gets a random number between 0 and 30 and gives each number to one of the two teams randomly until the combined total of both teams equals 1,000 or greater.

In Listing 27.10, lines 11 and 12 declare the observables `pass` and `run`. These `Observable` objects are both initialized and subscribed to within the `ngOnInit` function, which runs when the component is initialized.

The observable `pass` is initialized on lines 18 through 20, and `run` is initialized on lines 27 through 28. Once they are initialized, `pass` and `run` both use the function `playLoop` on lines 43 through 52. `playLoop` creates and sends an object that contains a random number between 0 and 1 to determine the team and a random number between 0 and 29 for yards. Each observable then interprets the team and applies the yards to either the team's pass yards or running yards.

Lines 57 through 59 create a random number generator that the rest of the application uses to create the random numbers for the timeout functions, teams, and yards.

Listing 27.11 shows the HTML for this example. This listing has three main parts. Lines 3 through 5 show data for an imaginary team's distance, in yards. Lines 8 through 10 show the same for a second team. Line 11 shows the combination of both teams' distances.

Figure 27.3 shows the rendered web page.

Listing 27.10 `observable.component.ts`: **Observables for Detecting Data Changes**

```
01 import { Component, OnInit } from '@angular/core';
02 import { Observable } from 'rxjs/observable';
03 import { Subscription } from 'rxjs/Subscription';
04 @Component({
05   selector: 'app-root',
06   templateUrl: "./observable.component.html",
07   styleUrls: ['./app.component.css']
08 })
09 export class AppComponent implements OnInit {
10   combinedTotal:number = 0;
11   private pass: Observable<any>;
12   private run: Observable<any>;
13   teams = [];
14   ngOnInit(){
15       this.teams.push({passing:0, running:0, total:0});
16       this.teams.push({passing:0, running:0, total:0});
17       //Passing
18       this.pass = new Observable(observer => {
19         this.playLoop(observer);
20       });
21       this.pass.subscribe(
22         data => {
23           this.teams[data.team].passing += data.yards;
24           this.addTotal(data.team, data.yards);
25       });
26       //Running
27       this.run = new Observable(observer => {
28         this.playLoop(observer);
29       });
30       this.run.subscribe(
31         data => {
32           this.teams[data.team].running += data.yards;
33           this.addTotal(data.team, data.yards);
34       });
```

```
    //Combined
    this.pass.subscribe(
      data => { this.combinedTotal += data.yards;
    });
    this.run.subscribe(
      data => { this.combinedTotal += data.yards;
    });
  }
  playLoop(observer){
    var time = this.getRandom(500, 2000);
    setTimeout(() => {
      observer.next(
        { team: this.getRandom(0,2),
          yards: this.getRandom(0,30)});
      if(this.combinedTotal < 1000){
        this.playLoop(observer);
      }
    }, time);
  }
  addTotal(team, yards){
    this.teams[team].total += yards;
  }
  getRandom(min, max) {
    return Math.floor(Math.random() * (max - min)) + min;
  }
}
```

Listing 27.11 `observable.component.html`: **A Template File for the Component**

```
<div>
  Team 1 Yards:<br>
  Passing: {{teams[0].passing}}<br>
  Running: {{teams[0].running}}<br>
  Total: {{teams[0].total}}<br>
  <hr>
  Team 2 Yards:<br>
  Passing: {{teams[1].passing}}<br>
  Running: {{teams[1].running}}<br>
  Total: {{teams[1].total}}<hr>
  Combined Total: {{combinedTotal}}
</div>
```

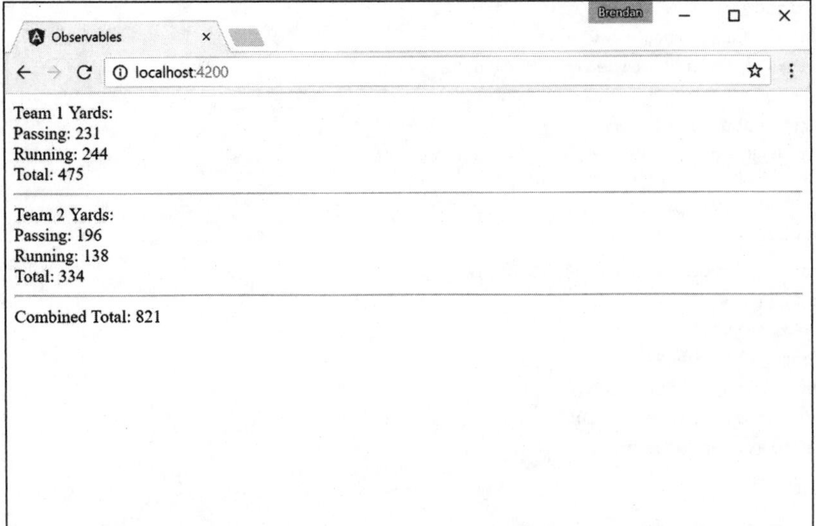

Figure 27.3 Using observables to watch for data changes over time

Summary

The capability to manage events is one of the most critical components in most Angular applications. You can use events in Angular applications to provide user interaction with elements as well as components of the application that communicate with each other so they know when to perform certain tasks.

Components are organized into hierarchies, and the root component is defined at the application level. In this chapter, you have learned how to emit events from within a component and then implement handlers that listen for those events and get executed when they are triggered. You have also learned about observables and how to implement them for asynchronous watching of values.

Next

The next chapter will introduce you to built-in Angular services. You will get a chance to see and implement some of the built-in services such as Http for communicating with back-end services and Router for managing routing in multi-view applications.

28

Implementing Angular Services in Web Applications

One of the most fundamental components of Angular functionality is services. *Services* provide task-based functionality to applications. You can think of a service as a chunk of reusable code that performs one or more related tasks. Angular provides several built-in services and also allows you to create your own customized services.

This chapter introduces built-in Angular services. You will get a chance to see and implement some of the built-in services, such as `http` for web server communication, `router` for managing and changing the state of an application, and `animate` to provide animation capabilities.

Understanding Angular Services

The purpose of a service is to provide a concise bit of code that performs specific tasks. A service does something as simple as providing a value definition or as complex as providing full HTTP communication to a web server.

A service provides a container for reusable functionality that is readily available to Angular applications. Services are defined and registered with the dependency injection mechanism in Angular. This allows you to inject services into modules, components, and other services.

Using the Built-in Services

Angular provides several built-in services that are included in the Angular module, using dependency injection. Once included within a module, services can be used throughout an application.

Table 28.1 describes some of the most common built-in services to give you an idea of what is available. The following sections cover the `http` and `router` services in more detail.

Table 28.1 **Common Services That Are Built in to Angular**

Service	Description
`animate`	Provides animation hooks to link into both CSS- and JavaScript-based animations
`http`	Provides a simple-to-use functionality to send HTTP requests to the web server or other service
`router`	Provides navigation between views and between sections within views
`forms`	Provides a service that allows for dynamic and reactive forms with simple form validation

Sending HTTP `GET` and `PUT` Requests with the `http` Service

The `http` service enables you to directly interact with the web server from your Angular code. The `http` service uses the browser's `XMLHttpRequest` object underneath but from the context of the Angular framework.

There are two ways to use the `http` service. The simplest is to use one of the following built-in shortcut methods that correspond to standard HTTP requests:

- `delete(url, [options])`
- `get(url, [options])`
- `head(url, [options])`
- `post(url, data, [options])`
- `put(url, data, [options])`
- `patch(url, data, [options])`

In these methods, the `url` parameter is the URL of the web request. The optional `options` parameter is a JavaScript object that specifies the options to use when implementing the request. Table 28.2 lists some the properties you can set in the `options` parameter.

Table 28.2 **Properties that Can Be Defined in the `config` Parameter for `http` Service Requests**

Property	Description
`method`	An HTTP method, such as `GET` or `POST`.
`url`	The URL of the resource that is being requested.
`params`	Parameters to be sent. This can be a string in the following format: `?key1=value1&key2=value2&...` Or it can be an object, in which case it is turned into a JSON string.

Property	Description
body	Data to be sent as the request message body.
headers	Headers to send with the request. You can specify an object containing the header names to be sent as properties. If a property in the object has a null value, the header is not sent.
withCredentials	A Boolean that, when true, indicates that the withCredentials flag on the XHR object is set.
responseType	The type of response to expect, such as JSON or text.

Configuring the HTTP Request

You can specify a request, a URL, and data by sending the options parameter directly to the http(options) method. For example, the following are exactly the same:

```
http.get('/myUrl');
http({method: 'GET', url:'/myUrl'});
```

Implementing the HTTP Response Callback Functions

When you call a request method by using the http object, you get back an Observable object, which allows the data sent or received to/from the server to be continuously observed. Observables have many operators that use the RxJS library to allow for the transformation and use of the data. The following are some useful methods:

- **map:** Applies a function to each value in the observable sequence. This allows you to dynamically transform the output of the observable stream into custom data formats.
- **toPromise:** Converts the observable into a Promise object, which has access to the methods available on a promise. Promise objects provide syntax to handle asynchronous operations.
- **catch:** Specifies a function to gracefully handle errors in the observable sequence.
- **debounce:** Specifies an interval at which the observable stream will emit values. Only the value of the observable at the interval is emitted; interim values are not emitted.

The following is a simple example of a GET request that returns an observable with syntax to add operators:

```
get(): Observable<any>{
  http.get(url)
    .map(response => response.JSON())
    .catch(err => Rx.Observable.of('the error was: ${err}'));
}
```

Implementing a Simple JSON File and Using the `http` Service to Access It

The code in Listings 28.1 through 28.5 implements a simple mock web server in the form of a JSON file and the Angular application that accesses it. Figure 28.1 shows the output. The web server contains a simple JSON object with a list of users. The web application allows a user to view the list of users. The example is very rudimentary to ensure that the code is easy to follow; it incorporates a `GET` request as well as an error-handling example.

Listing 28.1 shows the JSON file that contains the JSON object. This file can be accessed using an HTTP `GET` request, which allows `http` to grab the JSON object and return it to the Angular application as an observable.

Listing 28.1 `dummyDB.JSON`: A JSON Object that Contains Data for Users

```
[
  {
    "userId": 1,
    "userName": "brendan",
    "userEmail": "fake@email.com"
  },
  {
    "userId": 2,
    "userName": "brad",
    "userEmail": "email@notreal.com"
  },
  {
    "userId": 3,
    "userName": "caleb",
    "userEmail": "dummy@email.com"
  },
  {
    "userId": 4,
    "userName": "john",
    "userEmail": "ridiculous@email.com"
  },
  {
    "userId": 5,
    "userName": "doe",
    "userEmail": "some@email.com"
  }
]
```

Listing 28.2 implements the Angular component. `http` is imported on line 3, and `rxjs` is imported on line 5. (Note that you may need to install rxjs via npm.) `rxjs` allows `toPromise()` to be called on the observable object. Notice that the `constructor()` method instantiates `http` on line 15. Line 16 shows an HTTP `GET` request, which has the path to the `dummyDB.JSON` file passed in as `url`. The `toPromise()` method is called to convert the observable response from the `http.get()` method into a promise object. Once the promise completes, `.then()` is called, which takes in the promise object `data` and applies it to the array `users` so it can be displayed in the application. If an error occurs, `catch` is called, which passes the error response object to a callback function to be used.

Listing 28.2 `http.component.ts`: A Component that Implements the HTTP Service for a GET Request

```
import { Component } from '@angular/core';
import { Observable } from 'rxjs/Observable';
import { Http } from '@angular/http';

import 'rxjs/Rx';

@Component({
  selector: 'app-root',
  templateUrl: './app.component.html',
  styleUrls: ['./app.component.CSS']
})
export class AppComponent {
  users = [];

  constructor(private http: Http){
      http.get('../assets/dummyDB.JSON')
        .toPromise()
        .then((data) => {
          this.users = data.JSON()
        })
        .catch((err) =>{
          console.log(err);
        })
  }
}
```

Listing 28.3 implements an Angular module that imports `HttpModule` to allow the `http` service to be used throughout the application. `HttpModule` is imported from `@angular/http` on line 4 and then added to the `imports` array on line 15.

Listing 28.3 `app.module.ts`: An Angular Module that Imports `HttpModule` for Use in the Application

```
01 import { BrowserModule } from '@angular/platform-browser';
02 import { NgModule } from '@angular/core';
03 import { FormsModule } from '@angular/forms';
04 import { HttpModule } from '@angular/http';
05
```

```
import { AppComponent } from './app.component';

@NgModule({
  declarations: [
    AppComponent
  ],
  imports: [
    BrowserModule,
    FormsModule,
    HttpModule
  ],
  providers: [],
  bootstrap: [AppComponent]
})
export class AppModule { }
```

Listing 28.4 implements an Angular template that uses `ngFor` to create a list of users to be displayed in the application.

Listing 28.4 `http.component.html`: **An Angular Template that Displays a List of Users Received from the Database**

```
<h1>
  Users
</h1>
<div class="user" *ngFor="let user of users">
  <div><span>Id:</span> {{user.userId}}</div>
  <div><span>Username:</span> {{user.userName}}</div>
  <div><span>Email:</span> {{user.userEmail}}</div>
</div>
```

Listing 28.5 is a CSS file that styles the application so that each user is distinguishable from the rest and easy to see.

Listing 28.5 `http.component.CSS`: **A CSS File that Adds Styles to the Application**

```
span{
  width: 75px;
  text-align: right;
  font-weight: bold;
  display: inline-block;
}
.user{
  border: 2px ridge blue;
  margin: 10px 0px;
  padding: 5px;
}
```

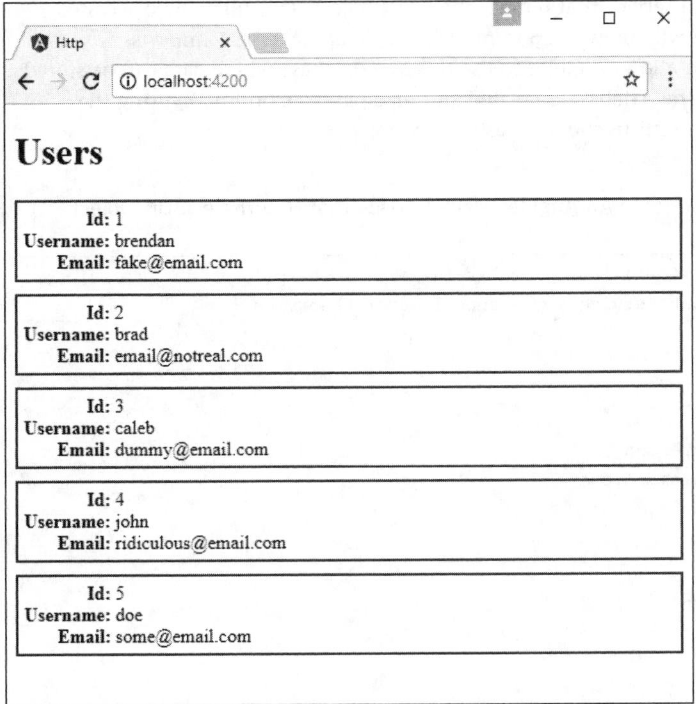

Figure 28.1 Implementing the `http` service to allow Angular components to interact with a web server

Implementing a Simple Mock Server Using the `http` Service

The code in Listings 28.6 through 28.11 implements a simple mock web server and the Angular application that accesses it. Figure 28.2 shows the output. The web server returns a simple JSON object with a list of users. The web application uses HTTP `GET`, `create`, and `delete` requests to allow the user to view, add to, and remove from the list of users.

> **Note**
>
> To create the mock service, you need to run the following command from the console:
>
> ```
> npm install Angular-in-memory-web-api
> ```
>
> This service is intended for development purposes only and shouldn't ever be used in a production application.

Listing 28.6 is the mock data service that returns the JSON object. This file will be accessed using HTTP requests, which will allow `http` to modify the database. Line 1 imports `InMemoryDbService`, which allows Angular to use this as a database where data can be stored while the session is active. The database is created and made useable on line 3, using the `createDb()` method, which returns the users as a JSON object.

Listing 28.6 `data.service.ts`: An Angular Mock Service that Returns a JSON Object Called Users

```
01 import { InMemoryDbService } from 'angular-in-memory-web-api';
02 export class InMemoryDataService implements InMemoryDbService {
03   createDb() {
04     const users = [
05       {
06         "id": 1,
07         "userName": "brendan",
08         "email": "fake@email.com"
09       },
10       {
11         "id": 2,
12         "userName": "brad",
13         "email": "email@notreal.com"
14       },
15       {
16         "id": 3,
17         "userName": "caleb",
18         "email": "dummy@email.com"
19       }
20     ]
21     return {users};
22   }
23 }
```

Listing 28.7 implements the Angular component. `UserService`, which is imported on line 7, contains all the HTTP functions that this application will be using. `UserService` is added to the component providers on line 13, making it available to the component. On line 19, `UserService` is implemented as a variable in the constructor.

Lines 21 through 37 define the `deleteUser()` function, which takes in a user object. On lines 32 and 33, the `deleteUser()` function on the `UserService` is called and passes in the user ID to let the database know which user to delete. The function has a callback in the `.then()` method that calls `this.getUsers()` to refresh the current list of users.

Lines 39 through 52 define the `createUser()` function. This function takes two parameters, `username` and `email`. It assigns those parameters to a `user` object on lines 41 through 44. Lines 48 through 51 call the `createUser()` method on the `UserService` and pass in the `user` object. Once the response is received, the `createUser()` method pushes the response into the `users` array, which is reflected immediately in the DOM.

Listing 28.7 `createDelete.component.ts`: An Angular Component that Gets and Modifies a List of Users with the `http` Service

```
import { Component, OnInit } from '@angular/core';
import { Observable } from 'rxjs/Observable';
import { Http } from '@angular/http';

import 'rxjs/Rx';

import { UserService } from './user.service';

@Component({
  selector: 'app-root',
  templateUrl: './app.component.html',
  styleUrls: ['./app.component.CSS'],
  providers: [UserService]
})
export class AppComponent implements OnInit {
  users = [];
  selectedUser;

  constructor(private UserService: UserService){ }

  ngOnInit(){
    this.getUsers()
  }

  getUsers(): void {
    this.UserService
        .getUsers()
        .then(users => this.users = users)
  }

  deleteUser(user){
    this.UserService
      .deleteUser(user.id)
      .then(() => {
        this.getUsers();
      });
  }

  createUser(userName, email){
    this.selectedUser = null;
    let user = {
      'userName': userName.trim(),
      'email': email.trim()
    };
    if (!user.userName || !user.email){
```

```
      return;
    }
    this.UserService.createUser(user)
        .then(res => {
          this.users.push(res);
        })
  }
}
```

Listing 28.8 implements the Angular service `UserService`, which handles all the HTTP requests for the application. Lines 16 through 21 define the `deleteUser()` method, which takes in the parameter `id`. An HTTP `delete` request is then created using `id` to go to the server and delete the user with the matching ID. Lines 22 through 31 define the `createUser()` method, which takes in a user object. A `post` request passes the user to the server as a JSON string, which is then added to the server.

Listing 28.8 `user.service.ts`: **An Angular Service that Uses `http` to Send and Get Data from a Server**

```
01 import { Injectable } from '@angular/core';
02 import { Http }       from '@angular/http';
03 import 'rxjs/add/operator/toPromise';
04
05 @Injectable()
06 export class UserService {
07   url = 'api/users'
08   constructor(private http: Http) { }
09
10   getUsers(): Promise<any[]> {
11     return this.http.get(this.url)
12                .toPromise()
13                .then(response => response.JSON().data)
14                .catch(this.handleError)
15   }
16   deleteUser(id: number): Promise<void>{
17     return this.http.delete(`${this.url}/${id}`)
18                     .toPromise()
19                     .then(() => null)
20                     .catch(this.handleError);
21   }
22   createUser(user): Promise<any>{
23     return this.http
24               .post(this.url, JSON.stringify({
25                 userName: user.userName,
26                 email: user.email
27               }))
28               .toPromise()
```

```
                .then(res => res.JSON().data)
                .catch(this.handleError)
  }

  private handleError(error: any): Promise<any> {
    console.error('An error occurred', error);
    return Promise.reject(error.message || error);
  }

}
```

Listing 28.9 implements an Angular template that utilizes `ngFor` to create a list of users to be displayed within the application.

Listing 28.9 `createDelete.component.html`: **An Angular Template that Displays a List of Users Received from the Database with Options to Create and Delete Users**

```
<div>
  <label>user name:</label> <input #userName />
  <label>user email:</label> <input #userEmail />
  <button (click)="createUser(userName.value, userEmail.value);
          userName.value=''; userEmail.value=''">
    Add
  </button>
</div>

<h1>
  Users
</h1>
<div class="userCard" *ngFor="let user of users">
  <div><span>Id:</span> {{user.id}}</div>
  <div><span>Username:</span> {{user.userName}}</div>
  <div><span>Email:</span> {{user.email}}</div>
  <button class="delete"
      (click)="deleteUser(user); $event.stopPropagation()">x</button>
</div>
```

Listing 28.10 is a CSS file that styles the application so that each user is distinguishable from the rest and easy to see.

Listing 28.10 `createDelete.component.CSS`: **A CSS Stylesheet that Styles the Application**

```
span{
  width: 75px;
  text-align: right;
  font-weight: bold;
```

```
  display: inline-block;
}
.userCard{
  border: 2px ridge blue;
  margin: 10px 0px;
  padding: 5px;
}
.selected{
  background-color: steelblue;
  color: white;
}
```

Listing 28.11 implements an Angular module that imports the mock data service. Line 5 imports `InMemoryWebApiModule` from `angular-in-memory-web-api`, which helps wire the mock database into the application. Line 8 imports `InMemoryDataService` from Listing 28.6. Line 18 shows `InMemoryWebApiModule` using its `forRoot` method on the `InMemoryDataService`, fully making the database service available to be used by the HTTP requests.

Listing 28.11 `app.module.ts`**: An Angular Module that Imports** `InMemoryWebApiModule` **to Be Used with the Application**

```
01 import { BrowserModule } from '@angular/platform-browser';
02 import { NgModule } from '@angular/core';
03 import { FormsModule } from '@angular/forms';
04 import { HttpModule } from '@angular/http';
05 import { InMemoryWebApiModule } from 'angular-in-memory-web-api';
06
07 import { AppComponent } from './app.component';
08 import { InMemoryDataService } from './data.service'
09
10 @NgModule({
11   declarations: [
12     AppComponent
13   ],
14   imports: [
15     BrowserModule,
16     FormsModule,
17     HttpModule,
18     InMemoryWebApiModule.forRoot(InMemoryDataService)
19   ],
20   providers: [],
21   bootstrap: [AppComponent]
22 })
23 export class AppModule { }
```

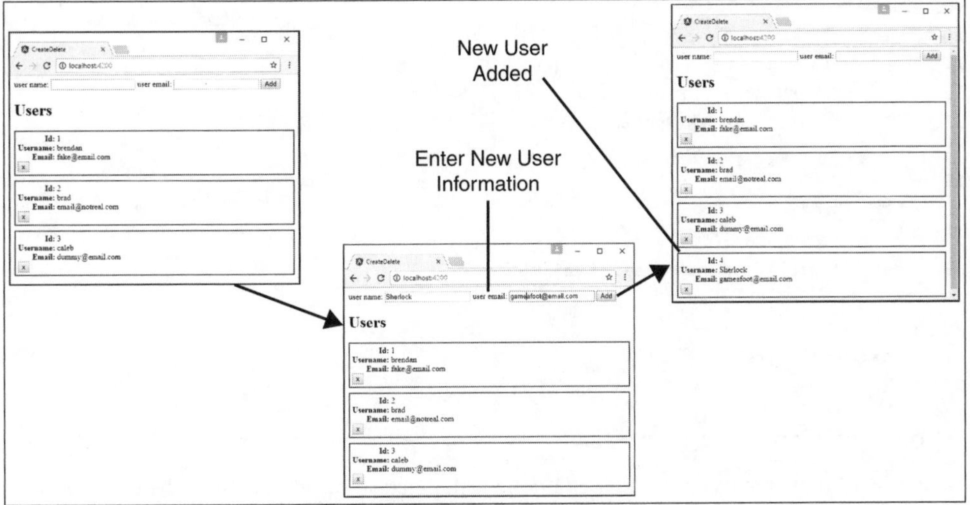

Figure 28.2 Implementing a simple mock server to create and delete items from a database

Implementing a Simple Mock Server and Using the `http` Service to Update Items on the Server

The code in Listings 28.12 through 28.16 implements the same mock web server from the previous example as well as the Angular application that accesses it. Figure 28.3 shows the output. The web application allows a user to view and edit the list of users, using HTTP `get` and `put` requests.

Listing 28.12 is the mock data service that returns the JSON object. This file will be accessed using HTTP requests, which will allow `http` to modify the database. Line 1 imports `InMemoryDbService`, which allows Angular to use this as a database where data can be stored while the session is active. The database is created and made usable on line 3, using the `createDb()` method, which returns the users as a JSON object.

Listing 28.12 `data.service.ts`: **An Angular Mock Service that Returns a JSON Object Called Users**

```
01 import { InMemoryDbService } from 'angular-in-memory-web-api';
02 export class InMemoryDataService implements InMemoryDbService {
03   createDb() {
04     const users = [
05       {
06         "id": 1,
07         "userName": "brendan",
08         "email": "fake@email.com"
```

```
      },
      {
        "id": 2,
        "userName": "brad",
        "email": "email@notreal.com"
      },
      {
        "id": 3,
        "userName": "caleb",
        "email": "dummy@email.com"
      }
    ]
    return {users};
  }
}
```

Listing 28.13 implements an Angular component that gets a list of users to be displayed in the template. This component also allows for the updating of users. Lines 7 and 13 import `UserService` and provide it to the component. In line 19, `UserService` is turned into a usable variable also named `UserService`. Lines 21 through 23 show the `ngOnInit` method, which calls the `getUsers` method when the component finishes loading. Lines 25 through 29 show the `getUsers` method, which calls the `getUsers` method on `UserService` and assigns the result to the variable `users`. Lines 31 through 33 show the `selectUser` method, which takes a parameter named `user`. This method assigns `user` to the variable `selectedUser`. Lines 35 through 39 show the `updateUser` method, which takes a parameter named `user`. The `updateUser` method sets the variable `selectedUser` to null and then invokes the `updateUser` method on `userService`, passing in `user` as a parameter. When the `updateUser` method completes, the `getUsers` method is called to refresh the list of users that is displayed.

Listing 28.13 `update.component.ts`: **An Angular Component that Uses `http` to Update Data in the Server**

```
01 import { Component, OnInit } from '@angular/core';
02 import { Observable } from 'rxjs/Observable';
03 import { Http } from '@angular/http';
04
05 import 'rxjs/Rx';
06
07 import { UserService } from './user.service';
08
09 @Component({
10   selector: 'app-root',
11   templateUrl: './app.component.html',
12   styleUrls: ['./app.component.CSS'],
13   providers: [UserService]
14 })
```

```
export class AppComponent implements OnInit {
  users = [];
  selectedUser;

  constructor(private UserService: UserService){ }

  ngOnInit(){
    this.getUsers()
  }

  getUsers(): void {
    this.UserService
        .getUsers()
        .then(users => this.users = users)
  }

  selectUser(user){
    this.selectedUser = user;
  }

  updateUser(user){
    this.selectedUser = null;
    this.UserService.updateUser(user)
    .then(() => this.getUsers());
  }
}
```

Listing 28.14 implements the Angular service UserService, which handles all the HTTP requests for the application. Lines 16 through 24 define the updateUser method, which takes in the parameter user. A URL is then generated to specify which user will be updated. An HTTP put request is made on line 20, taking in the generated URL and the user object, which is passed into the json.stringify method. The updateUser method then sends a response object on success or moves to the error handler on fail.

Listing 28.14 user.service.ts: **An Angular Service that Gets Users and Updates a User**

```
01 import { Injectable } from '@angular/core';
02 import { Http }       from '@angular/http';
03 import 'rxjs/add/operator/toPromise';
04
05 @Injectable()
06 export class UserService {
07   url = 'api/users'
08   constructor(private http: Http) { }
09
```

```
  getUsers(): Promise<any[]> {
    return this.http.get(this.url)
               .toPromise()
               .then(response => response.JSON().data)
               .catch(this.handleError)
  }
  updateUser(user): Promise<void>{
    console.log(user);
    const url = `${this.url}/${user.id}`;
    return this.http
      .put(url, JSON.stringify(user))
      .toPromise()
      .then(() => user)
      .catch(this.handleError)
  }

  private handleError(error: any): Promise<any> {
    console.error('An error occurred', error);
    return Promise.reject(error.message || error);
  }

}
```

Listing 28.15 implements an Angular template that uses ngFor to create a list of users to be displayed within the application. These users are each selectable. When one is selected, the information is shown in an editable form field that allows the user to be edited and saved. Lines 20 through 24 show the button that can be clicked to invoke the updateUser method and pass in an object with that user's updated information.

Listing 28.15 update.component.html: **An Angular Template that Displays a List of Users and Can Be Updated**

```
01 <h1>
02   Users
03 </h1>
04 <div class="userCard" *ngFor="let user of users"
05     (click)="selectUser(user)"
06     [class.selected]="user === selectedUser">
07   <div><span>Id:</span> {{user.id}}</div>
08   <div><span>Username:</span> {{user.userName}}</div>
09   <div><span>Email:</span> {{user.email}}</div>
10 </div>
11
```

```
<div *ngIf="selectedUser">
  <label>user name:</label>
  <input #updateName [ngModel]="selectedUser.userName"/>

  <label>user email:</label>
  <input #updateEmail [ngModel]="selectedUser.email" />


  <button (click)="updateUser(
      {'id': selectedUser.id,
       'userName': updateName.value,
       'email': updateEmail.value});
  ">
    Save
  </button>
</div>
```

Listing 28.16 is a CSS file that styles the application so that each user is distinguishable from the rest and easy to see. It provides some logic to help the user know that each user can be clicked on.

Listing 28.16 `update.component.CSS`: **A CSS File that Styles the Application**

```
span{
  width: 75px;
  text-align: right;
  font-weight: bold;
  display: inline-block;
}
.userCard{
  border: 2px ridge blue;
  margin: 10px 0px;
  padding: 5px;
  cursor: pointer;
}
.userCard:hover{
  background-color: lightblue;
}
.selected{
  background-color: steelblue;
  color: white;
}
```

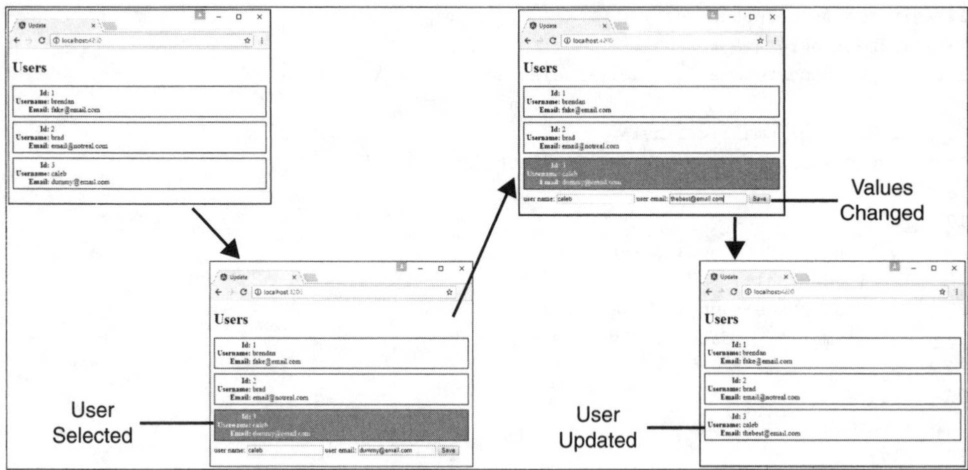

Figure 28.3 Implementing a simple mock server to update items in a database

Changing Views with the `router` Service

The `router` service enables you to change views on the web application so that you can route back and forth between components. This can be done as a full-page view change or can change smaller segments of a single-page application. The `router` service is in an external Angular module called `RouterModule` and needs to be included in the applications module to be used throughout the application.

To set up an app for routing, you need to import the `Routes` and `Router` modules from `@angular/router`. To help keep the application simple to maintain, `router` should get its own module that can be imported into the main application module.

Defining routes for an application is as simple as making an array of objects, with each object defining a specific route. The two required options for each of these routes are `path` and `component`. The `path` option specifies the tree to follow to reach the component. The `component` option defines which component will be loaded into the view. The following examples show the syntax for defining a `Routes` array:

```
Const routes: Routes = [
  {
    Path: '',
    Component: myComponent
  },
  {
    Path: 'route',
    Component: myComponent
  },
```

```
    {
      Path: 'routeWithParams/:param1/:param2',
      Component: myComponent
    }
]
```

Many more parameters can be added to the `route` object. Table 28.3 shows a list of some of them.

Table 28.3 **Properties that Can Be Defined in the `config` Parameter for `route` Service Object**

Property	Description
`path`	Shows where in the router tree this route belongs
`component`	Defines which component will be loaded once routed
`redirectTo`	Redirects to the defined path instead of the current route
`outlet`	Specifies the name used for the `RouterOutlet` that renders the route
`canActivate`	Protects the route by preventing activation when `false`
`canActivateChild`	Protects the child routes by preventing activation when `false`
`canDeactivate`	Specifies whether the route can be deactivated
`canLoad`	Allows you to protect specific modules from being loaded in the route
`Data`	Allows for data to be passed into the component
`Resolve`	Specifies a resolver that pre-fetches data for the route before activation
`Children`	Allows for a nested routes array that contains route objects (Each of these objects has the same options described in this table.)
`loadChildren`	Allows for lazy loading of child routes
`runGuardsAndResolvers`	Defines when the guards and resolvers are run

Once the `routes` array is defined, it needs to be implemented into the router so that the `router` service knows it exists and knows how to use it. This is done by using the `forRoot` method on `RouterModule`. The result of this is included in the `routing` module's `imports` array. The syntax for this looks as follows:

```
imports: [RouterModule.forRoot(routes)]
```

Using `routes` in Angular

To use `routes` in Angular, the `routing` module needs to be included within the main app module and included within the imports—the same as for built-in Angular modules. Once it is included within the application module, the defined routes become available throughout the application.

To be able to use `router` within a component, `Router` and `ActivatedRoute` need to be imported from `@angular/router`. Once they are imported, they need to be implemented via the constructor. The following code shows the syntax:

```
Constructor(
    private route: ActivatedRoute,
    private router: Router
){}
```

There are two ways to navigate between routes. The first way is from HTML directly, using the Angular directive `routerLink`, which has the following syntax:

```
<a routerLink="/myRoute">
```

The second way to navigate between routes is from the component class, using the following syntax:

```
myFunction(){
    this.router.navigate(['myRoute'])
}
```

When the router is all wired up and ready to be used, the last step is to make sure the routes get displayed on the application. You do this by using the Angular HTML tag `router-outlet`. It is important to note that the component that uses `router-outlet` will be outside the router, and anything besides `router-outlet` will always display, no matter what route is currently being shown. You can implement `router-outlet` by using the following syntax:

```
<router-outlet></router-outlet>
```

Implementing a Simple Router

Listings 28.17 through 28.23 implement a simple router that allows the user to navigate between two components. Figure 28.4 shows the output. This router is navigated using the Angular `routerLink` directive within the HTML, allowing it to change between the views.

Listing 28.17 shows the application module, which is the main module for the application. `App.module` imports the `Router` module from Listing 28.17. On line 6, this file loads `AppRoutingModule`, which is added to the `imports` array on line 21.

Listing 28.17 `app.module.ts`: An Angular Module that Imports the `Router` Module File

```
01 import { BrowserModule } from '@angular/platform-browser';
02 import { NgModule } from '@angular/core';
03 import { FormsModule } from '@angular/forms';
04 import { HttpModule } from '@angular/http';
05
```

```
import { AppRoutingModule } from './app-routing.module';
import { AppComponent } from './app.component';
import { Route2Component } from './route2/route2.component';
import { HomeComponent } from './home/home.component';

@NgModule({
  declarations: [
    AppComponent,
    Route2Component,
    HomeComponent
  ],
  imports: [
    BrowserModule,
    FormsModule,
    HttpModule,
    AppRoutingModule
  ],
  providers: [],
  bootstrap: [AppComponent]
})
export class AppModule { }
```

Listing 28.18 shows the `Router` module, which defines the routes for the application. The `Router` module imports `Routes` and `RouterModule` to enable routing within the application. The `Router` module also imports any components that will be used as routes. Lines 5 through 14 define the `routes` array, which contains the route definitions for the application. Lines 6 through 9 define the home route that the application will default to because the path is set to an empty string. The home route uses `HomeComponent` as the component that controls the view. Lines 10 through 13 define a second route object that will be displayed when the path is set to `route2`. This route uses `Route2Component`.

Listing 28.18 `app-routing.module.ts`: An Angular Module that Defines the `routes` for This Application

```
01 import { NgModule } from '@angular/core';
02 import { Routes, RouterModule } from '@angular/router';
03 import { Route2Component } from './route2/route2.component';
04 import { HomeComponent } from './home/home.component';
05 const routes: Routes = [
06   {
07     path: '',
08     component: HomeComponent
09   },
10   {
11     path: 'route2',
12     component: Route2Component
13   }
```

```
];

@NgModule({
  imports: [RouterModule.forRoot(routes)],
  exports: [RouterModule]
})
export class AppRoutingModule { }
```

Listing 28.19 shows the root component for the application. This component has a simple template that outputs `router-outlet` for `router` to display its routes.

Listing 28.19 `app.component.ts`**: An Angular Component that Defines the Router Outlet**

```
import { Component } from '@angular/core';

@Component({
  selector: 'app-root',
  template: '<router-outlet></router-outlet>'
})
export class AppComponent {}
```

Listing 28.20 shows the home component template file. This file displays a message that lets the user know that the route is working, followed by a link that uses `routerLink` to navigate the user to a separate view.

Listing 28.20 `home.component.html`**: An HTML File that Is the Default Displayed Route**

```
<p>
  Home Route works!
</p>
<a routerLink="/route2">Route 2</a>
```

Listing 28.21 shows the home component file. This file is as barebones as a component gets. Its main purpose is to load the template file and make it available to the router.

Listing 28.21 `home.component.ts`**: An Angular Component that Includes a Template with a Route**

```
import { Component} from '@angular/core';

@Component({
  selector: 'app-home',
  templateUrl: './home.component.html',
  styleUrls: ['./home.component.CSS']
})
export class HomeComponent{}
```

Listing 28.22 shows the `route2` component template file. This file displays a message that lets the user know the route is working, followed by a link that uses `routerLink` to navigate the user to a separate view.

Listing 28.22 `route2.component.html`: **A CSS File that Styles the Application**

```
<p>
  route 2 works!
</p>
<a routerLink="/">Route 1</a>
```

Listing 28.23 shows the barebones `route2` component file. Its main purpose is to load the template file and make it available to the router.

Listing 28.23 `route2.component.ts`: **An Angular Component that Includes a Template with a Route**

```
import { Component } from '@angular/core';

@Component({
  selector: 'app-route2',
  templateUrl: './route2.component.html'
})
export class Route2Component {}
```

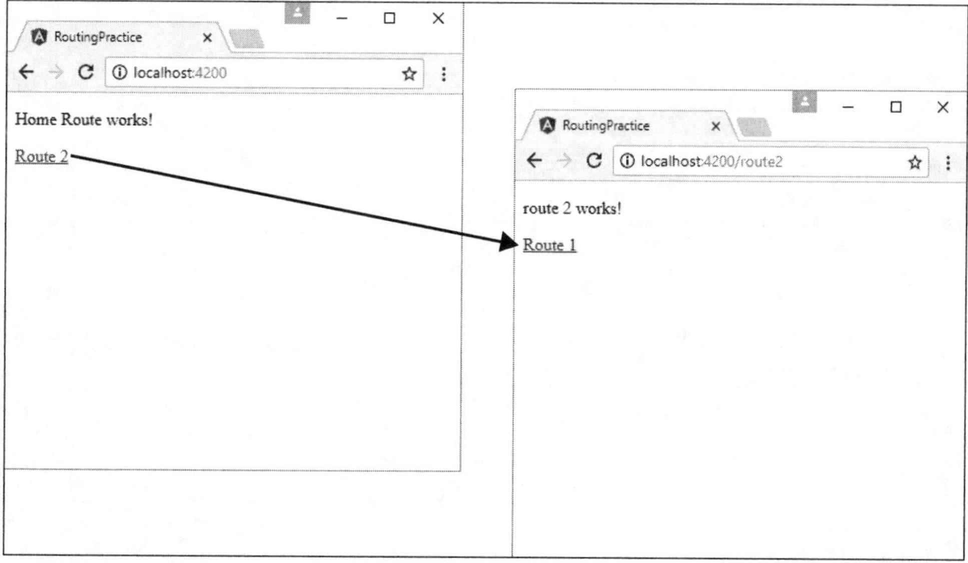

Figure 28.4 Implementing the `http` service to allow Angular components to interact with a web server

Implementing a Router with a Navigation Bar

The code in Listings 28.24 through 28.35 implements a router with a nav bar that allows the user to navigate between views that are nested. Figure 28.5 shows the output. This router is navigated using the Angular `routerLink` directive within the HTML, allowing it to change between the views.

Listing 28.24 shows the `Router` module, which defines the routes for the application. The `Router` module imports any components that will be used as routes. There isn't a home route for this example. If the route is empty, the router redirects to `page1`, as shown in lines 22 through 25. In addition, if an invalid route is typed into the URL, the router again redirects to `page1`, as shown in lines 27 through 30.

Listing 28.24 `app-routing.module.ts`: **An Angular Module that Defines the Routes for the Application**

```
01 import { NgModule } from '@angular/core';
02 import { Routes, RouterModule } from '@angular/router';
03 import { Page1Component } from './page1/page1.component';
04 import { Page2Component } from './page2/page2.component';
05 import { Page3Component } from './page3/page3.component';
06 import { Page4Component } from './page4/page4.component';
07 import { NavComponent } from './nav/nav.component';
08 const routes: Routes = [
09   {
10     path: 'page1',
11     component: Page1Component
12   },
13   {
14     path: 'page2',
15     component: Page2Component
16   },
17   {
18     path: 'page3',
19     component: Page3Component
20   },
21   {
22     path: '',
23     redirectTo: '/page1',
24     pathMatch: 'full'
25   },
26   {
27     path: '**',
28     redirectTo: '/page1',
29     pathMatch: 'full'
30   }
31 ];
32
```

```
@NgModule({
  imports: [RouterModule.forRoot(routes)],
  exports: [RouterModule]
})
export class AppRoutingModule { }
```

Listing 28.25 shows the nav component, which controls the nav bar and links to the views within the page. Lines 9 through 19 show an array of available pages which the nav bar can use to create buttons with links for navigation.

Listing 28.25 `nav.component.ts`: An Angular Component that Creates a Persisting Nav Bar That Navigates Between Views

```
01 import { Component, OnInit } from '@angular/core';
02
03 @Component({
04   selector: 'app-nav',
05   templateUrl: './nav.component.html',
06   styleUrls: ['./nav.component.CSS']
07 })
08 export class NavComponent{
09   pages = [
10     { 'url': 'page1',
11      'text': 'page 1'
12     },
13     { 'url': 'page2',
14      'text': 'page 2'
15     },
16     { 'url': 'page3',
17      'text': 'page 3'
18     }
19   ]
20 }
```

Listing 28.26 shows the nav component template file. It creates a list of buttons that allow for navigation between the named routes.

Listing 28.26 `nav.component.html`: An Angular Template that Creates the View for the Nav Bar

```
<span class="container" *ngFor="let page of pages">
  <a routerLink="/{{page.url}}">{{page.text}}</a>
</span>
```

Listing 28.27 shows the nav component CSS file. This file styles the nav bar buttons so they make sense. Lines 9 through 12 cause the color of the buttons and text to change when the user hovers the mouse over a button.

Listing 28.27 `nav.component.CSS`: **A CSS File that Styles the Navigation Buttons for the Application**

```
a{
  padding: 5px 10px;
  border: 1px solid darkblue;
  background-color: steelblue;
  color: white;
  text-decoration: none;
  border-radius: 3px;
}
a:hover{
  color: black;
  background-color: lightgrey;
}
```

Listing 28.28 shows the root component file `app.component.ts`, which serves as the entry to the application and loads the routed views and the nav component.

Listing 28.28 `app.comonent.ts`: **An Angular Component that Acts as the Root Component for the Application**

```
import { Component } from '@angular/core';

@Component({
  selector: 'app-root',
  templateUrl: './app.component.html',
  styleUrls: ['./app.component.CSS']
})
export class AppComponent { }
```

Listing 28.29 shows the root component template file, which loads the nav component followed by the router outlet, which is where the views are loaded for the application.

Listing 28.29 `app.component.html`: **An Angular Template that Loads the Nav Component Followed by the Router Outlet**

```
<div><app-nav></app-nav></div>
<div><router-outlet></router-outlet></div>
```

Listing 28.30 shows the root component CSS file, which provides some spacing for the nav bar so it is displayed nicely.

Listing 28.30 `app.component.CSS`: **An Angular Module that Imports the** `Router` **Module File**

```
div{
  margin: 15px 0px;
}
```

Listing 28.31 shows the `page1` component. This component loads a template that will be used as one of the views for this application. Line 5 loads an image to be displayed on the view.

Listing 28.31 `page1.component.ts`: **An Angular Module that Imports the** `Router` **Module File**

```
01 import { Component } from '@angular/core';
02
03 @Component({
04   selector: 'app-page1',
05   template: '<img src="../assets/images/lake.jpg" />'
06 })
07 export class Page1Component {}
```

Listing 28.32 shows the `page2` component. This component loads a template that will be used as one of the views for this application.

Listing 28.32 `page2.component.ts`: **An Angular Module that Imports the** `Router` **Module File**

```
import { Component } from '@angular/core';

@Component({
  selector: 'app-page2',
  templateUrl: './page2.component.html'
})
export class Page2Component { }
```

Listing 28.33 shows the `page2` template file, which contains some dummy text that will be loaded into the view.

Listing 28.33 `page2.component.html`: **An Angular Template that Creates the View for Page 2**

```
<p>
  Lorem ipsum dolor sit amet, consectetur adipiscing elit. Nam efficitur
  tristique ornare. Interdum et malesuada fames ac ante ipsum primis in
  faucibus. Proin id nulla vitae arcu laoreet consequat. Donec quis
  convallis felis. Mauris ultricies consectetur lectus, a hendrerit leo
  feugiat sit amet. Aliquam nec velit nibh. Nam interdum turpis ac dui
  congue maximus. Integer fringilla ante vitae arcu molestie finibus. Morbi
  eget ex pellentesque, convallis orci venenatis, vehicula nunc.
</p>
```

Listing 28.34 shows the `page3` component. This component loads a template that will be used as one of the views for this application.

Listing 28.34 `page3.component.ts`: **An Angular Module that Imports the `Router` Module File**

```
import { Component } from '@angular/core';

@Component({
  selector: 'app-page3',
  templateUrl: './page3.component.html'
})
export class Page3Component {}
```

Listing 28.35 shows the `page3` template file, which creates a text area box to be displayed on the view.

Listing 28.35 `page3.component.html`: **An Angular Template that Creates the View for Page 3**

```
<textarea rows="4" cols="50" placeHolder="Some Text Here">
</textarea>
```

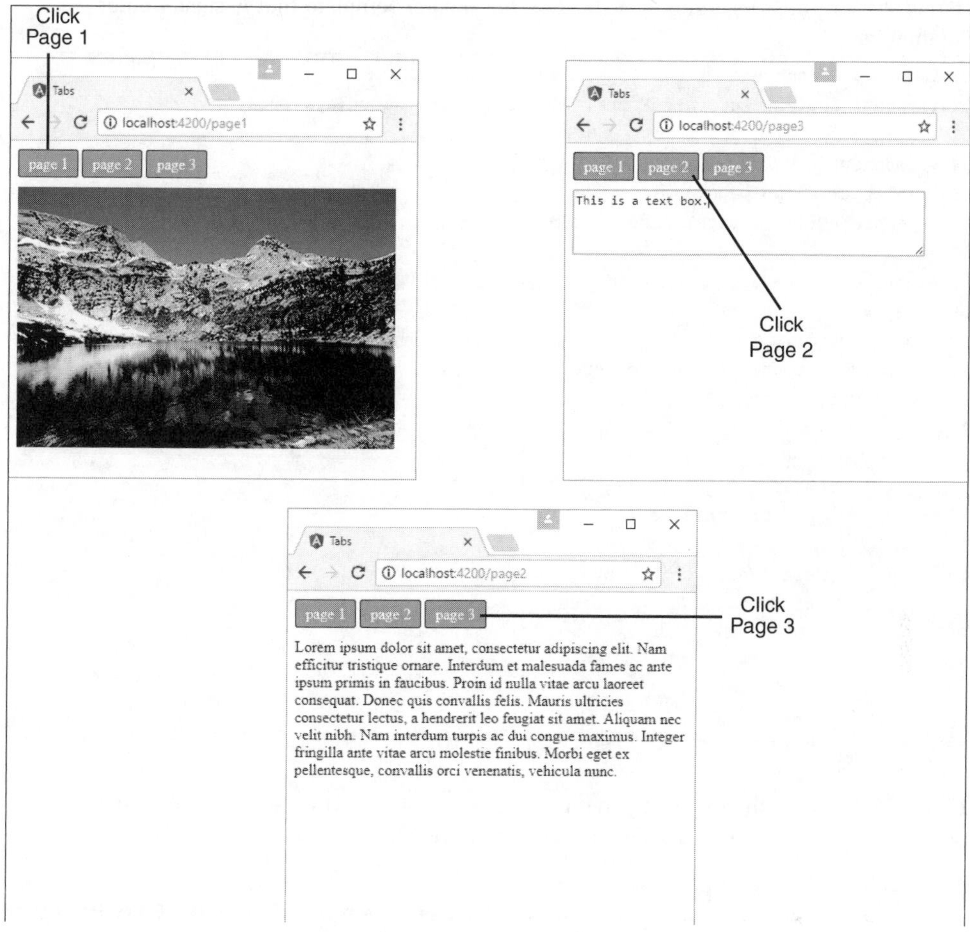

Figure 28.5 Implementing the `http` service to allow Angular components to interact with a web server

Implementing a Router with Parameters

Listings 28.36 through 28.40 implement a router with a route that takes in a parameter that allows for data to be transferred to that view through the `url` parameter. Figure 28.6 shows the output.

Listing 28.36 shows the `Router` module, which defines the routes for the application. The `Router` module imports any components that will be used as routes. Line 14 defines the path to page 2, which takes in the parameter `this.text`.

Listing 28.36 `app-routing.module.ts`: **An Angular Template that Assigns Router Parameters**

```
01 import { Component } from '@angular/core';
02 import { Router, ActivatedRoute, Params } from '@angular/router';
03
04 @Component({
05   selector: 'app-page1',
06   templateUrl: './page1.component.html'
07 })
08 export class Page1Component {
09   text='';
10   constructor(
11     private route: ActivatedRoute,
12     private router: Router,
13   ){ }
14   gotoPage2(){
15     this.router.navigate(
16         ['/page2', this.text],
17         {
18           relativeTo: this.route,
19           skipLocationChange: true
20         }
21     );
22   }
23 }
```

Listing 28.37 shows the root component `app.component.ts`. This file has a template that declares `router-outlet` to display the views from the router.

Listing 28.37 `app.component.ts`: **An Angular Component that Acts as the Entry Point to the Application**

```
import { Component } from '@angular/core';

@Component({
  selector: 'app-root',
  template: '<router-outlet></router-outlet>'
})
export class AppComponent { }
```

Listing 28.38 shows the `page1` component. This component imports `Router` and `ActivatedRoute` from `@angular/router` to allow this component to access the router and read or assign parameters to `RouterState`. Lines 10 through 13 define the constructor, which on lines 11 and 12 implements `ActivatedRoute` and `Router` as private variables `route` and `router`. Lines 14 through 22 define the function `gotoPage2()`, which navigates to `page2`, passing in a parameter. Line 16 navigates to `page2`, passing in `this.text` as the parameter. Lines 18 and 19 allow the application to change views without changing the URL in the browser.

Listing 28.38 `page1.component.ts`: **An Angular Component that Navigates to Page 2 with Parameters**

```
01 import { Component } from '@angular/core';
02 import { Router, ActivatedRoute } from '@angular/router';
03
04 @Component({
05   selector: 'app-page1',
06   templateUrl: './page1.component.html'
07 })
08 export class Page1Component {
09   text='';
10   constructor(
11     private route: ActivatedRoute,
12     private router: Router,
13   ){ }
14   gotoPage2(){
15     this.router.navigate(
16         ['/page2', this.text],
17         {
18           relativeTo: this.route,
19           skipLocationChange: true
20         }
21     );
22   }
23 }
```

Listing 28.39 shows the `page1` template file. Line 4 shows a text area that is bound to the variable text that is passed as a parameter when routed to page 2. Line 5 creates a button that invokes the `gotoPage2` function, changing the view. This button is available only when the variable text has a non-empty value.

Listing 28.39 `page1.component.html`: **An HTML Template that Provides an Input Field to Give a Value to Router Parameters**

```
01 <span>
02   Enter Text to Pass As Params:
03 </span>
04 <input type=text [(ngModel)]="text" />
05 <button [disabled]="!text" (click)="gotoPage2()">Page 2</button>
```

Listing 28.40 shows the `page2` component. This component imports `Router` and `ActivatedRoute` from `@angular/router` to allow this component to access the router and parameters that were set when the route was loaded. Lines 15 and 16 create a subscription to the `params` observable and assign the value to the variable `text` to be displayed in the view.

Listing 28.40 `page2.component.ts`: An Angular Component that Displays Router Parameters on the View

```
01 import { Component, OnInit } from '@angular/core';
02 import { Router, ActivatedRoute } from '@angular/router';
03
04 @Component({
05   selector: 'app-page2',
06   templateUrl: './page2.component.html'
07 })
08 export class Page2Component implements OnInit {
09   text;
10   constructor(
11     private route: ActivatedRoute,
12     private router: Router
13   ) { }
14   ngOnInit() {
15     this.route.params
16       .subscribe(text => this.text = text.params);
17   }
18
19   goBack(){
20     this.router.navigate(['/page1']);
21   }
22 }
```

Listing 28.41 shows the `page2` template file. Line 2 displays the variable `text`, which gets its value from the route `params`. Line 3 creates a button that can be clicked to navigate back to page 1.

Listing 28.41 `page2.component.html`: Parameters Passed from the Router

```
01 <h3>Params From Page 1</h3>
02 <p>{{text}}</p>
03 <button (click)="goBack()" >back</button>
```

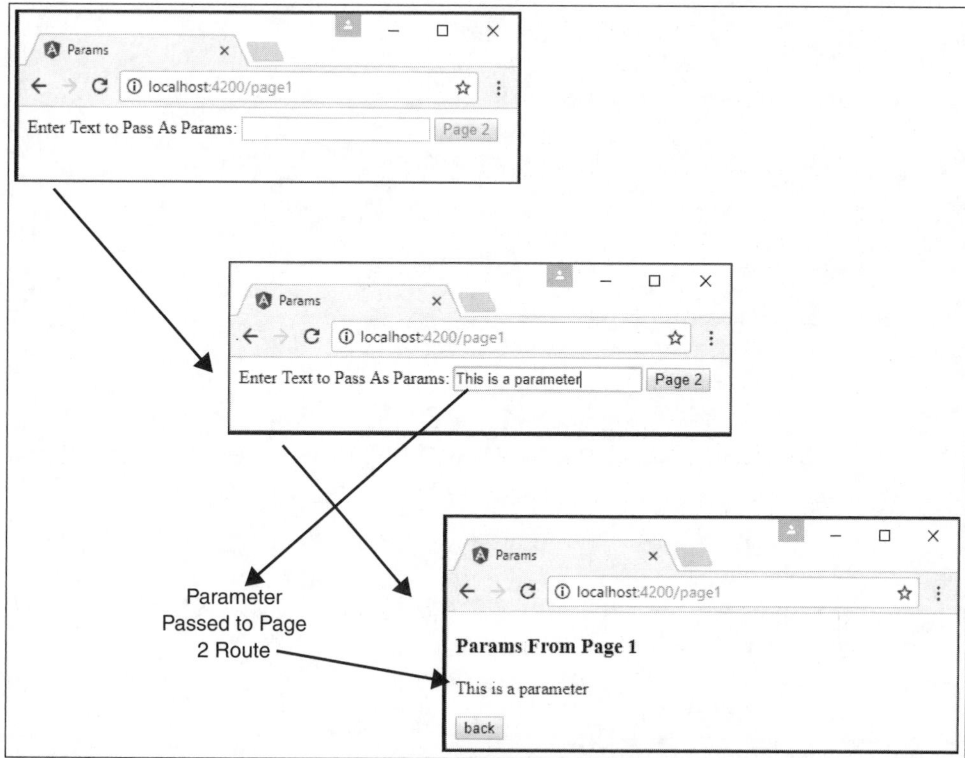

Figure 28.6 Implementing the `http` service to allow Angular components to interact with a web server

Summary

Angular services are objects that contain functionality you can inject into other Angular components. Angular's built-in services provide a lot of prebuilt functionality needed for your client code. For example, the `http` service allows you to easily integrate web server communication into your Angular applications, and the `router` service allows you to manage navigation between views.

Next

The next chapter introduces you to Angular custom services. While there is a lot of built-in functionality in Angular, the chapter shows you how you can create your own services for more control over your applications.

29

Creating Your Own Custom Angular Services

Angular provides a lot of functionality in its built-in services, but it also allows you to implement your own custom services to provide specific functionality. You should implement a custom service any time you need to provide task-based functionality to an application.

When implementing custom services, you need to think about each service as being a chunk of reusable code that performs one or more related tasks. Then you can design and group them together into libraries that can easily be consumed by several different Angular applications.

This chapter introduces Angular custom services. It provides several examples of custom Angular services to provide you with a clearer understanding of how to design and build your own.

Integrating Custom Services into Angular Applications

As you begin implementing Angular services for your applications, you will find that some will be very simple and others will be very complex. The complexity of the service typically reflects the complexity of the underlying data and the functionality it provides. The purpose of this section is to provide you with some basic examples of different types of custom services to illustrate how they can be implemented and used. Table 29.1 lists some uses for services.

Table 29.1 **Use Cases for Custom Services**

Service	Description
Mock service	Provides dummy data that can be used to test HTTP-based services while the back end is unavailable
Constant data	Returns data variables that need to remain constant, such as the mathematical value of pi
Variable data	Returns data variables that can be changed, with the changed value being saved to the service for other services to use

Service	Description
HTTP connection to the back end	Should be used within a custom service to create an interface with the back-end data
Data transformations	Takes in a form of data to be transformed, runs the transformation, and returns the transformed value (for example, a square service that takes in a number and returns the square)
Shared service	Any type of service that can be used by multiple components at once while the data is automatically updated for all components any time it changes

Adding an Angular Service to an Application

This section goes over how to create and implement a custom service in an application. When you create services, they have to be made injectable in order to be used throughout the application. The following example shows the syntax for creating an injectable service:

```
import { Injectable } from '@angular/core';
@Injectable()
export class CustomService { }
```

Once you've created an injectable service, it needs to be imported and provided to any Angular component that needs access to it. The following is the syntax for importing a custom service, along with the custom service being injected via the `providers` array in the component decorator metadata:

```
import { CustomService } from './path_to_service';

@Component({
  selector: 'app-root',
  template: '',
  providers: [ CustomService ]
})
```

The final step in making a custom service usable is to create an instance of that service to be used throughout the component. You do this in the constructor of the component, as shown in the following example:

```
constructor(
  private myService: CustomService
){}
```

When these steps are complete, the custom service and any of its methods are made available to the component through the instance `myService`.

The following sections provide examples that illustrate various ways of implementing custom services.

Implementing a Simple Application that Uses a Constant Data Service

This example shows how to build a constant data service. The purpose of this example is to create a simple service that returns a constant data variable.

Listing 29.1 shows the `pi` service, which returns the value of pi. Lines 1 and 3 import and implement `Injectable` to make the service available to be used externally. Line 4 creates the `PiService` class, which holds the definition for the service. Lines 5 through 7 define the `getPi` method, which returns the value of pi.

Listing 29.1 `pi.service.ts`: **Creating a Service that Returns the Value of Pi**

```
01 import { Injectable } from '@angular/core';
02
03 @Injectable()
04 export class PiService {
05   getPi(){
06     return Math.PI;
07   }
08 }
```

Listing 29.2 implements an Angular component that imports and implements `PiService`. Lines 2 and 7 show `PiService` being imported and then provided to make it available to use throughout the component. Line 12 shows `PiService` being instantiated as the variable `PiService`. Lines 14 through 16 show the `ngOnInit` method, which calls the `getPi` method from `PiService` and assigns it to the variable `pi`.

Listing 29.2 `app.component.ts`: **An Angular Component that Gets the Value of Pi from** `PiService`

```
01 import { Component, OnInit } from '@angular/core';
02 import { PiService } from './pi.service';
03
04 @Component({
05   selector: 'app-root',
06   templateUrl: './app.component.html',
07   providers: [ PiService ]
08 })
09 export class AppComponent implements OnInit {
10   pi: number;
11   constructor(
12     private PiService: PiService
13   ){}
14   ngOnInit(){
15     this.pi = this.PiService.getPi();
16   }
17 }
```

Listing 29.3 shows an Angular template that displays the value of pi to five places.

Listing 29.3 `app.component.html`: **An Angular Template That Displays the Value of Pi to Five Places**

```
<h1>
  Welcome. this app returns the value of pi
</h1>
<p> the value of pi is: {{pi | number:'1.1-5'}}</p>
```

Figure 29.1 shows the output of this example in a web browser.

Figure 29.1 An HTML page that shows the Angular component displaying the value of pi obtained from a constant service

Implementing a Data Transform Service

This example shows how to build a simple data transform service that takes in data variables, calculates the area of a shape, and returns the area for the shape.

Listing 29.4 shows a custom service named `AreaCalcService`, which has several methods named after various shapes. Each of these methods takes in variables that are then used to generate the areas of the shapes they are named after. Lines 1 and 3 import and implement `Injectable` to make the service available to be used externally.

Listing 29.4 `area-calc.service.ts`: **An Angular Service with Methods that Calculate the Areas of Shapes**

```
01 import { Injectable } from '@angular/core';
02
03 @Injectable()
04 export class AreaCalcService {
05   circle(radius:number): number {
06     return Math.PI * radius * radius;
07   }
```

```
  square(base:number): number {
    return base * base;
  }
  rectangle(base:number, height): number {
    return base * height;
  }
  triangle(base:number, height): number {
    return (base*height)/2;
  }
  trapezoid(base1:number,
            base2:number,
            height:number): number {
    return ((base1+base2)/2)*height;
  }
}
```

Listing 29.5 shows an Angular component that gets areas of shapes from `AreaCalcService`, based on the values received from the user. Lines 2 and 8 import `AreaCalcService` and add it to the providers to make it available to the component. Line 21 creates an instance of `AreaCalcService` as `areaCalc` to be used with the component methods.

Lines 23 through 25 define the `doCircle` method, which implements the `circle` method on `areaCalc` to get the area of a circle.

Lines 26 through 28 define the `doSquare` method, which implements the `square` method on `areaCalc` to get the area of a square.

Lines 29 through 31 define the `doRectangle` method, which implements the `rectangle` method on `areaCalc` to get the area of a rectangle.

Lines 32 through 34 define the `doTriangle` method, which implements the `triangle` method on `areaCalc` to get the area of a triangle.

Lines 35 through 39 define the `doTrapezoid` method, which implements the `trapezoid` method on `areaCalc` to get the area of a trapezoid.

Listing 29.5 `app.component.ts`: **An Angular Component that Gets Areas of Shapes from** `AreaCalcService` **Based on Values Received from the User**

```
01 import { Component } from '@angular/core';
02 import { AreaCalcService } from './area-calc.service';
03
04 @Component({
05   selector: 'app-root',
06   templateUrl: './app.component.html',
07   styleUrls: ['./app.component.css'],
08   providers: [ AreaCalcService ]
09 })
```

```
export class AppComponent {
  circleRadius: number = 0;
  squareBase: number = 0;
  rectangleBase: number = 0;
  rectangleHeight: number = 0;
  triangleBase: number = 0;
  triangleHeight: number = 0;
  trapezoidBase1: number = 0;
  trapezoidBase2: number = 0;
  trapezoidHeight: number = 0;

  constructor(private areaCalc: AreaCalcService){ }

  doCircle(){
    return this.areaCalc.circle(this.circleRadius);
  }
  doSquare(){
    return this.areaCalc.square(this.squareBase);
  }
  doRectangle(){
    return this.areaCalc.rectangle(this.rectangleBase, this.rectangleHeight);
  }
  doTriangle(){
    return this.areaCalc.triangle(this.triangleBase, this.triangleHeight);
  }
  doTrapezoid(){
    return this.areaCalc.trapezoid(this.trapezoidBase1,
                                   this.trapezoidBase2,
                                   this.trapezoidHeight);
  }
}
```

Listing 29.6 shows an Angular template file that creates form fields to input data required to calculate the areas of various shapes. When the data is input, the area is immediately calculated and displayed to the user.

Listing 29.6 `app.component.html`**: An Angular Template that Provides a User Interface to Create Form Fields to Receive the Areas of Shapes**

```
<label>Circle Radius:</label>
<input type="text" [(ngModel)]="circleRadius"/>
<span>Area: {{this.doCircle()}}</span>
<hr>

<label>Square Side:</label>
<input type="text" [(ngModel)]="squareBase" />
<span>Area: {{this.doSquare()}}</span>
```

```
<hr>

<label>Rectangle Base:</label>
<input type="text" [(ngModel)]="rectangleBase" /> <br>
<label>Rectangle Height:</label>
<input type="text" [(ngModel)]="rectangleHeight" />
<span>Area: {{this.doRectangle()}}</span>
<hr>

<label>Triangle Base:</label>
<input type="text"
  [(ngModel)]="triangleBase" /> <br>
<label>Triangle Height:</label>
<input type="text" [(ngModel)]="triangleHeight" />
<span>Area: {{this.doTriangle()}}</span>
<hr>

<label>Trapezoid Base1:</label>
<input type="text"  [(ngModel)]="trapezoidBase1" /><br>
<label>Trapezoid Base2:</label>
<input type="text"  [(ngModel)]="trapezoidBase2" /><br>
<label>Trapezoid Height:</label>
<input type="text"  [(ngModel)]="trapezoidHeight" />
<span>Area: {{this.doTrapezoid()}}</span>
```

Listing 29.7 shows a CSS file that styles the application, separating the individual forms for each shape.

Listing 29.7 `app.component.html`**: A CSS File that Styles the Application**

```
label{
    color: blue;
    font: bold 20px times new roman;
    width: 200px;
    display: inline-block;
    text-align: right;
}
input{
    width: 40px;
    text-align: right;
}
span{
    font: bold 20px courier new;
    padding-left: 10px;
}
```

Figure 29.2 shows the resulting Angular application web page. As values are added to the component, the areas are automatically calculated by the custom service.

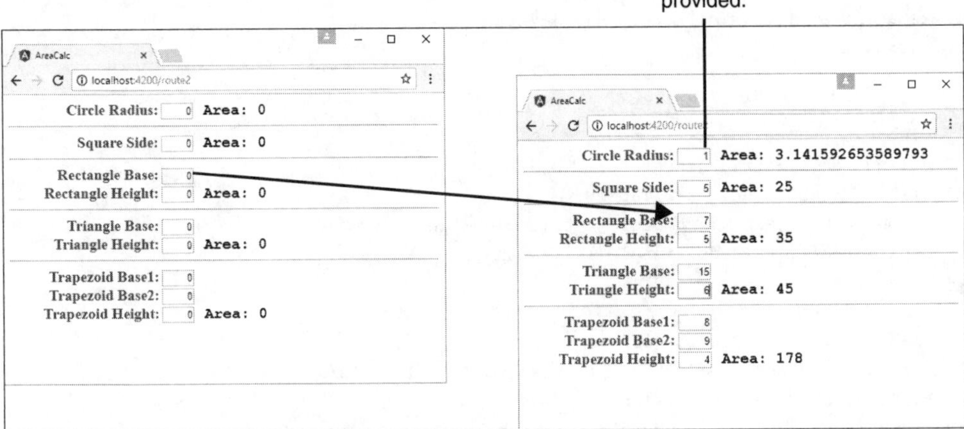

Figure 29.2 An Angular application that uses a custom service to automatically calculate the areas of different shapes

Implementing a Variable Data Service

This example shows how to build a variable data service that creates an image changer that at random times randomly selects an image from a list and sends it to the component to be displayed.

Listing 29.8 shows a custom service named `RandomImageService` that selects an image URL from a list and emits that URL at a random interval. Line 2 shows `Observable` being imported from `rxjs/observable`. Lines 33 through 37 show the constructor that initializes the observable `imageChange` and calls the method `changeLoop`, passing in the `observer` object. Lines 38 through 51 define the `changeLoop` method, which takes in the observable response object `observer`. A `setTimeout` function is called with a random time before it completes. Then a random image is selected from the `images` array. The image URL, title, and width are then emitted, and `changeLoop` recursively calls itself. Lines 52 through 54 define the `getRandom` function, which takes in two parameters, `min` and `max`, and gets a random number between those values.

Listing 29.8 `random-image.service.ts`: **An Angular Service that Returns an Observable that Contains a Random Image**

```
import { Injectable, OnInit } from '@angular/core';
import { Observable } from 'rxjs/observable';

@Injectable()
export class RandomImageService {
  imageChange: Observable<any>;
  private images = [
    {
      url: '../../assets/images/arch.jpg',
      title: "Delicate Arch"
    },
    {
      url: '../../assets/images/lake.jpg',
      title: "Silver Lake"
    },
    {
      url: '../../assets/images/cliff.jpg',
      title: "Desert Cliff"
    },
    {
      url: '../../assets/images/bison.jpg',
      title: "Bison"
    },
    {
      url: '../../assets/images/flower.jpg',
      title: "Flower"
    },
    {
      url: '../../assets/images/volcano.jpg',
      title: "Volcano"
    },
  ];
  constructor() {
    this.imageChange = new Observable(observer => {
        this.changeLoop(observer);
      });
  }
  changeLoop(observer){
    setTimeout(() => {
      let imgIndex = this.getRandom(0,6);
      let image = this.images[imgIndex];
      observer.next(
        {
          url: image.url,
```

```
          title: image.title,
          width: this.getRandom(200,400)
        }
      );
      this.changeLoop(observer);
    }, this.getRandom(100,1000));
  }
  getRandom(min, max) {
    return Math.floor(Math.random() * (max - min)) + min;
  }
  getRandomImage(): Observable<any> {
    return this.imageChange;
  }
}
```

Listing 29.9 shows an Angular component that gets a random image from `RandomImageService`, displays it in the main view, and adds it into the `imageHistory` array. Lines 4 and 10 show `RandomImageService` being imported and provided to the component. Line 18 instantiates the `RandomImageService` as the variable `randomImages`. Lines 20 through 24 create a default initial `imageInfo` object to hold a place until data can be received from `RandomImageService`. Lines 27 through 34 show the `ngOnInit` method, which calls the `getRandomImage` method on the `randomImages` service instance and assigns it to the observable `randomImage`. `imageInfo` is then assigned the value of anything emitted from the observable. `imageHistory` also adds the value of anything emitted from the observable.

Listing 29.9 `app.component.ts`: An Angular Component that Gets a Random Image from `RandomImageService` and Displays That Image

```
01 import { Component, OnInit } from '@angular/core';
02 import { Observable } from 'rxjs/observable';
03 import { Subscription } from 'rxjs/Subscription';
04 import { RandomImageService } from './random-image.service';
05
06 @Component({
07   selector: 'app-root',
08   templateUrl: './app.component.html',
09   styleUrls: ['./app.component.css'],
10   providers: [ RandomImageService ]
11 })
12 export class AppComponent {
13   title = 'app';
14   randomImage: Observable<any>;
15   imageInfo: any;
16   imageHistory: any[];
17   constructor(
18     private randomImages: RandomImageService
```

```
  ){
     this.imageInfo = {
      url: '',
      title: 'Loading . . .',
      width: 400
    };
    this.imageHistory = [];
  }
  ngOnInit(){
    this.randomImage = this.randomImages.getRandomImage();
    this.randomImage.subscribe(
      imageData => {
        this.imageInfo = imageData;
        this.imageHistory.push(imageData);
      });
  }
}
```

Listing 29.10 shows an Angular template that displays a random image in the main view. `ngFor` is used to display each image within the image history array.

Listing 29.10 `app.component.html`: **An Angular Template that Displays Images Emitted from** `RandomImageService`

```
<div>
  <img src="{{imageInfo.url}}"
       width="{{imageInfo.width}}">
  <p>{{imageInfo.title}}</p>
</div>
<hr>
<h3>Random Image History</h3>
<span *ngFor = "let image of imageHistory">
  <img src="{{image.url}}" height="50px">
</span>
```

Listing 29.11 shows a CSS file that styles the application with a border for the main image and text.

Listing 29.11 `app.component.css`: **A CSS File that Styles the Application Separating the Main View from the Smaller Pictures**

```
div {
    position: inline-block;
    width: fit-content;
    border: 3px solid black;
}
```

```
p {
    font: bold 25px 'Times New Roman';
    padding: 5px;
    text-align: center;
}
```

Figure 29.3 shows the running example. The main image URL and size are randomly changed by the service. A rolling history of the randomly displayed images is shown at the bottom.

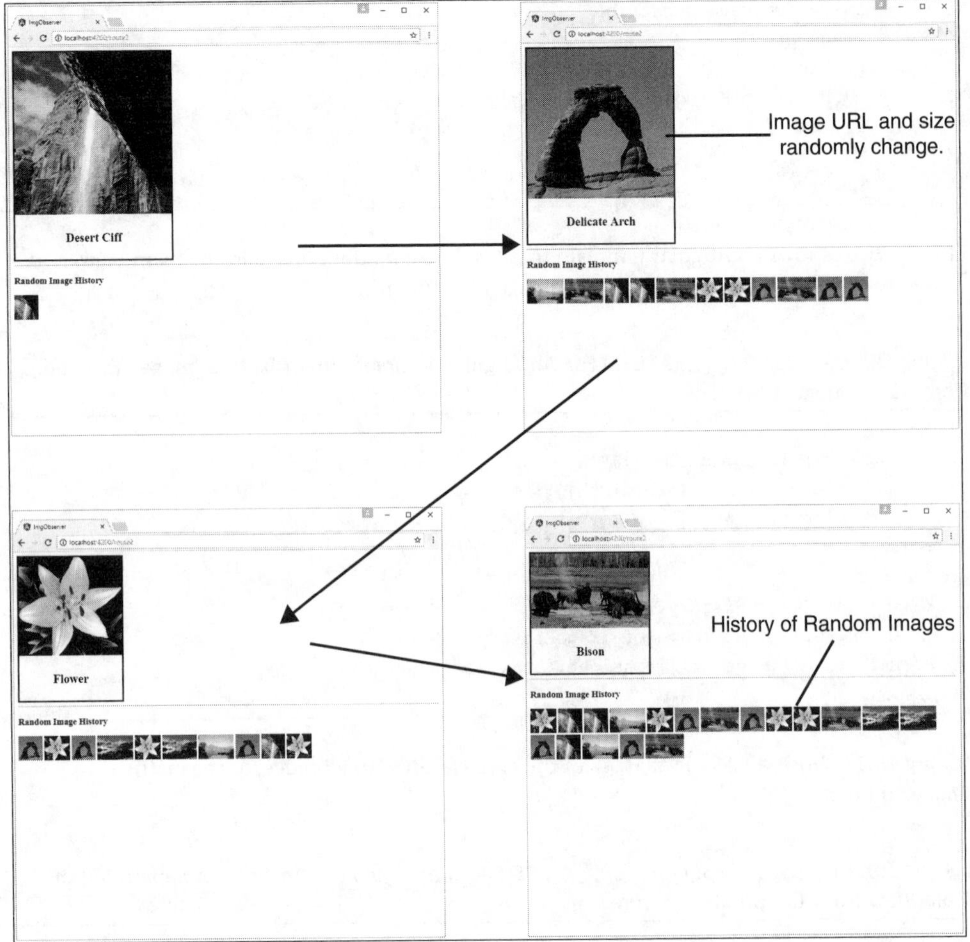

Figure 29.3 Implementing a variable data service that updates a component with random changes to image size and URL

Implementing a Service that Returns a Promise

This example shows how to build a service that creates and returns a promise.

Listing 29.12 shows a custom service named `PromiseService`, which creates an asynchronous timer that alerts the user after a particular number of seconds. Lines 6 through 13 define the method `createTimedAlert`, which takes in the parameter `seconds` and returns a promise. Lines 8 through 10 create a `resolve` function, which runs only after the promise completes. This function creates an alert that tells the user how long it took to run the alert.

Listing 29.12 `promise.service.ts`: **An Angular Service that Provides a Timer-Based Alert**

```
01 Import { Injectable } from '@angular/core';
02
03 @Injectable()
04 export class PromiseService {
05
06   createTimedAlert(seconds: number): Promise<any>{
07     return new Promise((resolve, reject) =>{
08       resolve(setTimeout(function(){
09           alert('this alert took ' + seconds + ' seconds to load');
10         }, (seconds * 1000))
11       );
12     })
13   }
```

Listing 29.13 shows an Angular component that uses `PromiseService` to create an asynchronous request that can be resolved at a later time. Lines 2 and 7 show `PromiseService` being imported and then added to the `providers` array so it is available to the component. Line 12 creates an instance of `PromiseService` called `alert`. Lines 15 through 17 define the `createAlert` method, which invokes the `createTimedAlert` method on `alert` and passes in the `seconds` variable.

Listing 29.13 `app.component.ts`: **An Angular Component that Uses the `PromiseService` Service**

```
01 import { Component } from '@angular/core';
02 import { PromiseService } from './promise.service';
03
04 @Component({
05   selector: 'app-root',
06   templateUrl: './app.component.html',
07   providers: [PromiseService]
08 })
09 export class AppComponent {
10   seconds: number = 0;
```

```
  constructor(
    private alert: PromiseService
  ){}

  createAlert(){
    this.alert.createTimedAlert(this.seconds);
  }
}
```

Listing 29.14 shows an Angular template that has an input the user can use to type the amount of time in seconds. The template has a button that invokes the function `createAlert`.

Listing 29.14 `app.component.htm`: **A Template that Displays a Button to Start the Asynchronous Alert Request**

```
<h3>set the time in seconds to create an alert</h3>
<input [(ngModel)]="seconds">
<button (click)="createAlert()">go</button>
```

Figure 29.4 shows the asynchronous alert being displayed by the service after the time has elapsed.

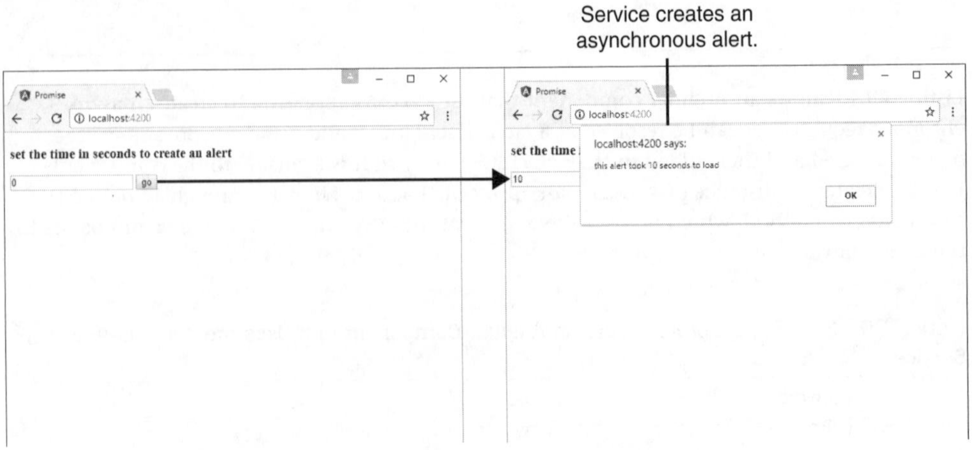

Figure 29.4 Using an Angular service to provide asynchronous alerts

Implementing a Shared Service

This example shows how to build a service that is shared between two components. There will only be one instance of this service, which means that when one component changes the data, the other component will see that data change as well.

Listing 29.15 shows a custom service named `SharedService`, which creates an observable of an array of characters. This observable is editable, which makes it useful for reducing characters' health. When the values are changed, the observable emits that change to all components that are subscribed to the observable.

Lines15 through 52 define the `characters` array, which contains the values `name`, `race`, `alignment`, and `health`. Lines 55 through 60 define the `constructor` method, which creates the observable `charObservable`. The observer object is saved to the service variable `observer`. Then the observer emits the `characters` array. Lines 62 through 64 define the `getCharacters` method, which returns the `charObservable`.

Lines 66 through 79 define the `hitCharacter` method, which takes two parameters: `character` and `damage`. The method then searches for the index of `character` within the `characters` array. If the character exists in the array, the method subtracts damage from that character's health. Then if the health is less than or equal to 0, the method removes the `character` from the array. Finally, the method emits the updated `characters` array.

Listing 29.15 `shared.service.ts`: **An Angular Service that Will Be Shared Between Components**

```
01 import { Injectable } from '@angular/core';
02
03 import { Observable }     from 'rxjs/Observable';
04 import 'rxjs';
05
06 export class character {
07   name: string;
08   race: string;
09   alignment: string;
10   health: number;
11 }
12
13 @Injectable()
14 export class SharedService{
15 characters: character[] = [
16       {
17         name: 'Aragon',
18         race: 'human',
19         alignment: 'good',
20         health: 100
21       },
22       {
23         name: 'Legolas',
24         race: 'elf',
25         alignment: 'good',
26         health: 100
27       },
28       {
29         name: 'Gimli',
```

```
      race: 'Dwarf',
      alignment: 'good',
      health: 100
    },
    {
      name: 'Witch King',
      race: 'Wraith',
      alignment: 'bad',
      health: 100
    },
    {
      name: 'Lurtz',
      race: 'Uruk-hai',
      alignment: 'bad',
      health: 100
    },
    {
      name: 'Sarumon',
      race: 'Wizard',
      alignment: 'bad',
      health: 100
    },
  ];
  charObservable: Observable<character[]>;
  observer;
  constructor(){
    this.charObservable = new Observable(observer => {
      this.observer = observer;
      this.observer.next(this.characters);
    })
  }

  getCharacters(): Observable<character[]>{
    return this.charObservable;
  }

  hitCharacter(character, damage){

    var index = this.characters.indexOf(character, 0);
      if(index > -1){
        this.characters[index].health -= damage;
        if(this.characters[index].health <= 0){
          this.characters.splice(index, 1);
        }
      }
    this.observer.next(this.characters);
  }
}
```

Listing 29.16 shows an Angular component that creates a single instance of `SharedService` that can be passed down to child components. Because each child receives the same instance of the service, all child components that inject the `SharedService` and subscribe to its observable will be updated anytime the data changes. Lines 2 and 7 import and provide `SharedService` for use within the component. Line 11 assigns `SharedService` to the variable `shared` to be used within the HTML.

Listing 29.16 `app.component.ts`: An Angular Component that Distributes `SharedService`

```
01 import { Component } from '@angular/core';
02 import { SharedService } from './shared.service';
03
04 @Component({
05   selector: 'app-root',
06   templateUrl: './app.component.html',
07   providers: [ SharedService ]
08 })
09 export class AppComponent {
10   constructor(
11      public shared: SharedService
12   ){}
13 }
```

Listing 29.17 shows an Angular template that displays two sections: one for good guys and one for bad guys. Line 2 shows the `Good Guys` component, which takes in an input `shared` and is passed the `shared` observable from `app.component` to `good-guys.component`. Line 5 shows the `Bad Guys` component, which takes in an input `shared` and is passed the `shared` observable from `app.component` to `badguys.component`.

Listing 29.17 `app.component.html`: An Angular Template File that Distributes `SharedService` to Two Components

```
01 <h2>Good Guys</h2>
02 <app-good-guys [shared]="shared"></app-good-guys>
03   <hr>
04 <h2>Bad Guys</h2>
05 <app-badguys [shared]="shared"></app-badguys>
```

Listing 29.18 shows the Angular component `good-guys.component`. Line 9 shows the input `shared` that gets the `SharedService` observable from `app.component`. Lines 14 through 16 show `getCharacters` being subscribed to on the `shared` service; this sets the variable `characters` to the emitted value from the observable returned from the method. Lines 18 through 20 define the `hitCharacter` method, which takes two parameters: `character` and `damage`. This method calls the `hitCharacter` method on the shared service and passes in `character` and `damage` as parameters.

Listing 29.18 `good-guys.component.ts`: **An Angular Component that Watches and Displays a Shared Observable**

```
import { Component, OnInit, Input } from '@angular/core';

@Component({
  selector: 'app-good-guys',
  templateUrl: './good-guys.component.html',
  styleUrls: ['./good-guys.component.css']
})
export class GoodGuysComponent implements OnInit {
  @Input('shared') shared;
  characters: Array<any>;
  constructor(){}

  ngOnInit(){
    this.shared.getCharacters().subscribe(
      characters => this.characters = characters
    );
  }
  hitCharacter(character, damage){
    this.shared.hitCharacter(character, damage)
  }
}
```

Listing 29.19 shows an Angular template that displays a list of characters. Lines 3 through 5 display the character's name, race, and health. Lines 6 through 8 show that characters with the alignment `'bad'` have a button that invokes the `hitCharacter` method which takes in the `character` object and the number `25` as parameters.

Listing 29.19 `good-guys.component.html`: **An Angular Template that Displays a List of Characters**

```
01 <div *ngFor="let character of characters">
02   <div class="character">
03         <b>Name:</b> {{character.name}}<br>
04         <b>Race:</b> {{character.race}}<br>
05         <b>Health:</b> {{character.health}}
06     <span *ngIf="character.alignment == 'bad'">
07       <button (click)="hitCharacter(character, 25)">hit</button>
08     </span>
09   </div>
10 </div>
```

Listing 29.20 shows a CSS file that adds borders to each character to help distinguish the characters as separate entities.

Listing 29.20 `good-guys.component.css`: **A CSS File that Visually Separates Characters into Their Own Cards**

```
b{
  font-weight: bold;
}
div {
  display: inline-block;
  margin: 10px;
  padding: 5px;
}
.character {
  border: 2px solid steelblue;
}
```

Listing 29.21 shows the Angular component `badguys.component`. Line 10 shows the input `shared` that gets the `SharedService` observable from `app.component`. Lines 15 through 17 show `getCharacters` being subscribed to on the `shared` service; this sets the variable `characters` to the emitted value from the observable returned from the method. Lines 19 through 21 define the `hitCharacter` method, which takes two parameters: `character` and `damage`. This method calls the `hitCharacter` method on the shared service to pass in `character` and `damage` as parameters.

Listing 29.21 `badguys.component.ts`: **An Angular Component that Watches and Displays a Shared Observable**

```
01 import { Component, OnInit, Input } from '@angular/core';
02
03 @Component({
04   selector: 'app-badguys',
05   templateUrl: './badguys.component.html',
06   styleUrls: ['./badguys.component.css']
07 })
08
09 export class BadguysComponent implements OnInit {
10   @Input('shared') shared;
11   characters: Array<any>;
12   constructor(){ }
13
14   ngOnInit(){
15    this.shared.getCharacters().subscribe(
16       characters => this.characters = characters
17     );
18   }
19   hitCharacter(character, damage){
20     this.shared.hitCharacter(character, damage);
21   }
22 }
```

Listing 29.22 shows an Angular template that displays a list of characters. Lines 3 through 5 display the character's name, race, and health. Lines 6 through 8 show that characters with the alignment `'good'` also have a button that invokes the `hitCharacter` method which takes in the `character` object and `25` as parameters.

Listing 29.22 `badguys.component.html`: **An Angular Template that Displays a List of Characters**

```
01 <div *ngFor="let character of characters">
02   <div class="character">
03     <b>Name:</b> {{character.name}}<br>
04     <b>Race:</b> {{character.race}}<br>
05     <b>Health:</b> {{character.health}}
06     <span *ngIf="character.alignment == 'good'">
07       <button (click)="hitCharacter(character, 25)">hit</button>
08     </span>
09   </div>
10 </div>
```

Listing 29.23 shows a CSS file that adds borders to each character to help distinguish the characters as separate entities.

Listing 29.23 `badguys.component.css`: **A CSS File that Visually Separates Characters into Their Own Cards**

```
b{
  font-weight: bold;
}
div {
  display: inline-block;
  margin: 10px;
  padding: 5px;
}
.character {
  border: 2px solid steelblue;
}
```

Figure 29.5 shows the application that connects a `Good Guys` component with a `Bad Guys` component. Clicking the hit button updates the shared service, which is observed by both components.

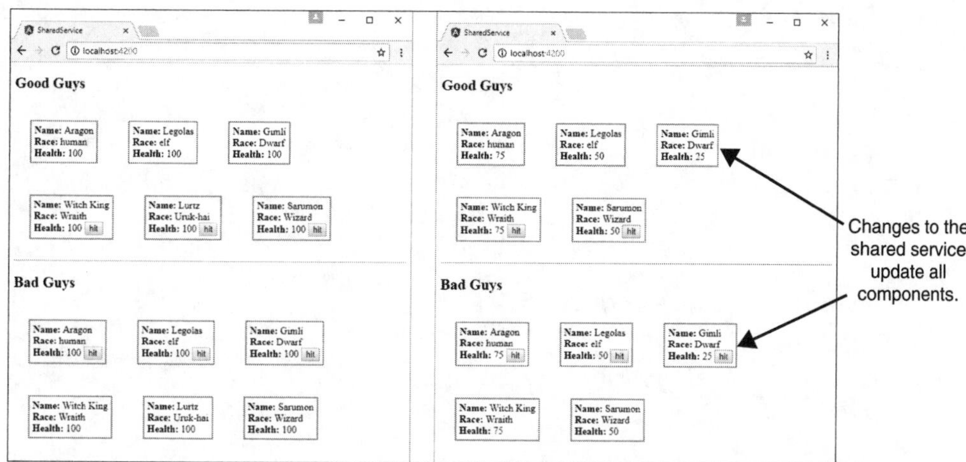

Figure 29.5 Using a shared Angular service to update multiple components

Summary

Angular custom services provide functionality that can be injected into other Angular services and components. Services allow you to organize your code into functional modules that can be used to create libraries of functionality available to Angular applications.

This chapter focuses on tools that enable you to implement your own custom Angular services for providing task-based functionality to applications. This chapter provides examples of implementing each of various types of custom Angular services.

Next

The next chapter focuses on expanding what you have learned so far with additional examples. It will take everything you have learned so far and show you how to use it to create fun and useful Angular components.

30

Having Fun with Angular

Angular provides a lot of functionality and is a well-featured framework. The previous chapters in this book have given you everything you need to understand what Angular has to offer. This chapter is a bit different from the previous ones. It provides some additional examples that expand on what you have learned so far. The examples in this chapter take bits and pieces from all the previous chapters and show you how to build fun and useful applications that demonstrate more of what Angular is capable of.

Implementing an Angular Application that Uses the Animation Service

Listings 30.1 through 30.6 show how to create an Angular application that uses the animation service to animate images. An image fades in and grows to the correct size when the mouse hovers over the image title. When the mouse leaves, the image shrinks and fades out of view.

The folder structure for this example is as follows:

- **`./app.module.ts:`** App module that imports animations (see Listing 30.1)
- **`./app.component.ts:`** Angular root component for the application (see Listing 30.2)
- **`./app.component.html:`** Angular template file for `app.component` (see Listing 30.3)
- **`./animated:`** Animated component folder
- **`./animated/animated.component.ts:`** Angular component that handles animations (see Listing 30.4)
- **`./animated/animated.component.html:`** Angular template for the `animated` component (see Listing 30.5)
- **`./animated/animated.component.css:`** CSS file for the `animated` component (see Listing 30.6)

Listing 30.1 shows the application module. For the application to use the animation service, `BrowserAnimationsModule` needs to be loaded. Lines 3 and 16 show `BrowserAnimationsModule` being imported from `@angular/platform-browser/animations` and then added to the `imports` array to make animations available to the application.

Listing 30.1 `app.module.ts`: **An Angular Module that Includes** `BrowserAnimationsModule`

```
01 import { BrowserModule } from '@angular/platform-browser';
02 import { NgModule } from '@angular/core';
03 import { BrowserAnimationsModule } from
04 '@angular/platform-browser/animations';
05
06 import { AppComponent } from './app.component';
07 import { AnimatedComponent } from './animated/animated.component';
08
09 @NgModule({
10   declarations: [
11     AppComponent,
12     AnimatedComponent
13   ],
14   imports: [
15     BrowserModule,
16     BrowserAnimationsModule
17   ],
18   providers: [],
19   bootstrap: [AppComponent]
20 })
21 export class AppModule { }
```

Listing 30.2 shows an Angular component that acts as the root of the application. This component loads a template file that uses the `animated` component.

Listing 30.2 `app.component.ts`: **An Angular Component that Acts as the Root to the Application**

```
import { Component } from '@angular/core';
import { AnimatedComponent } from './animated/animated.component';

@Component({
  selector: 'app-root',
  templateUrl: './app.component.html'
})
export class AppComponent {}
```

Listing 30.3 shows an Angular template that loads the `animated` component four times and passes in an image URL to the input `src`. It also adds a title to the input `title`.

Listing 30.3 `app.component.html`: **An Angular Template that Uses the** `animated` **Component**

```
<animated title="Arch"
          src="../../assets/images/arch.jpg">
</animated>
<animated title="Volcano"
          src="../../assets/images/volcano.jpg">
</animated>
<animated title="Flower"
          src="../../assets/images/flower.jpg">
</animated>
<animated title="Sunset"
          src="../../assets/images/jump.jpg">
</animated>
```

Listing 30.4 shows an Angular `animated` component which handles the animation of an image that is passed in via an input. Lines 1 through 3 import `animate`, `keyframes`, `state`, `style`, `transition`, and `trigger` from `@angular/core` to make animations for this application possible.

Lines 9 through 36 define the animations metadata for the component. Lines 10 through 23 show the trigger for the animation called `fadeState`, which when activated calls two states, `inactive` and `active`, and two transitions, `inactive => active` (which creates a 500 ms `ease-in` animation) and `active => inactive` (which creates a 500 ms `ease-out` animation).

Lines 24 through 34 show the trigger `bounceState`, which contains the transition `void => *`. This transition creates an animation that causes the menu items to bounce down and up when the application is first loaded. Lines 45 through 47 define the `enter` method, which sets the variable `state` to `active`. Lines 48 and 49 define the `leave` method, which sets the variable `state` to `inactive`.

Listing 30.4 `animated.component.ts`: **An Angular Component that Uses the Animation Service**

```
01 import { Component, OnInit, Input,
02          animate, keyframes, state,
03          style, transition, trigger } from '@angular/core';
04
05 @Component({
06   selector: 'animated',
07   templateUrl: './animated.component.html',
08   styleUrls: ['./animated.component.css'],
09   animations: [
10     trigger('fadeState', [
11       state('inactive', style({
12         transform: 'scale(.5) translateY(-50%)',
```

```
          opacity: 0
        })),
        state('active', style({
          transform: 'scale(1) translateY(0)',
          opacity: 1
        })),
        transition('inactive => active',
                   animate('500ms ease-in')),
        transition('active => inactive',
                   animate('500ms ease-out'))
      ]),
      trigger('bounceState', [
        transition('void => *', [
          animate(600, keyframes([
            style({ opacity: 0,
                    transform: 'translateY(-50px)' }),
            style({ opacity: .5,
                    transform: 'translateY(50px)' }),
            style({ opacity: 1,
                    transform: 'translateY(0)' }),
          ]))
        ])
      ])
    ]
})
export class AnimatedComponent implements OnInit {
  @Input ("src") src: string;
  @Input ("title") title: string;
  state: string = 'inactive';
  constructor() { }
  ngOnInit() {
  }
  enter(){
    this.state = 'active';
  }
  leave(){
    this.state = 'inactive';
  }
}
```

Listing 30.5 shows an Angular template that displays a title and an image. Line 1 shows the Angular animation `@bounceState` being used; it is passed in the variable `state` from the component to determine what animation sequence should be used. Lines 7 and 8 show `@fadeState` being implemented; it also has `state` passed in to determine the animation sequence.

Listing 30.5 `animated.Component.html`**: An Angular Template That Displays Image Titles with Images That Are Animated**

```
<div [@bounceState]='state'>
  <p
     (mouseenter)="enter()"
     (mouseleave)="leave()">
    {{title}}
  </p>
  <img src="{{src}}"
       [@fadeState]='state' />
</div>
```

Listing 30.6 shows a CSS file that styles the titles for the images and sets the dimensions for the images.

Listing 30.6 `animated.component.css`**: A CSS File That Styles the** `animated` **Component**

```
div {
  display: inline-block;
  padding: 0px;
  margin: 0px;
}
p {
  font: bold 16px/30px Times New Roman;
  color: #226bd8;
  border: 1px solid lightblue;
  background: linear-gradient(white, lightblue, skyblue);
  text-align: center;
  padding: 0px;
  margin: 0px;
  vertical-align: top;
}
img {
  width: 150px;
  vertical-align: top;
}
```

Figure 30.1 shows how the images animate in size and opacity when you click on the image name.

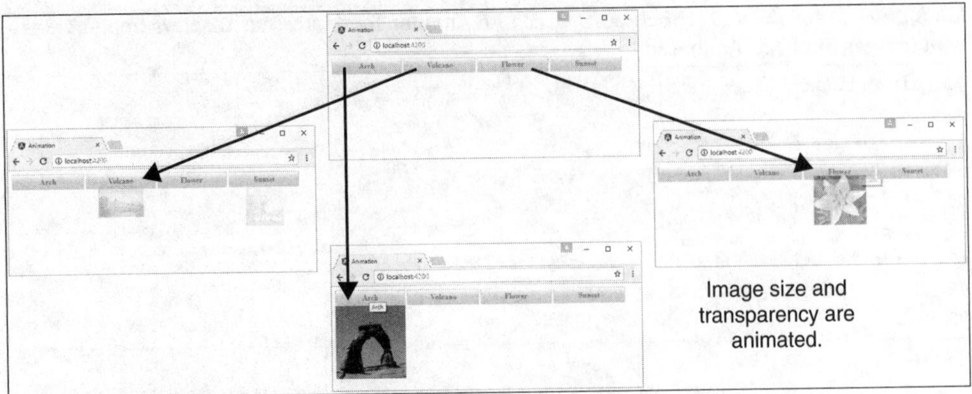

Figure 30.1 Using Angular's built-in animation service to animate images

Implementing an Angular Application that Zooms in on Images

Listings 30.7 through 30.11 show you how to create an Angular application that displays images that can be zoomed in on (via browser events) when they are clicked.

The folder structure for this example is as follows:

- **`./app/app.component.ts:`** Root component for the application (see Listing 30.7)
- **`./app/app.component.html:`** Angular template for the root component (see Listing 30.8)
- **`./app/zoomit:`** Folder containing the `zoomit` component
- **`./app/zoomit/zoomit.component.ts:`** Angular component called `zoomit` (see Listing 30.9)
- **`./app/zoomit/zoomit.component.html:`** Angular template for the `zoomit` component (see Listing 30.10)
- **`./app/zoomit/zoomit.component.html:`** CSS file for the `zoomit` component (see Listing 30.11)
- **`./assets/images:`** Folder where the image files for the example will be kept

Listing 30.7 shows an Angular component that acts as the root of the application. This component loads a template file that uses the `zoomit` component.

Listing 30.7 `app.component.ts`: **An Angular Component That Acts as the Root to the Application**

```
import { Component } from '@angular/core';
import { ZoomitComponent } from './zoomit/zoomit.component';

@Component({
  selector: 'app-root',
  templateUrl: './app.component.html'
})
export class AppComponent {}
```

Listing 30.8 shows an Angular template that creates three `zoomit` components by passing in the image URL as the attribute `zsrc`.

Listing 30.8 `app.component.html`: **An Angular Template That Implements the Component** `zoomit`

```
<hr>
<zoomit zsrc="../../assets/images/volcano.jpg"></zoomit>
<hr>
<zoomit zsrc="../../assets/images/flower2.jpg"></zoomit>
<hr>
<zoomit zsrc="../../assets/images/arch.jpg"></zoomit>
<hr>
```

Listing 30.9 shows the Angular `zoomit` component, which handles zooming in on a section of an image by using browser events. Lines 13 through 16 define the `ngOnInit` method, which generates a URL to get an image based on the name of the image passed into the component via the `zsrc` input. `ngOnInit` then sets a default position. Lines 18 through 23 define the `imageClick` event, which takes in a parameter `event`. Then it gets the element from the `event` object and uses that to set new x and y coordinates as the basis for the zoom of the image.

Listing 30.9 `zoomit.component.ts`: **An Angular Component That Uses Browser Events to Zoom In on Part of an Image**

```
01 import { Component, OnInit, Input } from '@angular/core';
02
03 @Component({
04   selector: 'zoomit',
05   templateUrl: './zoomit.component.html',
06   styleUrls: ['./zoomit.component.css']
07 })
08 export class ZoomitComponent implements OnInit {
09   @Input ("zsrc") zsrc: string;
10   public pos: string;
```

```
  public zUrl: string;

  ngOnInit() {
    this.zUrl = 'url("' + this.zsrc + '")';
    this.pos = "50% 50%";
  }

  imageClick(event: any){
    let element = event.target;
    let posX = Math.ceil(event.offsetX/element.width * 100);
    let posY = Math.ceil(event.offsetY/element.height * 100);
    this.pos = posX +"% " + posY + "%";
  }
}
```

Listing 30.10 shows an Angular template that displays an image and a zoomed-in portion of the image next to it, using the coordinates generated from the `imageClick` function.

Listing 30.10 `zoomit.component.html`: **An Angular Template That Displays an Image as Well as a Zoomed-In Portion of That Image**

```
<img src="{{zsrc}}" (click)="imageClick($event)"/>
<div class="zoombox"
      [style.background-image]="zUrl"
      [style.background-position]="pos">
</div>
```

Listing 30.11 shows a CSS file that styles the application by adding a border to the zoomed-in image. It also sets `width` and `height` to `100px`.

Listing 30.11 `zoomit.component.css`: **A CSS File That Styles the Application**

```
img {
  width: 200px;
}
.zoombox {
  display: inline-block;
  border: 3px ridge black;
  width: 100px;
  height: 100px;
  background-repeat: no-repeat;
}
```

Figure 30.2 shows how the custom component displays a zoomed-in portion of the image. When you click on the image, the position of the zoom is changed.

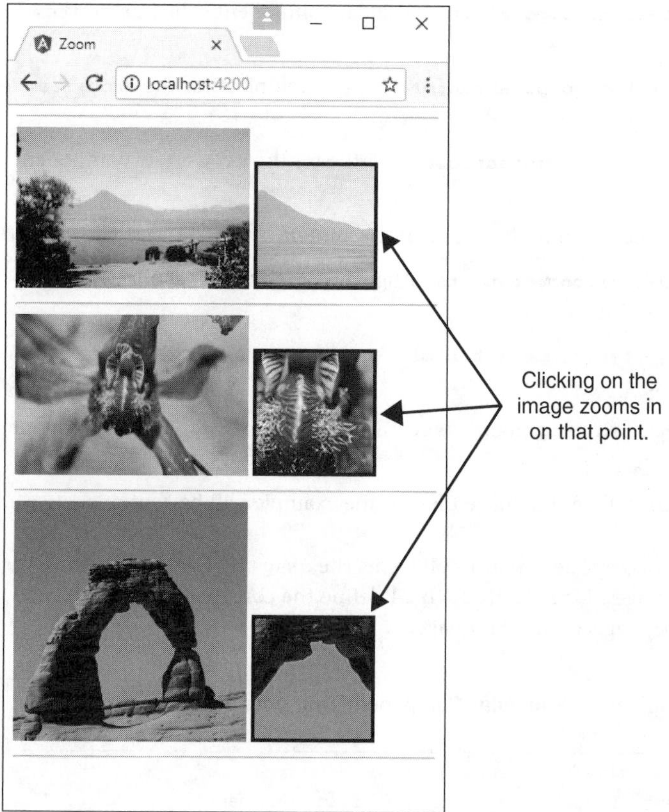

Figure 30.2 Implementing a custom Angular component that zooms in on a portion of an image

Implementing an Angular Application that Enables Drag and Drop

Listings 30.12 through 30.20 show how to create an Angular application that displays images that can have descriptive tags dragged and dropped onto them.

The folder structure for this example is as follows:

- **./app/app.component.ts:** Root component for the application (see Listing 30.12)
- **./app/app.component.html:** Angular template for the `root` component (see Listing 30.13)
- **./app/app.component.css:** CSS file for `app.component` (see Listing 30.14)
- **./app/drop-item:** Folder containing the `drop-item` component

- **./app/drop-item/drop-item.component.ts:** Angular component called `drop-item` (see Listing 30.15)
- **./app/drop-item/drop-item.component.html:** Angular template for the `drop-item` component (see Listing 30.16)
- **./app/drop-item/drop-item.component.css:** CSS file for the `drop-item` component (see Listing 30.17)
- **./app/drag-item:** Folder containing the `drag-item` component
- **./app/drag-item/drag-item.component.ts:** Angular component that allows the dragging of an element (see Listing 30.18)
- **./app/drag-item/drag-item.component.html:** Angular template for the `drag-item` component (see Listing 30.19)
- **./app/drag-item/drag-item.component.css:** CSS file for the `drag-item` component (see Listing 30.20)
- **./assets/images:** Folder where the image files for the example will be kept

Listing 30.12 shows an Angular component that implements the `drag-item` and `drop-item` components to apply tags to images. Lines 12 through 24 define the constructor, which initializes a list of tags available to be dragged onto an image.

Listing 30.12 `app.component.ts`: **An Angular Component That Acts as the Root to the Application**

```
01 import { Component } from '@angular/core';
02 import { DragItemComponent} from './drag-item/drag-item.component';
03 import { DropItemComponent} from './drop-item/drop-item.component';
04
05 @Component({
06   selector: 'app-root',
07   templateUrl: './app.component.html',
08   styleUrls: ['./app.component.css']
09 })
10 export class AppComponent {
11   tagList: string[];
12   constructor() {
13     this.tagList = [
14       'Nature',
15       'Landscape',
16       'Flora',
17       'Sunset',
18       'Desert',
19       'Beauty',
20       'Inspiring',
21       'Summer',
```

```
      'Fun'
    ]
  }
  ngOnInit() {
  }
}
```

Listing 30.13 shows an Angular template that implements the `drag-item` and `drop-item` components, which allow tags to be dragged and dropped onto images.

Listing 30.13 `app.component.html`**: An Angular Template That Implements the** `drag-item` **and** `drop-item` **Components**

```
<h1>Tagging Images</h1>
<hr>
<div class="tagBox">
    <span *ngFor="let tagText of tagList">
        <drag-item [tag]="tagText"></drag-item>
    </span>
</div>
<hr>

<drop-item
[imgsrc]="'../../assets/images/arch.jpg'">
</drop-item>
<drop-item
[imgsrc]="'../../assets/images/lake.jpg'">
</drop-item>
<drop-item
[imgsrc]="'../../assets/images/jump.jpg'">
</drop-item>
<drop-item
[imgsrc]="'../../assets/images/flower.jpg'">
</drop-item>
<drop-item
[imgsrc]="'../../assets/images/volcano.jpg'">
</drop-item>
```

Listing 30.14 shows a CSS file that styles the application to give direct styles to the `drop-item` custom HTML tag.

Listing 30.14 `app.component.css`**: A CSS File That Styles the Application**

```
.tagBox {
  width: 320px;
  padding: 5px;
}
```

```
drop-item{
  display: inline-block;
  vertical-align: top;
  margin-bottom: 5px;
}
```

Listing 30.15 shows the Angular component `drop-item`, which uses browser events to allow an element to be dropped onto the component element. Lines 11 through 13 define the constructor that initializes the `tags` variable as an empty array.

Lines 16 through 18 define the `allowDrop` method, which takes an `event` object as a parameter. The `preventDefault` method is invoked on the `event` object. Lines 19 through 25 define the `onDrop` method, which takes in an `event` object as a parameter. `preventDefault` is called on the event object. Then the variable data is assigned `tagData` from the event to allow Angular to add that data to the `tags` array and to the list on the image.

Listing 30.15 `drop.component.ts`: **An Angular Component That Allows for an Item to Be Dropped on the Element**

```
01 import { Component, OnInit, Input } from '@angular/core';
02
03 @Component({
04   selector: 'drop-item',
05   templateUrl: './drop-item.component.html',
06   styleUrls: ['./drop-item.component.css']
07 })
08 export class DropItemComponent implements OnInit {
09   @Input() imgsrc: string;
10   tags: string[];
11   constructor() {
12     this.tags = [];
13   }
14   ngOnInit() {
15   }
16   allowDrop(event) {
17     event.preventDefault();
18   }
19   onDrop(event) {
20     event.preventDefault();
21     let data = JSON.parse(event.dataTransfer.getData('tagData'));
22     if (!this.tags.includes(data.tag)){
23       this.tags.push(data.tag);
24     }
25   }
26 }
```

Listing 30.16 shows an Angular template that displays an image and any tags assigned to that image.

Listing 30.16 `drop.component.html`**: An Angular Template That Displays an Image and Any Image Tags Dropped onto That Image**

```
<div class="taggedImage"
     (dragover)="allowDrop($event)"
     (drop)="onDrop($event)">
  <img src="{{imgsrc}}" />
  <span class="imageTag"
        *ngFor="let tag of tags">
    {{tag}}
  </span>
</div>
```

Listing 30.17 shows a CSS file that styles the application by adding custom styles to the tags attached to the image.

Listing 30.17 `drop.component.css`**: A CSS File That Styles the Application**

```
img{
    width: 100px;
}
.taggedImage{
    display: inline-block;
    width: 100px;
    background: #000000;
}
.imageTag {
    display: inline-block;
    width: 100px;
    font: 16px/18px Georgia, serif;
    text-align: center;
    color: white;
    background: linear-gradient(#888888, #000000);
}
```

Listing 30.18 shows the Angular component `drag-item`, which uses browser events to allow elements to be dragged. Lines 14 through 17 define the `onDrag` method, which takes an `event` object as a parameter. This method adds data to the `dataTransfer` item on the `event` object to allow the tag data to be transferred when the element is dropped.

Listing 30.18 `drag.component.ts`**: An Angular Component That Allows an Element to Be Dragged**

```
import { Component, OnInit, Input } from '@angular/core';

@Component({
  selector: 'drag-item',
  templateUrl: './drag-item.component.html',
  styleUrls: ['./drag-item.component.css']
})
export class DragItemComponent implements OnInit {
  @Input() tag: string;
  constructor() {
  }
  ngOnInit() {
  }
  onDrag(event) {
    event.dataTransfer.setData('tagData',
       JSON.stringify({tag: this.tag}));
  }
}
```

Listing 30.19 shows an Angular template that displays a draggable tag.

Listing 30.19 `drag.component.html`**: An Angular Template That Displays an Image Tag**

```
<div class="tagItem"
     (dragstart)="onDrag($event)"
     draggable="true">
  {{tag}}
</div>
```

Listing 30.20 shows a CSS file that styles the application by adding custom styles to the tags.

Listing 30.20 `drag.component.css`**: A CSS File That Styles the Application**

```
.tagItem {
    display: inline-block;
    width: 100px;
    font: 16px/18px Georgia, serif;
    text-align: center;
    background: linear-gradient(#FFFFFF, #888888);
}
```

Figure 30.3 shows how the `drag-item` and `drop-item` components work in a browser: When you drag a tag onto an image, the tag is added to the list below.

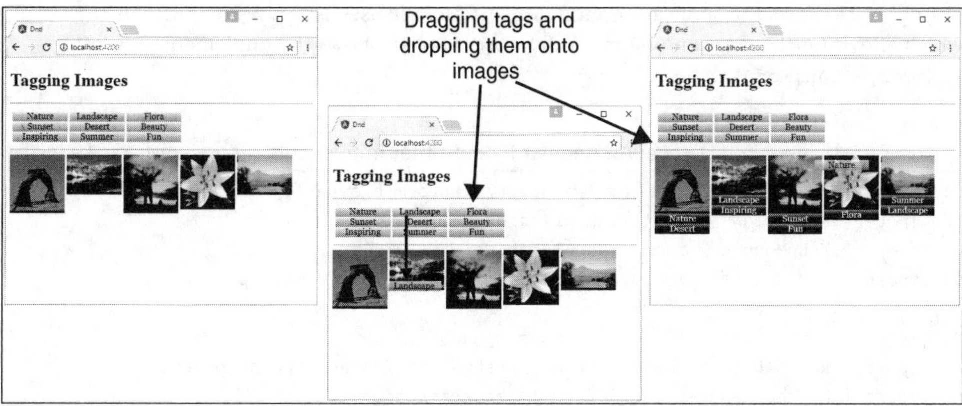

Figure 30.3 Implementing drag and drop using Angular components

Implementing a Star Rating Angular Component

Listings 30.21–30.29 show how to create an Angular application that creates a star rating system so a user can give ratings to items attached to the component (images in this case).

The folder structure for this example is as follows:

- **./app/app.module.ts:** Root component for the application (see Listing 30.21)
- **./app/mockbackend.service.ts:** Angular template for the `root` component (see Listing 30.22)
- **./app/app.module.ts:** CSS file for `app.component` (see Listing 30.23)
- **./app/app.component.ts:** Root component for the application (see Listing 30.24)
- **./app/app.component.html:** Angular template for the `root` component (see Listing 30.25)
- **./app/app.component.css:** CSS file for `app.component` (see Listing 30.26)
- **./app/rated-item:** Folder containing the `rated-item` component.
- **./app/rated-item/rated-item.component.ts:** Angular component that lets the user rate items (see Listing 30.27)
- **./app/rated-item/rated-item.component.html:** Angular template for the `rated-item` component (see Listing 30.28)
- **./app/rated-item/rated-item.component.css:** CSS file for the `rated-item` component (see Listing 30.29)

Listing 30.21 shows the application module. This module uses `InMemoryWebApiModule`, which allows for the creation of a mock database. Line 18 shows the implementation of `InMemoryWebApiModule`.

Listing 30.21 `app.module.ts`: **An Angular Module That Implements** `InMemoryWebApiModule`

```
01 import { BrowserModule } from '@angular/platform-browser';
02 import { NgModule } from '@angular/core';
03 import { HttpModule } from '@angular/http';
04 import { InMemoryWebApiModule } from 'angular-in-memory-web-api';
05
06 import { AppComponent } from './app.component';
07 import { RatedItemComponent } from './rated-item/rated-item.component';
08 import { MockbackendService } from './mockbackend.service';
09
10 @NgModule({
11   declarations: [
12     AppComponent,
13     RatedItemComponent
14   ],
15   imports: [
16     BrowserModule,
17     HttpModule,
18     InMemoryWebApiModule.forRoot(MockbackendService)
19   ],
20   providers: [],
21   bootstrap: [AppComponent]
22 })
23 export class AppModule { }
```

Listing 30.22 shows an Angular service that acts as a mock database for the application. Lines 4 through 29 create an array of items that can be retrieved and updated via HTTP requests.

Listing 30.22 `mockbackend.service.ts`: **An Angular Mock Back-end Service**

```
01 import { InMemoryDbService } from 'angular-in-memory-web-api';
02 export class MockbackendService implements InMemoryDbService{
03   createDb() {
04     const items = [
05       {
06         id: 1,
07         title: "Waterfall",
08         url: "../../assets/images/cliff.jpg",
09         rating: 4
10       },
11       {
```

```
        id: 2,
        title: "Flower",
        url: "../../assets/images/flower.jpg",
        rating: 5
      },
      {
        id: 3,
        title: "Pyramid",
        url: "../../assets/images/pyramid.jpg",
        rating: 3
      },
      {
        id: 4,
        title: "Lake",
        url: "../../assets/images/lake.jpg",
        rating: 5
      }
    ]
    return {items};
  }
}
```

Listing 30.23 shows an Angular service that uses HTTP to retrieve and update the items in the mock database. Lines 6 through 11 define the `RatedItem` interface with strictly typed variable names. Lines 19 through 24 define the constructor that creates an instance of `http` and a new observable called `itemObservable`.

Once a response is received from the observable, the `getItems` method is called. Lines 27 and 28 define the `getObservable` method, which returns `itemObservable`. Lines 30 through 38 define the `getItems` method, which uses an HTTP `get` to retrieve the items list from the mock database; it then assigns the `items` variable to the response and emits that response to the observer.

Lines 39 through 47 define the `updateRating` method, which takes two parameters: `item` and `newRating`. It assigns the item rating `newRating` and uses an HTTP `put` request to update the item in the database.

Listing 30.23 `ratings.service.ts`: An Angular Service That Uses HTTP to Retrieve a List of Items with Ratings

```
01 import { Injectable, OnInit } from '@angular/core';
02 import { Http } from '@angular/http';
03 import { Observable } from 'rxjs/observable';
04 import 'rxjs/add/operator/toPromise';
05
06 export class RatedItem {
07   id: number;
```

```
  url: string;
  title: string;
  rating: number;
}

@Injectable()
export class RatingsService {
  url = 'api/items';
  items: RatedItem[];
  public itemObservable: Observable<any>;
  observer;
  constructor(private http: Http) {
    this.itemObservable = new Observable(observer => {
      this.observer = observer;
      this.getItems();
    })
  }
  ngOnInit(){
  }
  getObservable(){
    return this.itemObservable;
  }
  getItems(){
    this.http.get(this.url)
             .toPromise()
             .then( response => {
               this.items = response.json().data;
               this.observer.next(this.items);
             })
             .catch(this.handleError);
  }
  updateRating(item, newRating){
    item.rating = newRating;
    const url = `${this.url}/${item.id}`;
    this.http
      .put(url, JSON.stringify(item))
      .toPromise()
      .then(() => this.getItems())
      .catch(this.handleError)
  }
  private handleError(error: any): Promise<any> {
    console.error('An error occurred', error);
    return Promise.reject(error.message || error);
  }
}
```

Listing 30.24 shows an Angular component that handles getting the items from `RatingsService`. Lines 21 through 27 define `ngOnInit`, which invokes the `getObservable` method on `RatingsService` to assign the `items` observable to `itemsObservable`. The `items` variable is then assigned the response received from `itemsObservable`.

Listing 30.24 `app.component.ts`: An Angular Component That Acts as the Root to the Application

```
01 import { Component } from '@angular/core';
02 import { RatedItemComponent } from './rated-item/rated-item.component';
03 import { Observable } from 'rxjs/observable';
04 import { RatingsService } from './ratings.service';
05
06 @Component({
07   selector: 'app-root',
08   templateUrl: './app.component.html',
09   styleUrls: ['./app.component.css'],
10   providers: [ RatingsService ]
11 })
12 export class AppComponent {
13   title = 'app';
14   itemsObservable: Observable<any>;
15   items: any[];
16   constructor(
17     public ratingsService: RatingsService
18   ){
19     this.items = [];
20   }
21   ngOnInit(){
22     this.itemsObservable = this.ratingsService.getObservable();
23     this.itemsObservable.subscribe(
24       itemList => {
25         this.items = itemList;
26       });
27   }
28 }
```

Listing 30.25 shows an Angular template that implements the `rated-item` component to display a list of rated items. `rated-item` takes two inputs: `item` and `RatingsService`.

Listing 30.25 `app.component.html`: An Angular Template That Creates a List of Rated Items, Using the Component `rated-item`

```
<h1> Rated Images </h1>
<hr>
<div class="item"
     *ngFor="let item of items">
   <rated-item
```

```
        [item]="item"
        [ratingsService]="ratingsService">
    </rated-item>
</div>
```

Listing 30.26 shows a CSS file that styles the `item` class on `app.component.html`.

Listing 30.26 `app.component.css`: A CSS File That Styles the Application

```
.item{
    border: .5px solid black;
    display: inline-block;
    width: 175px;
    text-align: center;
}
```

Listing 30.27 shows an Angular component that displays a rated item. Lines 13 through 15 define the `constructor` method, which initializes the `starArray` value.

Lines 18 through 20 define the `setRating` method, which takes the parameter `rating`. The method invokes the `updateRating` method on the `ratings` service and takes the parameters `item` and `rating`, which the ratings service uses to update the rating of the item.

Lines 21 through 27 define the `getStarClass` method, which takes the parameter `rating`. This method is used to assign the class of each star to accurately represent the rating of the item.

Listing 30.27 `rated-item.component.ts`: An Angular Component That Displays an Image as Well as a Rating for the Image

```
01 import { Component, OnInit, Input } from '@angular/core';
02 import { RatingsService } from '../ratings.service';
03
04 @Component({
05   selector: 'rated-item',
06   templateUrl: './rated-item.component.html',
07   styleUrls: ['./rated-item.component.css']
08 })
09 export class RatedItemComponent implements OnInit {
10   @Input ("item") item: any;
11   @Input ("ratingsService") ratingsService: RatingsService;
12   starArray: number[];
13   constructor() {
14     this.starArray = [1,2,3,4,5];
15   }
16   ngOnInit() {
17   }
```

```
  setRating(rating){
    this.ratingsService.updateRating(this.item, rating);
  }
  getStarClass(rating){
    if(rating <= this.item.rating){
      return "star";
    } else {
      return "empty";
    }
  }
}
```

Listing 30.28 shows an Angular template that displays a title, an image, and a rating. Lines 8 through 12 create the stars, which are used to visualize the rating. When a user clicks on a new rating, the overall rating is adjusted, using the `setRating` method. The `getStarClass` method determines whether the stars are filled in or blank.

Listing 30.28 `rated-item.component.html`**: An Angular Template That Displays a Title and an Image as Well as a Rating for the Image**

```
01 <p class="title">
02   {{item.title}}
03 </p>
04 <img src="{{item.url}}" />
05 <p>
06   Rating: {{item.rating}}
07 </p>
08 <span *ngFor="let rating of starArray"
09       (click)="setRating(rating)"
10       [ngClass]="getStarClass(rating)">
11    
12 </span>
```

Listing 30.29 shows a CSS file that styles the application by setting the dimensions of the rated item and adding stars to give that item a visualized rating.

Listing 30.29 `rated-item.component.css`**: A CSS File That Styles the Application**

```
* {
    margin: 5px;
}
img {
    height: 100px;
}
.title{
  font: bold 20px/24px Verdana;
```

```
}
span {
    float: left;
    width: 20px;
    background-repeat: no-repeat;
    cursor: pointer;
}
.star{
    background-image: url("../../assets/images/star.png");
}
.empty {
    background-image: url("../../assets/images/empty.png");
}
```

Figure 30.4 shows the star rating component in the browser. Clicking on a star changes the rating in the mock back-end service, which updates the UI component.

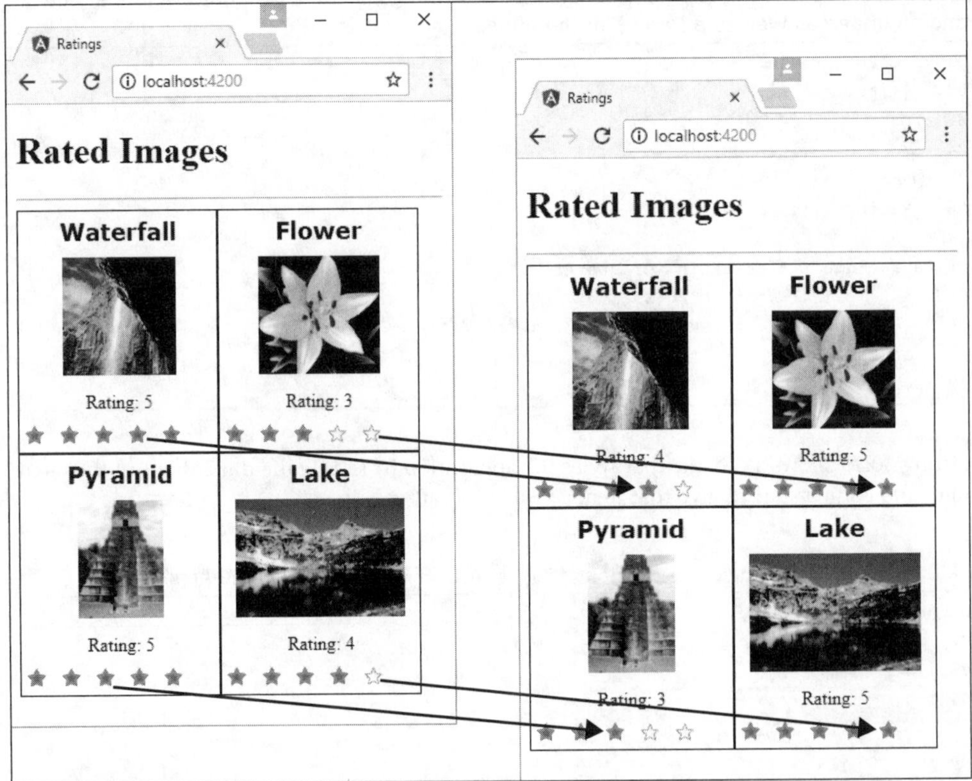

Figure 30.4 Using Angular components and services to implement star ratings on images with a mock back end

Summary

In this chapter, you got a chance to see how to extend what you have learned in the rest of the book to build some cool Angular components. You have seen how to implement animations, create a star rating component, and implement drag-and-drop capability. These are just some of the many ways to use Angular in real-world web applications. If you are interested in learning more about Angular, https://angular.io is a great resource.

Index

Symbols

A

B

C

D

E

F

G

H

I

J

K

L

M

N

O

P

S

U

V

W

X-Y-Z

Accessing the Free Web Edition

Your purchase of this book in any format includes access to the corresponding Web Edition, which provides several special online-only features:

- The complete text of the book
- Updates and corrections as they become available

The Web Edition can be viewed on all types of computers and mobile devices with any modern web browser that supports HTML5.

To get access to the Web Edition of *Node.js, MongoDB and Angular Web Development* all you need to do is register this book:

1. Go to www.informit.com/register.
2. Sign in or create a new account.
3. Enter the ISBN: 9780134655536.
4. Answer the questions as proof of purchase.
5. The Web Edition will appear under the Digital Purchases tab on your Account page. Click the Launch link to access the product.